THE REMINISCENCES OF
Rear Admiral James D. Ramage
U.S. Navy (Retired)

INTERVIEWED BY
Robert L. Lawson
and
Barrett Tillman

U.S. Naval Institute • Annapolis, Maryland

Copyright © 1999

Preface

For a number of years, retired Navy photographer Robert Lawson made a valuable contribution to the naval profession while serving as editor of The Hook magazine, published by the Tailhook Association. Under his editorship, the magazine did a remarkable job of documenting the activities and history of the carrier Navy.

One of the aviators who contributed articles to the magazine was retired Rear Admiral Ramage, whom I had come to know in the 1970s while editing his work for Proceedings. Thus I was receptive when Lawson nominated Ramage for the oral history program and especially gratified when Lawson and author Barrett Tillman offered to conduct the interviews on behalf of the Naval Institute. I am embarrassed that the press of other projects has kept the finished version from appearing for such a long time. In one of the interviews, Ramage remarked that his candid, to-the-point comments might need to be kept under wraps for a while. Though that was never the intent, that unfortunately proved to be the result. Now, at last, they are available for the benefit of history, and it is indeed his candor that makes them so useful

Several themes emerge in this story, foremost among them that Ramage was a warrior. He was eager to get into the fight in World War II and acquitted himself superbly as a dive-bomber pilot and squadron commanding officer. He had several combat tours in the Vietnam War, and then there were his numerous wars with the bureaucracy. As always, he was combative—preferring to call things as he saw them, rather than offering up diplomatic niceties. He moved up the ladder in naval aviation, serving as navigator of a jeep carrier, commanding a carrier air group during and after the Korean War, working in OP-05 on the OpNav staff, commanding a heavy attack wing as the Navy stepped up its capability for delivering nuclear weapons from aircraft carriers, commanding a seaplane tender, commanding the carrier Independence during a Mediterranean deployment, serving as chief of staff to CTF 77 during the bombing of North Vietnam, and then commanding a carrier division himself as the bombing continued.

Admiral Ramage's aggressiveness and outspokenness were basic components of his makeup throughout all these tours and, as he himself concedes, probably kept him from rising higher in rank. Another factor that held him back was the selection of

Admiral Elmo Zumwalt as Chief of Naval Operations in the early 1970s. Ramage's views were antithetical to Zumwalt's, as this oral history makes quite clear. Ramage essentially became personal non grata with the front office. The qualities that caused Washington to view him with disdain are especially valuable for the sake of history because the admiral felt no hesitation about speaking so candidly. He represents many others who felt a sense of disquiet when Zumwalt's directives were instituted. Both Ramage and Zumwalt had the objective of having a first-rate Navy; they differed markedly on how best to achieve that objective.

In the course of moving from the initial raw transcript of the oral interviews to this final version, both Admiral Ramage and I have done some editing in the interests of accuracy, smoothness, and clarity. In a few places, I have moved blocks of text from one place to another in order to improve the continuity of the story. Admiral Ramage looked into his personal files to track down information useful for the editing of the transcript. Debbie Reid, formerly of the oral history staff, did the original transcription. Paul Brawley, who previously worked in the Naval Academy's public affairs office, contributed to the process of annotating the transcript. Ann Hassinger of the Naval Institute's history division has made a significant contribution through her diligence in the overall process of printing, proofreading, and overseeing the binding of the completed volume.

Paul Stillwell
Director, History Division
U.S. Naval Institute
October 1999

REAR ADMIRAL JAMES DAVID RAMAGE
UNITED STATES NAVY (RETIRED)

James David Ramage was born in Waterloo, Iowa, on 19 July 1916, son of David S. and Flora Groat Ramage. He attended East Waterloo High School and Iowa State Teachers College, at Cedar Falls, prior to entering the U.S. Naval Academy, Annapolis, Maryland, on appointment from his native state in 1935. He was graduated and commissioned ensign on 1 June 1939.

Following graduation from the Naval Academy, he joined the aircraft carrier Enterprise (CV-6) and in August 1941 was detached for flight training at the Naval Air Station, Pensacola, Florida. Designated a naval aviator on 15 February 1942, he remained at the Pensacola Air Station until March of that year, then returned for duty in the Enterprise.

While in the ship he served from March 1943 until August 1944 as executive officer and commanding officer of Bombing Squadron Ten. While attached to that squadron, he participated in action in the Marshalls, Truk, Marianas, New Guinea, Palau, Battle of the Philippine Sea, Saipan, and Guam. He was awarded the Navy Cross, the Distinguished Flying Cross with gold star in lieu of a second similar award, and the Air Medal with gold stars in lieu of five additional awards.

In September 1944 he assumed command of Bombing Squadron 98 and in August 1946 reported for instruction at the Naval War College, Newport, Rhode Island. In July 1947 he was assigned as navigator of the USS Bairoko (CVE-115), while attached to that escort aircraft carrier, he participated in the atomic tests at Eniwetok in May 1948. Detached from the Bairoko in July 1948, he next had duty as personnel officer on the staff of Commander Air Force Pacific Fleet and in July 1950 became chief of operations and projects at the Armed Forces Special Weapons Project, Albuquerque, New Mexico.

He was Commander Air Group 19 from September 1952 to June 1954. During his time in command, the air group operated in the Korean area of hostilities. In June 1954 he was transferred to command of Composite Squadron Three. In July 1955 he became chief of the Sea Base Striking Forces Planning Unit in the Office of the Chief of Naval Operations, Navy Department, Washington, D.C. He remained there until July 1957, and after instruction at the National War College, Washington, D.C., he reported in July 1958 as wing commander of Heavy Attack Wing One. In July 1960 he assumed command of the seaplane tender Salisbury Sound (AV-13) and in July 1961 was detached for duty as head of the Special Weapons Plans Branch, Office of the Chief of Naval Operations. In 1963 he received the degree of master of arts in international affairs from George Washington University, Washington, D.C.

In August 1963 he assumed command of the aircraft carrier Independence (CVA-62) and in August 1964 was assigned to the Officer of the Chief of Naval Operations. After a month's duty there, he joined the staff of Commander Joint Task Force Two. From March 1966 to June 1967 he was chief of staff and aide to Commander Carrier Division Five, and "for exceptionally meritorious conduct . . . as Chief of Staff, Commander Attack Carrier

Striking Force SEVENTH Fleet/Commander Carrier Division FIVE, during combat operations in Southeast Asia from April 1966 to March 1967 . . . " he was awarded the Legion of Merit. His tour was interrupted by brief temporary additional duty in command of the aircraft carrier Franklin D. Roosevelt (CVA-42) in January 1967.

In June 1967 he became Commander Fleet Air Whidbey, with headquarters at the Naval Air Station, Whidbey Island, Oak Harbor, Washington, and in October of that year report as deputy chief of staff for plans and operations to the Commander in Chief, U.S. Pacific Fleet. He was awarded the Distinguished Service Medal "for exceptionally meritorious service . . . from October 1967 to May 1970. . . "

In May 1970 he became Commander Carrier Division Seven. "For exceptionally meritorious service from June to December 1970 as Commander Carrier Division SEVEN, Commander Task Group SEVENTY-SEVEN Point FIVE and for designated periods as Commander Task Group SEVENTY-SEVEN Point ZERO, during combat operations against enemy forces in Southeast Asia . . . " he was awarded a gold star in lieu of a second Legion of Merit. He was awarded a gold star in lieu of a third Legion of Merit for " . . . his dynamic leadership, tactical expertise and steadfast devotion to duty in the face of the changing situations in the unique combat environment of Southeast Asia . . . " during the period June to December 1971.

In April 1972 he reported as Commander Naval Air Reserve, headquartered at the Naval Air Station, Glenview, Illinois, and was assigned additionally as Commander Naval Air Reserve Force. In February 1973 he assumed further additional duty as Director of Naval Reserve, Office of the Chief of Naval Operations, and Deputy Chief of Naval Reserve (Air) and Commandant of the Ninth Naval District. He also served as Acting Chief of naval Reserve from February to April 1973. "For exceptionally meritorious conduct . . . from April 1972 to July 1973 . . . " he was awarded a gold star in lieu of the fourth Legion of Merit. The citation further states in part: "By his brilliant leadership, exceptional professional competence, perceptive judgment and perseverance in the face of many obstacle, Rear Admiral Ramage has contributed essentially to the Naval Air Reserve's high level of readiness and esprit de corps . . . "

From July 1973 to August 1975, Rear Admiral Ramage served as Commander of the Caribbean Sea Frontier with additional duty as Commandant of the Tenth Naval District, Commander Fleet Air Caribbean, and Commander Antilles Defense Command. His official retirement from active duty was in January 1976.

Dates of Rank

Ensign	1 June 1939
Lieutenant (junior grade)	1 June 1942
Lieutenant	1 August 1942
Lieutenant Commander	15 March 1944
Commander	29 July 1949

Captain   1 August 1957
Rear Admiral   1 July 1967

Chronological Record of Service:

June 1939 to August 1941   USS Enterprise (CV-6)
September 1941 to March 1942   Flight Training Pensacola Naval Air Station
May 1942 to October 1942   Squadron VS-3
November 1942-December 1942   Senior aviator, USS Salt Lake City (CA-25)
January 1943 to February 1943   USS Enterprise (CV-6)
March 1943 to August 1944   XO/CO, Bombing Squadron Ten
September 1944 to July 1946   CO, Bombing Squadron 98
August 1946 to June 1947   Student, Naval War College, Newport, Rhode Island
July 1947 to July 1948   Navigator, USS Bairoko (CVE-115)
August 1948 to June 1950   Staff, Commander Air Force Pacific Fleet
July 1950 to August 1952   Armed Forces Special Weapons Project, Albuquerque, New Mexico

September 1952 to June 1954   Commander Air Group 19
June 1954 to June 1955   CO, Composite Squadron Three
July 1955 to July 1957   Chief, Sea-Based Striking Forces Planning Unit, OpNav
August 1957 to June 1958   Student, National War College, Washington, D.C.
July 1958 to June 1960   Commander Heavy Attack Wing One
July 1960 to July 1961   CO, USS Salisbury Sound (AV-13)
July 1961 to August 1963   Head, Special Weapons Plans, OpNav
August 1963 to August 1964   CO, USS Independence (CVA-62)
July 1964 to December 1965   Director of Analysis and Reports, and Test Director, Joint Task Force Two, Sandia Base, New Mexico

January 1966 to March 1967   Chief of Staff, Carrier Division Five/Task Force 77
April 1967 to May 1967   Staff, Commander Naval Air Force Pacific Fleet
June 1967 to September 1967   Commander Fleet Air Whidbey
October 1967 to May 1970   Deputy Chief of Staff for Operations and Plans, Commander in Chief Pacific Fleet
May 1970 to February 1972   Commander Carrier Division Seven
April 1972 to July 1973   Commander Naval Air Reserve/Director of Naval Reserve
July 1973 to August 1975   Commandant Tenth Naval District; Commander Caribbean Sea Frontier; Commander Antilles Defense Command

1 January 1976   Retirement from active duty

Awards

Navy Cross
Distinguished Service Medal

Legion of Merit with three gold stars
Distinguished Flying Cross with gold star
Air Medal with five gold stars
Navy Unit Commendation awarded USS Enterprise
Navy Unit Commendation awarded Commander Carrier Division Five
American Defense Service Medal
American Campaign Medal
Asiatic-Pacific Campaign Medal with two silver stars and one bronze star (11 operations)
World War II Victory Medal
China Service Medal
Navy Occupation Service Medal
United Nations Service Medal
Armed Forces Expeditionary Medal
Vietnam Service Medal
Philippine Liberation Ribbon
Vietnam Gallantry Cross with Palm
National Order of Vietnam Fifth Class
Korean Presidential Unit Citation Badge
Republic of Vietnam Campaign Medal with device

Special Qualifications

Naval Aviator (HTA), 15 February 1942
Graduate of the senior course of the Naval War College, 1947
Graduate of National War College, 1958
Awarded master of arts degree in international affairs by the
George Washington University, 1963

Personal Data

Wife: Married Emeleen Tyler, 4 September 1941
         Married Virginia Keesling, 14 August 1964

Daughters: Jaleen T. Ramage, born 10 February 1951
                 Jamie T. Ramage, born 2 June 1955

Authorization

The U.S. Naval Institute is hereby authorized to make available to individuals, libraries, and other repositories of its choosing the transcripts of three oral history interviews concerning the life and naval career of the undersigned. The interviews were recorded on 23 February 1985, 30 March 1985, and 31 March 1985 in collaboration with Robert L. Lawson and Barrett Tillman for the U.S. Naval Institute.

The undersigned does hereby release and assign to the U.S. Naval Institute the rights and title to these interviews, with the exception that the undersigned retains the right to use the material for his own purposes, as he sees fit. The copyright in both the oral and transcribed versions shall be the sole property of the U.S. Naval Institute. The tape recordings of the interviews are and will remain the property of the U.S. Naval Institute.

Signed and sealed this __28__ day of __October__ 1996.

James D. Ramage
Rear Admiral, U.S. Navy (Retired)

Interview Number 1 with Rear Admiral James D. Ramage, U.S. Navy (Retired)

Place: Admiral Ramage's home, Bonita, California

Date: Saturday, 23 February 1985

Interviewers: Robert L. Lawson and Barrett Tillman

Admiral Ramage: When I received Paul Stillwell's letter concerning this oral history, I responded that I would be pleased to participate but wanted him to know my background. I outlined the many commands I was fortunate to have, probably considerably more than any contemporary, and also that I was very controversial. Perhaps he would want to put this on ice for about 20 years or so. His answering letter stated that he was more eager than before that I do the history. My views, however controversial and candid, would make the history more valuable. Hence, here we go. We will see that it is very subjective and also biased. I will name people who had great effects upon my life. Sometimes they will be people whom I admire, and sometimes they will be people whom I did not wish to emulate. My story is similar to my Navy career; I will call them as I see them.

I was born to David S. and Flora Groat Ramage at 11:15 A.M., 19 July 1916. I was born at home, at 261 Alta Vista Avenue in Waterloo, Iowa. I weighed nine and three-fourths pounds.

My father was of Scottish ancestry. His father, David Ramage, married Margaret Ferrie in Ayr, Scotland, and immigrated to the United States after our Civil War. He was a machinist by trade and worked for the Chicago and Alton Railroad in Bloomington, Illinois. My father was raised in Bloomington and remained there until he enlisted in the Army on the 26th of April 1898, to participate in the Yanko-Spanko War, as he called it, which was his name for the Spanish-American War.[*] He served in the First Regiment of Illinois Calvary, Troop B. He was 21 years old at the time and gave his occupation as a jeweler. He trained at Chickamauga, Georgia. He told me one time that it was very difficult to leave the base in Chickamauga, because they were still using Civil War uniforms, and the local

---

[*] During the Spanish-American War (April-August 1898), the United States acquired the Philippine Islands, Puerto Rico, and Guam.

people started yelling at the Yankees when they left camp. In other words, the Civil War was not dead in Georgia. His outfit was scheduled to go to Puerto Rico when the war ended. He was mustered out at Fort Sheridan, Illinois, six months later.

My mother was of Dutch, Irish, and English ancestry. Her father, James Monroe Groat, married Alvira Swan Weaver in October of 1867. Both were from Wyoming County, New York. Jim Groat enlisted in the 105th New York Infantry Regiment in December 1861 and was medically discharged five months later. He enlisted again in October 1863, at the age of 21. He gave his occupation as a farmer. He was mustered out on July 5, 1866, at Denver City, Colorado. He made his way back to Wyoming County, New York, married, and returned to Parkersburg, Iowa, where my mother was born in 1878. My grandfather achieved the rating of commissary sergeant. The Groat family moved to Waterloo, Iowa, shortly thereafter, where Flora, my mother, was raised. Grandfather Groat was apparently quite successful, as he was described to me later as being a man of substantial means. He owned several farms, a feed and coal company, started a bank and a savings and loan. He was mayor of the town and president of the waterworks. He died before I was born.

My mother, Flora, married George L. Humphreys in 1903 in Waterloo. He died in 1909, leaving a posthumous daughter, Mary, who has been an inspiration to me all my life. Mother married my father in 1914. She was taking in roomers on East Second Street in Waterloo at the time. He was a traveling salesman for the Heinz Pickle Company. They apparently made it permanent after he became used to the home. At that time, her daughter Mary was five years old.

I came along some two years later, in 1916. My younger sister Margaret, also known as Betty, was born in 1918. As a boy, I was certainly given privileged treatment at home, and my older half-sister Mary was always looked upon as being a real jewel, so far as her mother was concerned. Unfortunately, Betty was never really wanted, and as such, had a very difficult childhood.

Growing up in a small town in Iowa during the '20s was a pleasant experience. Allowing for the frustrations and problems of youth, which we all pass through, I can look back with happy thoughts. I was aware of the big financial changes in the Midwest during the late 1920s. The Depression hit the farmers in the mid-'20s, long before the big stock market crash in 1929.* First my father was forced to sell his farm, which he called the North Farm. Mother's farm went five years later.

Selling out that farm was a real experience to me; it had an impact on me the rest of my life. Dad let me be the clerk to record the sales of the various things, and when we went out to the farm, all I can say is that the various farmers were sullen. The auctioneers sold everything, including washboards, copper kettles. Everything that both my father and mother and the sharecropper, Harry Padgett, had that was on the farm, was sold. I made up my mind at that time that I would never be poor.

After marrying Mother, Dad went to work as a cashier for the Waterloo Trust and Savings Bank, which later went bankrupt with all the rest of the banks in town during the great bank freeze in '33.† He left the bank in order to take over the Maxwell-Chalmers auto agency, which I think the bank probably owned. He later bought out the agency and set up a distributorship for Maxwell and Chalmers. The Chalmers became the Chrysler, and ultimately Maxwell became the Plymouth.

He was a fairly large distributor for a section of northeast Iowa, and even if conditions were quite bad at the time, he could make a go of it as long as he had this distributorship. However, in about 1928, the Chrysler Corporation decided that it would distribute directly to the various garages around the state. He became simply a franchisee, and he couldn't make it with the very large building that he occupied. He went to work for the owner of the building, whose name was Clemens, and lived in Des Moines.

People who grew up during the Depression have a different view on life than almost anybody later. Things were extremely difficult. No one was starving, but there was certainly no ready cash anywhere. However, everybody was in the same boat, and so it wasn't all bad. We lived in a very nice house in a subdivision out from town in Waterloo, and gradually the house went into disrepair and decay, and we ultimately lost the house too.

---

* Following the crash of the New York Stock Exchange in late October 1929, the United States was plunged into the Great Depression, from which it did not recover until the nation geared up for World War II at the beginning of the 1940s. The Depression was marked by high unemployment and many business failures.
† The Emergency Banking Act went into effect on 9 March 1933, five days after Franklin D. Roosevelt became President.

I liked school and I liked my teachers. My first school was Francis Grout. It was kindergarten through fourth grade. Mother offered a dollar for each A that we children would get, and I ended up pretty wealthy at the end of every six weeks' period. Later on it became pretty apparent that Mother just couldn't pay the dollars, and I continued to get good grades anyway.

I had a job from the time I was nine years old. First it was selling Ladies Home Journal for ten cents and The Saturday Evening Post for a nickel. The profit on the Journal was three cents and on the Post it was a cent and a half. So we're not talking about much money. When I got to be about 11 years old, I was able to convince my neighbor, George Scully, that I should become his helper on his paper route for the Waterloo Daily Courier. Those paper routes were very difficult to get, and it was rather standard to become an apprentice for a year or so before you'd fleet up to get the big job.* My pay was $1.00 a week, six days a week. I figured out I was getting about eight cents an hour. I carried about 75 papers as an apprentice. A year or so later, I inherited the whole route, about 175 papers, and got the job of collecting. The papers went for 15 cents a week, and I got 10% of the take on the collection, plus a cent or two for carrying papers. So I would get between $4.00 and $5.00 a week for carrying papers, out of which I paid the new helper a buck. But that was pretty good money at that time, and it was a much-sought-for job.

Q: If I may, I'd like to interject a question here. Your reference to growing up in the Depression reminds me of the segment in William Manchester's Goodbye Darkness, where, if I remember correctly, he said that the World War II generation, having gone through the Depression, was in much better position to fight a global war like World War II than perhaps any other generation would have been.† What's your feeling on that?

Admiral Ramage: Well, that could be true. I don't know. The times were tough. The parents had the toughest time, the kids not nearly as difficult, but that could be so.

---

* "Fleet up" is Navy slang for a promotion within a particular organization.
† William Manchester, Goodbye Darkness: A Memoir of the Pacific War (Boston: Little Brown, 1980).

Q: Do you think it very generally prepared other people to cope with adverse situations?

Admiral Ramage: I think so. I certainly made up my mind that I would never be poor. That was one of the things. I also knew that whatever I did, I would have to do myself. That's the way it worked out.

I maintained the job carrying the papers on up through junior high school until I went to senior high school, which started in tenth grade. I always had a job of some kind: packing groceries or carrying something. I always had a job working for my dad, whether I wanted it or not, down in the garage, which he maintained and rented. I didn't ever get paid by him, however, so he always made it up to me somehow. But I didn't particularly like to work for him because there was no cash involved. The best job I got was later on, after high school, which was working in the Standard Glass and Paint Warehouse, stacking paint and hauling around these big 500- and 600-pound linoleum rolls. That was a well-paying job. I got 35 cents an hour during the summer when I worked. Then, during my year in college, I worked after school for about two or three hours a day. So this was good money, and I oftentimes helped Mother and Dad with expenses that they simply couldn't handle.

My first school, as I mentioned, was Francis Grout, which was kindergarten through four. It was only two blocks from home. My class had ten students. When I got into the fifth grade, we were transferred down to McKinley School and the classes jumped to about 30. McKinley School was down in another section of town which was fairly close to the Rath Packing Company. The students down there were a lot tougher than the ones that I was used to up around the area that we lived in. Let's say that I learned about life very early, on what not to do. From there I went to junior high, and that was downtown. That was eighth and ninth grade. Then high school started at the tenth grade, where I did various things that I'll go into later.

I mentioned that I liked all of my teachers, particularly my seventh grade teacher, who was Miss Koehm, of German extraction and probably the most patriotic American I've ever known. She was a wonderful teacher, and I can still see her marching along with the line of students as we entered the school to John Philip Sousa's marches as played on the hand wind-up phonograph.[*]

It was during this time that I had my first brush with music. My sister Mary was by this time a very good pianist, and my sister Betty, or Margaret, and I took lessons from Miss Abdill. It simply didn't take on me. I wouldn't practice, and I just didn't have it. But I wanted to play the cornet, so Dad got me a cornet. I think we paid 15 bucks for it. I wasn't much of a success at that either. Ultimately I was talked into playing the French horn, because they needed a French horn player in the high school orchestra, and I was equally poor at that.

I continued my paper route all the way through junior high, but when I went up to the high school in the tenth grade, I gave up the paper route in order to go out for football and do the various other things that I wanted to do.

When I was about five years old, my father began to chide me about sucking my thumb. It was my left thumb, and it was really good. One of his warnings was that if I didn't quit sucking my thumb, my thumb would be deformed and also my teeth would protrude and I couldn't go to West Point, whatever that was. A couple of years later, one of our neighbor's sons, Dick Cass, entered the Naval Academy.[†] A couple of years later, Mack Garrison, another neighbor, was appointed to the Naval Academy.[‡]

About that same time, my father took me to hear Commander Richard E. Byrd, who had returned from the South Pole and was going around the country giving these presentations, I think, to pay for the expedition.[§] I don't think his expedition was very well funded. He wore a white service uniform, I recall, and he had those wings of gold, and I thought that would be pretty neat.[**]

---

[*] John Philip Sousa (1854-1932), American composer and bandmaster known as the "March King." He was master of the Marine Band from 1880 to 1892 and later toured with a band of his own.
[†] Richard S. Cass graduated from the Naval Academy in the class of 1930 and later resigned while an ensign.
[‡] Malcolm E. Garrison graduated from the Naval Academy in the class of 1932 and eventually retired as a rear admiral.
[§] Commander Richard E. Byrd, Jr., USN (Ret.), explored Antarctica in 1928, 1933, 1939, 1947, 1955. He was retired for physical disability in 1916 but continued to be promoted, eventually becoming a rear admiral in 1929.
[**] White service was the dress uniform for naval officers in summertime; the uniform was--and is--distinguished by a high, stand-up collar.

My father thought this would be pretty fine too. He had always wanted to go to Annapolis but just had never been able to do it. He didn't have the background or the education, but at that time he decided his son would go, and I thought it was fine too. He gathered all the information available on how I would do this. He sent for the sample entrance exams, which I started studying when I was a freshman in high school. My mother strongly supported this idea also. Not the least of the reasons for my going to the Naval Academy was lack of funds in the Ramage treasury. It was really getting depleted about the time I was in high school. I wanted to go to Annapolis, but I really didn't connect the Naval Academy with the Navy. The Naval Academy was my goal, and that was as far as I could see. Whatever happened after that was something different. And also I could see myself in that blue uniform with all the gals around. I really wanted to do that.

I was a good student at East Waterloo High, perhaps not the best, but certainly in the top 5% or 10%. I played the lead in both the junior and senior class plays. The junior play was P.G. Wodehouse's Leave it to Psmith. It was kind of a light comedy and quite good. The second play, however, was a real bummer. I was the Duke of Athens in A Midsummer Night's Dream. I think that that's the first and last time that they ever tried a Shakespearean play. Even my father walked out on it. I played center on the football team, not well but with great enthusiasm. We did have one fine player on the team, Jake Stong, whom I will refer to later.[*] He was all-state in guard, and he entered the Naval Academy class with me in the summer of '35.

Q: Would that have been fairly unusual for two people from the same . . .

Admiral Ramage: It would be. He got an appointment through a different route, but it would be very unusual at the same high school.

The Ramages were very strong Episcopalians. We children were brought up in the church. Dad was on the vestry, sang in the choir, was coach of the Sunday school basketball teams. There were three of them: the senior, intermediate, and junior. My mother was everything in the church. I think she stoked the fire and cleaned up everything.

---

[*] Midshipman Jake Stong, USN.

She was really very dedicated. My sisters and I were in the choir. My older sister Mary by that time was quite an organist and used to fill in as organist. My younger sister and I sang in the junior choir, and I don't think that we added very much.

I can recall that one of my greatest problems of growing up was that I was extremely shy, particularly around girls. I had no regular girlfriend all the way through high school. As a matter of fact, the only girl that I was "sweet on" was already taken. She went steady with a good friend of mine named John Kyle. Her name was Phoebe Jane Eickelberg, and I never had enough courage to even look at her. I was so shy that my mother decided when I was 16 that I'd better go to dancing school, and I agreed I'd like to learn how to dance. So I was enrolled in the Esther Worrall School of Dance in the bottom of the Paramount Theater in Waterloo. I think the course was six lessons, and I learned the waltz and the fox-trot, and I think Esther probably gave up on me with sore feet. So I was all ready to go to the dances, but I couldn't get up enough courage to ask anybody for a date.

Q: There's good news and there's bad news.

Admiral Ramage: So nothing happened. Finally a friend of mine, Wirt Hoxie, who was a member of the De Molay club, which was the junior adjunct of the Masonic Lodge, asked me to go to a De Molay dance with him on a double date. Well, that put it to me. I had to get a date somewhere. So after hanging on the phone and sitting around for a matter of hours, I finally called a young lady and asked her if she wouldn't like to go, and she said she would. I don't remember the exact details of the dance, but I had a miserable time, and I'm sure that she had a worse time. That ended my dancing career for about six months.

I think it might be interesting to record the prejudices of our time in a small Midwest town. Waterloo was a city of about 35,000 at that time. There was no great prejudice against colored people or blacks, as we call them now. There weren't very many. In East High there were two or three that played on our football squad, and there was no great animosity one way or another. So far as Jews were concerned, there just weren't very many. I can remember later on dating a Ruthy Cohen, and my mother, who was very difficult about my dates, didn't seem to mind that. But we had one major prejudice, Catholics. I don't know exactly where my mother got it, but she was extremely biased against Roman Catholics; my father was also, to a lesser extent. I asked him one time why he was so prejudiced against Catholics, and he said, "Well, you know, your forefathers were Huguenots from northern France, and they fled to Scotland because of a great pogrom, a great campaign, really, against Protestants in France at that time." So therefore he was prejudiced against Catholics.

I indicated that that was 200 years ago, and it didn't seem that that should prevail now, but he mentioned that it still rankled him. Mother, I don't know exactly why, but she really disliked Catholics unless they were her particular friends, and then they were good Catholics. And wouldn't you know it? The first girl I really fell in love with, Jane Rhoads, came from a very nice but very Catholic family. Her father was a Purdue graduate and was a civil engineer for the Illinois Central Railroad. She was a very pretty girl and very smart, but that had no impact upon my mother. She was a Roman Catholic and, as such, every time I had a date with her, I would get a lecture about Catholicism before I left. Mother didn't mind me running around with Catholic boys, but I guess she feared that I would marry a Catholic, which would be the end of everything. I think that in our particular neighborhood this was quite prevalent. It was mainly a German-Swedish culture, and they were just anti-Catholic. I don't know exactly why. In any event, this did not rub off on me.

Q: What about the political climate of the times?

Admiral Ramage: During my senior year, my desire to go to Annapolis became even stronger, and I was studying real hard both in school and on the entrance exams. Now we'll go into the political situation. Iowa was strongly Republican and very conservative. Dad had already been working on our congressman. But in 1932, in the Roosevelt landslide, our Republican congressman was defeated, and we got a new congressman, Bert Willford, and there was no way he was going to appoint me to the Naval Academy.* He went through the

---

* Franklin D. Roosevelt defeated Herbert C. Hoover, capturing 57.4% of the popular vote. The Democrats also carried the House and Senate. Albert C. Willford.

discussion of giving me a chance to take the competitive exams, which I did, but I don't know exactly how I did relative to the rest of the competitors. I think I did quite well, but I really didn't ever get any results. As a matter of fact, I don't blame him, because my mother was extremely vociferous and so Republican that he just couldn't appoint me. That would be all there was to it.

However, now we get on into '34. The Republicans in our district got back in, and the congressman was John W. Gwynne, who had been our neighbor ever since I was born. As a matter of fact, I carried papers to him and knew him very well. However, he was very clever about it. He would not appoint me to be the principal to the Naval Academy; he gave me first alternate.* When my father went to him, he was really irate about it. But the congressman, said, "Dave, calm down. There's no way that this young man, who happens to be from Reinbeck, Iowa, can ever make it. Tell your son to get packed and he's in." And it worked out that way.

I've kind of skipped ahead here, because I'd like to talk about my year in college. I wasn't ready out of high school to go to the Naval Academy anyway. I simply didn't have the background in science and math. I went to Iowa State Teachers College, which is in Cedar Falls, about six miles away, to see a Dr. Kadesch, who was a physics professor.† He had been a professor at the Naval Academy, and he outlined pretty much what I should do the coming year at Iowa State Teachers, or the State Normal School, as my mother called it.‡

In the meantime, my sister Mary had married Tom Cranage, and he was working on getting me into the University of Michigan. I wasn't that good a football player, but he was making arrangements to get me some kind of a job sweeping up the gym or whatever they do for athletes there. He went so far as to get me invited to the Chi Psi House to be prepared to get into a fraternity if I went to the University of Michigan. Tom was a great

---

* The "principal" referred to here was the individual who received the congressman's principal appointment for a particular opening at the Naval Academy. Someone with an alternate appointment would get in only if the person with the principal appointment was found to be unqualified or if he decided not to accept the appointment.
† Iowa State Teachers College, now University of Northern Iowa. Dr. William H. Kadesch had been a professor of electrical engineering at the Naval Academy from 1913 to 1918.
‡ A normal school was a preparatory college for elementary school teachers; it was usually two years in duration.

inspiration to me also. He was an engineer and a very successful one. He kind of showed me the way in many ways as I went through life.

However, it was much easier to go to the State Normal School at $25.00 a semester and live at home, and also I could keep my job at the warehouse at Standard Glass and Paint. It was a simple decision; it was financial. I would work about three hours a day there and all day on Saturday. I'd bring in about seven bucks a week, which was good money at that time. A typical day was rather strenuous. I'd have to get up at 6:00 o'clock, which I sometimes didn't make, and would have to be routed out by my mother and be picked up shortly thereafter by Bill Fowler, who had a Ford V-8, and in the morning he would drive us up to the college for ten cents.

Q: How far was that?

Admiral Ramage: About five or six miles. I hitchhiked home every night because ten cents was ten cents. People were always hitchhiking, and drivers were very friendly at that time. I took the same basic courses at Iowa State Teachers as I was to take next year at the Naval Academy. About that time, the Vinson-Trammell Act was passed, which started to build up the Navy.* Vinson, you know, the famous congressman. There was a shipbuilding program, but also there was an extra appointment to the Naval Academy that year, and that's where my appointment came from. I was all ready to go, and I entered on certificate from high school and from Iowa State Teachers College.

Q: When you say there was an extra appointment, did that apply to each state?

Admiral Ramage: I think each congressman, although it couldn't be, because, golly, the class would be almost doubled that year with an extra appointment. In any event, Congressman Gwynne had an extra appointment and he sent me on that. I think the way it worked, a congressman was allowed to have four people in the academy at any one time,

---

* Representative Carl Vinson (Democrat-Georgia) and Senator Park Trammel (Democrat-Florida) were chairmen of the respective naval affairs committees. The Vinson-Trammel Act, 27 March 1934, called for the construction of 102 ships.

and this raised it to five. My class was one of the largest classes. I think we had 860 enter, which was substantially higher than had been previously because of this Vinson-Trammel bill.* So I was all ready to go. I bade goodbye to my parents, got on the Illinois Central train, went in to Chicago, spent a couple of days with my sister and brother-in-law. I went on to Annapolis by the Pennsylvania Railroad and the WB&A, the Washington, Baltimore, and Annapolis "Toonerville" trolley that served Annapolis at that time.

I got there on the 24th of July, 1935, and checked in at Carvel Hall, which was a hotel right across from the Naval Academy.† I immediately went across the road to take a look at the school. I was impressed. I thought it was the greatest place that I'd ever see. Boy, I really wanted to get in there.

One of the interesting things that happened to me that night, which brought up my first contact with race and prejudice, was I ran into a young man named Kermit Trim, who was from either Kentucky or Tennessee.‡ We were talking there in the hotel, and he said, "I've got to go down to the hardware store."

I said, "Why?"

He said, "I've got to get me a big knife. I've heard of these northern niggers, and I don't want to have any problem with them." I didn't agree with him at all, and he wanted to know if I wanted to go along.

I said, "No, I don't really want to do that." At that time I was aware of the fact that the toilets were separate for colored and white, and the drinking fountains were colored and white, even in Annapolis. Although Maryland was not part of the Confederacy, it was certainly part of the South at that time, as was Washington, D.C. I didn't like that at all. It simply wasn't right, and I'm glad things have changed since that time.

I was entered into the school the next day, passed the physical exam, had a little trouble with my eyes on color blindness. I think really that I was just so nervous and scared that I simply wasn't reading the charts right, because I really had never had any problems with it and never have since. So I went down into my new room and met my roommate.

---

* Of the 860, 581 graduated in 1939.
† Opened at the turn of the century, Carvel Hall was a favorite meeting place for officers and midshipmen. It has since been torn down.
‡ Midshipman Kermit M. Trim, USN. Trim subsequently dropped out of the academy.

I'm going to dwell a little bit now about my roommate Earl Carlsten, because he was my dancing partner later on.* He was a preacher's son from Bryan, Ohio. He was a small, towheaded youngster, very bright, and he was agnostic. Also, I think he was a Communist, or at least was extremely liberal. And, of course, coming from my church, Republican background, we just didn't see eye to eye on anything. He was smart, though, and he helped me a lot, particularly when I was having some scholastic troubles during plebe year.† But he stood for everything I didn't, and vice versa. I lived with him for four years. Every year I was considering getting a new roommate, but I didn't think anybody else would ever live with him, so it was just a cut-and-dried affair. We just let it hang on. Maybe he felt the same way about me, I don't know, but he was not a pleasant guy to live with, very caustic about many things. However, he helped me a lot. He was bright, particularly in science and math.

Anyway, we're getting back to plebe summer. I liked it. I thought the Naval Academy was going to be tough. Well, it was really right down my alley. They kept us running from morning till night. We did infantry drill, and we rowed cutters, we sailed, we went to the rifle range. It was really just what I wanted to do. I enjoyed it.

Q: Did you have any particular favorite activities among those?

Admiral Ramage: No, I just liked everything, and the food was excellent. Golly, that mess hall at the Naval Academy was really something. I think probably the food there is still equally good. It was very special. So I enjoyed that. During September we went into our first course in math, which was a very simple course. It was learning to manipulate the slide rule, because we were going to use that a lot in the coming year. At the same time, I went out for football. I ended up that first course in math with a 1.96, which is, of course, way below passing--2.5 being passing on a grade point system of 4.0. So I was unsat as I could

---

* Midshipman Earl E. Carlsten, USN. Carlsten graduated in the class of 1939 and retired as a commander in July 1959.
† A midshipman in his first year is called a plebe; second year, youngster or third classman; third year, second classman; fourth year, first classman.

be. Then the academic year started, and I immediately went unsat in chemistry, with a 2.23, and mechanical drawing, with a 2.4 something. In other words, I was really in deep trouble.

Well, the first thing I knew was that I'd better stop playing football. I wasn't doing all that well, but I was on the second plebe team, and I rather enjoyed it, although it was a heck of a lot tougher than high school football. I dropped football, and immediately Tom Hamilton, the coach, called me over.[*] I explained to him that I was unsat and that if I could pull sat, that I would come out again, but I just couldn't afford to bilge out of the Naval Academy.[†] I couldn't do it. Tom suggested I go back to my room and think it over. So I thought it over and decided that I was going to spend all my time studying.

About two or three days later, Captain Giffen, who was the athletic director, called me over.[‡] When a captain talks to a plebe, I mean, you stand at attention. I went through my problems with him, and he said, "Now, don't worry too much about it. You'll get on to the system. I think you ought to stay out for football." He said, "Now, in the event you do happen to flunk any subjects, why, when you go before the academic board, you'll always have somebody in your corner from the athletic department."

Well, I had no intention of going before the academic board for any reason, and Captain Giffen then indicated that I was somewhat less than manly and that I should go out for football. I went back to my room and that was it. I was not going to play football unless I could do a heck of a lot better in school.

I mentioned Jake Stong previously. Jake Stong was also out for football, and he was equally unsat. When he later went before the academic board, he didn't even get a firm handshake. He was back in Iowa, going to Iowa State, where he had gone the previous year. So I think that probably I was correct.

Q: This decision of going back to your room after talking to the athletic director--that must have been a very traumatic experience for a plebe to buck this four-striper and basically the

---

[*] Lieutenant (junior grade) Thomas J. Hamilton, USN, was tdhe Naval Academy's head football coach from 1934 to 1936, when he compiled a record of 19-8-0. The oral history of Hamilton, who retired as a rear admiral, is in the Naval Institute collection.
[†] Bilge out--to fail.
[‡] Captain Robert C. Giffen, USN, Naval Academy athletic director from 1934 to 1937.

system and go it on his own.

Admiral Ramage: Well, it wasn't much of a decision for me, because I knew that if I didn't make it at the Naval Academy, it would absolutely kill my parents; and if I flunked out, I would not go home. I don't know what would have happened to me, but I simply would not have gone back to my hometown.

So going into the first term, I was unsat in three subjects. By the end of November, I had all my grades on up to satisfactory. I had pulled them up. I had to be over the 3.0 mark in order to pull up those low grades, and I had learned the system of studying at the Naval Academy. It was different. They taught you nothing; you learned out of books. The professors, most of whom were naval officers, were simply referees. You were expected to recite or be tested every day in every subject, and you got a grade every day in every subject. I think it was probably a very good system in that it certainly taught you to do it yourself.

There was no teaching; there were no lectures. As a matter of fact, sometimes an instructor would ask, when you came into the classroom, if there were any questions. And if somebody happened to ask a question that was going to be on the quiz that day, he would say, "Unfortunately, I can't answer that because you're going to be asked that in about five minutes." The classes were only about 12 people in each class, so you got really direct attention. It was a fine experience.

As I go through this tape, I sometimes will make rather caustic remarks about the academy or some of the people that went there, but I don't want to ever give the impression that I wasn't both pleased and proud to go to the Naval Academy and graduate from it. My feeling is that they were somewhat lacking in certain things there, but I was very lucky to get into the academy and extremely pleased to be able to get out of it.

During that plebe year, I pulled myself sat in the various subjects, and I never again did go unsat. That was a good lesson to me. My father couldn't understand it. I had been a really good student in high school and a pretty good student in college for all the work I was doing there. Then here I was at the Naval Academy and just having a heck of a time. He thought I wasn't trying, and I was just trying as hard as I could. I kept telling him that the Naval Academy was a different league, that these people were a little smarter than most of the people in Waterloo or Iowa State Teachers. Consequently, I was struggling just to keep moving.

Q: Presumably you didn't play football again.

Admiral Ramage: No, no, I never did go out for football again. As a matter of fact, my time at the Naval Academy, unlike my time in high school, was very unexceptional. I did my work, I studied hard and so forth, but I certainly didn't star in anything.

Q: Was some type of athletic activity required?

Admiral Ramage: Oh, yes. You were always doing something. For a while I played battalion football, and I was always in athletics of some kind. Everybody was expected to do something. I'd wrestle a little bit and so forth, but I was never very good at any of it, but at the Naval Academy, you do things. They talk about the radiator squads; those are the people who sit on the radiator and don't do anything. I will say at times that I approached that because I was studying to stay sat. I used to study a lot, a lot more than the other people, because I had to work real hard just to keep moving along.

Q: Did you find from experience that you could skim material and sort out the pertinent from the unnecessary?

Admiral Ramage: Exactly. That's what I learned during this formative period when I was pulling sat, that I could pick out the high points, and I learned what they were. Now, there were a lot of guys that went in at the same time that I did that were a lot smarter than I was, who flunked out. Some of them were college graduates in engineering, and they flunked out simply because they couldn't sort out the important facts.

Q: They tried to absorb everything instead of what was important.

Admiral Ramage: Yes.

Q: That raises another question. From plebe year to graduation, what was the attrition?

Admiral Ramage: We went in with 860 and we graduated 581.

Q: Would that be representative of the period, do you think?

Admiral Ramage: I would say probably so. While some of them left voluntarily, most of them flunked out. They had a bell curve. I don't know exactly what it was, but they looked at the end result and knew how many commissions they had to offer when we graduated, so they kept everybody moving.

Although I did pretty well in the academics as time went on, I had one real problem, and that was aptitude for the service, or "grease," as they called it. I couldn't get above 2.5. It used to make me very angry, because I thought that I was a heck of a lot better candidate than most of these guys that were doing very well in "grease," as we called it. But I guess probably it was my independence--the fact that I wouldn't "suck ass," as they called it at the Naval Academy at that time. I didn't have any great disciplinary problems, but somehow or other the people that made up these things, whether it was the upperclassmen or the officers, I don't know. Because I never did get to be a midshipman officer, I don't know who was making out these report cards.

Q: Perhaps Captain Giffen.

Admiral Ramage: No. I simply couldn't get above a 2.5. Maybe I got a 2.6 one time, but I just couldn't do it. I guess it was my independent background. Also, I was very questioning of things that I thought were full of horseshit. When I saw somebody doing something dumb, I would say, "I just don't think that's right." Apparently that isn't the way you do it. However, that attitude and that low grease mark that I was getting was the same thing that I think was the reason for my success in the Navy later on--independence and questioning. Because I didn't change a bit, and all of a sudden when I got out into the fleet, I began to do real well. But I just couldn't get past that barrier. It's kind of a comical thing, because the two four-star guys in my class were also anchor men in "grease," Blackie Weinel and Means Johnston.[*] They were also down at the very bottom of the class in aptitude for the service. I think that that is indicative of something.

Incidentally, when I was out in Yankee Station out there in the Gulf of Tonkin years later, Blackie had made his third star, and I wrote him a congratulating letter.[†] He wrote an answer back that said, "I talked to a young officer here in Washington who said that you told him that you were anchor man in grease. I want to let you know that I nosed you out the last quarter." And he said, "Further, you were a greasy bastard."

He said, "I was carrying a rifle for all three sets of periods during first class year, and I noticed that you, you greasy bastard, got to be a 1-PO."[‡] Well, I didn't get to be a 1-PO; I got to be a guidon petty officer, which is up on the staff, and the only reason I was up there was because the company commander was over six feet, which I was, and they wanted somebody that would fit the size.[§] But I would have been a 2-PO in rank all three times, too, so I think that that accusation by Blackie Weinel is entirely wrong.[**] I would have been a 2-PO in rank staff all three sets of the first class year just like he was. So much for the grease marks there.

At the Naval Academy I did have a couple of interesting experiences. When I was a youngster, I was put on report by my battalion commander, Lieutenant Commander Wessell, known as the "Wooz."[††] I was guilty of the heinous crime of hands in pocket, aggravated offense. I was seen to enter the rotunda there at Bancroft Hall, with both hands

---

[*] John P. Weinel and Means Johnston, Jr., both wound up as four-star admirals. "Anchor man" is the slang term for a midshipman who finishes at the bottom of his class at the Naval Academy.
[†] As a rear admiral, Weinel commanded Carrier Division Three from 1967 to 1969. Yankee Station was the designation of the main operating area for aircraft carriers sending strikes against North Vietnam.
[‡] Set--semester at the Naval Academy; 1-PO--midshipman petty officer first class.
[§] The guidon petty officer carried numerical company flag during parades.
[**] 2-PO--petty officer second class.
[††] Lieutenant Commander Leonard P. Wessell, USN, battalion officer, 1934-1936.

in my overcoat pocket.* He, being my battalion officer, sent me down to the <u>Reina Mercedes</u>, which was the brig, for a weekend.† I always wanted to go to the <u>Reina Mercedes</u> because you got to be a black N guy, even for just the weekend, so that was one thing that I aspired to.‡ I got only 15 demerits for it, and most people that went down to the ship went down for a class A offense, and that was pretty rough.§

Q: Was it literally a brig?

Admiral Ramage: The <u>Reina Mercedes</u> was a Spanish ship that was captured during the Spanish-American War, and it was the station ship at the Naval Academy, so you'd go there and you'd attend all classes. You slept on canvas cots and were supposed to be penitent. It wasn't bad down there. It was kind of nice. Also, you met a fine class of people.

Q: Any future flag officers there?

Admiral Ramage: Yes, quite a few of the flag officers were down there.

One other experience I'd like to tell about, because it was kind of funny. "Frenching out" was one of the regular affairs that those of us that were a little sporty engaged in.** This experience happened during second class June Week, and really it was almost fatal. I was out, over the hill, seeing my girlfriend. It was a strange thing because midshipmen "Frenched out" in the same uniform. We didn't have any civilian clothes. The "Frenching out" uniform was blue shirt, blue trousers, and white tennis shoes, and if it was cold enough, you wore your blue sweater. If you saw anybody in town dressed that way, they

---

* Bancroft Hall is the large multi-wing dormitory that houses Naval Academy midshipmen. It also contains the offices of members of the executive department, including the commandant, executive officer, and battalion and company officers.
† USS <u>Reina Mercedes</u> (IX-25), captured during the Spanish-American War, served as a station ship at the Naval Academy from 1912 to 1957. Until 1940, midshipmen being punished for various disciplinary infractions slept and took meals on board the ship but continued to go to classes ashore.
‡ Each year's edition of the Naval Academy yearbook, the <u>Lucky Bag</u>, contained a boldface black N next to the photo and biography of each midshipman who had been confined to the <u>Reina Mercedes</u> for a time. It was a perverse badge of honor.
§ Class A offense--major infraction
** "Frenching out" meant climbing over the wall and spending time out in the town of Annapolis when not authorized.

were "Frenching out." So I got out, went around the fence there at Thompson Stadium, where everybody went around, and did whatever people do when they "French out."[*]

About 3:00 o'clock I was about to come back in and I went around the stadium fence, and the "Jimmy legs" as we called them--they're the civilian cops, nice old gentlemen--were there, and said, "You can't come in tonight. The duty officers are all out, and I can't let you in." So I went all the way around to the hospital gate, which was one of the places which generally wasn't manned. So I walked about half a mile to that gate, and they had Marines there. You could outrun the "Jimmy legs," but you couldn't outrun the Marines; they were different. So I went back to the main gate, and by that time it was getting light. I thought, "Well, maybe I'll just run the gate. I'll probably get caught, but God, I've got to get in before they muster." I wasn't getting anywhere.

About that time I ran into George Duncan and Duke David.[†] They were "Frenching in" also, and, God, I said I was really in a bad way. I'd been drinking a little beer, and I was in no great shape. They didn't think that rushing the gate was going to be a good thing; I'd get caught, and I'd really be turning myself in. So they said, "We have a place that's right here." It was right behind the chapel. The wall there around the academy is about a 10-foot brick and concrete wall, and then on top of it, behind the chapel, they had about an 8-foot wire mesh fence on top of that. I looked up at that, and, God, there was no way I could get up there. They said, "Come on, we're going over." So I got on up there. By that time it was broad daylight.

Just inside the wall was a commander's home. His name was Commander Larson, and he obviously was a very nice guy, because we made all the noise in the world climbing the fence.[‡] I think I fell off the fence coming down, and was stomping around in the shrubbery. I made it back to Bancroft Hall in time to get a shower. As a matter of fact, George Duncan said years later that he saw Commander Larson and that Commander Larson had seen us in broad daylight; he was such a nice guy, he didn't turn us in. Because that would have been a real class A, and with my wonderful reputation, I could have probably been kicked out for one or two things, including use of alcoholic beverages. In

---

[*] Thompson Stadium, near Dahlgren Hall, was the site of Naval Academy home football games.
[†] Midshipman George Duncan, USN; Midshipman Edmonds David, USN.
[‡] Commander William J. Larson, USN.

any event, that was the type of thing that went on for midshipmen at that time. I always rather felt sorry for these grease-balls that never had enough guts to go out over the fence--those who did everything exactly right--because I think they missed an awful lot at the Naval Academy.

Q: Annapolis was a pretty small town, even at that time.

Admiral Ramage: Yes. Probably about 10,000 to 12,000.

Q: The likelihood of you running into someone from the academy out in town was quite high.

Admiral Ramage: That's correct.

Q: What would have happened?

Admiral Ramage: Dressed the way we were, with everybody in the "Frenching out" uniform, everybody knew that you were from the academy and you were in "Frenching out" clothes.

Q: What if you had run across one of the academy officers?

Admiral Ramage: I think that the academy officers were all very well aware that it was going on.

Q: Because they did it when they were midshipmen.

Admiral Ramage: Right. I don't think there were very many of them that would go very much out of their way to turn in somebody unless he was a real goof-off. Very interesting, you bring up the academy officers. I don't think that I had a kind word spoken to me by a commissioned officer at the Naval Academy all the time I was there. There was a definite line, and I guess maybe the midshipmen stripers conversed with them, but it was always, rather, as far as I was concerned, an antagonistic confrontation.* It was we, the non-grease-balls, against them, and that was the way it was played. It was not unpleasant. There was always the idea of trying to see if you couldn't slip one over on them. But maybe this is why I got low grease marks. Maybe they knew that I was doing these things but couldn't catch me.

Q: Couldn't prove it.

Admiral Ramage: So rather than giving the demerits that go with it, they'd slide my grease mark down to 2.5.

Q: What's the origin of the term "Frenching out"?

Admiral Ramage: Golly, I don't know. During World War I, you used to hear of soldiers taking French leave, which was going AWOL.† I think probably it started there.

I graduated about a quarter of the way up from the bottom of my class, certainly the lowest quarter, which wasn't bad when you consider the extremely low grease marks that I was getting at that time.‡ I was very, very happy to graduate and very proud to be able to graduate.

At that time, you were obligated for only two years of service after graduation, and during that time you were also not permitted to get married, which was a real break because you could say, "Well, young lady, I really would like to marry you, but you know, you wouldn't want to ruin my naval career." That went away with the war and has never come back, but I always thought it was a pretty fine break. One of the things it did, of course, was to keep some of the youngsters from getting married right out of school. They were going to go to sea and leave some poor gal from Keokuk, Iowa, or someplace, in Long

---

* Stripers--midshipmen in positions of leadership and responsibility.
† AWOL--absent without leave
‡ Midshipman Ramage stood 518th of the 581 graduates in the class of 1939.

Beach, not knowing what the heck was going on. But I guess they decided during World War II that that just wouldn't sell, and had to do away with it.

The Navy's attitude at that time--and I still concur with it--was that if the Navy wanted you to have a wife, they'd issue you one.

Q: Right along with the seabag.

Admiral Ramage: Right. I thought it was a pretty good thing.

Q: As far as the Academy community goes, from time to time we hear about the Green Bowl Society.* What was the background on that?

Admiral Ramage: Well, I was going to get around to that when I got to the Enterprise because John Crommelin was such a great anti-Green Bowler.† I have the list of the Green Bowl at home that I got from John. I think probably we'd better go into that later, because it's part of John Crommelin's makeup. He, in my opinion, is one of the greatest guys I've ever met.

Also during these two years of obligated service, we ensigns were required to make book reports every quarter. We had to turn in eight book reports. This was to make up for the fact that they figured we didn't have a rounded education, that we were basically engineers and we didn't have any couth. So we were required to turn in these things every quarter, and they were a real pain in the neck to us who were doing them. I'm sure that it was worse on the Department of English and History at the Naval Academy, who had to correct these darn things. It was kind of a strange thing, but it was a part of the times. I don't know whether anything like that has ever been done since.

---

* Green Bowl Society was a secret clique of midshipmen who promoted their own interests while at the academy and later in the fleet, presumably by helping junior members of the organization get desirable, career-enhancing billets.
† Captain John G. Crommelin, Jr., USN, issued a diatribe against the Green Bowl Society shortly after World War II. During the war, as a commander, he served in the carrier Enterprise (CV-6).

Q: What was the prevailing attitude at the academy towards aviation at the time you went through?

Admiral Ramage: During first class year, we were given lectures on financial arrangements and various other things, and one of the things was on career planning.* This commander--and I don't remember his name--told us what we should look forward to in the Navy, and his first point was, "Avoid going to an aircraft carrier completely." He said that what you do as a junior officer is, you put in for a battleship, you join the junior officers' mess for two years, you get into the gunnery department, and you go with the largest guns possible, because that's the future of the Navy, the battleship. It made sense, because at that time the battle line was certainly it. I wanted to be an aviator pretty much all the time I was at the Naval Academy.

Q: Did you have that idea when you went to the academy?

Admiral Ramage: It came when I met certain people that were there. There were a few instructors who promoted aviation. One of them was Bob Pirie, who was in the department of seamanship and navigation.† There were two or three others, Ford Taylor being one.‡ They were very nice people, and I looked up to them. It seemed to me that naval aviation would give a lot more freedom of action. You could have more independence, and also I thought--which was proven to me later--that they were a heck of a lot better class of people in aviation than was in the regular line. This is where my prejudice shows.

Q: Had you ever seen a naval airplane or a naval vessel before you went to the academy?

Admiral Ramage: Yes. During second class summer, we took a short course in aviation.§

---

* First class year is a midshipman's fourth year at the Academy, the last before graduation.
† Lieutenant Robert B. Pirie, USN. The oral history of Pirie, who retired as a vice admiral, is in the Naval Institute collection.
‡ Lieutenant Ford N. Taylor, USN.
§ Second class summer--between the second and third academic years.

Q: But before you went to the academy?

Admiral Ramage: Oh, no.

Q: Had you ever seen a ship?

Admiral Ramage: I had never seen a ship or a service airplane. I had never seen the ocean. I'd never been anyplace, really, except once or twice I went up to Minnesota, and we would go to Bloomington, Illinois, where my dad came from. But other than that, I never left the state.

Q: Was there ever any thought of you going to West Point instead of Annapolis?

Admiral Ramage: Dad at first was talking about West Point, but later on he went all out as far as getting me into the Naval Academy. I took both exams just as a fallback position, but my desire was to get that blue uniform and impress the gals. That was really what it was all about.

Q: So your going to the Naval Academy really had no relationship to any kind of recruiting system of the Navy at that time?

Admiral Ramage: No. It was very much sought for, of course, because it was a good, free education, and people just didn't have any money. There weren't any freebies around like the colleges have today, including ROTCs and all that business.* There just wasn't anything you could do except to clean floors and do, as most of my friends did, hash at the various sororities. It was the usual thing to work your way through school, particularly among all my friends. I don't know any of them that went to school without working. It was just the times.

---

* ROTC--Reserve Officer Training Corps

Well, I went against this commander's advice and put in for the Enterprise. There were 16 of us ensigns that ended up on the Enterprise.[*] The normal draft out of the Academy was eight, but we got eight from the Wasp, which was not commissioned, and they wanted to send these guys to sea at the same time.[†]

Q: You could actually request a particular ship?

Admiral Ramage: Yes. You drew lots and you could ask for a ship. Both my roommate on the Enterprise, Grant Rogers, and I asked for that ship.[‡] I think that we were probably the only ones that did. I can remember the Enterprise was anchored out in the harbor here in San Diego, and she was a beauty. In reporting aboard, it was the biggest thing I'd ever seen, and I said, "This thing is just too big to move. I just don't think it will ever sail."

Q: Who was the captain at that time?

Admiral Ramage: Captain Pownall, who was one of the finest gentlemen I've ever met.[§] The ship was a beauty, the fittings throughout were stainless steel, the doors and so forth. It's never been done since. And they were polished. I'm going to go into this thing that I had in the Hook magazine here later to explain the Enterprise a little bit more.[**]

But you mentioned Captain Pownall. We 16 ensigns put on our full dress uniforms and our swords and went up to call on the captain. He was a pleasant man and, I think, an excellent naval officer. He asked how many had asked for the Enterprise, and I think Grant and I were the only two that raised our hands. Then he asked the same question that you did, Bob--what was the attitude at the Naval Academy. One of us explained to him how we

---

[*] USS Enterprise (CV-6) was commissioned 12 May 1938. She had a standard displacement of 19,800 tons, was 810 feet long, 83 feet in the beam, and had an extreme width of 114 feet. Her top speed was 33 knots. She had eight 5-inch guns and could accommodate approximately 90-100 aircraft.

[†] USS Wasp (CV-7) did not go into commission until 25 April 1940, nearly a year after Ensign Ramage's Naval Academy class graduated in June 1939.

[‡] Ensign Grant H. Rogers, USN.

[§] Captain Charles A. Pownall, USN, commanded the aircraft carrier Enterprise (CV-6) from 21 December 1938 to 21 March 1941. The oral history of Pownall, who retired as a vice admiral, is in the Naval Institute collection.

[**] The Hook, published quarterly by the Tailhook Association.

had been told not to go to a carrier under any circumstance. Captain Pownall's remark was, "None of you ensigns will ever regret coming to this ship." And, boy, I sure as heck didn't.

Q: Captain Pownall was an aviator?

Admiral Ramage: He was an aviator, of course, yes.

Q: Later he became a task group commander for a short time.[*]

Admiral Ramage: Yes. He was somewhat less than successful in that category because he was too damned kind. He just didn't like to take the losses, but he was a fine skipper. While I'm on that, I might talk about one of the experiences with Captain Pownall and one of the things that happened to me as a result of it. On board the carrier from time to time was ComAirBatFor, Commander Aircraft Battle Force. First that was Blakely, and then Halsey.[†] Halsey's chief of staff was a captain nicknamed Genial John Hoover.[‡] Maybe you've heard of him. That's what he wasn't.

I was in the deck division at the time, and so consequently I got to know Genial John pretty well, because I had the ceremonial gangway and five of the boats. Genial John was pretty rough, particularly on Captain Pownall. Although they were both captains, Genial John really wore Halsey's stripes around. As chief of staff, Genial John Hoover really directly ran the Enterprise, and Captain Baldy Pownall, as we called him, let him do it. It wasn't unusual at all for Hoover to give direct orders to the bridge over the voice tube.

I'm getting a little ahead of myself, but I'll mention it since we're on this particular situation and on Pownall, whom I admired very much. This occurred two years later, when I was standing deck watch. We were off Honolulu, and Captain George Murray, who had

---

[*] As a rear admiral, Pownall commanded the fast carrier task force in late 1943 in the Pacific. He was shortly afterward relieved by Rear Admiral Marc A. Mitscher, USN.
[†] Vice Admiral Charles A. Blakely, USN, served as Commander Aircraft Battle Force from June 1939 to June 1940. Vice Admiral William F. Halsey, Jr., USN, served as such from June 1940 to 10 April 1942, at which time the command was renamed Carriers Pacific Fleet. He was relieved of that command on 11 July 1942.
[‡] Captain John H. Hoover, USN.

relieved Pownall, was the skipper.* It was about 5:00 o'clock in the afternoon, and I got a direct order from Captain Hoover to change course. I sent the messenger immediately down to Captain Murray, who was in the in-port cabin taking a shower, to let him know that I had been directed to change course. There was a compass repeater down in Captain Murray's stateroom, and he ran to the bridge, and said to me, "Young man, what are you doing?"

I said, "I'm coming left to course so and so."

He said, "Why?"

I said, "I was directed to do so by the chief of staff."

He said, "Was the chief of staff on this bridge?"

I said, "Yes, sir."

He went up to the flag bridge, which was above, and got ahold of Genial John. They had it out, and you could hear it. It was loud. I'm sure that George Murray had known that Hoover had been running the Enterprise before he reported aboard, and was just waiting for the first occurrence. I happened to be in the middle of it.

After this very direct confrontation, Captain Murray came down on the bridge and he said, "Young man, who is the captain of this ship?"

I said, "You are, sir."

And he said, "Don't you ever forget it." He left the bridge, and, boy, that was the end of Captain Hoover running the Enterprise. There was a very cool relationship between the captain and the chief of staff thereafter. Well, so much for that.

Let's get back to my time on the ship. I was aboard the Enterprise for about 26 months, and all but four of them were spent in the deck department. I was a junior officer in the second division for the first year and then went down to engineering, mainly as a makee-learn to get qualified as engineering watch officer under way.†

Q: What year did you report?

---

* Captain George D. Murray, USN, commanded the Enterprise from 21 March 1941 to 30 June 1942.
† Makee-learn was essentially observation and on-the-job training before taking on the responsibility of the position.

Admiral Ramage: In 1939.

The policy at that time was to alternate the ensigns in the various departments. I was told when I was down in engineering that Captain Pownall wanted me back in deck. He considered me a good watch stander, which was very flattering to me, and I was very glad to get back up. When I came back to the second division, I was the division officer, and I learned a lot from being in a deck division. The deck division leading petty officer was first class petty officer named Van Keuren. He had a full-rigged ship tattooed on his chest, and he ran that division very smoothly. There was never a problem, and I learned very early not to meddle with things that are working right, because he had that division running just like a watch.

Another one who was on the ship that I really learned a lot from was the chief boatswain. His name was Filbry, and he was a real sea daddy.[*] As a junior officer, if you'd just listened to him, you learned how to do things. The boatswain was a great influence on me, in knowing how to handle men in the deck division, and making darn sure that I knew that the petty officers ran the division, and he put it very clearly. He said, "Always be around but don't interfere." I followed that.

As a matter of fact, I'll go into Felix Stump a little bit later, but Felix became our executive officer.[†] I used to get quite a lot of "at-a-boys" from Felix, because he knew that I was always around, not interfering, but always around the second division. I enjoyed my years on deck, but I was frustrated because I wanted to get up in that airplane. Nevertheless, the two years that we were required to do before flight training were good for me. I learned a lot, and it stood me in very good stead during my career in the Navy.

Q: Did you ever get an opportunity to fly off a ship while you were there?

Admiral Ramage: Never flew off the ship. I used to catch rides from anybody. While we're on it, I would even bum a ride with Felix Stump, who was considered to be the world's

---

[*] Chief Warrant Officer Frederick W. Filbry, USN; sea daddy--a person who teaches a newcomer the ins and outs of shipboard life.
[†] Commander Felix B. Stump, USN; Stump, later a four-star admiral, served as Commander in Chief Pacific Fleet in the 1950s. His oral history is in the Columbia University collection.

worst aviator. This was while we were in port. The ship was assigned a seaplane. I think it was probably an SOC attached to the ship.* In any event, I would ride with him, and the aviators that were in the air department on the ship, Bucky Lee and the two Taylor brothers--they weren't brothers at all but they called them that--J. I. Taylor and Ford Taylor would always ask me when I got back down whether I was alive and well.† They thought that I was probably the dumbest guy around to fly with old Felix because he really was erratic.

Stump was a very unusual guy. He wasn't very bright, in my opinion, but he was determined. The one thing I learned from him was to take care of my men. He was always taking care of the enlisted men on that ship. He was one tough cookie, particularly on the officers. But the men loved him, and I got to know him quite well. I didn't ever admire him, because he was so erratic and irrational. He was given to severe fits of temper, and he would bawl out officers in public, really chew them up. There was one particular officer that he really enjoyed going after. His name was Over, and he worked in the first lieutenant's department.‡ Lieutenant Over just couldn't do anything right as far, as Stump was concerned, and he would just absolutely tear this guy apart in front of everybody.

My immediate boss was Gus Roane, Virginius R. Roane, and he was a Virginian and a real gentleman, absolutely one of the finest men I've ever met.§ We got along quite well in spite of various things that went on. He was very close to me. As a matter of fact, when I put in for flight training, which I did almost immediately when I got there, I had quite a talk with Gus Roane. He indicated that I was doing very well in the gunnery department and that he thought that if I went into aviation that I'd be ruining my career. He was sincere about it. He wasn't anti-aviation. He was just telling me the facts of life at that time.

I'll go into a little episode here that I think is worth repeating. The <u>Enterprise</u> left for Pearl Harbor in September of 1939 to be the flagship of the Hawaiian detachment, and

---

* The SOC was the last Curtiss biplane to serve the Navy, operating from the mid-1930s through World War II.
† Lieutenant Commander James R. Lee, USN; Lieutenant Commander Joseph I. Taylor, USN; Lieutenant Ford N. Taylor, USN.
‡ Lieutenant George R. Over, USN.
§ Lieutenant Commander Virginius R. Roane, USN.

the flag that we carried with us was Vice Admiral Adolphus Andrews.* Adolphus Andrews was just as pompous as his name sounds. He was a real Lord Plushbottom. We didn't particularly like the staff that was on board, because they didn't like aviators at all. And this incident was kind of funny. We were tied up at Ten-Ten Dock there at Pearl in October of '39. They were having the normal Navy Day party at the Royal Hawaiian Hotel. Grant Rogers, my roommate, and I were all dressed for it. It was a dress occasion, black tie and so forth, so we were in dress uniform. We went to the party and did whatever people do at parties.

We had a borrowed car, and coming back sometime after midnight, we got hungry and decided to have a hamburger. So whoever was driving, I don't recall, parked on the wrong side of the street and went into the old Black Cat Cafe there in downtown Honolulu to get a hamburger. We immediately were arrested for parking on the wrong side of the street. Well, this wasn't a great crime, but at that time you had to have a Hawaiian driver's license. Any other driver's license would not fill the bill. So we were driving without a license, and the cop also said, "Where's the car's papers, the ownership papers?" Well, of course, it was a borrowed car, so we didn't have any idea where they were. So he said, "Well, I'm going to have to take you in." So we ended up in the police station with our car, and by that time it was getting kind of light. The police lieutenant that was there was a nice guy. We told him the situation and that if we were arrested it would probably mean our naval careers.

So he said, "Okay, I'm going to let you go. I understand this law on the license here is rather bad anyway. I know you didn't steal the car, but I can't let you drive the car back because you don't have a license."

So we were figuring out how we'd get back, when a shore patrol driver came up. He said, "I'll take you back. I'm going back about 7:30 in the morning. I'll get you out to Pearl by 8:00 o'clock quarters."

So we drove out--two ensigns in our dress uniforms, riding in the back end of the paddy wagon,. Well, we came up to Ten-Ten Dock just as Adolphus Andrews was arriving

---

* Vice Admiral Adolphus Andrews, USN, Commander Scouting Force, U.S. Fleet. In October 1939 the Navy Department directed the establishment of a Hawaiian Detachment of the U.S. Fleet, which was then based in California.

in his Cadillac, with all the pomp and circumstance that went on with the blackshoe Navy at that time.* Everybody was at quarters for muster. We drove up behind him, these two ensigns getting out of the back end of a paddy wagon. We reported aboard to the enjoyment of many people. I immediately went down to my room to change my clothes and get ready for the day's work. My old friend Gus Roane stuck his head in the door and said, "Mr. Ramage, I don't suppose you'll be going ashore much in the future."

I said, "No, sir, I hadn't planned on it." I was never officially in hack, and there was never anything said about it, but the ship was divided into two groups of people. One group thought that this was a great crime and reflected upon the good name of the USS Enterprise. Then there were the other people, mainly aviators, who thought it was pretty funny. So I gained a little and lost a little on that.

Q: I'd like to talk a little bit about the fleet organization at that time. During these big fleet problems that the Navy conducted prior to World War II, the flag carried aboard a carrier was actually a relative junior command, wasn't it?

Admiral Ramage: That's correct. Of course, the battleships ran the fleet, and you had CinCUS, Commander in Chief U.S. Fleet, who was first J. O. Richardson and then Kimmel while we were out there.† He was four stars. Then they had Commander Battle Force, who was also four stars. They had Commander Battleships. The aviators were way down the line.* The carrier really was not considered to be anything but a support for the battle line.

Q: And then the senior flag was carried in the battleships.

Admiral Ramage: Oh, yes. We were really way out in left field. We were part of the train.

---

* Blackshoe Navy--officers who served on surface ships; aviators were referred to as brownshoes.
† Admiral James O. Richardson, USN, served as Commander in Chief U.S. Fleet (CinCUS) from 6 January 1940 to 1 February 1941. His relief, Admiral Husband E. Kimmel, USN, was designated Commander in Chief Pacific Fleet rather than CinCUS. Kimmel was relieved of the fleet command on 17 December 1941 in the wake of the Japanese attack on Pearl Harbor.

Admiral Ramage: Oh, yes. We were really way out in left field. We were part of the train.

Q: Do you recall approximately how many of these battle problems you participated in?

Admiral Ramage: Well, probably three or four.

Q: They had one a year?

Admiral Ramage: They used to have the big fleet problem yearly. I don't think we had it that year or after the fleet left Long Beach, which was in '40. See, the Enterprise went out in '39, and then the fleet came out the following year.[*]

Q: Do you recall any change in attitude at all, or even a beginning of a change that aviation was starting to prove itself as being a valuable weapon in the Battle Force?

Admiral Ramage: None whatsoever. None whatsoever. There was a tremendous animosity against aviation at that time.

Q: What type of weapon then were the air groups considered?

Admiral Ramage: Well, first of all, they used them for scouting, to find the enemy so they could get the battle line up there. We did operate occasionally against the battleships with the torpedo squadrons with actual torpedoes--blind-loaded, of course--firing at the line itself with the depth set to go underneath the battleships. So we did have attacks from time to time upon the battle line, but really the decisive force was to be the battleships when they closed with the enemy and slugged it out as Lord Nelson did.[†]

---

[*] Fleet Problem XXI took place in the Hawaiian area in the spring of 1940. When it was completed, President Franklin D. Roosevelt directed that the fleet remain at Pearl Harbor rather than return to its bases on the West Coast. The idea was that leaving the fleet in Hawaii would serve as a deterrent to Japanese aggression in the Far East.

[†] Lord Horatio Viscount Nelson (1758-1805), British naval hero of the Battle of Cape St. Vincent, 1797, Battle of the Nile, 1798, Trafalgar, 1805.

Q: During this period, say, '39, '40, do you recall any discussion of Japanese naval air capability?

Admiral Ramage: Not much. Of course, I was in the blackshoe Navy at that time, and we used to ridicule the Japs, really didn't think they were capable of doing very much.

Q: That was until December 7, 1941.

Admiral Ramage: That was until December 7, when they knocked us out of our socks.

Q: Were the air groups used anywhere near like they were used at the beginning of the war, where they were both an offensive and defensive weapon?

Admiral Ramage: No, they didn't have the carrier strike as we knew it. They weren't organized at all to do a coordinated strike. Really, until after the Battle of Midway they weren't capable of it, and they learned the hard way that you must form a strike group, and it must be escorted.* This was a factor against the 90-knot TBDs.† Because of their very slow speed, there was no place for them in the strike group. The SBDs had arrived at that time and were reasonably fast.‡ The F4Fs were simply too short-legged to do very much.§ We started the war with a pretty poor stable of aircraft.

---

* From 4 to 6 June 1942, U.S. and Japanese naval forces fought a battle northwest of Midway Island in the Pacific. After Japanese bombers had struck the island, carrier-based U.S. dive-bombers attacked and sank the Japanese carriers Hiryu, Soryu, Kaga, and Akagi and the cruiser Mikuma. U.S. ships lost were the carrier Yorktown (CV-5) and the destroyer Hammann (DD-412). The battle was both a tactical and strategic victory for U.S. forces.
† The TBD Devastator, built by the Douglas Aircraft Company, was a monoplane torpedo bomber. The TBD-1 model had a wing span of 50 feet, length of 35 feet, gross weight of 10,194 pounds, and top speed of 206 miles per hour. It was armed with two .30-caliber machine guns. The first TBD-1 reached squadron VT-3 on 5 October 1937 and the following year was introduced to VT-2, VT-5, and VT-6.
‡ The Douglas-built SBD Dauntless, which entered fleet squadrons in 1941, was a most successful dive-bomber in the early part of World War II. It was instrumental in the sinking of four Japanese aircraft carriers in the Battle of Midway. The SBD-5 model had the following characteristics: length, 33 feet; wing span, 42 feet; gross weight, 10,855 pounds; top speed, 245 miles per hour.
§ Grumman F4F Wildcat fighters first entered fleet squadrons in late 1940. The F4F-4 was 28 feet, 9 inches long; wing span of 38 feet; gross weight of 7,952 pounds; and top speed of 318 miles per hour.

Q: I have a little difficulty understanding. We seem to have the aircraft carrier and this air group--they're the main battery of the aircraft carrier--not being considered a very worthwhile thing by the Navy.

Admiral Ramage: That's correct.

Q: However, we did have a pretty good carrier construction program going.

Admiral Ramage: That's correct. That's right. We had built the Yorktown class, which included the Enterprise and Hornet. And then we had Wasp coming along, which was somewhat less capable.

Q: The Essexes were already introduced to the plan and ordered.[*]

Admiral Ramage: The Essexes were ordered.

Q: Somebody thought this thing was important.

Admiral Ramage: Well, I think a lot of it was from civilian influence in Washington. Vinson was a real supporter of carrier aviation.[†] He didn't ever see a carrier, I guess, or never been on one. But a lot of the impetus for air power came from outside sources. As you probably know, the Yorktown and Enterprise were not Navy construction. They were built under the PWA, Public Works Administration; they were funded not out of Navy funds at all.[‡] They were built as a way to help us out of the Depression, to give Norfolk,

---

[*] First 11 ordered in 1940, these ships had a standard displacement of 27,100 tons each. The keel for the first ship, the Essex (CV-9), was laid 28 April 1941; she was commissioned 31 December 1942.
[†] Carl Vinson of Georgia entered the House of Representatives in 1913 and was appointed to the Naval Affairs Committee in 1917. He became the ranking Democrat in 1923 and chairman in 1931. When the Armed Services committee was formed in 1947 Vinson became chairman and held that position, except for two short periods when Republicans held the House, until his retirement from Congress in 1965.
[‡] PWA was formed in 1933 as a relief measure during the Depression.

Virginia, some jobs. It turned out that it was very fortuitous for the Navy and for the country.

Q: I don't know if the opinion has ever been advanced, but with a fairly intensive carrier construction program at a time when, as you say, the aircraft aboard those ships were second-rate at best, do you suppose there was a conscious decision that while it takes X number of years to build and develop the ships, maybe we better have the ships first and play catch-up with the airplanes later on?

Admiral Ramage: I'd like to think there was that much thinking. The aircraft carrier was simply not considered to be a major weapon in the prewar Navy. That's the fact. If we hadn't been blown out of our socks at Pearl Harbor, I think that they would have taken that battle line to sea. They'd have been sunk at sea just like they were at Pearl Harbor, and we'd never have been able to raise any of them. They were not thinking about carrier strike forces. In the meantime, of course, Yamamoto had this first strike fleet, which was a well-coordinated six-carrier outfit.[*]

Q: Tactically, doctrinally integrated?

Admiral Ramage: Yes. We were simply behind the times.

Q: I imagine you had some fun times down in Hotel Street in Honolulu running across some of your contemporaries from the battleships and defending your position as an aircraft carrier sailor.[†]

Admiral Ramage: As a young man, I never went ashore, so I wouldn't know about Hotel Street.

---

[*] Admiral Isoroku Yamamato, Commander in Chief, Japanese Combined Fleet. The six carriers--Akagi, Kaga, Kiryu, Soryu, Zuikaku, and Shokaku--attacked Pearl Harbor on 7 December 1941.
[†] Hotel Street was a well-known adult entertainment district.

Q: Not after you got arrested.

Admiral Ramage: No. Well, let's get on with some of these things. I went through the shore patrol problem there. I became immediately aware of the great animosity between the "airdales," as they were called, and the blackshoes. As a matter of fact, you know that there were only two real aviators admirals that made prewar flag rank. Halsey was not, you know; he came in as a captain, and so did Ernie King.*

Q: McCain the same.†

Admiral Ramage: That's right. Two admirals that made it all the way were Towers and Bellinger, and I don't think there were any others.‡

Q: Pete Mitscher?§

Admiral Ramage: No.

Q: He wasn't an admiral at that time.

Admiral Ramage: He didn't make admiral until just after Midway.

Let's talk a little bit about why I went into aviation. You can see right off that I enjoyed the people in aviation, although I rather enjoyed the gunnery department. Because I was a bachelor, I went to the gunnery schools, and married men didn't. They had other things to do. So I went to three of them. I went to one on the Brooklyn.** It was a fine

---

* Captain Ernest J. King, USN, took flight training in the 1920s, and Captain William F. Halsey, Jr., USN, took it in the 1930s; both were already senior officers before going into aviation.
† Captain John S. McCain, USN, was 52 years old when he became a naval aviator in August 1936.
‡ Rear Admiral John H. Towers, USN, date of rank 29 December 1939; Rear Admiral Patrick N.L. Bellinger, USN, date of rank 1 December 1941. Towers was naval aviator number three, and Bellinger was number eight.
§ Captain Marc A. Mitscher, USN, was the first commanding officer of the carrier Hornet (CV-8), which was commissioned 20 October 1941. He was promoted to rear admiral 30 June 1942.
** USS Brooklyn (CL-40), a light cruiser commissioned 30 September 1937.

antiaircraft gunnery ship and a good school, and I learned a lot. Then I went twice to the Utah to gunnery school, so as far as knowing antiaircraft gunnery at that time, I was in pretty good shape.*

The one thing I did know was that we couldn't hit anything, so I thought I was safer in the air. If we couldn't hit them, I was sure the Japs couldn't. But the main reason that I went into aviation, I think, was that it was a better life with better people. I enjoyed the aviators on the ship. I can remember the air group commanders, first Eddie Ewen and then later Dick Whitehead flying aboard and reporting up to the bridge in their khakis and their yellow Mae Wests.† Captain Pownall greeted them as friends. A feeling of camaraderie just didn't exist among the non-aviator community.

Also, the aviators, particularly after they knew that Grant Rogers and I were interested in going to flight training, were particularly nice to us. They took good care of us, and whenever Grant and I could catch a ride with the air group, we did it. It was a very pleasant life. It was frustrating, because I wanted to get to flight school so badly and couldn't do it in less than two years.

I'll tell you another little anecdote about the Enterprise which I think is pretty funny. This is after the big fleet got out to Pearl. Admiral J. O. Richardson was CinCUS at that time. He and his staff moved aboard the carrier for a week or two weeks of indoctrination. Well, this was hate at first sight. It was a big staff, as you might guess, nothing like the staffs we have today, but it must have had 60 or 70 people on it, maybe more. They reported aboard and immediately took over everything. The junior people, of course, went down in the wardroom with us. We just got along like cats and dogs. There wasn't anything about it that was pleasant. So when they left the ship, it was good riddance to them, as far as we were concerned, and they were delighted to get back on the "Pennsy," which was their home and a beautifully turned out ship.‡ We were kind of dirty and noisy.

---

* USS Utah (AG-16) was a gunnery training ship, converted from a battleship in the early 1930s. She was sunk at Pearl Harbor, 7 December 1941.
† Lieutenant Commander Edward C. Ewen, USN; Lieutenant Commander Richard F. Whitehead, USN; Mae West--inflatable life jacket named after the well-known actress.
‡ "Pennsy"--USS Pennsylvania (BB-38), flagship of the U.S. Fleet.

When the flag lieutenant, whose name was Eddy, left the ship, he had collected all the mess bills from the various people that were eating in the wardroom.* He put the checks and the money in an envelope. When he left the ship, he left it with the junior officer of the deck to give to Ensign Joe Roper, a classmate of mine, who was the mess treasurer.†

We had a young reserve ensign named Himmel aboard, and he thought he'd pull one on Joe.‡ When he got this envelope, he slipped in one of the little fornicating kits which were issued to liberty parties. They could pick up this little packet that contained a condom and a tube of something that we called Marine toothpaste. I don't know exactly what the name of it was. But, anyway, he slipped this into the envelope. When Joe opened up the envelope, this object fell out on his desk. Joe was an even-tempered guy, but he said, "Goddamn it, I've been around here long enough, and those guys think I'm screwing them."

So he took the packet in to see Felix Stump, the exec, and Felix had a low boiling point. Jesus, you know, very, very low, and he said, "Those goddamn blackshoes, they're insulting the Enterprise."

So they both went up to see Captain Pownall. He was a true gentleman, unruffled and courteous, but even Captain Pownall couldn't take this. So he called away the gig, and off the three went to the flagship Pennsylvania to see Admiral Richardson. They got to see the admiral, and pointed out this terrible thing that had been done, this terrible smear on the good name of the Enterprise, and they received a proper apology. Of course, nobody knew anything about the "crime."

About a week later, Himmel was talking to Roper, and he said, "Did you ever get that little thing I sent to you?"

Joe said, "What's that?"

He said, "That little item that I put in the envelope."

Roper said, "Oh, God." So back he went to see Stump, who had quite a reaction. They went to see Baldy. Then they called away the gig, went back over to the commander in chief, and apologized for this terrible thing that they had accused the flag lieutenant of

---

* Lieutenant Daniel T. Eddy, USN.
† Ensign Joseph C. Roper, USN.
‡ Ensign William Himmel, USNR.

doing.* I don't think it would be that funny today, but it was pretty funny then when you consider the spit and polish that existed at that time. That was particularly true going over to the Pennsylvania, where the deck was so clean that you wouldn't even dare step on it, and there was all the pomp and circumstance that went with CinCUS involved in this action.

Q: Is it true that terminology was changed shortly before the war because CinCUS had a poor connotation in naval circles?

Admiral Ramage: I think it was not changed until Ernie King came in.† Yes, he called it CominCh. Of course, he was commander in chief of everything, too, but I think CinCUS was kind of a bad title, particularly after what happened.

I might point out that in addition to these great aviators that were on the Enterprise at that time, there were also some of the ex-avcads.‡ See, I reported in '39, and this was about the time that the aviation cadets were becoming commissioned officers, and I enjoyed them very much. Of course, I wanted to be one of the aviators, so I pretty much ran around with the ex-avcads whenever I could. They were very dear friends of mine and have been all my life.

Q: Did you pick up any useful advice or information from those kind of folks that was useful in flight school?

Admiral Ramage: Well, not so much that, but during my time on the Enterprise I used to watch carrier landings. I couldn't fly, but when I finally got into carrier aviation on the

---

* "Gig" is the traditional name for the captain's boat on board a warship.
† Admiral Ernest J. King, USN, served as Commander in Chief U.S. Fleet from 20 December 1941 to 2 September 1945. Because CinCUS was pronounced "sink us," it had an unfortunate meaning after the attack on Pearl Harbor. King then inaugurated the abbreviation CominCh for the office of Commander in Chief U.S. Fleet.
‡ AvCad--aviation cadet, a program instituted in 1935 whereby individuals enlisted in the Naval Reserve, then were trained as aviators and sent to the fleet in cadet status until later being commissioned as officers. In 1939 the program was modified so that individuals were commissioned upon successful completion of flight training.

Enterprise, I think it stood me in very good stead, because I knew what a carrier pass looked like.

Q: Who were some of these avcads?

Admiral Ramage: Robin Lindsey and Jimmy Daniels were in VF-6; they were the two main guys that I admired.* There was a guy named Fogg in Scouting Six that I used to run around with.† He was killed in the first Kwajalein raid.‡ They were a pretty high-stepping outfit. They had pay and a half, and the girls liked that.

Q: Had a lot of personality.

Admiral Ramage: Yes, green charm.

Q: On a related subject, could we talk a little bit about the enlisted pilots? You had quite a few of those.

Admiral Ramage: Not in the Enterprise. We had two or three of them in the torpedo squadron. I can remember one of their names was Hoover. But they were, of course, very heavy in VF-2 in Lex.§ We had a few but very few. So they didn't really come through until VF-2 was split up. Later we got a lot of pilots in VF-10 out of VF-2. We got Bob Kanze, Pack Packard, and various others who were great pilots and a great addition.** But I don't recall knowing very many of them in Air Group Six on the Enterprise before the war.

---

* Ensign Robin M. Lindsey, USNR; Ensign James G. Daniels III, USNR. VF-6 was the abbreviation for Fighting Six, the fighter squadron in the Enterprise.
† Ensign Carleton T. Fogg, USN.
‡ As part of Task Force Eight, the Enterprise attacked Kwajalein Atoll in the Marshall Islands on 1 February 1942. For details see John B. Lundstrom, The First Team: Pacific Naval Air Combat from Pearl Harbor to Midway (Annapolis: Naval Institute Press, 1984), pages 63-66.
§ VF-2--Fighting Two in the aircraft carrier Lexington (CV-2).
** Aviation Pilot Second Class Robert F. Kanze, USN; Aviation Pilot First Class Howard S. Packard, USN.

Q: Do you recall anything about the relationship of these enlisted pilots with the other pilots?

Admiral Ramage: No, I don't.

Q: It had to be a very poor situation to be in.

Admiral Ramage: Yes, I think that it was, but there were only one or two of them involved, I think, with Air Group Six. I don't think they were in anything but the torpedo squadrons, and that was maybe just one or two. So I really don't know much about that.

    About the only other thing prior to going into flight training was the flight physical. I took it just before departing. I had a pilonidal cyst; that's a cyst on the base of your tailbone. The flight surgeon gave me a down until I had it corrected. So I had it corrected in a hurry in the naval hospital in San Diego. The Enterprise was temporarily back here from Pearl Harbor. I had it done, and then I was sitting on a rubber doughnut after I went back to the Enterprise. In my first flights in flight training, I was still sitting on this rubber doughnut.

Q: When did this take place that you first applied for flight training?

Admiral Ramage: This would be just before I left. This would be the summer of '41. I'll talk a little bit about Honolulu at the time.

    I got married out there just before I left. I had made a friend of Mr. Orville Tyler, who was executive vice president of Bishop Bank. He and his wife were exceptionally nice to service people. He had been a West Pointer. He was a classmate of MacArthur's and had been discharged from the Army.[*] When he was in the cavalry, a horse kicked him and broke his leg, and it never healed properly. He had become quite well-known in Honolulu.

---

[*] In 1941 Lieutenant General Douglas MacArthur, USA, commanded the U.S. Army forces in the Philippines. He had graduated in the class of 1903 from the Military Academy. Tyler had retired from the Army as a captain in 1916 because of physical disability.

Somehow, through some of the older officers on the Enterprise, I had met the Tylers. They were raising a niece named Ethel, who was known as "Sis." I got to know the older people much more than the niece. They did a lot of entertaining, and I used to fill in as a spare guy or if they wanted someone picked up or they wanted a bartender. It was just a great situation for me, because I didn't have anyplace to go. They did have a daughter who was in Puerto Rico, married to an Army officer. I didn't think much about that.

Here I was, spending many weekends out at the Tylers' house, enjoying everything. Then "Baby Ty," as they called her, came home from a former marriage.* She claimed she had to marry me to get her room back. She didn't come back until July of 1941, and we were married the fourth of September. It was a pretty fast operation. I don't think that Orville Tyler was putting much pressure on me, but certainly Mrs. Tyler was very much involved in indicating that she thought that Ty and I would make a fine couple. So in due course, the inevitable happened, and we were married just the day before I left for flight training.

Q: Before you get to flight training, I want to ask about the carriers out in Hawaii. Now, prior to World War II, we never sent a carrier west of Hawaii, did we?

Admiral Ramage: We had certain exercises. We went down for an exercise around Johnston Island one time, and that's as far west as we ever sailed.† Then, of course, just before Pearl was hit, the carriers went out to take the Marine planes to Wake and Midway.

Q: Do you recall any discussion of contingencies, if you'd run across a Japanese carrier force in peacetime?

Admiral Ramage: No. I was so far down the ladder as an ensign in a deck division that I kept my eyes pretty much in the boat.

---

* Her first name was Emeleen.
† Johnston Island is about 700 miles southwest of Honolulu.

Q: They never did ask you what you thought they should do in that situation.

Admiral Ramage: No. That was above my pay grade.

Okay. Flight training. I reported in to flight training in early October, and the first month was ground school. I can remember talking to one of my classmates. I won't give the name because it's one of two and I don't want to insult one of them. He met me when I was checking in, and he said, "You're going to like this. This is the cushiest place I've ever been. What you want to do is to go as slow as possible. I'm still in Squadron One, and I've been for three months. I have various physical things, I turn myself in as sick." This guy was actually there just trying to stay out of the fleet and have a free ride.

Q: This is Pensacola?

Admiral Ramage: In Pensacola. Yes. I never admired the guy before, and I admired him a hell of a lot less later on.

Q: Did he ever eventually get through flight training?

Admiral Ramage: He got through flight training, and then he put in for photo school or some goddamn thing. We'll get into this noncombatant situation of many of my classmates later on.

I went through flight training with very few problems. At that time you had to be real bad to flunk out, you know, and if I recall, I think I got one down going through primary.* I may not have. I worked real hard, and I worked real fast. I didn't really have any problems. I think my grades were pretty good going through. I loved flying, and it was just as great as I thought it was going to be. I really knew that this was my bag. So I went through primary there, Squadron One, and went up to Squadron Two.

Q: Excuse me a minute. In Squadron One, did you have N3Ns?

---

* "Down"--a down check for a particular flight, as graded by the instructor.

Admiral Ramage: N3Ns.* And in Squadron Two, we had OS2Us on wheels and Vultee "vibrators."† Then in Squadron Three, which was supposed to be the instrument deal, we had NJs, which were fixed-landing-gear SNJs.‡

This was the time they made the decision on where you were supposed to go and what type of training you would get. By this time, rather than take a full course, they had begun to specialize. So I immediately put in for carriers. I could see myself maybe going back to the Enterprise. All ten of us ring-knockers that were in the class got VO/VS, which was scout-observation.§ The thought behind this was that gunnery was still the main thing, and all of us had qualified in gunnery and deck watches on board ship. So it made sense to send us right back to the fleet in VO/VS. We were qualified top watch standers, and so it would be a saving of time.

Lem Cooke and I were classmates from the academy, and we immediately appealed.** He'd gone to the Ranger as a black shoe ensign, and, of course, I'd come from the Enterprise. The appeal went absolutely nowhere. We just didn't even know where to go. There just wasn't any argument about it; all ten of us in the class were going to go to VO/VS. So I went to Squadron Four there in Pensacola, which was OS2Us on floats.

Q: Were you still an ensign at this time, or were you jaygee?

Admiral Ramage: I made jaygee in about January of '42.††

---

* "Yellow Peril" was the nickname for the yellow-painted N3N trainer, a biplane equipped with a centerline pontoon. It was 26 feet long, had a wing span of 34 feet, gross weight of 2,792 pounds, and a top speed of 126 miles per hour.
† The Vought OS2U Kingfisher was the principal floatplane used by U.S. battleships and cruisers in World War II. It was 34 feet long, had a wing span of 36 feet, gross weight of 6,000 pounds, and maximum speed of 164 miles an hour. The Vultee-built SNV Valiant was a trainer that was 29 feet long, wing span of 42 feet, gross weight of 4,360 pounds, and top speed of 166 miles per hour.
‡ The SNJ Texan trainer, built by North American Aviation, first went into service in the late 1930s. Specifications for the NJ-1 model included a length of 27 feet, 2 inches; wing span of 42 feet, gross weight of 4,440 pounds, and maximum speed of 167 miles per hour.
§ Ring knockers is slang for Naval Academy graduates, who wore their heavy class rings.
** Lieutenant (junor grade) Lemuel D. Cooke, USN.
†† Jaygee--lieutenant (junor grade).

James D. Ramage #1 - 46

Q: While you were at Pensacola?

Admiral Ramage: While I was at Pensacola. The war had started on December 7. A bunch of us had the immediate reaction that maybe we ought to stop flight training and get the hell back out to the fleet, where we at least knew what to do. Of course, we had no idea what had happened to the fleet.

Q: There was fear the war would be over before you could get involved.

Admiral Ramage: Fear that the war would be over and also, of course, the President had announced that only one battleship was sunk and one was capsized. The Japanese knew what they had done to the fleet, so this had to be for the purpose of hiding it from the American people. That's the only reason. The Japs had pictures of the operation.

Q: Probably the whole thing was so demoralizing to begin with, the thought of losing the entire fleet, I'm sure, in the country . . .

Admiral Ramage: That's right. In any event, all ten of us finished off in VO/VS. I don't remember much about going through flight training, except I can say that I started flying on about the first of November, and I was through flight training certainly by April. I completed the whole course, and I recall having about 192 flight hours and only two-thirds of that was pilot time. The rest of it was back-seat time. So we got out of flight training with very little over 100 hours of actual training.

Q: In what categories do you feel that you were strong in under training?

Admiral Ramage: I was certainly safe for flying, and I had made up my mind that if I was ever going to get killed in an airplane accident, I was going to be shot down. I wasn't going to do it to myself. I was very confident of the fact that I could do a good job in the air.

Maybe it was a little bit overwhelming, but at the same time I was quite sure that I could do a pretty good job.

Q: How did you feel about instrument flying or navigation?

Admiral Ramage: We did very little instrument flying. Squadron Three was instrument, and it was the needle, ball, and airspeed. As a matter of fact, I think the guy that checked me let me fly most of my flight with the hood open. It was just indoctrination. They knew we weren't going to fly instruments. Nobody had an instrument card. Nobody cared about it. I didn't get an instrument card until after World War II. So it really was a VFR operation.[*]

I got out of flight training quite confident that I could do a job, and Ty and I started driving across the country to report in to the West Coast for transportation. I was to be assigned to the Salt Lake City.[†] Because of my seniority, being a ring-knocker, I would automatically be the senior aviator, which was kind of an awkward thing, speaking of bad things that happened, because of the seniority system.

Q: Was the ship based at Pearl?

Admiral Ramage: Based at Pearl, yes.

Q: How many aircraft were assigned?

Admiral Ramage: Four.

Q: Did you have a full crew for each?

---

[*] VFR--visual flight rules.
[†] The USS Salt Lake City (CA-25) had been commissioned in December 1929. She had a standard displacement of 9,100 tons, was 586 feet long, and 65 feet in the beam. Her top speed was 32.7 knots. She was armed with ten 8-inch main battery guns and four 5-inch/25-caliber antiaircraft guns.

Admiral Ramage: We had six crews, four aircraft.

I left San Francisco in May in a small seaplane tender, an AVP, for transportation. I don't remember the name of that ship, but we were escorting a convoy. It took eight days or so to get across, because a lot of ships were very slow. It was when we entered Pearl Harbor that I saw the utter devastation of the Pacific Fleet. I'd had no idea that it was this bad, and all I could think of was, "Those sons-of-bitches. I'm going to get them if there's any way I can do it." I was still a little shocked that the President would put the story across to the American people that he did, but mainly I was just plain angry at the Japs. I mean, there were these big ships, five or six of them down and oil still spewing out. There was still a smell of oil and smoke and crap around that harbor, just filthy with all sorts of stuff that was still coming out of the ships.

Q: What month was this?

Admiral Ramage: This was May of '42.

Q: The same time as the Coral Sea Battle.[*]

Admiral Ramage: Just about the same time. I got out there, I think, just before that. So I reported in to Pearl for transportation to the Salt Lake City. They said Salt Lake wasn't in, but they needed me there. They'd taken all of the VO/VS pilots off of these battleships and cruisers that had been demolished and had put them into an in-shore patrol outfit. I was to report there.

I started flying OS2Us on wheels off of Ford Island.[†] I would steal flight time any time. I would fly any extra flight, anything I could get in order to build up flight time. One of the things that was very nice at that time, in about July, Red Bullard, who had been senior aviator on one of the ships, was assigned a job of setting up a small VO/VS tactical

---

[*] The Battle of the Coral Sea, fought 4-8 May 1942, marked the first time that opposing fleets fought at sea without seeing each other. The battle helped prevent the Japanese from moving closer to Australia.
[†] Ford Island is in the center of Pearl Harbor.

training school, so I flew in his school and also flew my patrols.* I think I got as high as 140 hours of pilot time in one month, which is pretty hard in a single-piloted aircraft. I wanted the time, and the school was excellent. We had a little gunnery. Of course, we had the stuff that VO/VS did. We went down and observed gunfire down in the south coast of Hawaii.

In the meantime, the USS Pensacola, which was the sister ship of the "swayback Maru," as we called the Salt Lake City, came in. A classmate of mine, Deacon Reichel, was senior aviator there.† He took me out so I could qualify in cast recoveries, as they called them at that time.‡

Q: Under way.

Admiral Ramage: Yes. Where a ship would turn and make a slick, and you would land on the thing and bounce your way on up to the crane for hoisting. I made three of those, so I was all ready to go to the Salt Lake City, if I could get to her. The task forces were wandering all over the Pacific.

I went over from time to time to ComAirPac there at Pearl Harbor to try to see if I couldn't somehow sneak my way into a carrier.§ I knew many of the people who came back from the Battle of Midway, and I had never seen such a really destitute group of people in my life. They were the remnants of the three air groups that were out at Midway.** Everybody was just completely confused. Well, I thought, "Here's an opportunity." So I went tearing over to AirPac. I remember talking to a guy, Lieutenant Stever, and I said,

---

* Lieutenant (j.g.) George C. Bullard, USN, had been in VCS-5 in the heavy cruiser Pensacola (CA-24), the sister ship of the Salt Lake City.
† Lieutenant (j.g.) Leonard O. Reichel, USN.
‡ "Cast," which was a letter in the phonetic alphabet of the time, designated a recovery method whereby the airplane landed on the water, rode up on a sea sled, and was lifted aboard by a crane on the ship's fantail.
§ ComAirPac--Commander Air Force Pacific Fleet was the type commander for aircraft carriers and aircraft assigned to the fleet. That title was adopted on 1 September 1942, combining two predecessor organizations, Commander Carriers Pacific Fleet and Commander Patrol Wings Pacific Fleet.
** The three carriers in the Battle of Midway were the Yorktown, Enterprise, and Hornet. The Yorktown was sunk in the battle, and pilots were lost from all three ships.

"Now's the time. I'm ready, I've been on the Enterprise. Maybe I haven't made any carrier landings, but throw me in there. I'm ready to go."[*]

He said, "You? You need a lot of training. There's no way that you're going to get into one of those air groups. You get on back to do your job in the in-shore patrol squadron."

So I went back. I was pretty p-offed about this.

Then Air Group Ten came out, ready to go aboard the Enterprise as a replacement for this pickup group that was on the Enterprise at that time. They were at both Maui and out at Barbers Point.[†] I thought, "Boy, here's my opportunity," so I went on over to see Mr. Stever again. I told him that I now had maybe 450, 500 hours, and that I could certainly get ready in one month's time to get aboard ship. He threw me out. But I ran into an old friend of mine, and he still lives in Coronado. He was a first class yeoman named Jack Whitely. He had been assigned to the first lieutenant's department of the Enterprise. By this time he'd made chief and was working in personnel for AirPac. Whitely and I talked about how I was going to get into carriers and how I was to get back to the Enterprise.

After I got turned down for Air Group Ten, I went back to see the skipper of the in-shore patrol squadron, Lew Tamny.[‡] He said, "I just received a call from Lieutenant Stever, and he says for you to stay completely out of AirPac's personnel office, that you're not to come over there under any circumstance. Besides that, you'll never make it in carriers." He said, "Now, while we're at this, why don't you just think this thing out. You can bed down here in Pearl Harbor for the rest of the war if you want to. I need an exec, and you fit the bill. I can go to AirPac and tell them that you're a volunteer to join the in-shore patrol squadron at Pearl."

Well, I thanked him very kindly, but I said that wasn't in my game program, that I was going to get into aircraft carriers some way. Finally the Salt Lake City came back, and I reported aboard. This was maybe October, November. It was a nice ship, and the captain

---

[*] Lieutenant Elbert M. Stever, USN, who had been in VS-5 in the Yorktown.
[†] Maui is one of the islands of the Hawaiian chain. Barbers Point is a naval air station near Pearl Harbor on the island of Oahu.
[‡] Lieutenant Lewis D. Tamny, USN.

was a nice guy.* The aviation detachment was over at Ford Island where the in-shore patrol squadrons operated. I went over to see the captain and I made my rounds of calling on the various people in the ship. The gun boss, whom I would work for, was a commander and quite a nice guy.

I went around to call on the first lieutenant. The first lieutenant was responsible for the cranes and the cast recovery of the SOCs. I remember him very well because his name was Bitler, and I went in and presented myself to him.† He said, "I just want you to know that as long as you're on this ship, you're a red-haired orphan." That was a fine welcome, wasn't it?

I knew even better than ever that somehow I was going to get off that <u>Salt Lake City</u>. Sure enough, mainly through my associations with Chief Jack Whitley, I found out, number one, that there was a plan to take two SOCs and three crews off all the cruisers. They'd decided that the SOCs were a fire hazard, and they didn't use them much anyway. Also, simultaneously, Jack told me that Spud Monahan, who was working in the air department of the <u>Enterprise</u>, had broken his leg in a Jeep accident down in Espiritu Santo.‡ He said, "Now, you're going to have to move real fast on this. I can get you orders down there. I can write those. That will be no problem at all. But you've got to get yourself off <u>Salt Lake City</u>."

So I went over to see the captain, and I told him that two of the planes and three of the crews were going to be taken off. He said, "Well, who would you recommend?"

I said, "Well, myself and any two others."

Q: In that order.

Admiral Ramage: At first he was quite unhappy. I mean, after all, I'd only been aboard for two or three weeks, and it didn't look very good for me to think that about his ship. But

---

* Captain Ernest G. Small, USN, commanded the <u>Salt Lake City</u> from 28 May 1942 to 2 January 1943.
† Commander Worthington S. Bitler, USN.
‡ Lieutenant Commander Idris B. Monahan, USN. Espiritu Santo, an island in the New Hebrides chain, was a valuable base for the Allies in World War II because of its proximity to the Solomons. It was extensively developed with air, naval, and supply bases and served as a staging area for various operations.

then I said, "Captain, I have an opportunity to go down to the Enterprise if you'll let me go."

And he said, "Go on, tell them you've got my permission. Get the hell out of here." So off I went.

Q: See, all blackshoes aren't all that bad.

Admiral Ramage: No, he wasn't. He was a nice guy. So I went back over and said to Whitely, "Okay, I'm free. Now come forth with the orders." Sure enough, in due course the orders came up for me to report post haste down to USS Enterprise, which at that time was operating temporarily out of Espiritu Santo.

Q: Admiral, before we let you go on down to Espiritu Santo, you have previously mentioned to me about the situation that existed in Hawaii when the remnants of the air groups came back from the Battle of Midway. Can we talk about that a little bit?

Admiral Ramage: Yes. The first thing that happened was that the Air Force bomber pilots flew into Hickam Field within a day or so after the battle.* They had a mass awards presentation. They must have given away 100 Distinguished Service Crosses to these people who won the Battle of Midway. As you know, they hit nothing, but nevertheless, they reported hits, and I guess probably thought they had gotten hits. The only thing that they came close to was the submarine Grayling, as you recall.† They may have splashed some water on somebody, but they didn't hit anything.

Q: This was reported.

---

* Hickam Field, adjacent to Pearl Harbor, was a base of the Army Air Forces, as it was then officially designated.
† The Grayling (SS-209) and other U.S. submarines were arranged in a fanlike pattern west of Midway Island so they could watch the movements of the Japanese fleet. The submarines took little part in the battle. On the afternoon of 7 June three Army B-17s dropped 20 1,000-pound bombs on the Grayling, later claiming they had sunk a Japanese cruiser that went down in 15 seconds.

Admiral Ramage: This was reported. Not only that, I think that the original report by the Life magazine stated that this was a situation where land-based air power had finally proven itself and had defeated the Japanese at the Battle of Midway. It was terrible. So that when these Navy guys got back maybe about a week later, pretty well shot up, really shaken, their morale was utterly shaken by these Zeros, they were pretty unhappy and also reading the papers about the fact that they really hadn't done much at the battle up there.[*]

The second Battle of Midway really occurred at the Moana Hotel. This was where a bunch of our carrier guys were resting and recuperating, and it happened that a bunch of the Air Corps bomber pilots were there also.[†] This ended in a riot. It was an all-out melee between the two groups. I don't know exactly how it ended up, but it was quite a battle.

Q: You also mentioned the situation where one of the air group commanders had been ordered to report to someone.

Admiral Ramage: Well, the one story that I told you was about Wade McClusky, who led the Enterprise group in the morning strike when they got two of the carriers and the Yorktown got the other.[‡] He was out at Chris Holmes's place. This was a very wealthy man's private home that had been turned over to the Navy for kind of a rest home. I happened to be out there at the time trying to see if I couldn't somehow get into carrier aviation. Wade had gotten a call from--I'm pretty sure it was Admiral Spruance.[§] If it wasn't, it was Nimitz.[**] He wanted Wade to report out to Pearl the next day. Of course, everybody was kind of hanging on Wade's words after they knew that he was to talk to the admiral.

When it was over, he said, "Well, they want me to come out there to Pearl tomorrow. I'm not going. If they want to see me, I'm here." That was Wade McClusky.

---

[*] The Mitsubishi-built A6M Zero was the best-known fighter plane in the Japanese Navy in World War II. The standard A6M2 had a top speed of 317 miles per hour and was armed with two 7.7-millimeter machine guns and two 20-millimeter cannons.
[†] On 20 June 1941 the U.S. Army Air Corps had been officially redesignated the U.S. Army Air Forces.
[‡] Lieutenant Commander C. Wade McClusky, Jr., USN, was commander of the Enterprise air group.
[§] Rear Admiral Raymond A. Spruance, USN, was Commander Task Force 16 during the Battle of Midway.
[**] Admiral Chester W. Nimitz, USN, was Commander in Chief Pacific Fleet.

Q: Lieutenant commander.

Admiral Ramage: Lieutenant commander. He and the aviators were quite unhappy at this time. They were unhappy at the Air Corps, and they were really quite unhappy with the Navy too.

Q: I guess they had lost a lot of friends.

Admiral Ramage: They had lost a lot of people, and it was a very, very dreary time for carrier aviation.

Q: It must have been perhaps a shock to you to see <u>Enterprise</u>--how she looked when you left several months before and then after the battle.

Admiral Ramage: Yes. She still was pretty, but she was painted black or a very dark slate color.

Q: Gray.

Admiral Ramage: Yes. And the flight deck, which had been the color of the wood, had all been painted gray. And the hangar deck, with all that fancy gray deck painting, was greasy and dirty. It became a working ship.

Q: It's my understanding that the morale in air groups picked up rapidly after this. Is that true?

Admiral Ramage: I think it was. You see, they put together these makeup air groups after this for the carriers that were left. They only had the two because the <u>Yorktown</u> was gone. But as far as I know, they snapped back from it. It was just this week or so of real devastation. And, of course, they got rid of quite a few pilots. As a matter of fact, I know there were two or three of the bomber pilots that they simply took out of the bomber squadrons as being unfit for combat. They sent them on over to in-shore patrol, where I was flying in. That made me all the more desirous of getting the hell out of there.

Q: We had some people who actually had mental breakdowns.

Admiral Ramage: I know of one person in particular, and I'm not going to give his name. I mean, he was an ex-cadet, but I really won't talk about it. I think one of the most comical things at the Battle of Midway was when the dentist on the Enterprise shot himself in the foot. He had battle fatigue and got off the ship. I saw him from time to time later on, and boy, he always ran the other way.

Q: Was it about this time or was it before where you became "Jig Dog"?*

Admiral Ramage: I became "Jig Dog" at the Naval Academy. I didn't particularly like the name, but compared to some of the names people got, I'll settle for "Jig Dog."

Q: I've never heard you introduce yourself as anything other than James Ramage.

Admiral Ramage: Yes.

By late fall my wife had been able to come out to Honolulu. She was, of course, born in the islands and her family was out there. Through quite a bit of manipulation on the part of her father, she was able to return to her home. She took a job with the WARDs, which she called the "We Are Ready, Daddy" girls. They worked in the tunnel out at Fort Weaver, which was the air plot for the defense of the Hawaiian Islands, so she was doing her part at the same time.

I finally had my orders to join the Enterprise as a ship's company officer, and I departed Pearl in early January by the seaplane tender Curtiss. It was taking a CASU,

---

* In the phonetic alphabet of the time, Jig and Dog were the words used for Ramage's initials, J. D.

carrier aircraft service unit, later called FASRON, down to Nandi in the Fijis, where they were about to set up a naval air base.* We arrived there uneventfully, and after two or three days there I was transferred to the Army transport Sea Witch for a trip to Noumea.

The Sea Witch was correctly named, or perhaps incorrectly. It should have been called She Bitch. It was the worst ship that I've ever seen in my life. It was a C-2 cargo ship. The soldiers that were being carried on the transport were treated just like cattle. They even had armed guards over the scuttlebutts so that the soldiers couldn't have over one canteen full of water a day.† Of course, taking a bath was totally impossible. The enlisted men were stacked six or seven deep in their quarters. The officers had it pretty easy. We were only about four or five deep. It was an extremely uncomfortable voyage, but I did learn one thing.

They had a double bridge, and the skipper and officers were on one level and the helmsman was on a lower level. One day I was talking to the helmsman about pay. He was talking about the various bonuses that were available to merchant seamen. This man couldn't have been over 18 years old and probably really had nothing much to commend him, but he told me that when they entered port in Suva, which was on the other side of Fiji from Nandi, they received a bonus. When they came around the island, which was probably about 12 or 15 miles, and entered Nandi, he got another bonus, and when we would go into Noumea, New Caledonia, he would receive another bonus. All this, of course, was on top of an overall bonus for being in the war zone. If they were ever anywhere close to being shot at, they received another bonus. We figured out his pay, and I said, "My God, you make more money than General MacArthur does for running the whole war down this way." But that's the way it was.

I don't like to belittle the merchant marine, because certainly the people that were up on the Murmansk run deserved every dollar they got.‡ But when I hear complaints nowadays about the merchant marine not being fairly treated as far as receiving G.I. benefits and so forth, I remember what really happened.

---

* FASRON--fleet aircraft service squadron.
† "Scuttlebutt" is a Navy term for a drinking fountain.
‡ The convoy run from North America to Murmansk in north Russia was plagued by bad weather in addition to the German submarines, aircraft, and surface ships.

Q: Along that same line, did you hear any of the horror stories coming out of Australia or even the West Coast of the United States about stevedores and such union organizations refusing to help load the critically needed supplies without extra compensation?

Admiral Ramage: No, I don't recall those. I do remember when John L. Lewis took the coal miners on strike during the war, which wasn't very refreshing, sitting in the ready room there, getting ready to take off.* But, no, I don't recall anything about them.

I arrived in Noumea, which was a nice, clean French city. By that time Admiral Halsey's staff was shore-based down there.† I went on over to see several members of the staff that I remembered from being on the Enterprise previously.‡ I talked to them at length about what was going on.

About two days later I was able to bum a ride in a PBY-5 out of Noumea to Base Button, which was Espiritu Santo in the New Hebrides, where Enterprise was anchored.§ The flight up was uneventful. It was quite a shock to see some of the ships that were in there. There was one cruiser--I think it was the Minneapolis--with about 60 or 70 feet of the bow blown off. It had apparently been, I think, in that Savo Island affair just previous to that, and there were two or three ships pretty badly beaten up.**

We tied up to a buoy, and I was taken up to a seaplane tender called the Chandeleur. I had a day to spare, so I asked a classmate of mine, who was flying PBYs, to go on a patrol out of there on up into the northern area. I was interested to see what the PBYs did up there. It was a very slow and painful operation, but they earned their money,

---

* John L. Lewis was president of the United Mine Workers' Union.
† Vice Admiral William F. Halsey, Jr., USN, Commander South Pacific Force and Area from 18 October 1942 to 15 March 1943, when he became Commander Third Fleet. He was promoted to four-star admiral in November 1942.
‡ As a vice admiral, serving as Commander Aircraft Battle Force, Halsey was embarked in the Enterprise at the beginning of the war.
§ The PBY Catalina was a twin-engine flying boat that performed extensive service before and during World War II. Built by Consolidated, it first entered fleet squadrons in 1936. The PBY-2 model had a wing span of 104 feet, length of 65 feet, gross weight of 28,400 pounds, and top speed of 178 miles per hour. Cruising speed was 103 mph.
** In the Battle of Tassafaronga, off Guadalcanal the night of 30 November-1 December 1942, the Japanese used torpedoes to sink the heavy cruiser Northampton (CA-26) and knock the bows off the cruiser New Orleans (CA-32) and Minneapolis (CA-36).

because if there was anything up in the general area where they were going, they were going to get shot down. There wasn't any protection whatsoever for them.

On the morning of the first of February, 1943, I reported aboard Enterprise, and it was just like old home week. A lot of the same people were there that had been there when I was there for my two years as an ensign. They accused me of sitting out the war there in flight training. I very soon met John Crommelin, who was the executive officer and one of the most interesting people that I've ever met in my life.* He was a true warrior. He wanted to kill more Japs and get at them more than anybody I've ever known. On top of that he was a true leader and a pilot. He was an excellent pilot, and it's just a shame that he was just over the hill as far as flying in combat was concerned, because he was just an excellent aviator at the same time.

I told him that I was very happy to be back aboard the "Big E," but it wasn't my desire to be ship's company in the air department. I sure wanted to get into a squadron. He said, "Well, why don't you just look around a bit, and if you can find somebody that will hire you, I'll arrange for you to get transferred into a squadron." So that became my aim. I served in the ship for about two weeks up in Fly One, winding up airplanes and flagging them off. I gradually got to know the pilots in the various squadrons and the air group, which was quite an impressive group, I might say. They had been through two or three good combat sessions, and the majority of them were real gung-ho guys.

Q: This is still Air Group Ten?

Admiral Ramage: This was Ten, yes.

Q: Who was the air group commander at that time?

---

* Commander John G. Crommelin, Jr., USN. For a detailed description of Crommelin's service on board the ship, see Edward P. Stafford, The Big E: The Story of the USS Enterprise (New York: Random House, 1962).

Admiral Ramage: The air group commander at that time was Dick Gaines.[*] He wasn't really the greatest of all leaders, but they had Jimmy Flatley as skipper of VF-10.[†] For all purposes, he was the air group commander, and everybody pretty much paid attention to what he said and did. I think, again, talking about great heroes of the war, I would put Jimmy Flatley right up there at the top.

I worked on the flight deck, but I had been qualified top watch previously, so I went to the navigator, Oscar Pederson.[‡] I guess that's the Pederson that we're talking about that had been . . .

Q: He had been CAG of the Yorktown air group at Coral Sea and Midway, in a non-flying billet.[§]

Admiral Ramage: Yes. He was a fine guy, and I told him that I had been qualified previously under way and that I'd be very pleased to stand that top watch because I knew they were shorthanded. This was in spite of the fact that I was on the flight deck all day long. It certainly didn't make any difference to me. But I kind of got burned because I had quite some experiences with the commanding officer of the Enterprise at that time. His name was Captain O. B. Hardison, and he didn't impress me at all.[**]

About the third day I was aboard ship, I wanted to fly, and the only thing that they had was a J2F.[††] They had a daily run over to Bomber One, which was where the air group was on the beach. The procedure was that they would hoist you over the side, you'd take off and then land on the beach. Later, you would take off, land on the water, and then you'd be hoisted back aboard. When I was about to leave the Enterprise, John Crommelin

---

[*] Commander Richard K. Gaines, USN.
[†] Lieutenant Commander James H. Flatley, Jr., USN, commanding officer of Fighting Ten. For a book on VF-10 see Stanley Johnston, The Grim Reapers (New York: E. P. Dutton, 1943).
[‡] Commander Oscar Pederson, USN.
[§] CAG--commander of a carrier air group.
[**] Captain Osborne B. Hardison, USN, commanded the Enterprise from 21 October 1942 to 7 April 1943.
[††] The J2F Grumman Duck was a two-seat utility plane. It was an amphibian with a float on the bottom.

saw me and he asked me if I'd ever flown a J2F before. I said I hadn't. He said, "Well, have you ever flown on floats?"

I said, "Yes, I've been on floats."

He said, "Well, it won't be any problem for you, except for one thing. You have to watch out for the brakes when you land on the beach as your brake drums are going to be wet. Consequently, you might lose one or both brakes." Okay. No problem.

Sure enough, when I landed there, at Bomber One on Espiritu Santo, I had the use of only one brake. But by doing 270-degree turns when I wanted to make a 90-degree turn, I could go whichever way I wanted. By using the engine and tail, it wasn't a very complicated thing to do. So I taxied up to the shack, which was a Quonset hut, and Captain Hardison was there.[*] He had been over on the beach for something. The exec had mentioned that he may be there, and if he were there, to please pick him up and bring him back.

So I got the captain and put him in the J2F-5. I told him that I had bad brakes, so I might have a little trouble getting out. He apparently couldn't understand it, and about the first time I made a 270-degree turn to turn 90 degrees, he was jumping up and down and yelling. Then I got into a position where I almost ran into a mound of dirt on the end of the runway, and this bothered him. I guess he thought I was doing it on purpose. In any event, I finally lined up on the runway and got everything squared away. I took off and got the wheels cranked up, landed uneventfully, and ultimately was hoisted aboard.

When we deplaned, we were on the flight deck, the captain asked me who I was, and I said, "My name is Ramage."

He said, "How long have you been aboard?"

I said, "Only about three days."

He said, "Have you ever flown this plane before?"

I said, "No, sir."

He looked at me and said, "Well, thanks anyway." Then he turned and began to talk to the exec. The exec was kind of nodding his head and agreeing.

---

[*] A Quonset hut is a semi-cylindrical metal building that can be shipped to an advance base area and erected quickly.

Soon after the captain left, Crommelin came over to me and said, "What happened?"

I explained what happened, and he said, "Well, don't pay any attention to the son of a bitch. He doesn't know what's going on anyway." That was about the relationship between John Crommelin and O. B. Hardison.

As a matter of fact, one day Robin Lindsey and I were down in the wardroom, having a Coke with John. An announcement was made on the loudspeaker, and John said, "Oh, that son of a bitch on the bridge."

Robin Lindsey said, "Commander, I really don't think you should talk that way about the captain."

John said, "Okay, I won't. I'll say, 'Old Number One.' But if I say, 'Old Number One,' you'll know what I mean."

Well, in any event, I was standing top watch up there on the bridge, and I soon became aware of the fact that the captain really didn't even know anything about his ship. If he wanted to go up to 20 knots, he would ring up 25 knots on the engine room telegraph, which, of course, just raises hell down in the firerooms. They have to slip in extra burners to get ready for high speeds. Of course, there's a scheduled acceleration in engine speed that you can't exceed except in real emergency. So you can ring up anything you want, but you're going to get acceleration at about the same rate. I didn't feel that I should advise the captain of the Enterprise how the engine room worked, but I sure wanted to at times. That was at least once that I kept my mouth shut.

But it all kind of peaked one night. When we anchored in Segond Channel, we always kept the underway watch on and anchor detail ready to go, because we would possibly have to get under way in a hurry to get out of there. As a matter of fact, I don't know why the heck the Japs didn't come down and knock us out anyway, because we were the one carrier in the Pacific, but they didn't do it.

Q: Where is Segond Channel?

Admiral Ramage: It's in Espiritu Santo. That was our home over the winter of 1942-43.

So I had a midwatch that night, and everything was quiet. We listened to Tokyo Rose tell stories about how we were getting beaten up--the usual bull.* We received a warning of condition red, which came from the shore control. We were from time to time under attack from a Jap we used to call "Washing Machine Charlie" that had some kind of a small aircraft and he would come down and drop some kind of something on somebody. So we set general quarters immediately, and I sent the quartermaster down to advise the captain we were going to general quarters. I also advised the flag duty officer, who was on the upper bridge above us, about it, so everything was under control. The guns were manned. We were at general quarters.

Very shortly afterwards, we went from condition red back to green. Apparently it was either a false alarm or Charlie had gone home early. But about that time, Captain Hardison appeared on the bridge. Apparently the general alarm system had not functioned in his cabin. I can't imagine why he didn't wake up, with all the noise that was going on. And somehow the quartermaster either hadn't awakened him or he'd gone back to sleep. In any event, this was a total surprise to him when he got on the bridge and found that his ship was at general quarters. He turned to me and said, "Send for your relief," which is the same as being fired. So I went over and I wanted to explain to the captain that I had sent a messenger down to awaken him and so forth, and he just would have nothing to do with me. So I got my relief up to the bridge, and I went down to my room pretty unhappy. As far as I was concerned, I had done everything according to the book, exactly right.

The next morning the navigator, who runs the officers of the deck, sent for me and said, "What happened? The captain is really upset at you."

I told him, and he said, "Well, I don't see anything the matter with that." He said, "However, you'd better go and see the exec."

So I went in to see Commander Crommelin again. I told him exactly what transpired. He said, "Oh, that dumb son of a bitch. Don't pay any attention to him. He doesn't know what's going on anyway."

---

* "Tokyo Rose" was the nickname of an English-speaking Japanese woman who made radio broadcasts during World War II. Full of Japanese war propaganda, they were aimed at U.S. servicemen in an attempt to demoralize them. For the most part, she was entertaining rather than effective.

So I told the exec and later on the navigator, "I volunteered to be on this top watch job, and as far as I'm concerned, take me off the list. It was extra duty anyway, and I certainly don't want to have anything to do with that man."

Q: Do you think any of the animosity between them refers back to what we briefly mentioned yesterday about the Academy and the Green Bowlers?

Admiral Ramage: Yes. Let's go into that now. John was our hero, particularly to junior officers. He used to talk to us about all sorts of things: air power, carriers, anything that went on. He had discovered this list, which had apparently belonged to Lem Cooke, who had been on the Ranger as a ship's company ensign. The list contained the names of about 10 to 12 people from each Naval Academy class, going all the way back to probably around 1910, 1912. I have the list at home. It turned out in looking at the list that they were all very top-notch people. Most of them were athletes, and the Green Bowl was some kind of an elite group that liked to drink beer, which, of course, was illegal. They would go on out to a watering hole in Annapolis, and for some reason or other, their symbol was a green bowl, a bowling ball or something. I don't know exactly what it was. In any event, they were called Green Bowlers.

It was supposed to be a secret organization. I'll admit that I had never heard about it until John told me about it. John's claim was that this group actually controlled detailing of people and, as such, had unusual power over the future of officers. O. B. Hardison was one of the Green Bowlers, and so when John went public, as he did about this thing, he was directly opposing his commanding officer. But that's the story of the Green Bowl.

I since have talked to numerous members, all of whom are great people. Tom Hamilton, of course, is a Green Bowler who came on the ship following John, and so are Bush Bringle and Lem Cooke.[*] All the people that I knew that were Green Bowlers were quite good friends of mine, and I rather think that it was just what they claimed it was, a kind of a drinking society. In any event, that's what I choose to think.

---

[*] William F. Bringle was a football player who graduated from the Naval Academy in the class of 1937. He later became a naval aviator and eventually retired in 1973 as a four-star admiral.

Q: Does this society supposedly still exist?

Admiral Ramage: My list stops about 1946 or '47. So I don't know. I think that it probably does not. I kid some of the people about it from time to time and say, "Well, you Green Bowlers all had it made. We poor bastards had to make it our own way." But I really don't mean that. So much for the bowl.

Just as soon as I got an opportunity, I began to go to the various squadrons, looking for a job. The skipper of Scouting Squadron Ten, which was an SBD squadron, was Bucky Lee.* Bucky had been a ship's company officer when I was a blackshoe on the ship, so I knew Bucky better than anybody else in the air group. I told him that John Crommelin had told me that if I could find a job in a squadron, he'd be very happy to see that I got orders directly to the squadron. Bucky said, "Fine. Next time we're ashore at Espiritu Santo, come on over and we'll check you out in the SBD." I did so, of course, at the first opportunity, and he told Birney Strong to check me out.† He put himself in the back seat, and we flew around about an hour. Then he got out, and I flew around a couple more hours; that was my introduction to the SBD.

I'd like to talk about Birney Strong a little bit because he, again, is one of the people that helped me very much. There are people that certainly did. Birney was one of the biggest heroes I know. He had attacked, along with his wingman, a carrier single-handedly and had hit it.

Q: That was at Santa Cruz.‡

Admiral Ramage: He was a very determined young officer and a good pilot. He had a drawback, however. He simply couldn't get along with people. He could come into a room and for some reason or other, within five minutes everyone in the room would manage to

---

* Lieutenant Commander James R. Lee, USN.
† Lieutenant Stockton Birney Strong, USN.
‡ On 26 October 1942, in the Battle of Santa Cruz Islands, Lieutenant Strong and Ensign Charles B. Irvine, USNR, dropped two 500-pound bombs into the stern of the Japanese aircraft carrier Zuiho.

dislike him for one thing or another. He was rather small, good-looking, very arrogant, but as far as I'm concerned, he had a reason to be. He was good and he was a tough fighter, and, I think, one of the real heroes of World War II. So Birney pretty much took me under his wing at that time. He was number three in the squadron. Number two was Bill Martin, who later became skipper of Scouting Ten.* Birney moved over to Bombing Ten later on, and I ultimately ended up in Bombing Ten.

Q: But at this time Strong would have been flight officer in Scouting Ten.

Admiral Ramage: Yes. We talked at length, and I flew wing on Birney during the few flights I had before I got carrier qualified. This was the place for me to be, although I was quite senior to the rest of the pilots because of my two years as a blackshoe. My place was on his wing, and he taught me an awful lot.

Q: You had never flown from a carrier or landed?

Admiral Ramage: No, I had never flown from a carrier. So we're getting to the carrier qualifications. I have in my log book that after flying a total of 15.7 hours, I went in to the field carrier landing pattern at Espiritu Santo. I logged one field carrier landing program of eight-tenths of an hour, and if I recall correctly, Jim Daniels bounced me on that one. That was on the fifth of April, 1943. We must have gone to sea, because I didn't fly again until the 12th. I got an additional bounce drill there at Espiritu Santo with Robin Lindsey waving the paddles at me.† After it was over, I went on over to talk to Robin, and he said, "I'll get you aboard." So that was my training.

I will say that having observed carrier operations on the Enterprise for quite a long time probably helped me a lot. I knew what the pattern was supposed to look like. I just didn't know what the deck looked like when you were in an airplane over it. So I went out on the 13th of April and did three carrier landings, and from then on I was a carrier pilot.

---

* Lieutenant Commander William I. Martin, USN. The oral history of Martin, who eventually retired as a vice admiral, is in the Naval Institute collection.
† Lindsey was one of the ship's landing signal officers (LSO).

Q: What sort of dive-bombing training had you received, if any, up to this time?

Admiral Ramage: Back in Pensacola we did dive-bombing back in Squadron Four in OS2Us. It was very modified. I can recall we started our dive from 3,500 feet, rolling over on our backs and pulling straight through, releasing probably at about 2,000. Then at George Bullard's VO/VS school during the summer, we did additional dive-bombing, so I knew the technique. Of course, when I got to dive bomb in the SBD, it was just beautiful--just so stable and so good. Anybody that couldn't hit with that airplane really couldn't fly. It was that good.

So I had finally made my way to a carrier squadron, thanks to many people. I mentioned John Crommelin. Of course, the two LSOs, Jimmy Daniels and Robin Lindsey, Bucky Lee, skipper of VS-10, and Tommy Thomas, who went to VB-10, and that's where I went rather than VS-10.* Then ultimately Birney Strong went over to VB-10 and relieved Tommy Thomas, because Tommy became CAG, and Strong became skipper.

It was kind of a strange thing because we had a non-flying exec. He was a ground officer named John Dufficy, from New York, and he was a rotund, very happy little guy.† Birney wasn't very well pleased with him. He didn't want to call him exec, although he was the second senior. So he said, "Well, you're the exec. Do what you're supposed to do." So that worked out fine, and I continued to fly back where I should, as a wingman anyway, so it didn't make very much difference.

Q: Were you aware of any other carrier squadrons with non-flying execs?

Admiral Ramage: No, I think this was just a special case, because the air group had taken quite a few losses in the two previous battles, and we had a shortage of pilots. As a matter of fact, I think I could have gotten into either of the dive-bomber squadrons. I could have probably gotten in with Flatley in the fighter squadron, and I know I could have gotten into

---

* Lieutenant Commander James A. Thomas, USN.
† Lieutenant Commander John F. Dufficy, USNR.

the torpedo squadron. They were looking for anybody that would volunteer. They really, at that time, I think, had more aircraft than they had pilots. It was kind of a strange thing because they were all over the place, but there just didn't seem to be any on the Enterprise. It was good for me, because I was able to make this transition.

Q: Did you have any personal preferences at the time where you really wanted to fly?

Admiral Ramage: I figured probably I would be better in dive-bombers because after flying the SBD, I knew that it was a very nice plane to fly. I could handle it, and I liked the mission. I liked the idea of going out and killing people. I'm not much of a defense guy, so it was just what I wanted, and it worked out fine. So I was quite happy. Here I was in an operating squadron, deployed on the only carrier in the Pacific. All of my contemporaries that had gone through carrier training hadn't even gotten out of advanced carrier training unit back in San Diego. I was quite pleased with myself.

Q: Can we talk a minute about the relationship between the bombing and scouting squadrons on the carrier at that time? Did they really operate as independent squadrons, or did they kind of operate as one squadron?

Admiral Ramage: No, they operated as independent squadrons, but they both had the same aircraft and the same mission. We even flew the same aircraft. When you flew, you didn't know whether you were going to fly a scouting SBD or a bombing SBD. That's a simple way to do it. We were in adjacent ready rooms and there was a little competition between them. You'd say, "I've got to fly one of those goddamned scouting planes today, and you know how they maintain theirs." And I'm sure they said the same thing.

What you're leading up to is that when we reformed, Scouting-Bombing Ten became one squadron, which it should have been earlier. At that time, you'll notice that the carriers were all loaded three to one attack over fighters. Later on, when we reformed, we had to get more fighters on the carriers because we simply didn't have enough to escort our strike groups in to the target properly.

Q: And, of course, by then the nature of the threat had increased.

Admiral Ramage: Yes. One little story here. You could always tell, in making a carrier landing, who was on the paddles. If Robin Lindsey was bringing you aboard, you'd come around the bend and you'd see him talking to somebody, and he'd look at you, and he didn't even get his paddles up. If he thought that you needed any help, he'd give you a signal, which was rare, and then finally as you were coming down the groove, he'd give you a "Roger" and perhaps a signal and a cut and you were aboard. In other words, he indicated that he had absolute faith in you and, of course, that made you feel real good about it. People all loved Robin very much.

Jimmy Daniels, on the other hand, who, of course, is a very dear friend of mine, would pick you up as you came around the 180, give slants and dips and everything under the sun. I came aboard one day, and Jimmy came down to the ready room and asked me, "Why weren't you answering my signals?"

I said, "Jimmy, I just couldn't keep up with them. I was about three signals behind as I was coming up to the cut."

He said, "That's not funny."

I said, "Jimmy, I thought it was two gooney-birds screwing on the fantail." God, he got mad.

Q: Did LSOs grade each landing in those days as they do now?

Admiral Ramage: Oh, after every landing, they came down, and it was usually kind of a joke. That is, they'd usually have something rather funny to say about every one of them.

The funniest case happened about that time. One of the pilots--and I think he was in the scouting squadron--wanted to come aboard. There was a rain squall or something so that he had some kind of deferred landing. They had the yoke flag up back there, which meant the landing area was closed, but this guy came in and landed. The LSO was down under the overhang there along the catwalk when the guy landed. That really made Daniels mad. Of course, it was totally wrong, because you don't know whether the landing wires are rigged or up and so forth. It happened that they were, but I think mainly it hurt Jimmy's feelings that the guy could get aboard without his help.

Q: Was any action taken against the guy?

Admiral Ramage: I don't think so. I think he got a pretty good chewing, but that was it. You can't argue with success. I guess if he'd banged somebody up or the airplane up, they'd have been pretty unhappy about it.

So I was in the bombing squadron, very happy, and we got orders to return to Pearl Harbor. The air group was to be detached at that time to go back to the States on a transport and reform.

When we returned to Pearl Harbor with the Enterprise, the air group generally moved back to the Royal Hawaiian and Chris Holmes's place down on the beach. I, of course, went home because my wife had made it back to Honolulu. After two or three days, we were told what was going to happen, and when we were going to sail for the coast. I discussed with my wife and her family the desirability of her coming back to the States, because we didn't know how long the war was going to last, we didn't know how long I was going to be back there. We just had no idea of anything, and we all agreed that probably the best thing in the world was that she would go back to the coast if she could get there.

So I went out to Com 14, the 14th Naval District offices, to see about buying a ticket on some kind of a ship to get Ty, my wife, back to the States. All civilian travel was controlled by the Navy at that time. They didn't want people joyriding all over the ocean. I ultimately ended up with a Captain Robertson, and I told him who I was, that I'd just come in on the Enterprise, and that my wife was over here. I wanted permission to buy a ticket for her on some ship to go back to the coast because I didn't know how long I was going to be back there. He said, "Absolutely not."

I said, "Well, all I'm trying to do is get permission to buy a ticket. I'm not even asking for transportation."

Then he said, "If you will sign an agreement that she will not attempt to return to the Hawaiian Islands during the duration of the war, I will let you buy a ticket."

I said, "Captain, there's no way that I can say that. This is her home. I don't know what is going to happen to me, and anything that I would sign like that would be totally wrong." Looking at it later, I should have signed the damn thing because it couldn't hold water anyway, but being honest, I said, "No, Captain, I won't sign it."

So he said, "Well, she's going to have a nice time out here in Honolulu, then."

That afternoon I went back down to Chris Holmes's place and the CAG was there, Tommy Thomas. I told him about this, and he said, "Well, I'll be damned. I know who you should see." He made arrangements for me to go out and see Vice Admiral John Towers, who was ComAirPac.[*]

So the next morning I went in, and the first few minutes were taken up with the admiral asking me all sorts of questions about what was going on in the Western Pacific, what were the supply problems, did we have enough parts for our airplanes, anything that he could possibly do to make things better for the aviators out there. Finally we got around to my problem, and I told him how I was treated over at Com 14.

He said, "What's the guy's name?"

I said, "Captain Robertson."

He indicated that that was no surprise to him and told his aide to get Captain Robertson on the phone. He thereupon talked to me for a long time, five or ten minutes with Captain Robertson waiting on the line. It made me rather nervous, because a captain was a big shot as far as I was concerned. Admiral Towers was in no hurry to talk to him. He finally got on the phone and said, "I have a young pilot over here named Ramage who says that you won't let his wife go back to the coast." He conveyed to the captain that life in the forward area was somewhat more difficult than sitting on his ass over at Com 14. He then said, "Now, I'll tell you what you're going to do. You are going to issue her transportation on the same transport that her husband goes back to the coast on, and it will be free of charge."

---

[*] Vice Admiral John H. Towers, USN, served as Commander Air Force Pacific Fleet from 14 October 1942 to 28 February 1944.

There apparently was a cheery, "Aye, aye."

So then I thanked the good admiral, and he said, "You go over and see Captain Robertson, and I'm sure that everything will be taken care of."

I went over to Com 14. The good captain was waiting for me, and he said, "I didn't know you knew Admiral Towers."

I said, "I don't. I just went out to see him today."

He said, "I didn't understand exactly what you were talking about. Of course, that's a very reasonable thing, and you know, we're going to put her right on the same transport as you."

I didn't say anything but, "Thank you very much, Captain." Man, there was a different attitude than the previous afternoon. That was my only contact with John Towers, and I, of course, was very pleased with him.

The trip back was uneventful. In addition to my wife, Birney Strong's wife, Mani Strong, was aboard ship. The trip back was pleasant and, I might add, rather wet.

We arrived in Alameda, where we were processed, and the air group pilots were advised as to future assignments. I had no problem there. I was exactly where I wanted to be. The officer who handled this classification procedure was Captain Murr Arnold, and he was known as the "Coronado Cobra."[*] I guess this was probably because whenever anybody didn't want to go back to sea, he came right up like a cobra. The only alternative that he offered me, which was no problem at all, was he asked me if I wanted to be a landing signal officer. I said, "No, I want to go right back out to sea with Bombing Squadron Ten."

He said, "Well, go on up to Sand Point and you'll find the squadron already up there. Have a good cruise."[†]

Air Group Ten, in reorganizing up there, went from F4F-4s to F6Fs in the fighter

---

[*] Captain Murr E. Arnold, USN.
[†] Sand Point Naval Air Station, Seattle, Washington.

squadron, and that was a great improvement.*

Q: What month was that?

Admiral Ramage: This was in August of '43. We bombers went to the SBD-5, rather than the SBD-3, which we had flown previously. The newer version had additional horsepower in the engine. Better than that, even, it had the gun sight with the glass plate.

Q: The reflector plate.

Admiral Ramage: The reflector sight, so that you didn't have to stick your eye in that telescope, which was always fogging up. You really had a hard time bombing with that one. In the tropics, as a matter of fact, a lot of people didn't use the sight to bomb. It was useless. The reflector sight was fine.

Q: How would they compensate?

Admiral Ramage: They looked over the nose and they counted the number of rivets to use as an aiming system. It was another way of doing it. Of course, it wasn't as accurate, but that gun sight was a real problem. We still had a lot of people with gun sight faces in cases when they had a water landing or hit a barrier. They'd end up with the nose pretty well smashed up when it smashed into that sight. And, of course, the air group had the TBFs again, the TBF being a fine airplane.†

---

* Grumman F4F Wildcat fighters entered the fleet in 1940. The F4F-4 was 28 feet, 9 inches long; wing span of 38 feet; gross weight of 7,952 pounds; and top speed of 318 miles per hour; maximum range of 770 miles. Grumman F6F Hellcat fighters first entered the fleet in early 1943. The F6F-5 was 34 feet long, wing span of 43 feet, gross weight of 15,413 pounds, and top speed of 380 miles per hour; maximum range of 945 miles.

† The Grumman-built TBF Avenger was the U.S. Navy's standard carrier-based torpedo plane during the latter part of World War II. The TBf-1 model had a wing span of 54 feet, length of 40 feet, gross weight of 15,905 pounds, and top speed of 271 miles per hour. It was armed with one .30-caliber machine gun (two .50 caliber in the TBF-1C). The first TBF-1s reached the fleet in the spring of 1942.

Q: At the beginning of the war, the carrier planes weren't equipped with shoulder harnesses, were they?

Admiral Ramage: No. As a matter of fact, not until this period of time. We got shoulder harnesses at this time.

Q: It seems really amazing that it took so long to figure out that you really ought to strap this guy in a little better.

Admiral Ramage: That's right. The new air group commander was Roscoe Newman, who was a very aggressive guy.[*] He'd been a former landing signal officer. Killer Kane, who had relieved Flatley part way during the previous cruise, was to continue on as skipper of VF-10.[†] Bill Martin would move over from Scouting Ten to take over Torpedo Ten, because he was very interested in the capabilities of the TBF as a night attack aircraft. Dick Poor, out of the training command, came in to take over VB-10, which was now a combination of Scouting Ten and Bombing Ten.[‡]

There were to be 36 fighters, 36 bombers, and 18 torpedo planes. This would have been fine on an Essex carrier; they could handle that. But we couldn't do it on the "E." So when we finally went to sea three months later, we went to sea with the 36 fighters, I believe. Almost certainly we took a full load of fighters, but we took 24 bombers plus five, which we carried in the overhead of the hangar deck. They could be strapped up there. We took only 12 TBFs in Enterprise.

I won't dwell too much on the training. We got a fine group of replacement pilots. We operated Bombing Ten pretty much as two squadrons again, with Dick Poor in the first 18-plane outfit. He had Ira Hardman, who was a classmate of mine.[§] Believe it or not, he was a classmate that stood even lower than I did. It was impossible, but Ira did. As exec, I

---

[*] Commander Roscoe L. Newman, USN.
[†] Lieutenant Commander William R. Kane, USN.
[‡] Lieutenant Commander Richard L. Poor, USN.
[§] Lieutenant Ira S. Hardman, Jr., USN.

led the second unit, and I took Lou Bangs as my second.* Lou was just a fine aviator, a solid guy. So we had a good makeup of people.

Q: Did you have a regular rear-seat man?

Admiral Ramage: Yes. At that time I picked up Cawley.† He was a first class aviation radioman, second cruise, and just a fine, fine man. He was from Battle Mount, Oregon.

Q: That's the western part of the state.

Admiral Ramage: Yes. He was just a great guy. I was able to get him into flight training a year or so later. Unfortunately, I never heard of him after that.

They gave us a full load of pilots, however, for our 24 planes. I think they gave us 45 pilots, and so when we got ready to go to sea, we were able to pick the ones we really wanted to take. Some of them were very young, just out of high school, but I was very pleased with what we had. The bad thing about Sand Point--and also during our time at Maui--was that we had just terrible operational losses in training. The fighters in particular lost a lot of people, and we lost quite a number too. I've got all the figures, if it's important.

Q: What were the leading causes?

Admiral Ramage: Just doping off. Diving into the target. I can't put my finger on all of them. We had a lot of operational losses in training.

Q: Mostly pilot error, though?

Admiral Ramage: Yes.

---

* Lieutenant Louis L. Bangs, USN.
† Aviation Radioman First Class David J. Cawley, USN.

Q: Not maintenance problems?

Admiral Ramage: No. I know of no maintenance problems. No, just people maybe getting a little too overconfident for their ability. So we were back in Sand Point for about three months. The weather there is not good for training a carrier air group of that size, and Sand Point itself was somewhat restricted for a large air group like we had. However, the facilities were nice, and certainly the buildings and everything were beautiful. The weather was such, however, that we were quite restricted. We did very little night work there. It was just very difficult to get things done with that weather situation at night. Bombing training was fine--when we could get up. There were two or three targets out in the Puget Sound, and they were good, clear targets. We practiced an awful lot of IBP at that time, individual bombing practice.

Q: How would that normally shape up? Would you go up in squadron strength or two or three sections?

Admiral Ramage: We'd go out by division. That would be six planes.

Q: You'd have, what, three practice bombs on board?

Admiral Ramage: No, I think we carried six. By the time you climbed up to about 10,000 or 12,000 feet, it was a good session. All of our people were qualified. I think the qualification required 50-foot accuracy.

Q: That's a CEP?

Admiral Ramage: No, that's actual error. No, CEP is something the Air Force generated to do away with the fact that they threw a lot of bombs all over the area.[*]

---

[*] CEP--circular error probable.

Q: That's only talking about half of them. Right.

Admiral Ramage: And I would say that probably most of us had about a 25-foot error. The SBD was that good, and with our people, most of whom were just out of the training command, it was a very simple plane for simple people, and we could do a good job with it.

Q: Did you have an opportunity to practice on moving targets?

Admiral Ramage: Yes, we did have some target boats. They did send us over to Pasco, Washington, where they had a ship-sized target at Boardman Range. We generally used to have to simulate a moving target, and we would indicate that it had so many knots of speed. That was done mainly during skull practice.

So we finally were ready to go back aboard ship. My log book says that we flew aboard on the first of November. The Enterprise had been up in the yard there at Bremerton.* We were to go back on the same ship, which made us very happy. I'm not sure the ship was very happy with Air Group Ten when we flew aboard, though. We were wild as we could be; a lot of the kids had never really been aboard ship before. The captain, I know, had a heck of a time because he was running out of sea room there in Puget Sound during the recovery.

Q: Who was the captain at this time?

Admiral Ramage: We had gone through Hardison, Wieber, Ginder, and now Gardner.†

I notice I must have gotten aboard fairly easily and early because the duration of my flight was only seven-tenths of an hour. We took off from Whidbey Island rather than Sand Point. I guess we wanted to be sure that we were out in the area in case the weather closed in. The weather up in Whidbey is better than Sand Point. So we finally got aboard and

---

* Puget Sound Navy Yard, Bremerton, Washington.
† Command tenures were as follows: Captain Carlos W. Wieber, USN, 7 April 1943 to 16 April 1943; Captain Samuel P. Ginder, USN, 16 April 1943 to 7 November 1943; Captain Matthias B. Gardner, USN, 7 November 1943 to 10 July 1944.

started out for Maui, where we flew off on the sixth of November. We were shore-based at Maui for the next six weeks, during which time the Enterprise took a pickup air group aboard.* Bob, you probably know what they picked up in our place for the Gilberts operation. Was that Six again?

Q: Yes, it was.

Admiral Ramage: The Gilberts operation wasn't very complicated and not much of a problem except that we did lose Butch O'Hare there off the Enterprise at that time.† Another guy that we almost lost was John Crommelin again. He'd made captain and had become chief of staff of a jeep carrier division, which was on the Liscome Bay.‡ They were torpedoed, and he was blown right out of the shower and was pretty badly hurt, but he came back.

Maui was just fine for Air Group Ten.

Q: This is Kahului.

Admiral Ramage: The fighters were over at Kahului, and the bombers and torpedo planes were at Puunene. It was just ideal. You could take off with a load of anything you wanted, you could bomb, strafe, you could fly at night, you could do anything. There was all the sea room in the world. There was just nothing that you couldn't do.

Q: You used targets on Kahoolawe?

---

* Air Group Ten remained in Hawaii for additional training, while Air Group Six went aboard the Enterprise for the invasion of the Gilbert Islands in mid-November 1943.
† Lieutenant Commander Edward H. O'Hare, USN, was killed the night of 27 November 1943. He was the pilot of an F6F Hellcat while it flying with a radar-equipped TBF. See Eugene Burns, "Butch O'Hare's Last Flight," The Saturday Evening Post, 11 March 1944, page 19. See also Steve Ewing and John B. Lundstrom: Fateful Rendezvous: The Life of Butch O'Hare (Annpolis: Naval Institute Press, 1997).
‡ The escort carrier Liscome Bay (CVE-56) was torpedoed and sunk by the Japanese submarine I-175 on the morning of 24 November 1943 while supporting the invasion of the Gilbert Islands. Of those on board, 624 were lost and 272 were rescued. Among those killed was Rear Admiral Henry M. Mullinnix, USN, embarked as Commander Task Group 52.3.

Admiral Ramage: Well, that's where we did our live work, but there were lots of other targets around. There were targets in the water. There were boats at that time, moving target boats with armor on them that you could use, which again brought up the fact that we really were aiming for moving targets.

Q: You used it for practice bombs with small shotgun shell markers.

Admiral Ramage: That's right. They weighed about two or three pounds, I think, maybe not that much. They had a shotgun shell in them, left a little trace of white smoke. We really came alive there. The whole air group began to do group gropes and get into coordinated strikes, which we were going to have to use later on.

Q: Did you have night carrier quals here?

Admiral Ramage: Yes. We did our night bounce there at Maui and over the holidays. Looking at my log book here, I think we were out over Christmas of '43, January of '44. I see that I made two night carrier landings on the fifth of January 1944.

The entire group night qualified with only the two carrier landings, but those stood us in very good stead later on in the Battle of the Philippine Sea.[*] This was, I think, mainly because our leaders insisted that we night qual, and I think that a lot of the other leaders just didn't insist on it. I don't know how AirPac would let them get away without being night carqualed, but it worked out fine for us. And later on, as you will note, we had no problems with the Phil Sea Battle, as others really misbehaved, so far as I'm concerned.

Q: You mentioned the term "group grope." Can you describe that?

---

[*] This battle, which Admiral Ramage covers in greater detail later in the oral history, took place 19-20 June 1944.

Admiral Ramage: The group grope is where you launch your strike group; it is really a deck-load strike. In today's Navy they call it the Alfa strike, which is a combination of the aircraft that are going to go in to the target. We set it up so that we had a base element generally of 12 dive bombers and six torpedo planes, and 12 or 16 fighters overhead, depending upon what the opposition was. The procedure was that as we approached the targets, the low combat air patrol, which was weaving just over the bombers, would start in to the target just before the bombers went in. The bombers would then go in, and the torpedo planes simultaneously would pull out to either side and do a spiral and come on in low for their torpedo attack or from about 5,000 feet in the event they were going to drop bombs. We could get the full strike group on and off the target in less than two minutes' time. It was quite a devastating shot. Of course, the fighters would strafe ahead and then the high cover, providing there was nothing up there, would come on down and they would strafe afterwards.

Q: So you had continuous flak suppression during the attack.

Admiral Ramage: All the time, yes. It worked perfectly, and I think that was pretty standard among all the air groups. We learned the hard way at Midway, and every air group pretty much did the same thing. It was a devastating shot to be on the receiving end of, I know.

Q: On the subject of night flying, it was about this time, wasn't it, that Chick Harmer's four Corsairs came aboard?[*]

Admiral Ramage: That's right. Chick came aboard, and we were quite surprised that they would put F4Us aboard, because we knew that the F4Us had so much trouble in the past on

---

[*] Lieutenant Commander Richard E. Harmer, USN, commanding officer of VF-101(N), the first carrier-based night fighter squadron of F4U Corsairs.

the carriers.* We got Chick and his pilots, and they did a very, very good job. They had no problems with the airplane at all on the Enterprise, and they were used quite often. We used them occasionally during the daytime on strikes because they didn't want to be sitting there when the action was going on, but they flew quite a bit at night and later on got some planes. As I recall, we got some off Hollandia.†

Q: Yes, I think that was their first engagement. The reason that comes to mind is that when I was interviewing Chick for my Corsair book, he discussed the period coming aboard and said Tom Hamilton really hated to see him coming because he knew that was going to upset the respot procedures after dusk.‡

Admiral Ramage: Yes. Tom was air boss, and he later became exec.§ He again filled the same spot that John Crommelin did. He was very close to the pilots just like John was. Captain Gardner wasn't at all.** He didn't even know who I was.

Q: And you're one of the squadron commanders.

Admiral Ramage: Could care less, as a matter of fact. Maybe I'm doing him a disservice, but he didn't really do anything. On the other hand, Tom Hamilton was always around.

Q: You were the skipper of Bombing Ten now?

Admiral Ramage: No, I didn't take over as skipper of Bombing Ten until April 1944. Before that I was exec and strike leader, generally, so I was just happy as I could be.

---

* The Vought F4U Corsair was in production longer than any other U.S. fighter plane of World War II. It first entered fleet squadrons in 1942. The F4U-1 was 33 feet, 4 inches long; wing span of 41 feet; gross weight of 14,000 pounds; and top speed of 417 miles per hour.
† Allied troops began invading Hollandia, on the island of New Guinea, on 22 April 1944.
‡ See Barrett Tillman, Corsair: The F4U in World War II and Korea (Annapolis, Naval Institute Press, 1979), pages 109-110.
§ Commander Thomas J. Hamilton, USN, whose oral history is in the Naval Institute collection.
** Captain Matthias B. Gardner, USN, commanded the Enterprise from 7 November 1943 to 10 July 1944.

We're all ready to go into the Kwajalein operation.* We were to fly aboard the Enterprise. It shows here that we probably flew aboard on the 23rd of January, 1944, and the ship then entered port. It was an amazing sight to see what had happened in the year that we'd been gone. Actually it was less than a year. It was eight months. But Pearl Harbor was just chock-a-block with ships, just a tremendous sight to see, and, of course, really the last time that the fleet was ever together in Pearl Harbor. They were together out in Majuro and later in Ulithi. But we got under way, probably on the 24th of January, and those ships were nose to stern for hours. I think it took 24 or 36 hours to get that fleet out of Pearl. When you think of all the transports, we had the two divisions, we had the Army Seventh Infantry Division and the Fourth Marine Division. By that time we had probably eight escort carriers, and then we had five or six big carriers plus five or six CVLs.

Q: Independence class.†

Admiral Ramage: Yes, and then the bombardment battleships that went along with the amphibious force. It was an enormous fleet. When you looked around, you couldn't help but think, "These Japs are really going to get it this time."

My log book shows that our first strike of the new year, the new cruise, was against Taroa, which was an island in the Marshalls, and was one of those so-called unsinkable aircraft carriers the Japanese bragged so much about.

Q: It's also an area Enterprise knew well. She had launched strikes there in February or March of '42.

Admiral Ramage: Yes. It had crossed runways on it. It had various facilities, but the unsinkable aircraft carriers had one problem; they don't move. We could concentrate our

---

* U.S. troops invaded Kwajalein Atoll in the western Marshall Islands on 1 February 1944. Kwajalein fell on 6 February, and the entire atoll was declared secured.
† The Independence (CVL-22)-class light carriers were built on Cleveland-class cruiser hulls. Each had a standard displacement of 10,662 tons; full-load, 14,751 tons; length, 622 feet; beam, 72 feet, maximum width 109 feet, top speed of 31.6 knots; and capability of handling about 30 aircraft.

10 or 12 carriers on these guys one at a time, and it was no match. I can remember the first launch. The fighter sweep was to take off pre-dawn, and the strike group, which I led, was to take off at just about first light. The planes were all manned. The fighters took off directly into a rain squall, and it was probably the fourth and fifth of our fighters that had a mid-air collision with a tremendous explosion. It wasn't very reassuring.

But we went on in, of course, and found the target very easily. By that time the fighters had knocked down anything that was in the air. I don't recall just what the fighter action was on the fighter sweep, but there wasn't much there. I remember my specific target was a torpedo storage area, at least it was so called. I think I got a hit on it or close to it. We did a good job and came back. At least we started out the new inning with a nice strike.

Q: That was your first combat mission?

Admiral Ramage: Really it was, yes.

Q: Can you describe some of your thoughts and feelings as you sat in the ready room, briefed, and got ready for this thing? And then there's always some time up on the flight deck sitting in the cockpit before you start the engines. You must have had some thoughts about, "Gee, am I going to screw this up?" What was your biggest concern, or did you have any?

Admiral Ramage: Let's talk about that a little while, because I was going to talk a little bit about religion and prayer somewhere, and this is probably a good place. As I said previously, I came from a very religious family, and I did pray, but I never prayed for myself. I thought it would be a very arrogant thing for me to pray that I would live and somebody else would die. That wasn't in my way of thinking. I did pray, as you mentioned, from time to time, that I would do a good job, and that was what the prayers were about. I didn't think of praying for the longevity of myself or anybody else. We were out there to do a job, and everybody else knew that somebody was going to get killed. It's a fact of life during the war, no great problem. So much for religion. But I think everybody had about the same feeling. I don't know anybody that was too damned concerned about himself.

Now, as far as fear or apprehension, not really any more than any other carrier takeoff. You always take your nervous pee just before you man your plane, and when you get in your plane, you wish you could do it again. But no, I can remember sitting back and seeing the carrier swing on into the wind and the planes gradually take off, but you're thinking, you're checking, looking around to see what's going on, and there really isn't any great apprehension, at least in my case. Everything went just as briefed. We were well trained. As base element commander, I rendezvoused my bombers, then gathered up the torpedo planes and fighters. We were always last off because the SBD had fixed wings. We didn't have folding wings, and so consequently we were always on the stern, which was fine because we were the base element, and it gave the other two squadrons an opportunity to get themselves organized so they could join on us as a group. I think it saved time.

So Taroa was the first. My log says the following day I attacked Kwajalein, which apparently was part of the softening up. As a matter of fact, I had two more attacks on Kwajalein on the first. I notice that on the second I was the air coordinator for the various airborne forces at that time. I always carried a bomb too, and got rid of the bomb on the best target we could find. Then I tried to find targets for the other people as they reported in.

Q: What was the quality of radio communications?

Admiral Ramage: It was good. We had gone to VHF at that time, although we only had, I think, four channels plus guard.[*] But radio discipline was quite good. We did have a few loudmouths, like Jumping Joe Clifton.[†] He broadcast his whole flight history. We had the CAG on the Yorktown, Edgar Stebbins; he also was a talking CAG.[‡] He started talking when he was on the flight deck. But our squadron and our whole group was pretty well disciplined. You know, Killer Kane is a pretty big individual, and anyone would hate to

---

[*] VHF--very high frequency.
[†] Commander Joseph C. Clifton, Commander Air Group 12 in the Saratoga (CV-3).
[‡] Lieutenant Commander Edgar E. Stebbins, USN, Commander Air Group Five in the Yorktown (CV-10).

have him come on up and say, "Shut up. Be busy." He might make it so. So we had both good air discipline and radio discipline.

Q: Wasn't that unusual, though, for the air groups, generally speaking, during the war? I understand that the radio system wasn't that good.

Admiral Ramage: I thought that most of them were pretty good. The only ones that I remember were by individuals, like Clifton and Stebbins. I don't remember too many people shooting their mouths off, not enough to impact upon our operations, with only the four operating channels, and, of course, one of those was dedicated to combat air patrol. So we probably only had one strike channel for all the air groups, so you had to shut up, or you were going to screw up the whole operation.

So the log shows here operating off Kwajalein, first, two strikes again on the second, two on the third, and this is after the landings. We put the Seventh Infantry Division on the beach there, and it was a darn fine infantry division. There is a lot of argument about the Marines. They cleaned up Roi and Namur up north quicker because they operated in a different manner. But the Seventh Army Division was a good one and they did a fine job on Kwajalein. They took the main island and wound it up in four or five days.

Q: What was the means of coordinating tactical air support with the Army? Did you have people on the ground with them, or did they have their own forward controllers?

Admiral Ramage: We had people on the ground with the Army, and, of course, this was all handled by this time through the command ship. I forget what the name of it was at that time. But at that time Captain Dick Whitehead was the main aviation coordinator on the command ship.* It was no great problem. Of course, as the airborne coordinator, you would dig out targets of opportunity and report back to the command ship what you saw

---

* Captain Richard F. Whitehead, USN, was in the amphibious command ship Appalachian (AGC-1), flagship of Rear Admiral Richard L. Connolly, USN, for the Roi-Namur part of the operation.

and if there was anything that was needed. By the end of this time, we had so many planes in the air that you just couldn't use them all. Things had changed.

I will say this about Kwajalein. When those battleships and cruisers and the air that had been on it for four or five days got through with that place, it looked like the moon. It was plowed ground. I don't think there was a stick of anything standing. It looked just completely beaten up. We had certainly learned our lesson at Tarawa, where we lost so many Marines, and rather than underdo it this time, they certainly overdid it.* We just cleaned that place out completely. Those battleships, of course, laying off there, that's tremendous power. I just can't imagine being in a position of taking four or five of those 14- or 16-inch shells. It must be a terrifying thing to have happen to you.

Q: So at this point of the war, January of '44, what do you recall as the mood in the Navy, generally? Obviously most people would have concluded that we were no longer in danger of losing the war.

Admiral Ramage: I don't really remember. I had my head in the cockpit. I was interested in kicking the hell out of as many Japs as I could possibly get to, and I think that was the main desire. There was still a lot of hatred, you know.

Q: Yes.

Admiral Ramage: There wasn't any question about what they would do to us if they caught us, and we didn't hold back a darn bit, which I'll go into when we get to Truk.

Q: Was there ever, as far as you know, any doubt from the very beginning that we were going to win the war?

---

* U.S. Marines, supported by warships of the Central Pacific Force, invaded Tarawa on 20 November 1943 to begin the capture of the Gilbert Islands.

Admiral Ramage: I would say that during the first year, year and a half, there was a heck of a lot of doubt from the people that were out there and getting only 5% of the national effort, particularly when the Enterprise was all alone down there in '42 and '43. It was kind of Enterprise against the world. People felt pretty lonely. But I don't have any idea what the other people felt. I was mainly interested in doing a good job. I figured we were going to win, I guess, but I knew it was going to take forever. The motto was always, "The Golden Gate by '48," but we got back three years early.

We went back to Majuro, which became the fleet anchorage at that time and was for the next four to five months. It was a fine atoll. It was, again, just a tremendous sight to see the fleet enter Majuro.

Q: Where exactly was Majuro?

Admiral Ramage: Well, it's in the eastern Marshalls, and it's an atoll with a nice harbor in the midst of it, with probably two or three channels going into it, which are very easily guarded, could be mined and protected. It was an ideal anchorage. It was when we were in Majuro that the news began to get noised around, "What do you think of going into Truk?" This was something that everybody had heard about for so long, that Truk was such a tough target and invincible. And pretty soon we began to get the table layouts of the islands, the atolls around it, the relief maps of what the islands looked like, and what pictures we could get, which were scarce. I think they got all they had out of the National Geographics. We simply didn't have a darn thing.

Q: A Marine PB4Y went in there and got some pictures before the raid. They only had partial coverage, though, because of low clouds.

Admiral Ramage: As far as I know, we simply had surface pictures, which were taken sometime previously, and we did have the mockup on the table, though, and it was a good mockup of just what the islands looked like. Of course, it didn't show where the batteries were and where the anchorages were, but you could figure that out pretty easily. We got under way from Majuro, and my log book shows that on the 17th of February of 1944, we made the first attack on Truk.* The fighter sweep took off just about first light.†

I again was in the first strike group, and the fighters really had a field day. They went in and really did a job. I don't know how large the fighter sweep was, but it must have been 80 to 100 aircraft. By the time we got in there, yes, there were a few Zeros around, but certainly not enough to bother us. Our strike group was about standard size. We were escorted, I think, by probably 16 fighters. The only problem is that we were down to only two or three SBD squadrons in the fleet at that time. The SB2C had begun to come out by then.‡ We'd get tally-hoed from time to time as Zeros because the SBDs had rounded wingtips and kind of looked like the Zero.§ So I'd have to get on the air and say, "No, we're your friendly SBDs. Leave us alone," which they did.

As we approached the atoll, we were beginning to get good, bright sunlight. An ammo ship just plain erupted. I understand that a fighter had strafed it and blown himself up at the same time, but it was, I think, the biggest explosion I've ever seen--other than the atomic bombs later. It was just an enormous blast. As we got into the lagoon area, there must have been 40 to 45 ships in there--unfortunately, only one or two combatants--but it was a good bunch of targets. I picked out the biggest ship which was in there, which was a tanker, and put our guys on it, and we got some hits.

I went back again in the afternoon; I think all the ships were sunk. There were a few ships that were either up by the bow or down by the bow, but certainly they'd been hit. It was a good day to remember Pearl Harbor, because it was the first time that we'd really gotten an opportunity to get at their ships. Unfortunately, as I read in history later, the battle fleet left maybe three or four days prior. I guess they heard us coming.

Q: Was there much antiaircraft fire?

---

* On 17-18 February 1944, planes from nine carriers attacked Truk Atoll in the Carolines chain, and surface combatants later made a circuit around the atoll. All told, U.S. forces destroyed most of Truk's airstrips and sank a number of warships and merchant ships--a total tonnage of some 200,000.
† See Barrett Tillman, "Hellcats Over Truk," U.S. Naval Institute Proceedings, March 1977, pages 63 to 71.
‡ Curtiss SB2C Helldiver dive-bombers first entered combat in November 1943. The SB2C-4 version was 37 feet long, wing span of 50 feet, gross weight of 16,616 pounds, and top speed of 295 miles per hour. The Helldiver could carry 1,000 pounds of bombs internally and 1,000 pounds externally.
§ Tally-ho is the term used when a fighter pilot sights a designated target aircraft.

Admiral Ramage: Not too much at that time. The ships were in the lagoon within the islands, whereas we got an awful lot of antiaircraft fire the second time we went in, because we were after the shore targets. It wasn't bad. As a matter of fact, there wasn't really very much at all. We did lose one SBD, Dean, who went straight in.[*] So there was enough to keep you on your toes.

Q: Have you seen any of the television documentaries which appear from time to time about . . .

Admiral Ramage: I sure have, and it makes my heart glad every time I look at it. One of the interesting things about the Truk raid, it was either the second time I went in or the third time, there was a hospital ship in there. I'm afraid probably we had banged it up a little bit, but it was under way and it had two escorts with it that were smaller than destroyer escorts, probably about PC size, but there was an escort on either side of it.[†] We had dropped our bombs on other ships, and on the way out. This thing was moving out under escort.

There was nothing against cleaning out those escorts, so we immediately went to work and chopped them up pretty badly with our forward .50s to the point that both of them were sinking.[‡] They had a lot of people in the water, life boats, rafts, people in life jackets. But most of our .50s were out of ammo by that time, so I put all the SBDs into a circle and let the rear gunners kill all the rest of them. I don't know how many there were in the water, but if any of them lived, it wasn't our fault.

Q: How low were you?

Admiral Ramage: About 100 feet.

Q: So it was easy shooting.

---

[*] The crew was made up of Ensign Donald Dean and Aviation Radioman Second Class James J. McGorry.
[†] PC--patrol craft.
[‡] This is a reference to the airplanes' .50-caliber machine guns.

Admiral Ramage: Oh, yeah. After we thought we'd gotten every survivor, we joined up and went back. Another interesting thing, too, as we left the atoll, there was a Jap cruiser out there, and we had no bombs left, so I called "Bald Eagle," who was Mitscher over there in the Yorktown, and told him that we had this cruiser out here which apparently was damaged.[*]

It looked down by the stern and was going very slowly in circles, and that if they'd send a strike group over, I'd stay on station and we'd take care of the rest of him too. I got an immediate call back, "Cease and desist. You are not to hit the cruiser." It turned out later that Admiral Spruance had called the carrier planes off the cruiser because he wanted to give the battleships an opportunity to kill this poor little bastard.[†] So the big battleships finally drew blood against a cruiser that was almost dead in the water. It must have been a great victory. The Truk strike was quite successful. We pulled off on the third day. And the other three carrier task groups then proceeded to the Marianas, where they did the first sweep into the Marianas and did an excellent job there.

Enterprise and group 58.3 went back to Majuro by way of Jaluit. We were to attack Jaluit and use call signs of the carriers that were on the way to the Marianas, to try to fool them into the idea that we had the whole task force there. Jaluit wasn't much of a target. I got two strikes in there. I don't think there was much going on. It had been pretty badly beaten up, too, because it was fairly close to Majuro.

Q: Weren't some of these targets like Jaluit and Marcus kind of warm-up . . .

Admiral Ramage: Yes, they used Marcus. I never went into Marcus. Most of the new carriers were given an opportunity to get a shot at an easy target before they joined the big league.

Q: Let's do this before we really get serious.

---

[*] Rear Admiral Marc A. Mitscher, USN, Commander Task Force 58, the fast carrier task force.
[†] Vice Admiral Raymond A. Spruance, USN, Commander Task Force 50, embarked in the battleship New Jersey (BB-62).

Admiral Ramage: Yes. From there, I notice on the 20th of March, we find ourselves supporting landings at Emirau, which is down near Green Island.* That's quite a ways down in the southwest Pacific. It was not opposed, and I don't know exactly what we were doing there. Kind of an interesting story about that. Enterprise and the new Yorktown went into Espiritu Santo again. The old Yorktown and the old Enterprise, of course, had been great competitors and great enemies.† The new Yorktown was the same; we still had a bit of the same animosity towards each other.‡ So the air groups went ashore to the bar, which was a Quonset hut, and we were having a few drinks. The drinks there consisted of whatever they had. If they were serving gin, you drank gin, and maybe the next bottle might be brandy, and you had some brandy.

Q: They didn't care anyway.

Admiral Ramage: You didn't care. This led to a lot of problems. The last thing I remember, I was sitting in one of the camp chairs on the outside, and some guy yelled, "No Yorktown son-of-a-bitch can say that about the Enterprise." And somebody hit me about that time. I was down. I was down before the fight started. Anyway, it was a pretty good battle royal, and when I got home, back to the ship, I was kind of banged up. I had a place on the back of my head where somebody laid something on me, I don't know what it was. Tom Hamilton, who was our exec by this time, called me in. He said, "Were you over in the fight?"

I said, "I was in the fight, but I didn't last very long."

He said, "Well, I want to let you know that your squadron was the worst one." We had a lot of good athletes in that squadron, big guys, and apparently they were in the midst of it. And he said, "I just don't know what to do with you guys." He said, "I don't want to

---

* The Fourth Marine Division occupied Emirau, which was used as a naval and air base for the reduction of the Japanese stronghold of Rabaul on the island of New Britain.
† The USS Yorktown (CV-5), a sister ship of the Enterprise, was commissioned 30 September 1937. She was sunk on 7 June 1942 as a result of being bombed and torpedoed during the Battle of Midway.
‡ The new Yorktown (CV-10) was commissioned 15 April 1943.

restrict your squadron from going ashore tonight." We were only going to be there two days. "But I want you to go over there, and I don't want anything like this to happen again."

So I got the squadron together and told them, "Stop it. Take all the insults from those Yorktown bastards, but don't fight. Just leave them alone."

So we went over there and everything was quiet, and we were having a few drinks. And as you might guess, the same thing happened all over again. So we went back to our respective ships. We had our fights and we had our fun and were ready to get on with the war. So much for our second time back to Espiritu Santo.

Q: The real battle of Espiritu Santo.

Admiral Ramage: The real battle. We went back to Majuro again, and it shows here that the next time we were in combat was against Palau. That is a very interesting operation and not very well covered. I don't know why, because there were 30 to 35 ships in there, mainly tankers, and the old Mitscher Shampoo sunk them all the first day. It was another big day, and these tankers were loaded. It was a big day for Task Force 58.*

Q: Would you describe the Mitscher shampoo?

Admiral Ramage: Well, the Mitscher shampoo, really, was the attack, which consisted of the daily operation, which would start with the fighter sweep on the first day, and then deck load launches throughout the day, depending upon target distance, usually about eight strikes, eight carrier deck loads off each carrier.

Q: In other words, it would have been the World War II equivalent of cyclic ops on Yankee Station.

---

* Between 30 March and 2 April, aircraft from Task Force 38 hammered Japanese targets in the Western Carolines, including Palau, Yap, and Ulithi. The Japanese lost 150 airplanes, 6 combatant ships, and more than 100,000 tons of shipping. The U.S. forces lost 20 planes.

Admiral Ramage: Yes. That was about it. The same thing as deck load, Alfa Strike. Same thing.

Q: And a deck load is ...

Admiral Ramage: About an Alfa Strike.

Q: The number of aircraft you can have ready on the flight deck.

Admiral Ramage: That's right. It's about half the air group. It's a pretty good process, because once you cock the ship and you start the first deck load and you shoot the second deck load off and land the first, and then it just keeps going until you've either run out of ammo or run out of targets. It's an extremely successful way to get to the enemy.

Q: Do you remember exactly when we started using this procedure? That was not the case at the beginning of the war.

Admiral Ramage: I think it probably started with the big sweep across the Pacific, because that's when Mitscher took over.

Q: Early 1944.

Admiral Ramage: Early 1944, yes. And, of course, that's when we had enough carrier power to really make it stick. We had enough fighters to defend ourselves, mainly because of the CVLs. They were fighter heavy. They had 24 fighters and 12 torpedo planes. So we were fighter heavy by that time. The CVLs at first were supposed to be used mainly as defensive forces and, of course, the CVL guys bitched like the dickens about being on the second team, so they later got a good crack at the strikes as well as being the combat air patrol.

Q: Weren't the CVLs kind of unsung heroes of the Pacific War? You just never hear as much about those guys as you do the Essex class.

Admiral Ramage: I thought they were. To begin with, just operating off them was always kind of a challenge. They were narrower than the CVEs, and they were a little longer.[*] Of course, the CVLs were high speed and could keep up with the fast carriers, but I always thought that they had a very challenging job, and they did a darn good job.

So much for Palau. It was another big day. I notice that on the 31st of March, we went into Yap, and Yap was nothing but the south end of the cable from Japan, the cable station. I think we only sent probably one carrier load in. It was no great target. On the first of April, we went into Woleai, which was another one of these unsinkable carriers, had a lot of Zeros on it, but by the time we got there, there were a lot of Zeros spread all over the landscape. I don't think we were opposed since we bombed installations. It wasn't much of a strike.

By this time I had taken over from Dick Poor as commanding officer. I believe it was some time in March. This was a double shuffle. Incidentally, Roscoe Newman, our CAG, was ordered to Black Jack Reeves's staff, the admiral that was our admiral in 58.3.[†] Simultaneously, Killer Kane was ordered to be the air boss on the Enterprise. That would have made Dick Poor CAG, and there was no way that was going to happen. The double shuffle was, of course, that Killer got his orders changed and became CAG, and Dick Poor went from Bombing Ten to air boss. I guess you can call that the Green Bowl at work, I don't know, but Killer certainly was better equipped in every way to be the air group commander. I don't think anybody that I know, other than Dick, minded it. He probably felt rather bad about it.

We went back to Majuro after the Woleai strike. We were briefed on a very interesting operation. Some Army people from Australia came up and briefed us on an operation for a landing in Hollandia, New Guinea. Hollandia is about in the middle of the island on the north side. It was very interesting because the Army people told--I believe it

---

[*] CVE--an escort aircraft carrier.
[†] Rear Admiral John W. Reeves, Jr., USN, Commander Task Group 58.3, a subdivision of Task Force 58.

was Admiral Mitscher--what they wanted, Admiral Mitscher said, "Tell me what time you want how many planes, and we'll put them there."

I can remember this general in the Army, he was very surprised because he said, "You mean that you will do what we tell you to do?"

And the admiral said, "Absolutely. What time do you want them?"

And the general then said, "You know, we don't get the same kind of cooperation out of the Army Air Corps."

The Hollandia operation was another case of overkill. That's the farthest south, I think, and west, that Task Force 58 ever went. We stood off the beach there and launched aircraft. The main target area was completely fogged in, which is unusual in the tropics. The three airfields in the area were on a lake called Lake Sentani, back of a mountain called Cyclops Mountain. Somehow the fog had gathered in there the evening before, so when our fighter sweep and the first strike were over the target, there was nothing in the air.

Gradually the Japs would try to come on up through the overcast, and our fighters would knock them down one at a time. Then the fog lifted all of a sudden, and they got jumped on by about 200 airplanes. It was a massacre. That was the end of all air opposition in Hollandia. I notice I have three strikes into Hollandia. Other than planes on the ground, there wasn't much in the way of targets. The landing took place, and it was virtually unopposed. It was a very successful operation. We gave MacArthur a fine victory.*

On the way back from Hollandia, we stopped by and gave Truk another shampoo.† It shows that on the 29th of April, we went on in. This time there were no ships. We were to destroy the shore installations, fuel tanks, the shipyard, and anything that was in there. This time the Triple A opposition was really heavy.‡ We cleaned out about everything that was worthwhile the first day. Kind of an interesting anecdote--we had begun to get

---

* General Douglas MacArthur, USA, Commander Southwest Pacific Area and Force. For detail on amphibious operations in the area, see Vice Admiral Daniel E. Barbey, USN (Ret.), MacArthur's Amphibious Navy: Seventh Amphibious Force Operations, 1943-1945 (Annapolis: U.S. Naval Institute, 1969).

† On 29-30 April 1944 Task Force 58 returned to Truk. About 120 Japanese aircraft were destroyed, along with large amounts of arms and petroleum supplies. Truk was never of significant use to the Japanese from that point.

‡ Triple A--antiaircraft artillery.

replacement aircraft flown out by jeep carriers to the carriers at that time, and a friend of mine was ferrying an F6F aboard Enterprise.* He asked me if I thought that I could get him a strike into Truk. I said, "I'm sure I can." So I went in to see Killer Kane, and I said, "This guy wants to fly with you today."

Killer said, "Okay, get him in here." He said, "He's going to be on my wing."

Well, after that flight was over, this guy came in to me. He said, "That's the last time I'll ever do that." He said, "That man is a mad man. We were down at the streets looking in the windows, shooting up everything we could possibly find." He said, "I've had my strike. I'm going back to the jeep."

Q: Didn't Killer Kane later on become one of the most rescued individuals of the war?

Admiral Ramage: No. Killer was in the water only twice at the Marianas, and I don't think he was ever downed other than that.

Q: I must be confusing him with someone else.

Admiral Ramage: Yes. At Truk, I notice I had two strikes the first day against installations. The second day, however, was a Sunday. I remember it very well because the weather was particularly bad, and I had a strike in about 11:00 o'clock. The area was overcast with clouds at about 1,000 feet. I took my strike group on in under the overcast, and there was antiaircraft firing at us down out of the hills. They were higher than we were going through the shipyard area, and, of course, we were bombing straight and level, which isn't good bombing. It turned out that we had a lot of bomb damage from our own fragments.

Q: Had you ever had occasion to practice shooting level?

---

* Jeep carriers was a nickname for the escort aircraft carriers (CVEs).

Admiral Ramage: No, we certainly didn't want to throw our ordnance in the general direction of the enemy like some of the sister service people did. As long as we were carrying these 1,000-pounders in, we wanted to do something with them. We didn't lose anybody, but we got quite a bit of damage to the aircraft from our own stuff. However, as I pulled out, and I think it was to the south, I don't know how many airplanes of ours that I saw in the water--10, 12, 15 that had the same problem and also from the Triple A fire. We had SOCs in there, inside the lagoon, picking up people. We had, of course, the rescue subs off the atoll and they were picking up people. It was really not a very good day. I don't know how many planes were lost that day, but I'd suggest maybe 20 or 30.*

In any event, when I landed I went up to see Admiral Reeves, and Captain Gardner was there. I told them as far as I could see, that we'd done about all the damage that was worthwhile. Also, I pointed out that we'd lost an awful lot of airplanes. This is when I first heard about the law of diminishing returns. Admiral Reeves turned to Captain Gardner, and he said, "I think we've run into the law of diminishing returns. I'm going to recommend to Admiral Mitscher that we cease this operation," which he did. It just wasn't worth the risk.

Q: You were mentioning about this time the confidence factor in the air groups was such that you just said, "Bring 'em on, we'll lick 'em, we don't care what it is." Is that true?

Admiral Ramage: That's absolutely correct. We knew that in the F6F we had the greatest fighter around, and by this time we had one by one knocked out these unsinkable aircraft carriers. We could concentrate on each of these targets singly, whereas they may have had an overall advantage in numbers of fighters or aircraft in the Pacific Ocean, we could put all ours at one point. And when you get about 1,500 airplanes coming at you, you usually give up something. They were pretty well beaten by that time. We felt that we could do anything by this time.

Let me see. We're through the second Truk raid. While we're on the second Truk raid, I'd like to make a comment. I can't remember the exact timing, but some time after

---

* While on lifeguard duty near Truk the submarine Tang (SS-306) rescued 22 downed aviators, including seven from the Enterprise.

this when we were at sea, we in the ready room received the information that Admiral Reeves had sent a message to Admiral Mitscher as follows. "Would I be stretching my glide too far if I recommended that we detach 58.3 [which was the Enterprise task group, of course] and give Truk the treatment one more time?"

Well, this didn't make much sense to us down there. If you've got 12 carriers, don't send three, one big one and two little. We were kind of concerned and, of course, interested to know what Admiral Mitscher's response would be. And it came back shortly: "I will not be badgered into an unwise decision." Mitscher, of course, was our friend forever.

Q: This seems to contradict his previous attitude of the law of diminishing returns.

Admiral Ramage: Yes, it does. It didn't make sense. We could have gone in there and probably done a reasonable job, but why not take the whole load in if you're going in?

So we're through the second Truk strike and back in Majuro again. That seemed to be our home that winter of '44. We're preparing now for the invasion of the Marianas. The invasion of the Marianas was scheduled for the 15th of June, 1944. My log book shows that I flew aboard on the eighth of June to get ready for the attack. The fighter sweep was supposed to go on the morning of the 12th of June, but a Betty had snooped around the day before and the task force was reported.[*] So Admiral Mitscher decided that he'd launch the fighter sweep the afternoon of the 11th of June. The only aircraft in the air other than fighters were some torpedo planes that carried extra life rafts. The submarines that we normally used as lifeguards off the target area apparently weren't in position by that time, and so consequently if somebody went in close offshore, there would not be the regular submarine on duty for lifeguard protection.

The attack on the Marianas was extremely successful. We completely annihilated everything that flew the afternoon before, and we started in on the regular softening-up process on the beaches on the 12th. My log book shows two strikes on the 12th. It shows

---

[*] The G4M (known by the Allied code name Betty) was a Mitsubishi Type 1 two-engine, land-based torpedo bomber.

two strikes on the 13th, one strike on the 14th, and the actual landing was to take place on the 15th.* This was kind of an interesting incident. Killer Kane, our CAG, was to be the air coordinator of all of the aviation over the beach for the actual target time. I was to be the <u>Enterprise</u> strike leader.

We took off on a pre-dawn launch and Killer was going on ahead with his wingman, King Kirchwey.† All of a sudden, Killer got on the air saying, "Stop it! You're shooting at me." What had happened was that our own amphibious force, which was in position off the beach, was shooting at him. He finally said, "Well, damn it, you've shot me down now." So Killer was a casualty of our own antiaircraft fire. Thank God he wasn't hurt. So I then moved up to be air coordinator for all aviation over the target. Lou Bangs moved up as the strike leader of the <u>Enterprise</u> strike group.‡

Q: Was he your exec?

Admiral Ramage: No. My exec was Ira Hardman, but Lou was a dependable guy.§ If there was anything to do, I always asked Lou to do it. This was a very interesting operation to watch from right over the beach. I watched the tremendous power of this fleet putting those people ashore. The big carriers were pre-targeted into areas, and the CVE planes would go in to strafe just ahead of the beach where their fighters were strafing just ahead of the troops as they landed. We had the carrier aircraft orbiting down to the south, and my job was to call them up as targets developed. We simply had so darn much air power over the area that it was hard to find targets for them, and I was looking around down into the area, and unfortunately I got too low. I had inherited Killer's wingman, and this wingman was shot off my wing by AAA. This really was kind of dumb on my part, because I didn't need a wingman, and he simply shouldn't have been with me. I felt very badly about that.

---

* On 15 June 1944 the Second and Fourth Marine divisions landed on Saipan against a Japanese force of 17,600 men. The Marines secured a five-mile-wide beachhead on the first day. The Japanese 136th Infantry Regiment counterattacked the Sixth Marines. In eight hours of combat, 700 Japanese were killed.
† Lieutenant (junior grade) Karl W. Kirchwey, USNR.
‡ Lieutenant Louis L. Bangs, USNR.
§ Lieutenant Commander Ira S. Hardman, Jr., USN.

So the invasion took place, and it was very successful at the start. They had some problems later on. About that time we began to get some rumblings of the possibility of the Japanese fleet being in the area. We continued to strike into Saipan, and some of the other carriers were going into Guam. I led a strike in because there was a ship reported still afloat in Garapan; Tanapag, I think, is the name of the harbor. I took a strike group in on it. We went in and got hits on it, and as we came out I circled to rendezvous the group.

I saw that one of my planes had become a flamer; it was Leonard and his gunner Wynne.* He went straight in right off the ship in the harbor. We were out far enough so we were out of the way of the antiaircraft fire, and I detached myself and again turned the strike over to Bangs. I went back to see if I could find what had really happened to Leonard, the name of the pilot. And there was just no question that he had gone straight in, and there was no way of possibly saving him, no chute, no nothing. So I made a tour of the harbor and let them take a few shots at me.

I came on back and landed aboard late, which never makes you very popular, and went up and reported to Admiral Reeves. I told him that we had lost a plane and also that I had gone back and there was absolutely nothing that we could do about it. He said, "Well, that's fine. Now, what I want you to do is to get yourself a couple of planes and go on back into the harbor and make absolutely sure that there is no way that the pilot can be alive." And it's that type of thinking that we knew that our admirals did. I mean, we knew darn well that if there was any time, that there was any chance whatsoever of being rescued, that they'd come after us. Whereas I thought it was rather a useless mission, it still was a very fine thing to know that those admirals knew that you were out there too.

Q: Can we talk a little bit here about resupply? When you had a combat loss of an airplane and the crew, did you just do without them?

Admiral Ramage: We had no problems. We lost only three crews in combat. I mentioned Dean at Truk; Stubby Pearson, who was an all-American football player, at Palau; and Irish

---

* Lieutenant J. G. Leonard and Aviation Radioman Second Class R. P. Wynne.

Leonard here in Saipan.* We had enough spare air crews to make up for the losses, and, of course, we had the five spare SBDs in the overhead, so we didn't really need any replacement planes. But they did have the replacement situation where they would bring aircraft out in the CVEs with the ferry pilots to ferry them aboard. So resupply by this time had gotten quite efficient.

Q: How about replacement of pilots, though?

Admiral Ramage: The CVEs had replacement pilots too.

Q: They came too.

Admiral Ramage: They would send somebody over. That's what my job was when I got back to the States later on in the year of '44, setting up replacement Air Group 98.

Q: How close would the escort carrier force normally keep to Task Force 58?

Admiral Ramage: We rarely saw them. They were so slow, you know, their top speed was 18 to 20 knots, and that was all out. They generally stayed pretty close to the amphibious forces. They furnished air cover for the amphibious forces if they needed it. If they really needed help, they'd send Task Force 58 close by and we could take care of them.

Q: Things got a little more exciting for the CVEs off Samar a little later.

Admiral Ramage: Yes, a little bit later. But we're still striking into Saipan and getting ready for the big Turkey Shoot on the 19th and the assault on the Japanese fleet on the

---

* Lieutenant (junior grade) Charles B. "Stubby" Pearson, USNR, had graduated from Dartmouth, where he was captain of the football and basketball teams. His gunner was Aviation Radioman Second Class T. W. Watterson.

20th.* We were down in the ready rooms wondering when we were going to get a crack at those Japs, and we knew at the time that Mitscher wanted to detach Task Force 58 and go after the fleet, because it was out there somewhere. We all felt that we ought to go get them.

Q: Do you recall at what point the squadrons or the air groups began to feel that fleet engagement was likely?

Admiral Ramage: I'd say about the 16th. We were kept close to Saipan, and we continued to support the troops. We had a couple of strikes into Orote Peninsula, which was an airfield on Guam. I'd say around the 16th we heard that the Japanese fleet was coming. Of course, we were getting ready for it.

Q: I imagine at that point probably not 10% of the pilots in Task Force 58 had ever seen a Japanese carrier.

Admiral Ramage: That's right. Very, very few, because the last time was in '42.

Q: Santa Cruz in October.†

Admiral Ramage: Yes. So we're on to the 19th of June. I'd say about 10:00 o'clock in the morning we launched all fighters, and we had also a strike group all loaded up ready to go in case somebody found the Japanese fleet. They picked up the Japanese aircraft about 100 miles to the west of us, and for some reason or other, the Japanese decided that they would circle and get all the aircraft into one group rather than come on in, which gave us

---

* The "Great Marianas Turkey Shoot" took place on 19 June 1944 while U.S. carriers were supporting the invasion of Saipan. That day U.S. planes shot down more than 300 Japanese aircraft.
† On 26 October 1942, U.S. and Japanese carrier aircraft were involved in the Battle of the Santa Cruz Islands, near the Solomons. The Enterprise and Hornet (CV-8) faced the Japanese carriers Shokaku, Zuikaku, Zuiho, and Junyo. The Hornet was sunk as a result of the encounter and the Shokaku badly damaged.

additional time to get everything into the air. So we had all the fighters in the air that we wanted to have in the air.

Then we had the strike groups, the first deck load, launched from each carrier in the air also. We were back of the force, whereas the fighters were heading on out in front. There were something like 350 to 400 airplanes attacking Task Force 58. I could see an occasional flamer going on down, but we were about 15 to 20 miles back towards Guam. Of course, we didn't have any fighters with us; they were all up topside. I put my dive bombers into the fluid four formation rather than in the tight division that we used, because I thought possibly some of the Japs would break through, and we might be able to get a shot at them. We would jettison our bombs and go after them.

After about two or three hours, we received a message to go on in and drop our bombs on the fields in Guam. Actually it was Orote Peninsula. We were to get down in there and see if we couldn't keep the field at least temporarily knocked out in case some of the Japs got through and tried to land on Guam. We got over there in time to see several shoot-downs. It was kind of interesting because our F6Fs were right down at treetop level chasing these poor guys up and down the landscape. I don't know if any Jap ever landed. I think there were some enemy pilots that either force landed or actually were so scared, they just landed right in the water. It was a real massacre. They ended up that day with their whole striking force gone, plus a pretty good percentage of their fighters that they sent along as escorts. All that they had aboard the ships on out the west of us was maybe 60 or 70 Zeros.

Q: You were never attacked?

Admiral Ramage: The Enterprise was never attacked. I don't think they came close to anything.

Q: But while you were flying?

Admiral Ramage: No.

Q: Would this be a good place to talk about the change in tactics? Early in the war we were using a stepped-up echelon formation, that gunners couldn't fire because our own aircraft were in their field of fire.

Admiral Ramage: Well, we can talk about it. That change took place very early in the war. When we went through flight training, the wingmen were stepped up and, of course, it did blank out the view of the fire on both sides from the rear gunners. And it was after the Kwajalein operations in early '42 that they then began to fly a step-down formation.

So we're ready for the big battle on the 20th, which became known as the Battle of the Philippine Sea.* On the morning of the 20th, we finally began to get some contacts, and in the afternoon of the 20th, Stu Nelson, who was in VT-10, finally did locate the Japanese fleet.† We'd been in the ready room all day, and we had the flight plan. We had completely gone through all of the best ways to save gas, to see how much we could get out of the SBDs. There really was nothing that we had overlooked in being prepared for this. We'd been at sea for five months by the time and had quite a bit of combat, and we certainly felt that we were ready to go. The one thing that we did know was that as it got later, probably we'd come back at night, which didn't bother us, because we were all night qualed and there wouldn't be any problem.

Finally about 1600, 4:00 o'clock, we finally got the word to launch. I had with me the 12 SBDs and I think only five torpedo planes this time, and 12 fighters, I think--maybe 16. We had been briefed that we knew that it was a long distance out. The fighters and torpedoes would take off first as they always did, get themselves grouped, and we bombers would take off and immediately make a 180-degree turn because the prevailing wind was from the east and the targets were almost due west. So I would make a turn immediately and slow down, and the other bombers would simply fly up and join me on the wing. In other words, we didn't have the luxury of doing a normal rendezvous. We called it the running rendezvous. Everything worked out fine.

---

* During the battle, which included the Marianas Turkey shoot, U.S. aircraft sank the Japanese carrier Hiyo. Prior to the battle, American submarines had sunk the carriers Shokaku and Taiho.
† Lieutenant Robert S. Nelson, USNR.

We finally got all the bombers together. I was flying along about 5,000 feet and climbing, when all of a sudden I got a cloud of smoke in my cockpit. I thought, "Oh, God, I'm on fire. Here's my big time and here this damn thing is happening to me."

Cawley, my rear-seat gunner, said, "I think it might be just spilled oil." He said that one time previously that the plane captain had spilled oil around the engine, and when it got heated up, the oil burned off the cylinders, causing smoke. And that's apparently what happened, because within about three or four minutes, the smoke cleared out. I wasn't going to turn around anyway, but it was just one of those nuisances that came up.

What I'm going to do here is read from a pamphlet that was put out by one of the pilots, Lieutenant (junior grade) Don Lewis, to tell about the strike.* I'm doing this because of my mother's admonition that self-praise stinks, and I'd rather have somebody else say anything good about me than try to say it myself. So this is from Don. We called it Hound Dog Lewis's account of the strike on the Japanese fleet on the 20th of June of 1944.

He says, "That afternoon at 1615, with beating heart, I manned my plane and wondered for the hundredth time of the merits of this poor, old, tired-out SBD, Dauntless dive bomber, if it still had anyplace in the war where planes were slow if they cruised at less than 250 knots. I'm ashamed now of my doubts. I was to have ample proof before that day was out that tenacity and the ability to keep going can sometimes make up for speed and show. Of course, the behavior of the plane depends a lot on its pilot, its crew, and its squadron. It can be handled rough, and it will probably balk. We handled ours gently that day.

"My crew consisted of one John Mankin, once a good citizen of Wyoming. He was both radioman and gunner. He represented, I thought, the best there was. I had confidence in the other squadron members. I felt that they, too, were the best, and I know to this day that my story would be a lot different if our skipper had merely gone by the rules.

"Lieutenant Commander Ramage, our skipper, was different. Sometimes in this business the rules are inadequate and things happen so quickly there isn't time to consult an admiral's committee about some new ones. They have to be made right on the spot. The skipper made quite a few that night. The Jap losses which we had helped to inflict and the

---

* Lieutenant (junior grade) Donald Lewis, USNR.

fact that 12 pilots and 12 air crewmen went up that night and all returned to their ships speaks more for his leadership than anything I might write here.

"My regular place in the division was flying number two position in Lieutenant Bangs' division. He had at one time been an instructor in Pensacola for Wayne Morris.* By 1630, all of our planes were in the air. We were rendezvoused with Commander Bill Martin's Grumman Avenger torpedo planes, this flight being led by the exec of the squadron, Lieutenant Commander Van Eason, our Hellcat fighter escort was under Commander William Killer Kane, destined to become an ace with five planes to his credit as a result of this day's work.† At last on a heading of 290 degrees and throttle back to the maximum to ensure the most economic fuel consumption, we started out after the Jap fleet."

I can interject one thing, that we thought at that time that the Jap fleet was out 260 miles, and after we were launched, we got a correction in the position report. Nelson's position was one degree off in the wrong direction. In other words, it was about 60 miles farther out. The radius of action of the SBD was about 250 miles, and it was as plotted about 260 miles, which wasn't a bad chance to take. But when you add on the extra 50 or 60 miles, which takes you well out over 300 miles, it becomes pretty much a one-way mission as far as SBDs are concerned. I now go back to Al Lewis's story.

"Our navigation boards told us it would be 250 miles at least. I burned out my left auxiliary tank, 52 gallons gone already, I thought, and we were scarcely at the halfway mark. We were then 6,000 feet and it was 1800. I could see more air groups from some of our other carriers to one side and, of course, headed at the same target. I felt good to see them there. At least we were not doing this alone. I heard a contact report from a TBF scout plane piloted by Lieutenant Robert S. Nelson, apparently over the Jap fleet. He gave their strength as consisting of three separate task forces, one consisting of six fleet oilers plus a number of destroyers, another containing battleships and more destroyers, and third, containing the carriers, of which the search plane said there were seven, three large and four small.

---

* Ensign Bert D. Morris, Jr., USNR, had received flight training early in the war. He was a Hollywood movie actor who got a legitimate combat role in the war.
† Lieutenant Commander Van V. Eason, Jr., USNR.

"At 11,000 feet I put my engine in high blower, adjusted my oxygen mask, and called my gunner to see how he was doing. John said he was cold. For days while we had been about the ship, I had been too hot, but now because of the altitude, the pure oxygen I was breathing, and the nervous drain on my energies, I was beginning to feel cold too. Not even the heat from my engines seemed enough to kill the chill. We were now at 14,000 feet. I had just run out of gas on my right wing auxiliary tank. It was 1845. I was thinking to myself that if we would only go into our dives right now, my chances of a hit would be the best, as with my gas tanks evened off, the plane would trim up just about perfectly. I wanted to have as many things in my favor as possible, as I knew that once over the target, there would be quite a few things decidedly not in my favor.

"At any rate, I decided to keep my two main tanks of fuel, approximately 250 gallons, exactly equal up to the moment I actually did nose into my dive. I imagine some of the other pilots of my flight were worrying about the same thing, as it meant changing tanks every five minutes. It was now almost 7:00 o'clock, and we had already covered 225 miles. I thought of my gunner again and knew he was almost frozen to death. The back seat of an SBD is a pretty exposed place, and he must make it even more so in order to keep his guns ready for quick use. I think the real credit of naval aviation goes to those rear seat gunners. Their job is the hardest and requires more downright nerve and guts than anything I can think of.

"We were at 15,000 feet when I heard our fighters tally-ho the Jap force. The first report gave their positions as 15 miles to our port. This force consisted of six fleet tankers and a half a dozen destroyers. The TBF had sighted them now and even as their report was given, I could see several thin strips of white far below, which were the wakes of those ships. They were moving fast with everything they had. Even at this altitude I could tell that.

"I heard my skipper on the air. '41 Sniper to 85 Sniper. We will not attack. We will not attack. Where are the Charlie Victors?'* I think he must have been exasperated that anyone would even suggest that we would come 300 miles to dump a load of bombs on a few oilers when there were carriers around. I started to get squared away. I took notice

---
* Charlie Victors is the phonetic expression of the letters CV, the designation for a large aircraft carrier.

where the wind was from in relation to the direction we were now heading. I changed my gas tanks again, checked my bomb release, flipped on my gun switches and bomb sights, and did as many things as could be done this much in advance of the dive.

"Then I heard another contact report. More ships had been seen still further north about 20 miles. There were many cruisers and destroyers, some battleships, and best of all, and my heart turned over when I heard this, seven carriers, four small CVs and three large CVs. I started to get ready in earnest now. I was scared. I couldn't really believe this was happening to me. I went over my check-off list again, closed my formation. In a few minutes I could see them. Yes, even as I thought this, I could make out several black forms ahead, way below and partly concealed by some clouds. They were already starting to maneuver. Some were going in circles, others were zigzagging. Their formation was well spread out, just the opposite battle procedure from our task force. '41 Sniper to all bombers,' I heard my skipper call again. 'The first division will dive on the largest CV. The other sections will dive on the small jobs unless the big one is still not hit. Out.'

"We were beginning to spread a little now. From 16,500 feet we started what was to be a high-speed break-up into our dives. Three carriers I could see plainly trying to make cover under a cloud. Another large one, I'm sure of the Shokaku class, was on my left without a cloud near it. We had 200 knots now. I checked everything. Once more my gas seemed to be evened up, the plane well trimmed. When I came back to low blower because of the natural decrease in power at this altitude, I had lost a little distance.

"Tip Mester, the other wingman in my section, filled in quickly, keeping the interval between planes just about right.* We had agreed before the flight to make a close-in diving interval as that keeps the men on the gun crews on the deck below taking cover most of the time. So quickly does one bomb follow another. This then is the way I would try to keep it. I glanced quickly at my altimeter, I saw 13,000 feet. For the first time now I took notice. AA fire. I couldn't help thinking how unlike our ships those Japs were, for I knew we would never let two divisions of dive bombers get as near as we were now without sending out every available fighter and throwing up a virtual barrage as well.

---

* Lieutenant (junior grade) Cecil R. Mester, USNR.

"I saw a pair of our fighters on the other side of my cockpit. One of them was Lieutenant (j.g.) John Shinneman.* He had been just off my starboard, watching the other bombers steepen up into their dives. Now he would go down with me. I was the last plane to dive, and I knew there was little chance of anything besides an F6F Hellcat getting on my tail. There were great black puffs all over now and smaller white ones, looking for all the world like small balls of cotton. Things started to happen fast. It was a blur from here on in. Now it was 10,000 feet. I was starting to overspeed and then overshoot the carrier I had picked out. That meant the last thing on my check-off list, dive flaps. I pushed the actuator, glancing out to see if they had operated successfully, saw a plane smoking horribly away on my port, wondered if it was one of ours.

"I heard Japs talking on our radio frequency. They were counting, then more talk. They were excited. Who wasn't? I heard someone tally-ho again, 'Enemy aircraft, 4:00 o'clock, Angel 5.' It seemed to take an eternity. Never had a dive taken so long. The wind was from my right. I was overshooting. I corkscrewed toward the left and then back again. It helped. The carrier below looked big, tremendous, almost make-believe. I had a moment of real joy. I had often dreamed of something like this. Then I was horrified with myself. What a spot to be in. I must be crazy. I was straight up and down now in my dive. I was right in the middle of all those white puffs, and for the first time I could see where they were coming from.

"From each side of the carrier below seemed to be a mass of flashing red dots. It had been turning slowly to port. It stopped, and I noticed a larger red flash, which was a bomb hit on the side and well forward, but unmistakably a hit. I figured it must have been scored by 'Banger,' as we called Lou Bangs. The carrier below had stopped moving. Who could ask for more? I thanked whoever it was who laid on the last one, as it had stopped the carrier right up and down in my sights. I kept trying to move my point of aim to the right to allow more for the wind. First I could move so that it rested squarely on that side of the carrier. That wouldn't be enough, I knew, but it was too late to do any of the violent maneuvers necessary to move it more. I could allow for the error in one other way, however, and that would be by going lower.

---

* Lieutenant (junior grade) John R. Shinneman, USNR.

"The last time I glanced at my altimeter it registered 3,000 feet. Stopped below, the big carrier looked even larger. It was completely enveloped in a sort of smoke haze. It was hard to stay in my dive this long. Under some conditions a person can live a lifetime in a few seconds. It was time. I couldn't go any lower. Now! I pulled my bomb release, felt the bomb go away, started my pull-out. My eyes watered, my ears hurt, and my altimeter indicated 1,500 feet. Too low, I thought, but what had I done? I turned back to see that there was more smoke and flame on the same side as the first hit, the first hit I had seen, only this was way aft. That could be mine, but even with my low pull-out, the wind had apparently carried it way to the starboard side. I experienced a momentary disappointment. I had expected much more of a conflagration to follow a direct hit on something as vulnerable as a carrier.

"Then I remembered that our section carried semi-armor piercing bombs which would, of course, pierce the flight deck and burst below. My ears still hurt. I had already closed my dive flaps and had 280 knots, but I couldn't seem to go fast enough. There were ships all about. They were all shooting far above the carrier, which was dark with smoke and its own AA. I saw a plane burst into flames and then slowly float downward. I saw a smaller carrier off my other wing with its flight deck a mass of flames. A torpedo plane flying at only a few thousand feet left a vicious path of black smoke and dark flames before it plunged into the sea. I wondered if I would get out of this yet. I had felt good and a little surprised after pulling out of my dive still unhit. Now I had to do it all over.

"For a moment I was almost panic-stricken. Everywhere I looked there seemed to be ships with every gun blazing. The sky was just a mass of black and white puffs, and in the midst of it planes already hit, burning and crashing into the water below. It's strange how a person can be fascinated even in the midst of horror. I'd see orange bursts from some ships, a moment later a billowy puff would blossom out too nearby, a second later another, still nearer. They were getting the word. I was employing the wildest evasive tactics possible. I would be down low on the water and then pull up quick and pick up hard rudder one way, hold it for a moment, then kick rudder the opposite way. I had decided it didn't make much difference which way I went. Our prearranged retirement course was 090 degrees. I would take that. Any direction I went, I would still have to run the gauntlet.

"I saw now the Japs' advantage in spreading out their formation of ships. I would no sooner exceed the range of one ship than I would fall into the sights of another further along. I seemed to spend an eternity in the midst of their AA. I began to think that real low on the water was the best place. I flew there for a few seconds, a temporary lull. Suddenly a tremendous geyser suddenly ahead, another to starboard. I pulled up quickly and realized that a cruiser was using its large deck guns to drop shells in front of us, hoping we would run into some of the columns of water, even if the shell itself did miss.

"There were other planes all about now. I saw a Helldiver flying low over the water, as I had been a moment before, lose a wing and disappear almost instantly without either smoke or fire, scarcely a ripple on the sea below. I found myself with a cruiser on one side and a destroyer on the other. Resulting crossfire was effective. I believe they were closer to getting me than any of the other little yellow men I had been a target for. Some of the shells burst so near that the concussion would lift my plane a few feet higher in the air. A few times I was surrounded by black bursts and I could hear the hollow metal sound that concussion made when it came against the metal fuselage.

"The Japanese should have had one more SBD Dauntless to their credit that day, and if it had been our gun batteries, they would have. I saw a bomber, one of our own, it was Lieutenant (junior grade) William Schaefer and his rear seat man, Santulli.[*] I joined up on him. My own gunner called, 'Jap fighters, high starboard.' I looked to my right and saw half a dozen fighters fighting off in that position, even as I watched. I saw one literally blown to pieces in the air and another catch fire and slowly descend, disappearing in a cloud. Schaefer and I joined on some other planes. We were about out of the AA now, except for an occasional burst. I began to feel better. These were planes from the Lexington. I wondered where my own bombers were. There was no other interference from the Jap fighters. They had apparently been well taken care of. My attention was taken by a tremendous explosion fire off on the horizon. I looked, seeing the remains of one of the fleet tankers, which we had seen going in. Some other group had decided to concentrate on that task force after all.

---

[*] Lieutenant (junior grade) William W. Schaefer, USNR; George W. Santulli.

"I stayed with this group of planes for 15 minutes. It was rapidly getting dark. I took stock of my gas and immediately decided that I would have to leave this formation. Much as I liked their company, I knew I would never make it back at the engine settings they were using. I had 32 inches of manifold pressure and 2,100 RPM, and I could barely stay up with them. I couldn't help wondering if they would make it back either.

"John called and pointed out another formation of bombers way to starboard. I broke away and joined them. It was our own air group. I counted them like a mother hen counting her chickens. There were eight and I would make nine. We had come with 12. Well, I would not try to think about that now. Perhaps they had joined with one of the other groups. I joined up with number three position on Lieutenant (junior grade) Hubert Grubiss.* Grube gave me a smile and started wiping his brow as though he were hot. He probably had been shortly before in more ways than one.

"I felt better. Our skipper was using his head. We were conserving what little fuel we had left, for it was quite dark already, and we were still a long way from our ships. I could only imagine what would go on when we did get back and 300 or 400 planes started trying to make night landings, some of them for the first time, aboard a dozen carriers. We ran into a few rain squalls. It was now pitch dark. I turned on my lights, dim, ate an apple which I brought along, and then readjusted my oxygen mask, as I was feeling tired and my eyes were seeing things that weren't there. The pure oxygen, even at 2,000 feet, would both relieve fatigue and help my vision at the same time.

"Apparently there were many of our planes that day who hadn't used their fuel economically. The results began to show. It was 8:30. I heard one pilot tell his rear seat man to get ready for a water landing. I heard a fighter pilot call his wingman and say he had been hit in one tank and was going down. The wingman called back and said that he would land with him. I saw a group of lights to my right getting lower and lower, then there weren't any more. Apparently a whole section of planes had been low on gas and decided to land together, thus giving a greater chance of being picked up. I heard some pilot, apparently lost, calling desperately for a carrier. His base was too far away to pick him up. Finally he called again, he was out of gas, bailing out. Then silence.

---

* Lieutenant (junior grade) Hubert F. Grubiss, USNR.

"Another hour had passed, leaving the time after 9:00 o'clock. I was worrying about my own gas. I had three of my four tanks completely dry and a good deal gone from the last one. With good luck, I might make it back. My eyes were tired and my back was stiff, my head ached, and I was hungry. In short, I had had enough for that day. Everyone felt the same way, I could tell by the loose formation, but we hung on.

"Every few minutes now I could hear a plane falling, calling its wingman, its base, announcing it was going in, then silence for a little more. At 9:20 I thought I could see star shells off the starboard, but I wasn't sure. There was also lighting around. A moment later there was no mistaking it. They were star shells, and the searchlights as well. We were still a long ways off, but it made me feel good. I realized that a tremendous concession was being made in our favor. I heard pilots express the opinion that the admirals looked upon the fliers as quite expendable, and I suppose they must be to a certain extent, but I shall never again feel that they wouldn't do everything conceivable in their power to bring a pilot back.

"I know there were subs about the fleet that night, and enemy planes had followed us back, for one actually got in the landing circle for one of our carriers, and yet when we approached the outer screen of our fleet, it seemed that almost every ship had a light of some kind on. In the utter darkness, the intensity of some of the lights was blinding. The largeness of the carriers seemed to stretch off into infinity. It was a demonstration I shall never forget.

"Every group seemed to get over the fleet at the same time and, of course, everyone being low on gas wanted to land immediately. We were told to land on any base available, that is, which had a clear deck. The skipper found a carrier landing planes, the first two sections broke up. I could see them break away and head down for the landing circle. It was a little before 10:00 o'clock now. I figured I had about 15 minutes more fuel, then I would have to make preparations for a water landing too.

"My best bet, I thought, would be to circle, for I was at 1,500 feet, and try to spot a carrier not only with a clear deck but with no one in the landing circle, for I thought if I once put my wheels and flaps down and started operating at full power, the little gas I had left would be gone in no time. Some carrier was on the air, their deck was clear, they said, furthermore they would signal their position by two flashes from their largest searchlight. That was what I was waiting for. I watched for the signal. Finally I saw it off to the left. I felt good again. Perhaps I would make it after all.

"When I drew near, I saw one plane in the traffic circle. I started to get squared away myself, mixture rich, wheels down, shoulder straps tight, and so forth. I made my turn a little way ahead. I could just barely see the lights of the ship. The plane I had noticed before was in his cross leg. I saw his lights steadily approaching for his final turn into the groove, then there was just blackness where he had been. He had gone through all the incredible experiences of this day and night, and then scarcely a minute before he would have been safely landed aboard, his gas had run out.

"I checked my own gas again. Even my last tank registered empty. It was ten minutes after 10:00. I felt I had enough gas left for three passes at this ship. I was in the groove now and could plainly make out the long line of lights down the flight deck. There was a signal officer to the left. He looked grotesque, like a mechanical man with arms of light where the electric wands were that are used for night carrier landings. I was near enough now to pick up his signals. My heart stopped. He was waving me off. I was mad, frustrated. I would land anyway. Still I couldn't. He was under me now. As I gunned it, I heard the engine gobble up still more of my last precious gallon. I called him everything I could think of. Well, perhaps he was right. Maybe I had been too low.

"I would try again, and this time concentrate what energy I had on making my approach perfect. Just the right speed, just the right altitude. Once again I was in the groove. Another wave-off. I was really mad now, but as I went by, I saw the reason. On the deck just after the island structure was a plane on its back and thoroughly cracked up. They couldn't land me without wires or barriers. I pulled up my wheels and flaps, throttled back as much as possible, and gained a little altitude. Perhaps a destroyer would pick me up in the water. After such a day, I was too tired to have much concern now over a mere water landing in the middle of the Pacific enemy waters. I think this must have been the attitude of most of those pilots that night who actually did make water landings, as a surprisingly high number of them were made successfully.

"I decided if I could find a carrier shortly, I would have enough fuel for one pass. Surely, I thought, there must be one carrier with a clear deck around. I saw more lights further ahead. I gained on them slowly. Yes, it was another carrier, and what luck, I was approaching from its stern. For a moment my impulse was to let my wheels and flaps down immediately and come right in for a landing, a very unorthodox procedure. I decided against it, mostly because I had lost sight of the landing signal officer. I went by the port side and looked down. He was giving me the wheels-down land signal. The deck looked clear. It was a big carrier of the Essex class.

"I got squared away once again. This would be my last chance, as I must be at the very end of my gas. Again I was on my cross leg and got in the groove, picking up the signal man. He was giving me a high and fast. I dropped my nose, took off a little throttle, pick up with a little back stick pressure, and now I was right over the ramp, and there it was at last, the cut. The deck looked big after so many landings on our smaller E. I dropped my nose and guided her down, felt the hook catch a wire. It was all over. I was taxiing on the deck following the plane director's lights, cutting my engine. I heard myself talking as in a dream. Everyone seemed friendly. What carrier was this? The Yorktown, I was told. Another plane was coming in to land. There had been accidents that night. I was told to clear the deck quickly. I felt tired but elated.

"From the side, I watched this next plane land. It was an SBD also, and a good landing followed. I saw the number on the side, it was the skipper's plane. We were glad to see each other. It had only been seven hours since I had seen him last, but it seemed like a year. He had done a swell job that day. I told him so, but he scarcely heard me, he was so glad just to be back. I was grateful to my old SBD, still the most dependable plane in the fleet, grateful to my skipper for a fine job in leading us out and back, to every admiral and captain who willingly took 1,000 risks to help us back, and last but surely not the least, to my God who knows when a fellow needs help."

Q: I'm sorry. I feel about the same way and I wasn't there. Getting back to the strike itself, when you reached the target, it must have been getting pretty dark. It was after 7:00.

Admiral Ramage: It was dusk, but there was plenty of visibility, and the Japanese ships were making high speed, so the wakes were very visible.

Q: Can you describe your personal dive there?

Admiral Ramage: Well, mine is about the same as his. It was a very nice, clean dive. I dove on the carrier easily. I too went much lower than we normally did, for the same reason that he did, that we wanted to make sure we got a hit. I put my pipper on the port bow, which was the way I figured the ship's motion and the wind at the time.

Q: At this stage of life, do you know exactly which carrier this was?

Admiral Ramage: I don't know. Do you?

Q: Not for certain. There's contradictory evidence on both sides.

Admiral Ramage: Yes. I'm not sure exactly what it was. Barrett Tillman, you've researched this strike. What do you think?

Q: We know that Air Group Ten attacked the center of the three Japanese carrier task groups, and by juggling American and Japanese accounts, I'm convinced that Bombing Ten probably went down on Ryuho, which was identified at the time as a Zuiho-class ship, but it's definitely known for sure that Ryuho took bomb damage, so there's not much doubt that Bombing Ten did score hits on her.

Admiral Ramage: That's the first division, though. Now, the second division, which Bangs led, went on another one, and they definitely hit that one. That was much more sure than ours. As Hound Dog Lewis states in this case, he actually saw Bangs's bomb go off. This was, I think, a converted ship, Junyo.

Q: Apparently Bangs, Mester, and Lewis dived on Junyo, while Grubiss, Bolton, and one of the VB-16 fellows, Jack Wright, went down on Hiyo. Hiyo was the one ship sunk in this strike, primarily by CVL torpedo planes, but she also sustained bomb damage. So it's possible to say that Bombing Ten helped sink one and damaged two others.

Were you attacked by Zeros at any time during this strike?

Admiral Ramage: As we approached the fleet, I would say about 20 miles out, when we were still in a fairly tight formation, we got a tally-ho on a number of Zeros. My gunner, Cawley, again said Zeros up at 4:00 o'clock. But because of our fighter escort, and VF-10 was darn good at this, they would not in any way ever leave a strike group in order to shoot down an enemy airplane. They hung right in there, and every time the Zeros would start an attack towards us, Killer and his guys would nose into them, and then the Zeros would back off. In other words, they weren't very determined on getting us before the time of break-up.

As I dived, the Zeros began to come after me, and I think two of them went down with me, one in particular, and, with my dive brakes out, he zipped past me so fast that I could hardly see him. Cawley called out to me that he was coming, and was trying to shoot at him. He was afraid the Jap would hit us, and it could be very possible that he might have been a kind of kamikaze plane, as far as trying to knock me out of the sky, because he missed me by a matter of just a few feet. It didn't disconcert me too much. By this time I had that pipper right where I wanted it. There wasn't anything that was going to stop me. The Triple A was coming up, and it was shallow, that is, going under my belly. A dive bomber coming down is nearly vertical, and it's awfully hard to shoot straight up. Most of their stuff was going beneath me.

Q: During the retirement, did you stay low?

Admiral Ramage: Again, my trusty gunner would call it out, and I would respond to what he said, and I would either go up or go down, depending upon what he could see was going on. When we finally joined up, there were still some Zeros in the air, and they were, of all things, doing slow rolls and various things around the area. I don't know exactly why. This was not unusual for Zeros, but they were doing it even at this time when the whole world was falling apart on them. Kane and group by this time were right with us, and they knocked down two or more of them. We had absolutely no problem after that.

I might talk a little bit about the return to the ship, because I was very unhappy with the air discipline of the other air groups that were there. We went back very slowly, of course, because we planned it that way. But a lot of them became frustrated, and I think they went into the water unnecessarily. Some of the people actually dived into carrier decks when they got wave-offs. They showed poor air discipline by doing that--knocking carriers out. I had a lot more with me than just the SBDs and the TBFs of the Air Group Ten. I had quite a few stragglers, and I was the last one in there against the Jap fleet. They all joined up, so I don't know how many planes I had. We came back directly over the Enterprise because I wanted to get back to my own ship, and my first break-up, when I came back and went around the first time, I could see that somebody had gone into the Enterprise, and they had a wreck on the deck.

Q: This is the one that Lewis refers to?

Admiral Ramage: I think that probably is. We'd broken up by that time. It was kind of every man to himself because the air discipline had just gone apart. I was lined up for a straight-in approach on a CVL, and was coming on in, and just ahead of it I saw one of these large, fat carriers, and so I just kind of pulled my nose up and dropped it again and made a pass at the Yorktown.

Getting aboard the Yorktown was great, but it was a real unhappy situation because they had an SB2C squadron aboard, and I think every one of them went in the drink. In my opinion, there's no excuse for this type of thing, in that the SB2C had far greater range than we did in the SBDs. I just think that they'd hadn't planned their flight correctly.

Q: A lot has been made about turning the lights on. Would you like to talk about that a little bit?

Admiral Ramage: Yes, I would, because there's a negative to it, too, that Lewis refers to. The turning on the lights, in spite of what a certain admiral has to say, was planned in the afternoon, and Admiral Arleigh Burke, who was Mitscher's chief of staff, has described the fact that they knew that they would possibly have this affair going on in this manner, and he had separated the task groups by a greater distance.* They had prepared ahead of time to turn on the lights, so it wasn't any spur of the moment operation. It was a well-considered plan.

The drawback of the thing was that if the signal had been for only the carriers to turn on their lights, it would have been absolutely perfect, but because in that mass of ships down there, it was very, very difficult to tell the carriers apart from other surface ships.

Q: There were literally hundreds of lights.

Admiral Ramage: Yes, there were lights all over the place. It could very well be that many people made passes at ships that weren't carriers.

Q: That's for sure. A Lexington pilot told me that, I think, his first pass was on a destroyer.

Admiral Ramage: Yes.

Q: Of course, hindsight is always easier.

Admiral Ramage: That's right. And we got aboard. I guess it is in your book that says we lost 104 planes.

Q: Yes, and, I think, 40 out of the 45 SB2Cs, so that's a 90% loss rate.

---

* Captain Arleigh A. Burke, USN, became chief of staff in March 1944; Mitscher was promoted to vice admiral that same month. Later, as a four-star admiral, Burke served as Chief of Naval Operations, 1955-61. See Burke's article, "Admiral Marc Mitscher: A Naval Aviator," U.S. Naval Institute Proceedings, April 1975, pages 53-63.

Admiral Ramage: In our squadron, we had the 12 planes, we actually only put one in the water, and I think that's the plane that Hound Dog describes as going in when he was in the groove. That was Lou Bangs, and the only reason he went in the water was because his ass was too big--at least, that is what I told him later.

Q: He was overgross?

Admiral Ramage: He was overgross. We brought them all back, and we got Lou back. Incidentally, Killer Kane went in the water again that night, so he'd been in twice within a week. He had black eyes under black eyes when they finally sent him back from the destroyer.

Q: Now, the recovery rate on these downed crewmen was very good, about 80%. Do you recall any of the search and rescue procedures that were used?

Admiral Ramage: No. I landed on the Yorktown, and we were prepared to launch again from the Yorktown. They still had some SB2Cs there, and I pointed out that if I went out the following morning, I couldn't go with the SB2Cs because they cruised a lot faster than we did. We always went max cruise, and that was only about 145 knots indicated, and they cruised at 165, 170, and they'd burn me out of fuel in no time at all.

Q: You're talking about the second strike.

Admiral Ramage: The second strike the following morning. They did launch quite a lot of search planes. They launched me directly back to the Enterprise.

Q: Did you spend the night on Yorktown?

Admiral Ramage: Yes, and it was rather an unhappy time. As I say, they lost a lot of their aircraft, and it was quite a difficult situation. One interesting thing is that John Crommelin, my old hero, was chief of staff to the carrier division aboard. He came down to the wardroom where I was having a late dinner, and asked me about the strike. He was quite exuberant. He said, "Well, we finally got to them."

And I said, "Captain, I think that these reports that you're getting are very exaggerated. I think we got two carriers out there."

One of the ones I thought we got, which we may not have gotten, was one when we were pulling away, my gunner Cawley said, "Can you look back? You've got to see it. It's burning from asshole to appetite." And I never did see it. Then I think Bangs and group got one, and there were other carriers beaten up, but it really wasn't that good. I just didn't want to have the same thing happen that happened in the past, where the senior officers got carried away with the idea that this had been a great, great victory. It was a victory, there's no question about it, when we tied it all together, but it wasn't the way it looked at first.

Q: I guess controversial points is the fact that I believe it was <u>Wasp</u>'s air group went after the oilers instead of the carriers. Do you recall any discussion of that at the time?

Admiral Ramage: Well, very much so. We were in the SBDs; they were equipped with SB2Cs. We were coming along late on the way in and late on the way out, so when I sighted them over there, I could see that there was a strike group getting ready to go in on the oiler force, and I said, "Unknown air group going on the oilers. What are you trying to do, sink their merchant marine? Their carriers are up ahead about 20 or 30 miles." Heck, you could see the Triple A up there, it was all over the place.

Later on, I understand that the strike group commander, whose name was Jack Blitch, he's departed now, claimed that the reason he went on them was because he was low on fuel.* What the hell, so was everybody else. However, he did, and getting back to that, the following morning when I did get back and was debriefing Black Jack Reeves, he asked

---

* Lieutenant Commander John D. Blitch, USN, was commanding officer of VB-14, an SB2C squadron from the USS <u>Wasp</u> (CV-18).

me about the thing. He was really mad, because specifically the target was the carriers. I mean, there wasn't any consideration of any other type of ship. I think maybe Lewis may be wrong. I think there were probably eight carriers out there, weren't there? I don't know.

Q: The number that sticks in my mind is nine Japanese and 14 American carriers.

Admiral Ramage: There was enough out there for everybody to be a hero.

Q: Enough to go around.

Admiral Ramage: Yes. But in any event, getting back to John Crommelin, I told him that I really didn't think that it was that big, and he really looked at me a little askance. I think he really wanted to believe that it had been the day the way the reports were coming in, but I also think that he believed me because I had known him. And it turned out that I think my figures were about right. Of course, we didn't know about the submarines doing the great job they did at the same time, and they also got two, so it was a great victory.

Q: When do you recall hearing about the two carriers sunk by the submarines?

Admiral Ramage: Oh, long after the war.

Q: Much later?

Admiral Ramage: Yes. The one thing about this battle, it was the last carrier battle, although the Japanese carriers, or what were left of them, did show up in the northern attack in the Leyte Gulf affair, they really had no airplanes.* They were simply decoys.

---

* In the Battle of Leyte Gulf was a complex engagement that lasted from 23 to 26 October 1944. The Japanese lost the cariers Zuikaku, Chiyoda, Zuiho, and Chitose, along with the battleships Musashi, Fuso, and Yamashiro; ten cruisers; 13 destroyers, and 5 submarines. U.S. losses were the light carrier Princeton (CVL-23), two escort carriers, two destroyers, and a destroyer escort.

Again, Task Force 38 and their planes took care of the rest of them. But this was the last big carrier battle where both sides really had at each other.

Q: The two points which seem to most occur in the wake of the first Philippine Sea are the decision not to pursue the Japanese, and as we know, Admiral Spruance took some criticism for that, and then the temporary discussion, as I understand it, of the possibility of reinstituting the SBD as the primary dive bomber.* Taking the first of those initially, what do you recall as the aviation attitude, say, the day after? Was there a feeling that this had somehow been a lost opportunity?

Admiral Ramage: Well, we in the ready rooms thought so for two days before that if there was any chance of getting out there, we'd sure like to do it. I did have the opportunity several years later, when I was at the Naval War College, to talk to Admiral Spruance about it personally, and he was very honest about it. He said, "I know of the criticism. However, you have to look at the information that I had at the time." He said, "I didn't know exactly where the Japanese fleet was, and I knew that they had a habit of splitting their forces, and I also knew what my mission was, which was to seize, occupy, and defend the Marianas. As such, I certainly didn't want any end run into my amphibious force." So I think even the most steadfast of aviators, including myself, will recognize that Spruance's decision was correct. It was safe. But Spruance was honest about it. He said, "Maybe I was wrong, but this is the way I saw it and this is what I did."

Q: Yes. Now, at what point do you recall Admiral Mitscher or anybody at the staff level having second thoughts, or perhaps by this time third thoughts about the SB2C?

Admiral Ramage: After the battle was over, we stayed around the Marianas for a little while, and we continued to furnish close air support at Guam. We headed back to Kwajalein, and the whole fleet was in the harbor. I got this message from the flagship,

---

* Admiral Raymond A. Spruance, USN, was Commander Fifth Fleet during the battle. His biographer, Thomas B. Buell, devotes an entire chapter to the battle in his book The Quiet Warrior: A Biography of Admiral Raymond A. Spruance (Boston: Little, Brown, 1974), pages 256-280.

which was the Lex, that Admiral Mitscher wanted to talk to me. I went over there, cap in hand, of course, and he was with several of his staff members. I can remember looking at that man, he was such a slight little person, and whereas I had seen him before at awards ceremonies, I had never really had a chance to talk to him.

The thing that impressed me so much was the way he looked at me. I felt as though that man thought that I was about the greatest thing coming, and I felt that way about him. This man, in spite of the fact that he had to commit his pilots to this almost one-way mission, really felt for them, and I think that he was just a great, great person. But after discussing the strike, he said, "It looks like you and Ralph Weymouth got in and got out, and probably got the most hits. What do you think of returning back to the SBD as far as the bomber plane?"[*]

I pointed out that in my opinion the SBD was still a finer airplane, but I didn't think that it was possible to do it out in the forward area. There was a discussion that ensued with the supply people and so forth, and it finally became just a matter of discussion, because we couldn't get spare parts and other support. So when Weymouth and I flew our two squadrons off at Eniwetok, where we left them, that was the last of the SBDs on the strike carriers.

Q: At this stage of the discussion we were down to two air groups with SBDs, Lexington and Enterprise.

Admiral Ramage: Right.

Q: The entire question of the SB2C arose later, I guess, that fall, October and November, when Admiral McCain had moved in with Task Force 38.[†] I know Bill Leonard, who at that time was the assistant ops officer to Jimmy Thach, had pursued the suggestion that McCain thought was in effect on the West Coast, phasing out the SB2C and having the

---

[*] Lieutenant Commander Ralph Weymouth, USN, commanding officer of VB-16, an SBD squadron in the Lexington (CV-16).
[†] Vice Admiral John S. McCain, USN, Commander Task Force 38, which was the designation of the fast carrier task force when it operated as part of the Third Fleet rather than the Fifth Fleet.

F6Fs and F4Us accomplish a good deal of the dive bombing.[*] And it's been said from at least two sources I can think of that apparently Curtiss Wright's political influence interfered.[†] Do you recall any such discussion?

Admiral Ramage: No. The only place where I know about any political influence or any argument came in a discussion with Ed Heinemann, who built the SBD.[‡] He said that the Wright engine people would not go for increasing the horsepower on the R-1820 engine until after the SB2C was sold and flying. See, when we got the SBD-5s, we got an extra 200 horsepower over the SBD-3s that we were flying before. But, according to Heinemann, they weren't about to let that occur until the Wright aircraft was sold. But the change of going into more fighters, of course, was absolutely necessary. The SB2C was not an adequate airplane, but also the whole complexion of the war had changed. The threat had disappeared, and other than those two big battleships, which they ultimately got with bombers and torpedo planes, the main thing was to try to protect the fleet. The kamikazes were about to come at us.[§]

Q: And that was the time in which fighter squadron strength had expanded to 72 airplanes.

Admiral Ramage: Yes.

Q: So obviously they couldn't hold as many SB2Cs as they had.

Admiral Ramage: Yes. On the ninth of July, 1944, our combat cruise was over, and we sailed with Enterprise back to Pearl Harbor, where we ultimately went back on a jeep

---

[*] Lieutenant Commander William N. Leonard, USN; Captain John S. Thach, USN. The oral history of Thach, who retired as a four-star admiral, is in the Naval Institute collection.
[†] Curtiss Wright was the manufacturer of the SB2C Helldiver.
[‡] Edward H. Heinemann was a highly respected designer for the Douglas Aircraft Company, which later merged with McDonnell. He collaborated with Rosario Rausa on the book Ed Heinemann: Combat Aircraft Designer (Annapolis: Naval Institute Press, 1980).
[§] Kamikazes were Japanese suicide aircraft that began showing up in the Philippines campaign in the autumn of 1944. The pilots attempted to crash their bomb-armed aircraft directly into American warships. Hundreds of them successfully hit their targets and inflicted great damage.

carrier to the West Coast. We were going to again go through the process of stating what we wanted to do. I didn't really have any great ideas. I felt that I was certainly competent to be an air group commander. Although I had reached the age of 28 by that time, I certainly had as much or more experience than anybody around, and that's what I wanted to do.

By this time Captain Crommelin had become the force training officer down at Commander Fleet Air West Coast, in San Diego, and he had decided that we should put together a replacement air group. He selected Killer Kane to be the air group commander, and Bruce Weber was to take over the fighter squadron.[*] Tex Harris was to take over the fighter-bomber squadron, which was F4Us, Tom Bash would take over the torpedoes, and I would take over the bomber squadron.[†] This pleased me, of course, to go with Killer again, but it turned out that Killer didn't take the job. He was sent back to Annapolis to be athletic director, which I always disagreed with, but nevertheless, that's what the jocks looked upon as a great job.

I was pleased to stay with the fleet, and in one of my first visits down to see Captain Crommelin I pointed out that I would like to be an air group commander. He indicated that if I'd stick around in this replacement air group training for a year, that he would guarantee that I got an air group. That would be pretty nice. Not only I was one of the youngest squadron commanders, but I'm sure I'd be the youngest air group commander. That promise didn't materialize because the war ended.

The idea of the replacement air group was to do just what it indicates in its title, was to give the pilots and air crews a certain amount of training and prepare them to either be replacement pilots directly in the squadrons or to proceed down into squadrons that were reforming. One of the other reasons that we needed it badly is about that time the carriers began to get pretty well banged up in the Western Pacific, and we had too many air groups. We just didn't have anyplace for people to go. I don't know how many of our carriers were knocked out in the fall of '44. They weren't sunk, but they were knocked out, and we just had a lot of carrier pilots available.

---

[*] Lieutenant Commander Bruce S. Weber, USNR.
[†] Lieutenant Commander Leroy E. Harris, USN; Lieutenant Commander Tom B. Bash, USNR.

In addition to being skipper of the bombing squadron, which was a pretty big squadron, probably 50 to 60 airplanes, I also had the job of running the pilot pool, which I'll get into later. The air group formed up at Ventura County Airport, which is in Oxnard, and it was totally inadequate for the job it had to do. Ultimately we were moved after three months, about the first of the year, 1945, down to NAS Los Alamitos.[*] Of course, that was much, much more desirable. In the meantime they ended up with maybe 400 or 500 spare pilots that we didn't know what to do with. So I was given the extra job of trying to take care of these 400 or 500 pilots, and if you got that number of 20-year-old studs without enough to keep them busy and not enough airplanes to keep them flying, you've got a real problem.

So I finally got Al Lewis, who'd been in VB-14, out of a returning air group, and sent him up there to be the boss man of that thing, the on-scene commander, and he was tough enough to at least make some semblance of order. In VB-98, like the rest of the squadrons in the replacement air group, I was given a choice of pretty much what I wanted, so I went right back to Air Group Ten, because I knew they were tried. I got Red Carmody, who had been in Scouting Ten in the first cruise, and, of course, Lou Bangs out of Bombing Ten in the second cruise.[†] Then I got Frank West, who had been in Bombing Ten the first cruise, a real aggressive, scrappy guy. I got a couple of rather young guys out of VB-1, one named Regester, and another named Kiernan, whom I hadn't asked for, and so far as I was concerned, didn't have the necessary background to serve in the capacity as instructor in this type of training. Nevertheless, I got them and they worked out well.

Q: At what point did you part company with Bombing Ten?

Admiral Ramage: That would be July of 1944.

Q: Was that on the West Coast?

---

[*] Naval Air Station Los Alamitos, about six miles east of Long Beach, California.
[†] Lieutenant Martin D. Carmody, USNR.

Admiral Ramage: Yes. We went through the reassignment process. It probably would be August of '44 and then they broke up the air group. As a matter of fact, Air Group Ten reformed on the East Coast. Not too many people stayed with them, but they had a lot of other first- and second-tour pilots. We were in the land of plenty, finally, as far as personnel was concerned.

Q: You had to be very pleased to be home and happy. What kind of feelings did you have leaving these guys that you had flown in combat with?

Admiral Ramage: Well, I loved them, but every good thing can't go forever. I hoped that I would see them again in the future, and I have seen many of them. A couple of them went out on additional cruises and got bagged, a chap named Powell was killed in the next cruise, and also a pilot named Hubbard, who was one of the finest young officers I ever knew.[*] But war is war, and when it's over, that's it. I still look backwards at those guys as being really the best. They sure performed.

I can't say too much about the replacement air group. We did our job. It was a very difficult job to keep track of, because I would have detachments training at 29 Palms, Holtville, we had a field at Thermal, California, that the Air Force had given up. We had people out on the carriers, and then I had the pool, so I was every day somewhere else, and it was kind of hard to keep track of what was going on.

Q: When pilots reported in to VB-98, were they already current in the SB2C?

Admiral Ramage: Some were, but most weren't, no. No, most of them had never seen the Beast, as we called it.

Q: Was the operational training system still in effect, or did you guys take over that mission?

---

[*] Lieutenant (junior grade) Stanley W. Powell, USNR; Lieutenant (junior grade) Oliver W. Hubbard, USNR.

Admiral Ramage: Yes, we took over the mission that had been ACTG, Advanced Carrier Training Group, which included the car quals. We had a CVE, which became our main qualifying carrier, it was called the Matanikau, CVE, and the skipper was Captain Skee Erdmann, who, as far as I know, had never served on a carrier.* At least he didn't know much about it.

I learned something about him very early. He was a bully, and when you'd send a detachment out for car quals, if one of the younger people and smaller people, Regester or Kiernan, would go out, they inevitably had trouble, and Erdmann would throw them right off the ship. However, if I or Lou Bangs or Red Carmody, who were all big guys, went aboard, everything went fine. It was just one of the strange things in the mental makeup of this guy. It was not a pleasant time to be on that ship, and he had a reputation for being extremely difficult.†

I stayed there for about a year and a half. The promise of the air group, of course, evaporated on V-J Day, and we really didn't have anything to do.‡ I learned that Admiral Spruance was going to go to the Naval War College.§ I couldn't get another flying job, so I applied for and went to the Naval War College first postwar class in the spring of 1946.

When I reported in to the Naval War College, it became apparent right away that World War II had not touched the Naval War College. In spite of the fact that we had one of the real heroes, Admiral Spruance, as the new president, he hadn't had a chance to change any of the curriculum. Consequently, we started doing the same old thing, pushing battleships around on the floor. They would arbitrarily rule out the use of air in battle problems. They would just say, "Well, either the weather's too bad or you're operating in a climate that the weather prevails, so we will rule out air for this problem." Other than, I'd say, two or three of the monthly problems, we did not use air power whatsoever.

---

* Captain William L. Erdmann, USN, was the first commanding officer when the escort carrier Matanikau (CVE-101) was commissioned on 24 June 1944. He served in that billet until 27 March 1945.
† For further examples of Erdmann's difficult personality, see the Naval Institute oral history of Captain Daniel W. Tomlinson IV, USNR (Ret.).
‡ V-J Day--Victory-over-Japan Day, 15 August 1945, marking the end of hostilities in the war in the Pacific. The formal Japanese surrender was on 2 September on board the battleship Missouri (BB-63) in Tokyo Bay.
§ Admiral Raymond A. Spruance, USN, served as president of the Naval War College from 1 March 1946 to 1 July 1948.

James D. Ramage #1 - 129

Q: Who was responsible for this type of thing?

Admiral Ramage: Well, what happened was that they had three or four commodores still on the staff. You know, a commodore during the war was somebody who just couldn't quite make it, and they were kind of old-timers. The war had simply passed the Naval War College by. The one advantage was that Admiral Spruance would make himself available personally if you wanted to go down and talk to him. I went down from time to time and talked to him, particularly about that decision at the Philippine Sea battle. But Admiral Spruance was an exceedingly shy man, and he rarely got on the platform. I got quite a bit out of the course.

Q: Was Wade McClusky an instructor? Was he at the war college the same time as you were there?

Admiral Ramage: Wade was not at the war college; he was the executive officer of the line school, which was started just after the war in order to provide the ex-cadets with some background that the Navy Department felt that they needed.[*] I myself felt that the Navy needed more background than the ex-cadets did, but that's a personal affair. Wade was there, and I talked to him from time to time because we had been together for quite a long time. I was such an admirer of his.

Incidentally, Admiral Spruance once on the platform was asked about the Battle of Midway, and he said that if there was any one man responsible for the victory at Midway, it was Wade McClusky. So Spruance was well aware of everything that went on there, and I admired him for it.

Q: You'd had some discussions with McClusky about the battle. Would you care to address that?

---

[*] On 4 June 1942, in the Battle of Midway, Lieutenant Commander C. Wade McClusky, Jr., USN, was the commander of the air group from the carrier Enterprise (CV-6). McClusky trailed a Japanese destroyer from the air and thus led the American strike force to the Japanese carriers. He had been promoted to captain during the war.

Admiral Ramage: Well, the one thing that he indicated was that he was not as unhappy with Jim Gray, the skipper of VF-6, as a lot of people were at the time.* Jim had a very unfortunate day that day. It was something that could happen to anybody. Very fortunately it didn't happen to me, but it could, I guess. I don't think I really want to get into that.

Q: Who else was at the war college with you?

Admiral Ramage: Well, of my buddies, Robin Lindsey, Bob Elder, Jim Daniels, and all of the first early group of ex-cadets were at the line school, and I played around with them.†

Q: Did you do any studying at all? That was a pretty bad group you were with there.

Admiral Ramage: I studied quite hard and learned a lot. I did two theses. The first one was on the aircraft carrier and the atomic bomb, outlining how and why we had to get the A-bombs aboard the carrier. The other one was a study of the future arrangements with Russia. It was a very good year, and it was kind of a sabbatical in that I'd been so close to aviation and the war for so long, maybe it was a good thing. I didn't think at the time that I got an awful lot out of it, but as I look back on it, I think probably it was a plus. And, as I say, I didn't have anyplace else to go. They wouldn't give me another flying job. I'd been skipper of two squadrons, and many of my classmates had not showed at all. I was told that we had to give these people a chance to command; they didn't deserve it.

Q: As far as your thesis on carrier aviation and nuclear weapons, did that include the flip side, defending against nuclear weapons at sea?

---

* Lieutenant James S. Gray, USN, was commanding officer of Fighting Six from the Enterprise during the Battle of Midway. His planes got separated from the air group's torpedo planes and did not provide them protection against attack by the Japanese.
† Commander Robin M. Lindsey, USN; Lieutenant Commander Robert M. Elder, USN; Lieutenant Commander James G. Daniels III, USN. The general line school was intended to provide officers with a broad range of naval knowledge. It was particularly useful for those who had been in a particular specialty, such as aviation, and not exposed to the Navy as a whole.

Admiral Ramage: No. This was mainly concerned with obtaining nuclear capability, as it really was a must. I could see that even from my capacity, and quite obviously other people did, mainly Chick Hayward and that group.*

Q: Presumably North American was at work on the AJ at this time.

Admiral Ramage: I guess so. I didn't learn of that until later. So I graduated from the war college in the spring of '47, and immediately asked for another flying job. The answer was not only, "No," but "Hell no. We've got to give these people who haven't ever had a chance to command a carrier squadron a chance." Well, what that did was bring carrier aviation to its lowest ebb during the period of time up to the Korean War. They simply did not let anybody get into any position in carrier aviation that knew much about it. I disagreed with the Navy system quite a bit, but I considered that if carriers were that important, that they ought to put the best people in them, but they sure didn't at that time.

Q: Where were these decisions coming from, BuPers?†

Admiral Ramage: Well, wherever the Navy policymakers were. At that time the Navy was still imbued with the idea of the rounded officer, which is fine, but they had not accepted the fact that naval aviation was really one of the most, if not the most important element of the fleet. And I don't know exactly why they should try to spread out these commands, particularly to these people that hadn't availed themselves of the opportunity to get shot at during the war, but that was the general policy. I will talk a little bit about that.

The Naval Academy classes of my time, and mine really the most, was in a very proper position to be in combat during that war. We had to have the two years as surface officers to get qualified under way, and although, as I said, I opposed it at the time, I think that it was a good thing for me. But the Navy system of personnel permitted academy graduates to attend postgraduate school during the war. At the same time, various other

---

* Commander John T. Hayward, USN, had an important role in getting nuclear weapons to sea on board carriers. The oral history of Hayward, who retired as a vice admiral, is in the Naval Institute collection.
† BuPers--Bureau of Naval Personnel.

people, including the reserves and the aviation cadets, were out fighting the war. And I think it was wrong.

They not only let people go to postgraduate school, but they let aviators become aviation engineering duty officer only during the war, without even going to postgraduate school, just by saying you wanted to be an AEDO, which, of course, was the deepest foxhole you could possibly find during the war. So what I ran into was that the various people that showed during the war were generally cadets and a few of the Naval Academy people. I didn't really like to be known as an academy graduate, and I stopped wearing my class ring at that time. This was about 1942, and I haven't worn it since.

Q: Do you know of anyone else from the class who shared that opinion?

Admiral Ramage: I think probably Gene Fairfax shared it, and I think Tex Harris shared it.[*] George Duncan.[†] The people that got out there, I think, all felt the same way.

Q: Them that got shot at.

Admiral Ramage: Because those that got to the carriers, the loss rate was pretty high. The loss in aviation itself was about 25%, but the majority of the people were not in carriers, so when you take a look at that . . .

Q: It's disproportionate.

Admiral Ramage: Yes. It was probably well over 50% of the people who went into carriers are no longer with us.

Q: Do you think that things have turned around in the period since then, or is it still possible to, as you say, find the deepest foxhole?

---

[*] Lieutenant Commander Eugene G. Fairfax, USN; Lieutenant Commander Leroy E. Harris, USN.
[†] Lieuteant Commander George C. Duncan, USN.

Admiral Ramage: Well, yes, they definitely turned around during the Vietnam War, but the Korean War was more of the same. The reserves basically fought the Korean War. We'll get into that later.

Q: All right. So you graduated from the Naval War College. Where did you go from there?

Admiral Ramage: My next job was navigator of the CVE Bairoko.* Again I didn't particularly seek the job, but it turned out quite well because by checking that off as navigator, they never forced me into a ship's company job again until I was skipper. So that served its purpose. The Bairoko was a converted fleet tanker, which was operating out of San Diego. It had two air groups, one of them was an ASW group flying Grumman AFs, and then from time to time we had Marine F4Us that would operate with us.†

I was allowed to do everything on that ship. The first day I reported aboard I got under way and operated aircraft. One of the reasons was that the skipper was a drunk, and consequently, generally was incompetent to get the ship under way, so it worked out fine for me. I'd get under way and start conducting flight operations. About Wednesday he'd be ready to take a look at things.

We ultimately got a new skipper, Bill Harris, a heck of a nice guy.‡ He took us out to Eniwetok. We went out to Operation Sandstone.§ We had a helo detachment aboard, and we were the sniffers, as they called them, we took the samples after the three bombs

---

* USS Bairoko (CVE-115), a Commencement Bay-class escort carrier, was commissioned 16 July 1945. She had a standard displacement of 10,330 tons, was 557 feet long, 75 feet in the beam, and had an extreme width of 105 feet. Her top speed was 19.1 knots. The ship was originally armed with two 5-inch guns and could accommodate approximately 33 aircraft. She was eventually decommissioned in 1955.
† Grumman's AF Guardian was conceived as a torpedo bomber replacement for the TBF Avenger. Subsequently the AF was modified to be an antisubmarine warfare aircraft with two configurations that operated in hunter-killer pairs: the radar-equipped AF-2W and the weapon-carrying AF-2S. Deliveries of the AF-2 to fleet squadrons began in October 1950. The AF-2S version was 43 feet long, wing span of 61 feet, gross weight of 25,500 pounds, and top speed of 317 miles per hour.
‡ Captain William S. Harris, USN, commanded the Bairoko, 1948-49.
§ Operation Sandstone comprised a series of atmospheric tests of nuclear weapons at Eniwetok in the Marshall Islands in 1948. The series included tests X-Ray on 15 April, Yoke on 1 May, and Zebra on 15 May.

went off. It was an interesting thing to watch the bombs go and to meet some of the scientific people that they put aboard ship to be part of the exercise.

The year on the Bairoko was very pleasant. There was no great problem. I liked everybody, and I think they liked me. So on the way back from Operation Sandstone, I stopped by ComAirPac, which was in Pearl at that time. I dropped in to see Frank Upham, who was a former commander of Air Group 98.[*] I told Frank that I was looking for a job, that I'd like to come out to Honolulu because my wife had come from there. I thought that now would be a good time to get on the staff if I had to be on one. He said he'd look around and see what he could find.

The job that he found was one that I wasn't particularly eager for, which was enlisted personnel officer. So in due course, about June of 1947, I was ordered to ComNavAirPac in Honolulu as enlisted personnel officer. Again, that was a job that I learned a lot in, as you always do in the Navy, you look at something and say, "I don't particularly want it," and it turns out to be a fine job.

One of the things that became readily apparent, the person I relieved, who was a lieutenant, had been a real politician. He would send people all over the place at the request of anybody. There were people stashed away in the Hawaiian area without jobs, without billets, without anything. As an example, we had a chief petty officer living down in Hilo whose job was to meet people getting their flight time down to Hilo and make sure that they got a ride in to pick up their orchids and the beef. There was a jaygee on the staff named Homer Giddens.[†] They called him "The Judge," and "The Judge" was just ready for me. He had a listing of all of these things that he didn't like, which he couldn't remedy with the former personnel officer, so we went to work on cleaning up all these odds and ends that had existed all during World War II. It was very sloppy.

One of the funny ones that Frank Upham likes to tell is about the skipper of NAS Ford Island at that time. He was a captain, of course, as Ford Island was an important base. He had come up to my office. I was still a lieutenant commander at the time. He had asked

---

[*] Commander Frank K. Upham, USN.
[†] Lieutenant (junior grade) Homer A. Giddens, USN, a limited duty officer who specialized in the field of administration.

for certain people that were on a carrier that was en route to WestPac.* I knew that ComFAir West Coast had a hell of a time during these very difficult days trying to load up these ships for deployment, and there was no way I was going to pull anybody off that ship. I said, "No, I'm sorry, these people are ship's company, and that's the way it's going to be."

And the captain said, "Well, where am I going to get my people, then?"

I responded, "Just about the way that everybody else does."

Apparently Frank had overheard this and thought it was the funniest thing. Within two hours it was all over the base that the skipper of Ford Island had finally lost his special way of loading up Ford Island with people.

Ultimately ComNavAirPac moved back to San Diego. This was in 1949. ComFAir West Coast was decommissioned, and ComAirPac was where it should be. Admiral Sallada, who was ComNavAirPac at the time, opposed it.† He felt that we should be close to CinCPacFlt because of the importance of air power, and he felt that we would lose some clout.‡ But there was no getting around the fact that we were double-staffing. ComFAir West Coast was doing the job that ComAirPac should do, so we moved back.

When I got back to ComFAir West Coast, I brought Giddens with me, and we started doing the same thing at North Island that we had done out at Ford Island, trying to root out some of these people that had never been to sea. There were people that had been on North Island in San Diego since before the war and all during the war, and then never been to sea.

Q: Yes. I know photographers that were swapping fleet air boats at North Island to fleet air boat at Barbers Point, and that's all they did. They made careers of it.

Admiral Ramage: We started working on this, and by this time Tommy Sprague, Admiral Sprague, had just come out of BuPers and become ComAirNavPac.§ I didn't know him, but

---

* WestPac--Western Pacific.
† Vice Admiral Harold B. Sallada, USN, served as Commander Air Force Pacific Fleet from 5 January 1948 to 1 October 1949.
‡ CinCPacFlt--Commander in Chief Pacific Fleet.
§ Vice Admiral Thomas L. Sprague, USN, served as Commander Air Force Pacific Fleet from 1 October 1949 to 1 April 1952.

I knew that I would have support. And we'd get these calls from these flag officers, retired officers, that would say, "Why are you sending Chief So-and-so to the Philippines?"

I'd point out that he'd been on shore duty for 15 years and it was time he move out. And usually when you told them that, they'd say, "Oh, I understand." But there would be an occasional one who would say, "Well, he's a particular friend of mine, and I'd like to see if you couldn't do so and so."

I'd always say, "You can take this up with Admiral Sprague." So far as I know, no one ever went to Admiral Sprague. I know that they knew what kind of response they'd get.

The other thing that was kind of interesting at that time, ComFAir West Coast was running a monster receiving station, and all of the people that came to the NavAirPac ships, squadrons, or bases physically went through the receiving station that was run out at North Island. This is a hell of a waste of time and effort. Also ComFAir West Coast was doing all of the accounting by hand in large trays of cards. We'd had a personnel accounting machine there in the Navy since just after the war, and it was available, but they claimed that that was not what they wanted.

So my first dictation was to start making the personnel accounting machinery work. Secondly, to decommission the receiving station, because we had as many as 1,000 people on hand there from time to time. So we then set up the procedure of picking up the people as they became available at whatever shore station, making them available for assignment by our immediate subordinate commands. They in turn would make the assignment directly to the squadron or activity without the man showing up at North Island. It's amazing to me that that thing had gone on that long. We must have wasted just millions and millions of dollars and man-hours in forcing all these people through the receiving station.

Q: From a personal experience of having been in a receiving station, it was the most ridiculous experience.

Admiral Ramage: I felt that I learned a lot from being there. But, more than that, for some reason or other, Giddens also had the job of maintaining the fitness reports that were written by admirals on admirals and captains. They went through him, and I was able to get a look at how senior officers wrote up people that they really wanted to get promoted and how they wrote up people whom they didn't want to be promoted. The point is that a lot of people don't know that the fitness report system is very inflated, too much so, but if everybody knows that, then the system works. Unfortunately, you'll get somebody who doesn't know the system, and he will write out a fitness report just the way he sees it. All you have to do is write the truth on a report card, and the guy's going home the next week. This is just the nature of the beast.

Q: 99.9 doesn't cut it.

Admiral Ramage: 99.9 doesn't cut it. It's a game. Before I leave ComAirPac, I'd like to point out that at that time enlisted personnel were handled completely within the force. There was no detailing of anything below the rank of commander by Washington, so it was a good job. We had all of the ships, squadrons, and air stations in the Pacific, plus all of the group nine, that is, the aviation ratings, as far as distribution was concerned. I learned quite a bit about personnel handling at that time.

In the spring of 1950 the coming of the heavy attack program had quite an impact upon the personnel situation in the Air Force Pacific Fleet. We had a staff meeting in which Admiral Sprague pointed out that the VC squadrons that were to form would get absolutely the highest priority as far as we were concerned. VC-5 was the first, up at Moffett.[*]

Q: These are the Navy's first nuclear strike.

Admiral Ramage: These were the strike aircraft. Of course, this caused a lot of discontent among the other squadrons, because qualified personnel were very difficult to come by at that time. We were briefed as to just what the VC squadron was to do and how they would operate off the ship by Chick Hayward, who was quite a guy, incidentally.[†]

---

[*] Moffett Field Naval Air Station, Sunnyvale, California, is located ten miles north of San Jose, at the southern tip of San Francisco Bay. It was named in honor of Rear Admiral William A. Moffett, USN, first Chief of the Bureau of Aeronautics. Fleet Composite Squadron Five (VC-5) was commissioned 13 September 1948.
[†] Commander John T. Hayward, USN, commanded VC-5 from 1948 to 1951.

I really wanted to know more and more about this nuclear capability. So in about March of 1950 I had an opportunity to go over to Sandia Base to attend an indoctrination school for about a week on the nuclear bomb.* People knew nothing about the bomb, and I wanted to know more about it. The week's course was fascinating. We had only two weapons at that time. The big 10,000-pound Fat Man was an implosion weapon.† We also had the Little Boy, which was the gun-type weapon.‡ It was still a heavy weapon, but it had a much smaller diameter.

In one of the briefings, looking into the future, the briefer indicated that there was a possibility that we could get a smaller implosion-type weapon with a 30-inch sphere rather than a 60-inch sphere. This really interested me, because if you get a weapon with that small a diameter, you could use it on lots of aircraft that we had on the carriers at that time, without going to the special-mission aircraft like the AJ.§

At the same time, I was again looking for a job and told again that I couldn't get a flying job because I'd had too much of everything. I had orders to the Armed Forces Staff College, which was rather stupid, because I'd already graduated from the senior course at the Naval War College. Nevertheless, they simply didn't know what to do with me. When Tom Walker, who was stationed over at Kirtland Air Force Base with the special weapons project, asked me if I wouldn't like to come on over to Albuquerque, I said I'd sure be delighted if he could arrange it.**

I went back to San Diego, and I talked to various people on the staff about these new weapons that were coming along, that I felt that we should proceed on into the nuclear field. I said we should pursue the smaller bombs that could be carried on the AD and the

---

* Sandia Base was near Albuquerque, New Mexico.
† Fat Man was the nickname of the U.S. atomic bomb dropped on Nagasaki, Japan, on 9 August 1945. It weighed 10,000 pounds and measured 10 feet, 8 inches in length and 5 feet in diameter.
‡ Little Boy was the nickname of the U.S. atomic bomb dropped on Hiroshima, Japan, on 6 August 1945. It weighed 9,000 pounds and measured 10 feet in length and 28 inches in diameter.
§ The AJ Savage was a propeller-driven carrier-based nuclear strike aircraft built by North American Aviation, Inc. It first entered the fleet in squadron VC-5 in September 1949. It was reclassified A-2 in 1962. The AJ-1 version was 63 feet long; wing span of 75 feet; gross weight of 52,862 pounds; and top speed of 471 miles per hour. It had a maximum bomb capacity of 12,000 pounds.
** Lieutenant Commander Thomas J. Walker III, USN, a Naval Academy classmate of Ramage and also a naval aviator.

F2H-2.* I talked to Admiral Sprague about it, and I told him I had a chance to go to Sandia Base. He said, "Good luck. Just keep me advised on these things as they develop in the nuclear weapons field."

I was promoted to the rank of commander in May of 1950, and in June took off for Albuquerque for duty in the field command of the Armed Forces Special Weapons Project, which was at Sandia Base, near Albuquerque. While I was on leave during that June, the Korean War started, which made me feel that I was going in the wrong direction.† Because if there was one going on, I sure wanted to be in it. When we got to Albuquerque, we got a house in the valley at 3118 Rio Grande Boulevard. It was an adobe house and really very nice. My daughter Jaleen was born in February of 1951.

When I reported in to the field command of the Armed Forces Special Weapons Projects, I couldn't go to work immediately, because my Q clearance had not come through. The Q clearance is that clearance which is required to handle information on nuclear weapons. So I was put in charge of an AJ accident board.

Q: That's the AJ-1 Savage.

Admiral Ramage: That's the Savage, AJ-1, which was built by North American. The plane had blown up in the air south of Albuquerque and had strewn parts of people and aircraft all over the area. It was quite a gory accident and one which seemed to be almost insolvable. The pieces were minute. It just seemed that there was no place to go on this thing. I might say that at that time we didn't have anything like the Navy Safety Center.

---

* Douglas AD Skyraider propeller-driven attack planes first entered fleet squadrons in late 1946. The AD-2 version was 38 feet long, wing span of 50 feet, gross weight of 18,263 pounds, and top speed of 321 miles per hour. It had a bomb capacity of 8,000 pounds. McDonnell's F2H Banshee was a jet-powered fighter-bomber that first entered the fleet with squadron VF-171 in March 1949. The F2H-2 version was 40 feet long, wing span of 45 feet, gross weight of 22,312 pounds, and top speed of 532 miles per hour. It had four fixed forward-firing 20-millimeter guns and provision to carry two 500-pound bombs.
† The Korean War began on 25 June 1950, when six North Korean infantry division and three border constabulary brigades invaded the South Korea. The troops were supported by approximately 100 Russian-made T-34 tanks. In New York that same day the United Nations Security Council adopted a resolution condemning the invasion.

I began to look at the specifications of the AJ, and I might say that I was very unimpressed. It had two propellers on high wing mountings, on the parasol-type wing, and it had a small jet stinger in the tail. It was a high-altitude level bomber, which was just exactly what I didn't like. It was totally foreign to the Navy method of delivering weapons. At that time it had already become known as the "human barbecue pit." As it went into the fleet, it became known as the "drut," which means "turd," spelled backwards.

The accident board was pretty well confused. We didn't know where to go until finally I received a call from Ray Rice, who was the chief engineer at North American. They felt that they had some kind of a handle on this accident. When I got to El Segundo, there was an AJ on the line that was almost completely purple aft of the wing. What the engineers had done was to put purple dye in the fuel and then discharged some of the fuel through the overboard vents which were up in the wing. It was quite apparent then that the fuel, when discharged, went down over the fuselage and drifted aft. And when they looked into the fuselage, it was very clear that the dye had penetrated inside of the plating, so that there was fuel leaking into the after part of the fuselage. It was apparent that the fuel had actually gone all the way aft and entered into the plenum chamber of the jet stinger aperture in the tail. So there was a way that aviation fuel could get into that plenum chamber.

Apparently what had happened was that the pilot had lit off the jet stinger engine in the tail and blown the plane up. There were other things that I ran into about the plane that I didn't like. I found out that they carried extra open containers of hydraulic fluid in the cockpit, because they had so many hydraulic fluid leaks that they were running out of hydraulic fluid while they were in flight. Also, the third crewman carried a fire ax with him because they wanted to be able to get out of the thing. Escape from the airplane was very difficult, and apparently this fire ax would help them get out. It was just a mess!

Q: Had this airplane been designed in a hurry? It sounds like not much thought went into it.

Admiral Ramage: Well, I'm not sure of that. I just saw it as the finished product. I knew that it was coming along. I have talked to people that had it at Patuxent, particularly Don

Runyon, who did some of the flight testing on it, and he said it was a decent airplane to fly.[*] I don't think it completed all the tests at Patuxent. I think that there was so much pressure to get the thing into the fleet that it hadn't been completely wrung out at the test center.

You've got to realize that this aircraft was expedited because of political reasons more than anything. The Navy had to get into the nuclear weapons field, and it had to be able to carry the only bomb that was in stockpile at that time, which was the Mark 4. The Mark 4 I can only describe as looking like one of these cement mixers that you see riding around on the back of cement trucks on the highway. It was an ungainly thing. It was an adaptation of the Fat Man.

Q: What was the size and configuration of the early nuclear weapons?[†]

Admiral Ramage: We had two types. One was the implosion type, which rather than exploding like normal bombs do, the shaped charges, which surrounded the nuclear core, were directed inward. The great pressure that these shaped charges generated would compress the plutonium in the middle of the sphere to the point that it became critical, and then it in turn detonated. Of course, the bigger the squeeze, then the more critical the nuclear material became and the larger the detonation was. That was the principle of the Fat Man that was dropped in Nagasaki.

The other weapon was in very limited supply. They built only three of them. The Mark 8 was similar to the Little Boy. This was a very simple weapon. It was a tube into which two masses of nuclear material were fired into each other, and the mass then became of sufficient size to become critical. And if you inserted some nuclear flux at the same time, you got a detonation. This was a very inefficient and also a very dirty weapon, as far as nuclear material is concerned.

---

[*] Naval Air Test Center at Patuxent River Naval Air Station, Lexington Park, Maryland. Lieutenant Commander Donald E. Runyon, USN.
[†] For details and illustrations of these various weapons, see Chuck Hansen, U.S. Nuclear Weapons: The Secret History (New York: Orion Books [Crown Publishers, Inc.], 1988).

Q: Probably that was simpler from an engineering standpoint, thought, wasn't it, than implosion, which would require equal force in a 360-degree . . . ?

Admiral Ramage: That's correct. Anybody could build a Little Boy, which later became the Mark 8. While I'm at it, I'll discuss the weapons of that time that were either in the stockpile or coming along. I mentioned the Mark 4, which was the one which was in stockpile and the one which the Navy had to be able to carry in order to get in the A-bomb business, because certainly the Strategic Air Command was not going to recommend building anything smaller if it could help it.[*] The Mark 4 had a 60-inch sphere and was only about 12 feet long. So you can see that it had a very poor fineness ratio. As a matter of fact, people were asked from time to time which end was the front. It was a very ungainly thing. It weighed 10,000 pounds, which is an awful lot of weight to be carrying around.

The next one up, not necessarily in line, was the Mark 5, and the Mark 5 had a 45-inch sphere. It was an implosion weapon, and it was built for internal carriage also. The Mark 5 had been established as a Navy requirement, and I could never figure exactly why, because it didn't give us the advantage of external carriage. It could fly only in the AJ, and although it was lighter, really didn't add much, plus because of the smaller warhead didn't give the same amount of yield as the Mark 4. If I recall right, this thing probably weighed about 4,500 pounds.

Q: What was considered minimum acceptable yield at that time?

Admiral Ramage: Well, certainly they didn't want to go under 20 KT, which was the Hiroshima bomb.[†]

The next weapon up was the Mark 6, which was simply a cleaned-up version of the Mark 4. It had the 60-inch sphere also, and they'd improved the fuzing and firing system. They'd lightened it up a little bit so it weighed only 8,000 pounds. But it was the same size and shape as the Mark 4, so really didn't do too much as far as improvement is concerned.

---

[*] The Strategic Air Command was the element of the U.S. Air Force that had the responsibility for long-range delivery of nuclear weapons by manned bombers.
[†] KT--kilotons, a means of measuring the equivalent weight of TNT to achieve a given explosive effect.

Then we come to the Mark 7, which was the one which we really had to have in the Navy. This was built around a 30-inch sphere, and obviously it gave us a great capability because it had an external carriage capability. It had a lesser yield, because, of course, it had lesser squeeze.

The only other one was the Mark 8, and there was only a limited number of them. As far as I know, there were only three in existence, and that had to do with the P2V-2 capability that VC-5 had before it had the AJ.[*] So far as I know, those were the only ones built.

The reason that the 60-inch sphere was the standard was that it was the largest size that a B-29 could carry.[†] At the time they were the only delivery aircraft of the Strategic Air Command. Consequently, the B-29 sized the Mark 4 bomb and the Mark 4 bomb sized the bomb bays of the AJ and A3D when they came out.[‡] It was kind of an indirect connection.

Q: Was there a Mark 1, 2, or 3, or were those simply paper?

Admiral Ramage: I believe there was a Mark 3, which was a Fat Man, but I really don't remember that very well. I rather suspect that Mark 1 and Mark 2 were the bombs that were dropped on Japan.

Q: Okay.

---

[*] The Lockheed P2V Neptune was a propeller-drive land-based patrol aircraft that entered the fleet in March 1947. A modified P2V-3, equipped with jet-assisted takeoff, was launched from the carrier <u>Midway</u> (CVB-41) on 5 October 1949 to demonstrate the carrier suitability for a nuclear strike aircraft. The pilot during the test was Commander Frederick L. Ashworth, USN. The oral history of Ashworth, who retired as a vice admiral, is in the Naval Institute collection.
[†] The Army's Boeing B-29 Superfortress was the most advanced bomber of World War II. It had four 2,220-horsepower engines that gave it a top speed of 365 miles per hour at 25,000 feet. It had a maximum range of 5,830 miles. B-29s were used from the strikes against Hiroshima and Nagasaki in August 1945.
[‡] The Douglas A3D Skywarrior first entered fleet squadrons in 1956 as a carrier-based heavy bomber. It was reclassified as the A-3 in 1962. The A3D-2 version was 76 feet long; wing span of 72 feet; gross weight of 82,000 pounds; and top speed of 610 miles per hour. It had a maximum bomb capacity of 12,000 pounds.

Admiral Ramage: After I completed the accident report on the AJ, my Q clearance finally came in, and I reported in for duty at Sandia Base. The senior naval officer present at that time was a Captain Dave Young, who really spent most of his time trying to get the Navy into the nuclear weapons business.[*] When he briefed me on my duties, I said that I had some views that I'd like to discuss with him first. As I looked up at the artist's concept of the A3D on the bulkhead, I said that I didn't think that was the way to go, that I felt that the Navy should be trying to develop as soon as possible the light weapons capability, because about half of the aircraft on the aircraft carriers could then become potential nuclear weapons carriers. I told him that I intended to try to do everything I could to expedite the light weapon capability. He didn't say no, so I presumed that I had his concurrence.

In the meantime, Commander Tom Walker was over at Kirtland Air Force Base with the Navy weapons facility over there.

Q: He was a classmate of yours, wasn't he?

Admiral Ramage: Yes, he was a classmate, and he was an ordnance PG.[†] What he was trying to do was be sure that both the AD and the F2H-2 were capable of carrying the light weapon and that the shapes would separate correctly from the aircraft when they were in flight. He did have an AJ or two over there. As a matter of fact, the one that blew up had been one of his aircraft.

Q: Had the Navy been dealing with doctrine and tactics for nuclear delivery at this time?

Admiral Ramage: Not a thing. That didn't come until much later on, when Tom I went out to Norfolk and talked to the commander of the Operational Development Force, who was Rear Admiral Entwistle.[‡] He set up VX-5, and Tom Walker was the first skipper.[§] His job

---

[*] Captain David B. Young, USN.
[†] PG--postgraduate.
[‡] Rear Admiral Frederick I. Entwistle, USN, commanded the Operational Development Force from October 1950 to February 1954.
[§] VX-5—Air Development Squadron Five.

was to try to expedite weapon delivery tactics into the fleet, but this was a good two years later.

Q: But we still had AJs in the fleet at this time.

Admiral Ramage: Oh, yes.

Q: With nuclear weapons.

Admiral Ramage: They were just coming into the fleet, actually, at this time.

Q: I think 1950 is when they first started in. What was your job? What was your billet at Sandia?

Admiral Ramage: My job was in the operations division. By the time I'd gotten there, the Air Force had stacked it so completely with people senior to me that I was four or five down the list in seniority. The job of the operations division was to support the SAC war plan and the Navy, if they ever developed a plan.* Secondly it was to operate the three assembly bases. We had a weapons assembly plant at Albuquerque, one at Killeen, Texas, and one at Clarksville, Kentucky. The field command operated these three assembly plants.

SAC in turn had a certain number of weapons under their control, but they didn't have the nuclear components. Consequently, SAC's capability was definitely limited. You might recall that Harry Truman distrusted the military, and he once stated that he didn't want some colonel to start the war before breakfast.† So SAC, although it was developing a fine organization, really, when you talk about readiness, didn't have any, because the President of the United States would not let the commander of SAC have any nuclear components under his control.

---

* SAC--Strategic Air Command.
† Harry S. Truman served as President of the United States from 12 April 1945 to 20 January 1953.

Q: How do you feel about that decision?

Admiral Ramage: Well, it was absolutely ridiculous, and, of course, the Navy at that time was putting the three CVBs--that is, the Roosevelt, Coral Sea, and Midway--into the business with the big Mark 4 weapons.* And if you didn't have the nuclear components aboard ships, you certainly had no readiness whatsoever.

Q: This came shortly after the congressional fight that centered around the elimination of the Marine Corps and reduction of the Navy.

Admiral Ramage: That was a year or two earlier, but for all purposes, in spite of the fact that some fine officers got canned, the Navy won that, mainly because of Forrestal and Vinson.† Arthur Radford was also very successful in that fight.‡ My old friend John Crommelin was involved in it.§ I think he was kind of dancing around the sidelines, and I've been told by people in the know that perhaps he was a little more harmful than good as far as the fight was concerned. But John was a crusader, and if there was a fight, particularly for naval aviation, he was going to be in it.

Q: So with your job, what exactly were your duties?

Admiral Ramage: That was reviewing the SAC war plans and then writing the Armed Forces Special Weapons Field Command plans to support the SAC war plans. Then we would watch the SAC maneuvers, and I learned a lot about how airplanes should be flown from SAC. It was a real first-class outfit. They were a professional outfit compared to the

---

* At the time the three newest and biggest aircraft carriers in the fleet were the Midway (CVB-41), Franklin D. Roosevelt (CVB-42), and Coral Sea (CVB-43).
† James V. Forrestal was Secretary of Defense, and Representative Carl Vinson was chairman of the House Armed Services Committee. See Jeffrey G. Barlow, Revolt of the Admirals: The Fight for Naval Aviation, 1945-1950 (Washington, D.C.: U.S. Government Printing Office, 1994).
‡ Admiral Arthur W. Radford, USN, served as Vice Chief of Naval Operations from 3 January 1948 to 16 April 1949.
§ For a description of the role of Captain John G. Crommelin, USN, in the "revolt of the admirals," see Edward P. Stafford, "Saving Carrier Aviation--1949 Style," U.S. Naval Institute Proceedings, January 1990, pages 44-51.

Navy, as far as aviation was concerned. The Navy had at that time still not accepted the fact that naval aviation was a career. You were a naval officer first, and naval aviation came along as kind of a specialty.

Q: Collateral duty.

Admiral Ramage: Exactly. Collateral duty. Whereas when you moved into the SAC squadrons, you knew darn well that they were professional aviators, and they behaved in that manner. Sometimes they were a little bit overwhelming in some things, but I was a great admirer of SAC and also Curtis LeMay.[*]

I'd like to tell a little story about Curtis LeMay. The bomb wing commander down at Biggs Air Force Base, which was at El Paso, was a friend of my boss up at Albuquerque, an Air Force colonel. The wing commander wanted him to fly up to Omaha with him to see General LeMay.[†] Any time there was an accident in a bomb wing, the wing commander reported to LeMay post haste. The next day they came back, and everything was very quiet. Finally the general went back to Biggs, and I asked my boss what went on. He said, "Well, the wing commander went in to see Curtis LeMay, and LeMay told him that if there was another accident in his wing, he'd better be in it, and he'd better be dead." That gets your attention!

Q: We're jumping ahead probably a couple of years here, but it's probably not widely known that LeMay was actively recruiting naval aviators to transfer to SAC. How big a program was that?

Admiral Ramage: That had taken place long before.

---

[*] General Curtis E. LeMay, USAF, served as Commander in Chief of the Strategic Air Command from 19 October 1948 to 30 June 1957. He was a lieutenant general until 29 October 1951. The original title was Commanding General, changed to Commander in June 1953 and changed to Commander in Chief in April 1955.
[†] SAC headquarters were at Offutt Air Force Base, near Omaha, Nebraska.

Q: Oh, it had?

Admiral Ramage: Yes. I had an approach from General McKee, who was Assistant Vice Chief of the Air Force, in about 1947.[*] He indicated that there was a place for me and for others. The procedure would be that I would resign from the Navy, go into the Air Force Reserve as a major, and then the following year he indicated that I would become a full colonel in the regular Air Force. I know of maybe two other people that were so approached. I don't know anybody else. I'll have to say that it was very interesting to me, but also at the same time there was an interest in the Navy to try to fight this by saying, "Look, you do have a career in the Navy as a naval aviator."

Q: The first B-52 crash. That was Pat Fleming.[†]

Admiral Ramage: Pat Fleming. Pat was the only other guy that I knew that had a direct approach. I heard that there were others, but I knew that Pat had been asked, and Pat went in. But, yes, that happened previously, and as far as I know, at the time that we're talking about, there was no great effort to get any Navy pilots into SAC. As a matter of fact, they were so professional that they really didn't need us.

Just after I reported in, I got my first warning from my immediate boss, whose name was George Jumper. He was a colonel in the Air Force and a West Point graduate, class of '39.[‡] He was a fine officer. One night, after we'd had a few drinks, he said, "I understand that you're a hotshot, and you've been sent over here to fight the Air Force."

I said, "No, whether I'm a hotshot or not is a matter of question. I was sent over here to try to expedite the Navy in the bomb business. As far as I'm concerned, I'm basically interested in getting the light weapons delivery capability." I also added, "As far as my doing my job over here in this joint command, you'll find that I can be as joint as

---

[*] Major General William F. McKee, USAF, Assistant Vice Chief of Staff.
[†] Colonel Patrick D. Fleming, USAF, had graduated from the Naval Academy in the class of 1941 and subsequently transferred to the Air Force. He was killed 16 February 1956 neary Tracy, California, in the first accident involving a B-52, the large Boeing jet bomber that entered active service in the 1950s.
[‡] Colonel George Y. Jumper, USAF.

anybody else as far as supporting the Strategic Air Command." I didn't have any more problems at all as far as the Air Force was concerned.

The big problem with the Mark 7 was that it was relatively inefficient as far as an implosion weapon was concerned. Every time we tried to put pressure on expediting the Mark 7, SAC--and, to a certain extent, the Navy, because the Navy was in the same category--would say that the nuclear material was so scarce that the bigger the weapon, the bigger the bang. They didn't emphasize the ability to carry the weapons externally. The Navy's priority at that time was Mark 5 and Mark 6, and somewhere down the line, Mark 7. So our problem was to try to see if we couldn't get the Navy to jump on the Mark 7 and get it into the fleet.

Q: Was weapons procurement a problem at this time? Any idea of annual production, anything like that?

Admiral Ramage: Yes, I know what the production was because I counted stockpiles. But we had a lot of bombs then.

Q: So there were enough bombs to hang on airplanes.

Admiral Ramage: Oh, yes. It was in the several hundreds. So there wasn't that problem. But you could say that they were right insofar as the nuclear material, which was relatively scarce. But certainly the ability to deliver, particularly by the Navy, was not emphasized at all by the people in OP-36, which was the OpNav office that had responsibility for nuclear weapons.[*]

About that time I contacted Jack Sloatman, who was one of the smartest naval officers that I ever knew.[†] He was a commander working for the Sandia Corporation in their analysis division. He was working for a Dr. Ted Youngs, who was on loan to the Sandia Corporation by the University of Indiana, where he had the mathematics chair, so he

---

[*] OpNav refers to the large extended staff of the Chief of Naval Operations.
[†] Commander John K. Sloatman, Jr., USN.

was a pretty high-level mathematician. We talked at length over this nuclear efficiency problem, and Dr. Youngs said, "This should be no problem. If you can indicate a lower CEP or error in delivery, I can certainly prove that the Mark 7 is not an inferior weapon. As a matter of fact, I think I can prove that it's definitely better off than dropping this bomb from 40,000 feet when the miss distance would be so great." So they went to work on this study, which ultimately became yield versus accuracy.

In the meantime, I was keeping contact with both AirLant and AirPac, basically in trying to get the three big carriers going in the weapons business with the big weapons, but also doing a little selling, pointing out that the light weapons were possible. Over at AirPac, of course, they didn't have any CVBs, so they were really straining to get some kind of capability.

On one of my trips I took Lieutenant Doyle Stone, who was a mustang officer and very bright.* He was located in one of the special weapons assembly teams that went out on the carriers to give us the operational capability. He also was very interested in the Mark 7 weapon. In discussing future plans there with AirPac, Doyle said, "You know, we could bring a Mark 7 weapon--of course it would be an inert one, but with the full electronic gadgetry on it--over here and assemble it on any carrier you want. We could load it and give you an emergency capability." This went over like gangbusters, of course, with AirPac, so we went back over and Doyle laid out how it was to be done. He'd been chief engineer on the Yorktown, which is now a museum.†

He had picked up a machine shop on the aft side port on the hangar bay. He said it would be completely adequate for assembling and wringing out a Mark 7. We would load an AD aboard, and he would take the bomb right through from stockpile configuration to loading. They were very happy about it in AirPac and immediately announced to OpNav that they had an emergency capability. This didn't go over at all well in OP-36. As far as they were concerned, I think one of the problems was that they were afraid that if we gave

---

* Lieutenant Doyle L. Stone, USN. "Mustang" is Navy slang for a former enlisted man who has risen through the ranks to become an officer.

† The aircraft carrier Yorktown, which at various times carried the hull numbers CV-10, CVA-10, and CVS-10, was decommissioned on 27 June 1970 and placed in mothballs. In June 1975 she was towed to Charleston, South Carolina, to become the centerpiece of a naval memorial named Patriot's Point. She was formally dedicated in that role on 13 October 1975, the U.S. Navy's 200th birthday.

an emergency capability to these carriers that perhaps the full capability that was coming along later might not be funded. On the other hand, there was still a lot of reticence on the part of the heavy attack mind that ruled in OP-36--that perhaps we were somehow impinging upon the heavy attack wing. But other than being told by several people in Washington that the emergency capability in AirPac went over like a lead balloon, nothing really happened. What later happened, though, was that Sloatman and Youngs completed their study of yield versus accuracy, and we gave it to Admiral Trapnell. Trapnell replaced Dave Young as the senior naval officer present.

Q: This is Fred Trapnell.

Admiral Ramage: Fred Trapnell, the famous test pilot.[*] He was great. And in turn, Dave Young went to be executive assistant to the Secretary of the Navy, so this opened the road down to being able to do something about this light weapon.

Admiral Trapnell concurred completely, as you might guess. Of course, he had flown the F2H and the AD. In spite of the fact that he was reasonably old at that time, he was still pretty darn current in airplanes.[†] He liked them. So in turn I contacted Commander Steve Morrison, who was in OP-05. I think he was the executive assistant to OpNav 05, DCNO for Air, and told him that we had this study that I thought the people there ought to get. And perhaps the people in OP-36 ought to hear it, too, because it really indicated that the Navy had a great potential right in their hands if we just did it with the Mark 7 weapon.

We went in and gave the presentation to relatively junior people there. I don't think there was any rank over a captain. I don't think anybody from OP-36 even attended. The people in the aviation business understood it right away, but that didn't mean that they could do anything about it.

---

[*] Rear Admiral Frederick M. Trapnell, USN. On 21 April 1943, when he was a captain, Trapnell made a flight in the Bell XP-59A jet Airacomet at Muroc, California--the first jet flight by a U.S. naval aviator.
[†] Trapnell was born 9 July 1902.

That afternoon Jack Sloatman and I and Ted went in to see Captain Dave Young, who at that time was the executive assistant to SecNav, and told him we had the study.[*] Ted ran through it, and Dave said, "I think the Secretary would like to hear this."

And we went right into it. The Secretary said, "I think we're going in the wrong direction. I want Admiral Fechteler [who was the CNO at that time] to get this right away."[†] He had his aide call Fechteler, and he said, "You have got to get this." This was about 5:00 or 6:00 o'clock in the afternoon. So they set us up to go in there first thing in the morning to give this presentation to the Chief of Naval Operations.

We were in there bright and early, and the CNO was waiting. As a matter of fact, he was in the chair getting a haircut. The barber was in the CNO's office, and Fechteler was kind of a rough guy, and he said, "What's so goddamned important that you guys have to come here so early in the morning?"

So Ted Youngs gave the presentation. I was simply the front man. Ted, who was the Ph.D. mathematician, spoke with authority. What it was based on was simply the fact that the yield only went up as the cube root--the blast damage decreased by the square of the bombing error. So if you came closer to the target, you were doing far more damage than you could with a hell of a big bang off but considerable error. A very simple thing, and he had curves to prove it.

The thing that really sold Admiral Fechteler was something Youngs said when he got through. He said, "In India, where I was raised, we have an old saying that he who passes the loudest wind does not necessarily have the biggest set of testicles." And Fechteler thought that was wonderful. He said, "I understand that completely." He said, "It's just like a Marine with a rifle, shooting a guy in the forehead, it's just as effective as a 16-inch shell going off 100 yards from the guy." Fechteler hit it right on the head. That was it. He said, "I think this is important. Would you put this study into a form that I can pass around OpNav? Because I think that we've got something here."

---

[*] Dan A. Kimball served as Secretary of the Navy from 31 July 1951 to 20 January 1953. Captain David B. Young, USN, was his executive assistant.
[†] Admiral William M. Fechteler, USN, served as Chief of Naval Operations from 16 August 1951 to 17 August 1953.

Apparently Admiral Fechteler didn't know that there was a light weapon potential, or at least he didn't know that it was within our grasp. As we left the chief's office that morning, I said, "Oh, boy, we're in trouble."

So I went in to OP-36 because I wanted to see Admiral Withington, who quite obviously hadn't kept the CNO advised of various developments in weaponry.[*] I didn't want to get him blindsided by the CNO. I went in to see him to make sure that he knew what was going on, because in due course there was going to be a great change in emphasis there in Washington. He wasn't in. So I talked to a captain in the office, and I told him exactly what had happened. I told him that there was bound to be some increased pressure from above on this Mark 7 weapon, and that I sure didn't want to have his boss be surprised by it. Whether he didn't tell his boss or whether he couldn't tell his boss or what happened, I'm not sure, but I'll tell you, when the explosion went off, the reverberation reached Albuquerque.

About a day or so later, I received a call from General Stranathan, who was a brigadier general in the Air Force, to see him immediately.[†]

Q: What was his position?

Admiral Ramage: He was commanding general of the field command of the Armed Forces Special Weapons Project. I presumed that it was something to do with our last visit, so I dropped by to see Admiral Trapnell on the way, and I said, "It looks like we've struck a nerve in Washington, and General Stranathan has sent for me."

Trap said, "Run through exactly what happened now." So I went through the whole procedure. I told him I was afraid that perhaps Admiral Withington had been caught up in this thing.

He said, "Don't you go in there. I'll go in to see General Stranathan." So he went in. In about 15 minutes he came out, and first of all, he said, "I think that you and Jack

---

[*] From 1949 to 1951 Rear Admiral Frederic S. Withington, USN, served as Assistant Director of the Atomic Energy Division in the Navy Department. He was director of the division, 1951-52. His oral history is in the Naval Institute collection.
[†] Brigadier General Leland S. Stranathan, USAF.

Sloatman have a very short time left in Albuquerque. As a matter of fact, your stay here has become somewhat tenuous."

What had happened, he explained, was that Admiral Withington apparently went directly in to CNO's office, obviously unwarned, and Admiral Fechteler had had a piece of him. Withington had gone back to his office and called Army General Graham, who was chief of the whole Armed Forces Special Weapons Project in Washington, and said, "You've got two Navy commanders working for you down in Albuquerque. They think they're setting Navy policy. If you think that's the way to do it, you come on up and sit in my office here and run it." Hence, the call from Graham to Stranathan. However Trap was able to save me, as I completed a normal tour of duty.

Jack got immediate orders to CinCLantFlt and became Admiral Lynde McCormick's nuclear planner, and he did a fine job there.[*] Admiral Trapnell told me that I could look around for a job and that he would guarantee that I got what I wanted. I said, "I want an air group."

He said, "You go on in, and I'll call the people in OP-54 and tell them that you'll be leaving here shortly."

Q: It's nice to be able to pick and choose.

Admiral Ramage: And to have such support.

Q: Can we talk a little bit about who developed the method of delivery for the small weapons being externally carried, and what methods were considered? Do you have any knowledge on that?

---

[*] Admiral Lynde D. McCormick, USN, served as Supreme Allied Commander Atlantic and Commander in Chief Atlantic Fleet from 1951 to 1954.

Admiral Ramage: As we went along, as I mentioned previously, Tom Walker was doing the separation tests, that is, the shapes from the two aircraft there at his outfit over at Kirtland Air Force Base. At one time we went to Norfolk, contacted Admiral Entwistle, who in turn set up VX-5, which was to be charged with developing the tactics for the fleet use of the nuclear weapons. Tom Walker then became the first skipper of VX-5, so I would say that that whole process was due to the success of Commander Tom Walker at that time. So with Admiral Trapnell's clearance, I went into Washington. At that time OP-54 did the detailing. It hadn't been moved over to BuPers at that time. Later I was told in OP-54 that I was going to get Air Group Six, which was on the East Coast.

Q: What time period is this?

Admiral Ramage: This is now 1952. I told them that I felt that I should go west because the war was going on, and they said, "Yes, but you have this nuclear knowledge, the CVBs are getting into the business in a big way, and you've been asked for by the Atlantic Fleet, and Air Group Six is attached to one of the CVBs, and that's where you're going."

Q: At this time we put all the CVBs on the East Coast.

Admiral Ramage: That's right.

Q: Was that because the perceived threat was strictly from the Soviets in Europe?

Admiral Ramage: Well, even during the Korean War, our major emphasis was in Europe. The Korean War was kind of a bastard child. It really wasn't popular, and all of the smart guys stayed in the Atlantic. Also it was a nice foxhole. The people who wanted to fight, which included a lot of reserves, I might say, fought the war in the Pacific.

Q: So basically things had not changed at all since early in World War II when the Allied powers decided that Europe had priority.

Admiral Ramage: That's correct. We still were pointing towards Europe all the way through the Korean War. After I left Washington, I went back to Albuquerque, of course, and ultimately flew back to San Diego to my old buddies in AirPac. Lou Kirn was in operations at that time, and I told him that I was leaving and indicated that I'd gotten Air Group Six on the East Coast.* And he said, "Hell, you're going the wrong way."

And I said, "I know it."

He said, "I've got vacancies for command of Air Groups Two, 11, or 19."

I said, "I'd like to have one of them."

He said, "I think I can arrange it for you."

I said, "Please be my guest," and they in turn, in AirPac, asked for me.

Q: Would there have been any security considerations of somebody with your nuclear knowledge flying in a combat zone?

Admiral Ramage: It became a point later on, and I know that it went through OP-36 and became a stick point for a while. I think that it was dropped. I think probably the people in OP-36 thought I was so stupid, it didn't make any difference.

Q: Maybe they thought they could get rid of you forever.

Admiral Ramage: That might be part of it.

Q: Anybody who wants to get shot at can't be all there.

Admiral Ramage: Yes. Well, I got immediate orders out of Albuquerque, but they were not to Air Group 19. They were to Fleet Airborne Electronics Unit Pacific, which was on North Island. This was devastating. Here I had an air group in hand on the East Coast, and they were sending me to FAETUPac.

---

* Captain Louis J. Kirn, USN.

Q: Did you even know what it was?

Admiral Ramage: I knew what it was. They were interested in airborne electronics. It wasn't my bag at all. What had happened was that AirPac in the Pacific Fleet had put in for a guy that was knowledgeable in nuclear weapons, and I was the only guy that was available. So I got ordered into that damn job out here. I was really wounded. Here I thought I had everything greased. So I reported in to FAETUPac. There was a Captain Hawkins in there, and I told him that I really felt I'd been screwed, that I thought I was getting Air Group 19.[*] And he said, "Well, we've been fighting to get this school going." As a matter of fact, his predecessor, Wes Byng, had put the finger on me to come on over there and work for him and set up this school.[†] He said, "I agree with you. This is bad." He also said, "If you can get a qualified relief, I certainly will let you go."

So I went over to the personnel department at AirPac, and we went through every possibility, and sure enough, there was one. Lieutenant Commander Charlie Carr had been in a Navy squadron and had been wounded; he was over in the hospital in Balboa.[‡] He had had a good nuclear background, been through the schools in one of the heavy attack squadrons, and he was acceptable as far as Hawkins was concerned. So I had that thing solved, and I had already negotiated to go to the Fleet Air Gunnery Unit in class number two, starting about the following week, so I felt as long as I had things rolling, I might as well hit hard. I told Captain Hawkins that that was fine, Carr was acceptable, but I wanted to depart next week for El Centro to go through the Fleet Air Gunnery School. He kind of shook his head and said, "You really want everything, don't you?"

I said, "Well, I've got to go through something," because I really was not jet qualified, just one or two flights in a jet, and I had to get some jet time somehow. There wasn't any other way to get it. I talked him into the idea that I would fly back on the weekends and check how the various people were setting up this class until Charlie Carr could report in.

---
[*] Captain Carson Hawkins, USN.
[†] Captain John Weston Byng, USN.
[‡] Lieutenant Commander Charles H. Carr, USN. Balboa Naval Hospital, San Diego, California.

He said, "Okay, go on over."

So about the first of November in 1952, I reported in to FAGU, and about the same time, Bill Elliott, who had been with me over in Albuquerque, reported in to go through the course in ADs.* We'd already figured out that he ought to get VA-195, so he was going through FAGU too. FAGU was probably the best Navy school I've ever been through, particularly considering the real shoestring they were operating under. I think they had not over 12 aircraft there and just a handful of people. They had six or eight instructors and were darn good. Boogie Hoffman, the skipper, had been an old ex-NAP in VF-2, and he knew gunnery.† It was really a real strip-down fly-all-day type of operation.

Q: What were you flying?

Admiral Ramage: F9F-5s.‡ I put four weeks in F9F-5s in gunnery and they went into some rocketry also. Then I put in two weeks in the ADs, because I wanted to be qualified in the high-altitude delivery of the nuclear weapons. So about six weeks later, which would put us about the middle of December, Bill Elliot and I headed up for Air Group 19.

Q: They were at Alameda at this time?

Admiral Ramage: They were in hangar two at Moffett Field. I relieved Commander Bill Denton as CAG of Air Group 19 in early December 1952, in hangar two, with all personnel present.* The uniform was blues. However, my uniforms hadn't arrived, so I relieved in greens and a garrison cap, which was completely out of uniform, but I think the younger aviators thought that this was pretty neat. They didn't particularly like to wear blues anyway.

---

* Lieutenant Commander August William Elliott, Jr., USN.
† Commander Melvin C. Hoffman, USN.
‡ The Grumman F9F-2 Panther was first delivered to an operational unit, VF-51, in May 1949. On 3 July 1950 the Panther became the first U.S. Navy jet ever used in combat. The F9F-5 model was 39 feet long; wing span of 38 feet; gross weight of 18,721 pounds; and top speed of 579 miles per hour. It was armed with four 20-millimeter guns.

Q: They knew they had a flying CAG.

Admiral Ramage: I hope so. I immediately went into the personnel situation, because we had a severe problem in the Navy at that time. We were transitioning from three prop squadrons and one jet squadron, in the air groups, to just the reverse, three jet squadrons and one prop squadron. The Navy had simply not kept up with the aircraft that were coming along, and they didn't have the trained people. What we had, in essence, was untrained people being trained by untrained people. And so consequently, we wanted to get a handle on where the good guys were.

Very fortunately the prospective skipper of VF-191 was Bob Elder, who again, like Trapnell, was one of the finest aviators of his time.[*] He knew not only tactics and aircraft, but he knew where the good aviators were. And we began to negotiate around to see if we couldn't do something about getting the best qualified people. Also my experience, again, in the personnel division of AirPac was of benefit, because they let me go back into the cards of the reporting in pilots there at AirPac. I don't think this was done by anybody else. I don't think anybody knew enough to do it. So I was able to thumb through the cards of people that were coming in, and try to pick out the people that looked like they would be the best qualified.

You've got to remember that the people coming in were basically non-voluntary-recall reservists. They may have been somewhat lackadaisical in some of the things they did, but they had good carrier operational backgrounds, and I would look for that type of guy, even though he was a little bit raunchy or radical, in preference to some of the other people who couldn't make their hands and feet work properly.

Q: Getting aboard the boat was a little more important than cutting your hair.

---

[*] Commander Robert M. Elder, USN.

Admiral Ramage: That's right. Yes. Bob Elder was able to dig up people like Ed Holley, Jeff Davis, Tiny Graning, and he got Al Shepherd right out of Patuxent River.[*] We got quite a number of other good pilots who were becoming available at that time, mainly because we could identify them.

The air group, the four squadrons, I mentioned Bob Elder, commander just out of Pax River, where he had done an outstanding job, was to take over VF-191. He's probably one of the best naval aviators I've ever known. They flew the F9F-6, which was the first swept wing they put on the carriers.

Concurrently, VF-24 was going into Cougars under Duke Windsor up in Air Group Two.[†] Fighter Squadron 192 was to be skippered by Lieutenant Commander John Dinneen.[‡] He was a second-tour pilot, who'd been exec before in 192. They were transitioning from F4Us into F9F-5s, which was a real fine airplane, much better than the other series that preceded it.

VF-193 was only a 12-plane squadron. It was to fly F2H-3s, the reason being that we would get the additional four F2H-3s from VC-3, which was across the field, when we deployed. VC-3 was supposed to provide the real night fighter capability, plus the F2H-3 was also in the nuclear weapons field. The Mark 7s were beginning to come along at that time. All the ADs were in nuclear weapons, so we ended up with probably about 36 to 38 aircraft that could carry nuclear weapons. Plus Bill Elliot in 195 was a real expert in the use of weapons. Bill had a 16-plane squadron which was augmented by the cats and dogs from VC-35 and also the early-warning outfit. So he had about 22 or 23 ADs that he was responsible for. It was a fine squadron with good leadership, and a very good cadre of people that knew how to fly.

I flew with VF-193 aboard ship. I flew all the other aircraft, but as the CAG, I felt that I had my hands full with my first jet cruise, just mastering one aircraft. The F2H-3 was

---

[*] Commander Edward B. Holley, USN; Commander Jefferson Davis, USN; Commander Leonard G. Graning, USN; Lieutenant Alan B. Shepard, Jr., USN. Shepard later became an astronaut and was the first American to go into space.
[†] Commander Robert W. Windsor, Jr., USN.
[‡] Lieutenant Commander John H. Dinneen, USN.

also a nuclear-capable aircraft, and if we were going to ever drop a bomb, I sure wanted to be one of the delivery pilots.

Q: Would you have had nuclear weapons training as part of your workup schedule?

Admiral Ramage: Oh, yes, and we accented it. We advertised it. I tried to get Doyle Stone, as an example, attached to the CAG's staff, to guarantee that we were configured correctly and so forth. I was turned down on it, but we were very heavy in the nuclear weapons business, I think probably more so than any other air group at that time, because we had the talent there. I think we had a real capability.

Q: Had the previous dilemma been solved about availability of weapons on an emergency basis such as you mentioned previously in AirPac?

Admiral Ramage: Yes, we were beginning to get carriers out with an assembly capability, and also, more importantly, General Eisenhower had relieved Truman as President of the United States.* One of the first things that he did was to permit the military to have control of the nuclear components.

Now, let's go into the same old thing. Remember we're talking about a nuclear capability, and we neither confirm nor deny the fact that . . .

Q: That they're aboard.

Admiral Ramage: That's right. Because that was the policy at that time and still is, but we certainly were working on the capability.

Q: What was the delivery method with the ADs and F2H-3s at that time?

---

* Dwight D. Eisenhower served as President of the United States from 20 January 1953 to 20 January 1961.

Admiral Ramage: We had both. We had the high altitude dive bombing attack and the loft, and we exercised at both of them. The reason we went into the loft capability, of course, was that we didn't have a lay-down weapon except for those very few Mark 8s, and so therefore we had to have an air-burst capability, because the Mark 7 would disintegrate it if it hit the ground. So you couldn't lay it down. So loft delivery was originated in order to get in with a low-altitude approach, which we felt that we had to have, and throw the bomb in the general direction of the target. It wasn't as accurate as a dive bombing delivery, but you could get the bomb on the target with it. Besides, it was fun to do.

Q: What kind of CEPs could you get with this thing?

Admiral Ramage: We figured about 1,500 feet, which was better than the high-altitude bombers, so we were in the ballpark with them.

Q: For a nuke, that ought to be fine.

Admiral Ramage: Yes.

Q: Air Force missed Bikini by a mile and a half.[*]

Admiral Ramage: In getting Air Group 19 ready for sea, one of the things that I wanted to guarantee was the group grope capability, the Alfa Strike, as better known at the present time, the deck-load launch. So we started out very early, maybe after six weeks, in combined operations in order to get the fighters and bombers going together. I think that's probably the earliest that any air group at that time ever tried to do it.

By the 15th of April, in briefing Admiral Ewen, I noticed that we were 29% through our syllabus with only one-sixth of the time used up.[†] So we were going along pretty well,

---

[*] In July 1946 a joint Army-Navy task force conducted tests at Bikini Atoll in the Marshall Islands to determine the effects of atomic bombs on moored warships. Along with an array of U.S. ships were captured German and Japanese warships.
[†] Rear Admiral Edward C. Ewen, USN.

and by that time Eddie Ewen, who had been a real hero of mine there on the old Enterprise, and I were getting along famously. I admitted to him at one time that I was lying, cheating, and stealing to get the best aviators, and he said, "Well, that's the way to do it." He said, "You know, it's better to be like Knute Rockne getting his football team with the best proselyting system that's available at that time, which was a Catholic church, rather than Alonzo Stagg building character over at the University of Chicago."* I took that as a kind of a plan for the future.

Q: What was Ewen?

Admiral Ramage: He was ComFAir Alameda, rear admiral. He was a great guy. In June we started our carquals aboard the Yorktown, and by the 19th of June, we were pretty well through.

Q: Out of curiosity, did you have any special feelings about landing aboard Yorktown the first time after--that was the ship you landed on in the Battle of the Philippine Sea, wasn't it?

Admiral Ramage: I kind of liked the idea. I had made my first jet landing on it. It's always been kind of--I also did my night quals on it in VC-3, so the Yorktown has been a good ship to me.

Q: You'd actually been away from carriers about eight years.

Admiral Ramage: From 1946 to 1952. I couldn't get a flying job. I was too well qualified. We completed our carquals for the whole group by the end of June, and our total accidents for the entire carquals were only two, actually one and a half. We had a broken wheel on a VF-191 landing. He scraped the wing at the same time. Whether this was pilot error, I don't remember. We got a barrier in VF-192, F9F-5. Qualification on a straight-deck

---

* Knute Rocke, head football coach at Notre Dame University from 1918 to 1931, was one of the most successful college football coaches in history. Amos Alonzo Stagg, in addition to the character-building, won 314 games in his long career that ended when he was 89.

carrier at that time, with that load of aircraft was not easy. I had an excellent landing signal officer, Roy Farmer.* Maybe you've heard of him. VF-193 and VA-195 went through all the carquals without a blown tire. This, of course, made both Admiral Ewen and Admiral Beauty Martin down at ComAirPac, sit up and take notice, because they were just having terrible times with carrier operations, mainly because of the fact that we were transitioning so many people into jets who simply didn't have the background to do it.†

We completed our training and went through the final debriefing with Admiral Ewen up at ComFAir Alameda, and he was very flattering. He said he thought that we had the best air group that had gone through training during his tenure there. I again pointed out that it was people; I thought that I had the best people available, and add to that first-class maintenance.

Q: Was maintenance a problem with the jets as far as experienced mechanics, that sort of thing?

Admiral Ramage: No, not really, not with those very simple jets because the maintenance of the jet engine is really simple.

Q: What about some of the other systems?

Admiral Ramage: Well, the F2H-3, of course, was an all-weather fighter, and as such, our radars weren't really peaked, but everything was pretty much a VFR operation at that time. We had the special teams that were supposed to take care of the night work, as you recall. VC-3 had the night fighters, VC-35, the night attack. Although we emphasized it, they were supposed to be the specialists.

---

* Lieutenant Roy E. Farmer, USN.
† Vice Admiral Harold M. Martin, USN, served as Commander Air Force Pacific Fleet from 1 April 1952 to 1 February 1956.

We reported in to the under way training unit out at Pearl at that time, and got ready for our ORI.* I'll look at some of my notes here on the critique, which was on the fifth of October, 1953.

Q: This is on Oriskany.

Admiral Ramage: This is on Oriskany.† I might talk a little bit about Oriskany before we go on. It was really a fine ship, and I was in a real nice position because the former CAG apparently had been a real horse's ass. As P. K. Blesh, the exec, said, "You guys are so good compared to what we had last time, even if you crapped on the quarterdeck, we'd still like you."‡ So it was kind of like shooting fish.

Q: Who was the skipper?

Admiral Ramage: Don Griffin.§ I would say that if I ever followed anybody on how to run a carrier, I'd follow Captain Don Griffin. He just went all out for the air group. We liked the ship and the ship liked us. It was a good combination.

Q: How long were you aboard?

Admiral Ramage: We were aboard about ten months. The debriefing, by Captain Vieweg, at ComFAir Hawaii, was quite flattering.** He was an ordnance guy, and he was quite pleased that we were so good around the target.

---

* ORI--operational readiness inspection.
† USS Oriskany (CVA-34) was an improved Essex-class aircraft carrier, commissioned 25 September 1950. She had a standard displacement of 33,000 tons, was 888 feet long, 93 feet in the beam, and had an extreme width of 148 feet. Her top speed was 33 knots. She had eight 5-inch guns and could accommodate approximately 90 aircraft.
‡ Commander Paul K. Blesh, USN.
§ Captain Charles Donald Griffin, USN, commanded the Oriskany from June 1953 to August 1954. The oral history of Griffin, who retired as a four-star admiral, is in the Naval Institute collection.
** Captain Walter V. R. Vieweg, USN.

Q: He'd been skipper of Gambier Bay.*

Admiral Ramage: Yes. Also, he came from NOTS Inyokern.† He said that we were outstanding in the quality of strikes and we made most of our money around the target. He said it was the most effective air group around the target that he'd seen. Our landings on the ship were good, but our intervals were poor, which we accepted. We had no air control at that time. We were still running a VFR deck, of course, with a flat pass, because it was a straight deck. Consequently, we needed a lot of improvement in timing. Everything was pretty much handled as it was in the old props.

A special weapons operation was particularly noted, as it should have been, no deficiencies, overall grade of the ship was good, which is standard.‡ The air group was excellent, bordering on outstanding. As far as I know, they just didn't give outstanding, but anyway, they liked us, and they made recommendations that we have a better call-down system for our jets, which we were aware of, and better CIC group coordination; we were aware of that. We just hadn't gone into that yet in the carriers. We just didn't know about handling jets and how to keep the landing pattern full, which again is part of control, which was a ship function.

I might tell one little anecdote about that time. It was one of the most embarrassing things that ever happened to me. During the ORI, we operated both off the ship and off the base at Barbers Point. We would often take off the ship and do gunnery exercises, land at the base, refuel, try to do something else, and land at the ship so that they could exercise more of everything simultaneously. I was on a gunnery hop, and we landed at Barbers Point. It was an expedited refueling situation, because we had our landing time back at the ship, and you know the worst crime you can ever do is to be late back at the boat.

When we got ready to go, there was an F2H that they hadn't refueled, so I told the flight that I would take that one. I think we had eight Banshees on this flight. I would take

---
* The escort carrier Gambier Bay (CVE-73) was sunk on the morning of 25 October 1944, during the Battle of Leyte Gulf, while Captain Vieweg was in command. She was the victim of close-range gunfire from Japanese cruisers.
† Naval Ordnance Test Station at Inyokern, California.
‡ "Special weapons" is a term sometimes used for nuclear weapons.

the unrefueled plane, because the ship was just offshore. There would be no problem, even though I was low on fuel, about 3,500 pounds. So we took off and Murphy was alive and well.* The ship had gone out through the channel between Oahu and Molokai and was operating on the other side, where the wind was stronger. Well, that wasn't too bad. As Murphy will tell you, things can go wrong.

Somehow the next takeoff was slow, so I found myself up over the ship low on fuel, but I was certainly not going to admit that I started out low because that would be most embarrassing. I thought things would work out, and it was a good, clear day, so we could see what was going on down there on the ship. I got to the position where I was at the point of no return, that I didn't have enough fuel to go back to Barbers Point or to Kaneohe, and, of course, there was no field on Molokai at that time, not even a dry strip. So I got myself to the point where I was going to have to land on the ship. I was committed. I didn't want to call down to the ship and tell them that I had a fuel emergency. I thought things would work out.

Pretty soon, the old red light began to bob, which indicated that I was down to 1,000 pounds. Nothing was happening down there. I was watching. It was clear enough at 20,000 feet where we usually orbited, I could see what was going on down there. Very slowly I could see that ship turn into the wind, and I thought, "Well, it's going to be close, but I'll keep my mouth shut here because, you know, if you have an emergency on a straight deck carrier, you've got to push everything forward and then pull everything back to get ready to go again," and I sure didn't want to cause that.

So finally they begin to take off. I've never seen a slower takeoff in my life. About that time I eased back on my throttle and began to take my flight down, you know, easing on down in the pattern, spirals, using no fuel whatsoever, just barely cruising along. About that time I was down to maybe 300 or 400 pounds or less, and I could see that the last plane was about to be launched. I came in for a straight-in approach and zinged it right into the arresting gear and taxied forward, and the other planes followed. God, it was a beautiful recovery. I went on up to see the captain, and he said, "That is just the way we've got to operate these aircraft. You were right on the button there."

---

* Murpphy's so-called law, "If something can go wrong, it will."

I said, "Thank you very much, Captain," and left the bridge. This is the first time I've ever told anybody about this stupid action. I guess after 32 years I'm safe.

I went down to the ready room, and I think there was only one guy that knew that I was sweating it out up there, and that was Al Shepherd, who had my second section. I think he looked at me and laughed a little bit. I don't think the other pilots were bright enough to know that I was really sweating the thing out.

Q: Now it can be told.

Admiral Ramage: Now it can be told. Shortly thereafter, we departed for WestPac and arrived there in early October. We debriefed from the Lake Champlain. It was a question of getting the strike frequencies and all that business squared away. The carriers were retained in the Sea of Japan simply to provide presence, I think. There apparently was still some kind of negotiating going on, and the President didn't want to stand down immediately from the war.

Q: The cease-fire had gone into effect July 23.

Admiral Ramage: During our stay in port, half of the air group flew off and was based at Atsugi, which went on all during that cruise, in order to try to keep some kind of readiness in weapons.* We were able to put half of them up at Atsugi, and that was a real blessing to us. During the time half of the group was off the ship, Oriskany got under way for carquals for our AJ detachment. They went out one day and were back the next. The detachment had made a very feeble effort, whether it was the first or second landing, the pilot hard-landed and detached both engines from the wings.

Q: Common in the AJ.

---

* Atsugi is the site of a U.S. naval air station, not far from the naval base at Yokosuka, Japan.

Admiral Ramage: And Captain Griffin simply turned around and came back to Yokosuka. I was talking to him about it later. I said, "Captain, you don't have to worry about the nuclear capability. We've got 36 planes that can be configured, and we've got at least 40 pilots that are trained in nuclear weapons delivery. I also can tell you that they're more apt to get into the target area than the AJs, so please don't worry about it."

Q: What was the background of the AJ crews? Did they tend to be VP people?*

Admiral Ramage: At the time that the AJ program started in 1947-48, it was supposed to be half and half, and there were some pretty good carrier pilots that went with it, such as Eddie Outlaw and Birney Strong.[†] But as the bloom wore off the program, the carrier pilots had a tendency to try to avoid it. As a matter of fact, when I was in Albuquerque, Paul Ramsey, who was ComHAtWing 1 asked me if I wouldn't like to have one of the AJ squadrons, and I said, "Paul, I'm scheduled to get an air group, and I think I'd rather have it."[‡]

And Paul said, "I don't blame you."

Yes, there were only a few really gung-ho carrier aviators that I knew that were out at Atsugi detachment at that time, one of them being Norman McInnis.[§] When I saw him in that VC detachment, I asked him what a nice carrier guy like him was doing with these other people. He said, "Just lucky, I guess." But they had a tendency to go towards the VP. As a matter of fact, the skipper of the detachment that came out to qualify was a classmate of mine named Ronald Stultz, and he'd been VP all the way.[**] I think he was the pilot of that airplane. They were very much looked down upon in the carriers. If you had a dud AJ on a 27 Charlie, you know, straight deck, you had a real deck problem.[††] You just plain had to go home.

---

* VP--patrol planes.
[†] Commander Edward C. Outlaw, USN; Commander Stockton Birney Strong, USN.
[‡] Captain Paul H. Ramsey, USN.
[§] Lieutenant Norman K. McInnis, USN.
[**] Lieutenant Commander Ronald F. Stultz, USN.
[††] The designation 27C was used to designate a package of modernization items to update the Essex (CVA-9) class carriers. Later modification included the installation of an angled landing deck.

Q: The AJs were actually based at Atsugi and would operate off the on-station carriers.

Admiral Ramage: That's correct. If they ever did. I never saw any operate.

Q: I think they just came out for CQs, is the only thing I've heard of.*

Admiral Ramage: I never saw one in the Sea of Japan. They went out, like Griffin took his bunch out, just to see if they could be warmed up.

While we're on this nuclear thing, and I can't define the time because it doesn't seem to concur with anything that happened, but at about that time, we were told--and I can't define by whom--to stand by for a nuclear strike.

Q: This was when?

Admiral Ramage: This would probably be in October, which is why I can't understand why at this time, because the prisoners were all out.

Q: That's three months after the war ended.

Admiral Ramage: Yes. So I can't put my finger on the reason. But, in any event, I never saw a directive on this, but I was told, I guess by the skipper, to stand by. Of course, having all the talent that we had in nuclear knowledge, we went along and weaponeered the whole strike, I think, maybe 10 or 12 nukes. We were probably whistling in the dark, but anyway, we thought we were prepared to go. We picked the crews; we had everything ready. One item about picking the crews, the skipper of the VC-3 detachment, which was F2Hs that were working with VF-193, came to me and said that one of his guys had come to him saying that he'd like to be excused from the strike because he didn't feel that he could morally drop an A-bomb.

---
* CQs--carrier qualifications.

I said, "Well, I suggest you send the pilot in to see me and tell him to have his wings in hand, because he's going to present them to me." I don't know whether I could have actually done it, but I certainly would have tried. That was the end of that subject, and, of course, after a day or so this whole thing just passed away. I have no idea what the reasoning behind it was, and I can't seem to tie it in with anything that went on at that time in history.

Q: Would you like to discuss any further your personal feelings or philosophy of the moral aspect of the nuclear weapons?

Admiral Ramage: As far as I'm concerned, I'd drop it. If the President said go, I'd go. And I think that the other pilots who were involved and everybody else on the carrier would have carried out the mission.

Q: Obviously the end result is identical, dead bodies, and what difference does the weapon make?

Admiral Ramage: That's my feeling, that if anybody is involved in killing people, preferably the enemy, he can't let his feelings overrule his duties.

Q: 'Tis more blessed to give than receive.

Admiral Ramage: Our times at sea, which were entirely in the Sea of Japan, were not unpleasant. We did operate over South Korea. We flew in and out. The only thing that I can remember markedly about that winter is the damn cold. The Sea of Japan is no place to operate during the winter months if you can help it.

Q: You had a rather spectacular ramp strike that had kind of a humorous aspect.

Admiral Ramage: Yes.

Q: Would you like to tell that story?

Admiral Ramage: Yes. The pilot was a reserve lieutenant named Frank Repp, from Glenview, Illinois.* He got low in the groove and hit the ramp right smack in the middle of the fuselage.

Q: This is an AD?

Admiral Ramage: F2H-3. Part of the fuselage, including the two engines, and Frank came rolling up the deck. The tail went down into the spud locker, and there were flames shooting 200 or 300 feet in the air. I mean, this was obviously a fatality. I was up on the bridge at the time, and it was really a screamer. Imagine my surprise when about three minutes later the pilot, Frank Repp, comes walking up on the bridge. I said, "Frank, were you in that airplane?"

He said, "Sure. Pretty colorful, wasn't it?"

Well, we got him in the air in the next flight, which we did at that time. I think nowadays they send everybody down and hold their hands for a little while, but we got him in the air just as soon as possible afterwards.

As I mentioned previously, Captain Don Griffin gave us an excellent cruise, and it was a pleasant cruise from almost all aspects. We had hardly any accidents, and we had a good time while we were there. One of the stories I like to tell about Captain Griffin had to do with a heads of department meeting one evening. The exec, Commander Blesh, held the meeting in his cabin. The doctor, a commander, claimed that the air group was harboring venereal disease and that they were treating themselves, and that this was a very bad thing. He wanted to hold a short-arm inspection for the air group. I didn't think this was a very good idea, so I said, "Well, Commander, you hold the short-arm inspection and I'll be first in line."

---

* Lieutenant Frank J. Repp, USNR.

I went up on the bridge shortly thereafter and told the captain this. I thought it was rather humorous. He said, "No, you won't be first in line; I'll be first in line." That was the end of the short-arm inspection.

Another rather comical thing that happened almost caused a heart attack for the exec. We were getting under way out of Yokosuka one time, and we decided to really pull one on him. The captain was coming down for evening meal in the wardroom, and we always tried to put something special on when he came down. This was quite special. VF-192 had a young Japanese-American boy in the squadron, and their ready room was in the forward part of the wardroom. So unbeknownst to the exec, we put this Nisei boy into civilian clothes and hung a lot of clothes in the front end of the wardroom. He hung a tape measure around his neck and had two or three people in there getting measured for suits. It appeared that one of the tailors was staying aboard for the cruise. So we were all set.

The exec, P. K. Blesh, brought Captain Griffin in the wardroom, and P. K. was absolutely astounded. He looked at me, and he didn't know what to say. Finally, after two or three minutes, I got it across to him. I said, "P. K., it's a joke. It's a joke." God, he was just about going wild until he got calmed down. The captain, of course, was laughing like hell at him. P. K. turned to me and said, "Don't ever do that again to me. That's the worst thing that ever has happened." He said, "I almost died."

Another rather comical thing occurred with Griffin. Bill Elliot and I, in particular, used to go up on the bridge and talk to him because he'd been a test pilot and was very friendly, and we liked to tell sea stories. We were about to fly off before we went into port at Atsugi. The captain said to me, "Jig, I think it would be a good idea if you stayed with me on the ship because some day you're going to be skipper of one of these carriers, and you're going to have to know how you enter port and how we dock the ship."

I said, "Well, Captain, you know, I'm the air group commander, and at least half of the air group is flying ashore, and I've got to be in the lead."

So then he turned to Bill Elliot and said, "Bill, you're going to do the same thing one of these days. Why don't you come on in with me. The <u>Lake Champlain</u> is in the dry dock over there. It had an accident and she's got a bent shaft. We'll go down and take a look at it."

Bill Elliot said, "Captain, I'm not much of a shaft man myself."

And Griffin said, "Both of you, get the hell off my bridge."

I've been asked many times about fear. That is, fear of going into combat, fear of flying, and so forth, and I don't know of ever having any fear. A good carrier pilot certainly is apprehensive. He has those two or three nervous pees before he gets in the catapults, particularly for a night launch, and in combat he obviously is going to try to do everything he can not to be shot down, but to me, fear means that you actually lose control of yourself and you can't react properly. And as far as that is concerned, I don't think that I ever had any real fear. However, I did have one incident that really was a terrifying one.

I remember the date very well because it was the Ides of March of 1954. We were at sea doing a joint exercise with the fleet flagship, which was the Wisconsin at that time. It was to be a pre-dawn launch with a dawn strike on the Wisconsin. The weather was absolutely terrible. In the Sea of Japan I hadn't seen weather like that. We were not in the Sea of Japan; we were operating just to the south. That night I went to the skipper and told him that I thought that we ought to cancel out the F9F-6s and the F9F-5s because the ADs and the F2H-3s at least had some kind of an all-weather capability. And the skipper right away scratched them.

So we get on up in the morning for this pre-dawn launch, and it was one of those mornings that you know you're not going to go because only a fool would shoot anybody off into this blinding snowstorm. So I went up to my aircraft, finally finding it, which is not easy.

Q: What type of airplane?

Admiral Ramage: F2H-3. All the time, of course, I was going through the check off, but there was no way we would be launched. All of a sudden, wham!, and I was airborne--and I was airborne into a storm that was just impossible to believe. So I started climbing. In this flight Al Shepard was my wingman. We very carefully picked the people that we thought wouldn't kill themselves in this operation. I started climbing on through, and it was black. My windscreen began to freeze over to the point that I only had just a little hole up in the front to see out. I remember turning on the heat full bore. It was really cold. I wanted to get that ice melted off if there was any way possible.

We began climbing through and climbing and climbing, and, of course, the old Banshee didn't have much performance. I passed about 24,000 or 25,000 feet, and I remember very well I looked down at my gauge, and I was flying in about a 45% or 50% bank. I snapped it back up and reminded myself I'd better shape up, because we didn't want to spin in. I climbed about 2,000 or 3,000 feet more. In my ear was, "Nose down CAG, nose down, you're going in." I had apparently just completely passed out.

I snapped that old nose forward and tried to get myself organized, and gradually began to climb through. I think the overcast was maybe 29,000 feet. I had the greatest tendency to roll it on its back and just dive right back down into that storm. I was really confused. Of course, at the same time, I got sick, and if you've never been sick in a mask, you don't know the pleasure of it. So finally I got on top, and I was straight and level and I was beginning to make some sense, and Al was talking to me at the time. Of course, at that time we got word from the flagship that the strike had been canceled and that they were in zero-zero weather down there.

Q: Return immediately.

Admiral Ramage: So I was on top, and my flight was fine. We got all of our people up there. The ADs, of course, were going in low. They stayed down at 500 feet, so they didn't have this great pleasure of going back in the storm. What I was left with was whether I should turn the lead over to Al and fly wing on him, let him take us back down to the ship, or whether I'd better keep the lead and let Al keep talking to me. And I decided on the latter. I didn't know if I could fly decent wing under the situation, although my head was clearing up. So we got down to the ship uneventfully, back down through the snowstorm. It was a lot easier going down than coming up. I got down, began to get some air, and I began to feel pretty good.

When I got down, the ship was ready, and I snapped her right in there. Of course, I was pretty messy. I can remember very clearly telling the plane captain, "Don't you clean this thing up. I did it; I'll clean it."

So I went up to the skipper on the bridge, which I usually did after a flight. He looked at me and he said, "What happened?"

And I told him.

He said, "Boy, you're really lucky."

I went down to the ready room. By that time, they'd taken a look at the oxygen system on the airplane, and I had no oxygen the whole time I was up there, just cabin pressure the whole time, so I was really suffering from anoxia, but I think the intense heat that I'd turned on had much more impact upon me than the oxygen at that time. What that left me with, of course, was an understanding of a lot of these unexplained accidents that occur to people. You say everything is fine, the guy's a good pilot, he's safe, and so forth, and all of a sudden he disappears. And if it hadn't been for Al Shepard on that day, I wouldn't be here today, and I really thanked him when I got down. He really got me right through this thing.

We left Yokosuka in April of 1954 and returned to Alameda in May of 1954. I've got in my book here, hints for my relief: conduct car quals as late as possible, and emphasize contact with the deck. Those wooden decks on the Oriskany class with three jet squadrons really didn't last. The poor darn flight deck crew was changing planks all the time. They just weren't built to handle jets until they got the flash plating later. It was a real problem.

Q: You mentioned previously that before the war, we were primarily land-based squadrons that occasionally operated off of aircraft carriers. During the period of the Korean War, had this situation improved greatly, even slightly?

Admiral Ramage: They improved during World War II.

Q: But did we have any relapse after the war?

Admiral Ramage: No, no.

Q: We learned that you have to emphasize training in getting aboard carriers?

Admiral Ramage: That's correct. That weakness of the deck left us in quite a quandary, because on the straight-deck carrier, particularly with the F9F-6, getting aboard was rather difficult, and you almost had to wipe it out, that is, get a little nose over in order to land it. And I put down here not to dive for the deck, because the struts, particularly in the F2H-3, were so weak, you were going to put your wheels on up through the wings. So you had a proposition there where you didn't want to float into the barrier, although that was really no great problem. It didn't do much damage when a plane hit the barrier. We still had to watch out for the struts, particularly in the F2H-3, and also we had to watch out for the flight deck. We didn't want to knock it out of business. I think that probably handling those planes on that carrier was the most demanding of any carrier aviation that I've run into. Of course, then the angled deck came along, and the jets were really no great problem. I don't know how we got away with it on the straight decks.

I've also got a note to myself, "You are not aiding the individual or the Navy by retaining a weakling. Get rid of him early. He will only cause you trouble in the end." I don't recall what that was caused by, but I had said that before we left, that I thought that probably maybe one or two of the people had slipped through the squadron commanders, who were warned that I had no sympathy with a weakling on the ship. If we were going to operate first class aircraft, we certainly had to have first-class people.

Q: You mentioned earlier that you had a lot of recalled reservists at this time. Do you have any idea what the percentage was of recalled reserves, and where were the regulars?

Admiral Ramage: I would say that in Air Group 19, we had about 50% recalled reservists, and these were not people out of regularly organized squadrons. These were generally casuals. Some of these people hadn't flown for four or five years or six years.

Q: I think that point was brought out in The Bridges at Toko-ri, Lieutenant Brubaker.*

Admiral Ramage: Yes. Then let's say we had about 30% nuggets, people out of the training command.† The other 20% were regulars.

Q: Where were the rest of the regulars?

Admiral Ramage: Well, at that time the Atlantic Fleet was a fine foxhole. Only the Lake Champlain and the Leyte made it around to the war.

Q: Leyte, at the beginning of the war.

Admiral Ramage: That was the total participation of the Atlantic Fleet. It was a rather pathetic thing, and I think it had a great impact upon the Naval Air Reserve, because we had reserves going back two or even three times in the Korean War, and many, many regular naval officers that had never shown out there.

Q: Do you know what the percentages were in the Atlantic Fleet squadrons?

Admiral Ramage: They were much higher and much better qualified people.

Q: This raises a point I intended to cover during World War II, that being the effectiveness of the Naval Academy's preparation process for teaching people to lead men in combat. What's your overall impression? How effective or how useful was the Annapolis education in leading a wing or a squadron or an air group into combat?

Admiral Ramage: Let me comment first on what happened during Vietnam.

---

* This is a reference to James Michener's Korean War novel The Bridges at Toko-ri (New York: Random House, 1953), later made into a movie starring William Holden and Grace Kelly.
† Nuggets is a nickname for newly trained pilots, just reporting to their first operational fleet squadrons.

Q: All right.

Admiral Ramage: It was entirely different. Everybody got their shot at the Vietnamese War two or three times, regardless of who they were. The Atlantic Fleet foxhole no longer was in being. I think I mentioned this earlier about the Naval Academy system. I don't feel that they really emphasized combat very much. I don't recall it. I previously have mentioned how many aviators went to postgraduate school during the war, pointing out that the Navy system permitted it. On the other hand, these individuals shouldn't have requested it. And I have also mentioned that a lot of naval aviators went AEDO without going to postgraduate school, which is another foxhole. So I really can't answer the question, except to say that in my opinion, in the first two wars that I'm talking about, the Naval Academy was not a great plus, as far as providing replacement combat pilots. The reserves fought the war, in other words, and they'll let you know it every time.

Q: What about academy courses in leadership, generally?

Admiral Ramage: I don't remember any. I'm sure that there's been a great change at the Naval Academy recently, but I don't recall anything in leadership. And, of course, as I previously said, I was so close to being anchorman in grease that I wasn't considered to be an adequate leader, so maybe they didn't spend much time on me.

When we returned to the coast, I was asked to debrief Vice Admiral Beauty Martin at ComAirNavPac, and it was a very pleasant briefing because we had done well. I pointed out the same thing that I previously pointed out, that I had more than my fair share of the talent available. I think he agreed to that, but nevertheless, he was very pleased with what we'd been able to do with Air Group 19, plus the fact that we had a pretty unusual deck load there of F9F-6s, F9F-5s, F2H-3s, plus the ADs, which wasn't a good mix at all. He asked me if there was any great weakness that I noticed, and I said, yes, I thought that the VC-3 night fighter detachment was not up to where I would like to see it, and he kind of smiled a little bit.

He said, "How would you like to move across the field from hangar two to hangar one?" Which meant go over to VC-3. Of course, I was delighted at the opportunity.

What had happened was that the people in AirPac had decided that we had to set up some kind of a fleet training for the new aircraft that were coming in, and VC-3 was probably a good squadron to hang this training on. It was a large squadron of over 1,000 people. It provided the night detachments, F2H-3s, and it even had some F4Us at that time. It did have a permanent base at Moffett Field, good maintenance, and that it was decided to set up a transitional training unit there under VC-3.

The skipper of VF-24, Commander Duke Windsor, had made quite a successful cruise with the F9F-6s also, and I might say that Elder and Windsor were about the only people that were successful. The rest of the people were breaking up airplanes all over the place. The plan was that Duke would come over and be my exec, I would take over the F2H-3 and the whole unit, but Duke would spend a lot of time trying to set up this transitional training unit, which we called Project Checkout. So after quite a bit of negotiating, I went over there.

I had tentative orders to OpNav 05W in Washington, and Admiral Martin had to do everything possible to keep me from going to Washington at that time. There was quite an exchange of dispatches, pointing out that I was required, and all this business, and Washington saying that they needed a man of my capabilities, whatever that was, in Washington, and so forth. But being ComNavAirPac, Beauty Martin won. So I moved over. They said it was for only one year's time and I'd have to carry out my orders to OpNav. Of course, I was delighted with any job to keep flying.

The first thing that I did when I moved over there was to go to the skipper, who was Captain Dick Burns, and when I found him, finally . . .[*]

Q: He was skipper of Moffett?

---

[*] Captain Richard H. Burns, USN.

Admiral Ramage: VC-3. I hadn't relieved him yet. I said, "You've got a team qualifying out in Monterey Bay on a carrier. How about letting me fly out and shoot a couple of landings and see how they're doing?"

He said, "No, I wish you wouldn't do that."

I later found out why he wished I wouldn't do it was because he'd been aboard VC-3 for a year or two, and he had never made a carrier landing himself. As a matter of fact, I don't think he'd ever checked out in the F2H-3. He was a few years older; he was class of '35.[*]

I relieved him, and the first afternoon I perceived that what they needed was a shot in the ass. So my first order was, "Everything in the air this afternoon. I don't care what it is. We're all going to get in the air, and you're going to have a big parade over Moffett." I think we even had a couple of Beechcraft in the air.

Q: VC-3 had quite a mix of aircraft at that time, didn't they?

Admiral Ramage: Well, the F3D was just leaving.[†] They had had F3Ds, but the F3D was never used as a carrier plane, at least in the Pacific. We had the F4U, the N version. Was that the 5N?

Q: Yes.

Admiral Ramage: And the F2H-3, but that's about all we had. We had everything that flew up in one massive flight that afternoon and kind of pumped everybody up. They realized that they were going to really get into aviation and were going to be pressed. So we went on, first of all, to get the F2H-3 going, and I asked for help from Admiral Martin in that. I said, "There's nothing, getting some good people into the night-flying program won't help."

---

[*] Burns was born 12 January 1913. Ramage was born 19 July 1916.
[†] The Douglas F3D Skyknight was an all-weather jet fighter used by the Marines as a night fighter and for electronic countermeasures. It was first delivered to VC-3 in 1951. The plane's two-man crew of pilot and radar operator sat side by side. The F3D-2 version was 46 feet long, wing span of 50 feet, gross weight of 26,850 pounds, and top speed of 600 miles per hour. It had four fixed forward-firing 20-millimeter guns.

So I got a good look again at the cards of the incoming pilots into AirPac, and I nailed quite a few people who were scheduled for other units, to come in to night fighters. In the meantime, Duke Windsor was setting up his transitional training unit. He selected Lieutenant Commander Bud Sickel as the guy to run it, and it was a good choice.[*] Bud probably had more jet time than anybody in the Navy. He had an exchange tour in the Air Force and had been a Patuxent River test pilot, and was extremely well qualified for this job.

The idea of this unit was to take four pilots, preferably the senior four, that were coming in to one of these squadrons that was reforming and a cadre of maintenance people up to VC-3, and check them out in these airplanes. We're not talking about anything very great. We're talking about maybe 50 flight hours. In the maintenance crew, just basic understanding of the parts of the new aircraft, to give the oncoming squadrons better preparation for the new planes that were coming in. It really performed the same function that the old Air Group 98 did in World War II. They had decommissioned all these replacement air groups. VC-3 really was a training and replacement air group on a very small scale. Of course, later on the replacement air groups came back into effect in 1958, after the Navy realized that we just couldn't make this transition into these high-performance airplanes without some kind of a fleet training.

Q: Now, in 1958, were they actually replacement air groups, or were they the independent squadron structure such as we have now?

Admiral Ramage: It was the same thing as Air Group 98, a training squadron.

Q: Replacement air groups.

Admiral Ramage: Training, yes. In other words, you could get through your training in Pensacola or wherever you came from, but you hadn't done anything in high-performance aircraft, so consequently you were being placed into that same situation that I mentioned

---

[*] Lieutenant Commander Horatio G. Sickel, USN.

before, untrained people training untrained people. It was pretty bad in the 1953-54 period of time.

I didn't realize, among other things, how much we'd taken on, but I had good people. I didn't realize, first of all, that we were going to get into the Cutlass.[*] I thought that the Cutlass was dead.

Q: You probably would have gone to Washington if you had known.

Admiral Ramage: Well, it wasn't that bad. But one day I looked up and I saw six Cutlasses on the flight line. We got them out of the Project Cutlass, which had been set up by Bud Brown, who introduced the Cutlass to the fleet.[†]

Q: That was out at Miramar.

Admiral Ramage: At Miramar. And we got six aircraft and a cadre of maintenance people plus three pilots. The pilots were outstanding. We got Wally Schirra and Don Shelton, who made rear admiral, and Burt Shepherd, who also made rear admiral.[‡] They were very competent.

Q: They were all test pilots?

Admiral Ramage: No, I don't think any of them had been. I'm not sure where they came from, but they came from Brown's outfit, and they let me know in no uncertain terms when they came up there that they weren't fond of the Cutlass. I halfway promised them that if they'd do a good job with me, they'd never go to sea in a Cutlass.

---

[*] The Vought F7U Cutlass was a swept-wing jet fighter of an experimental design. It had two vertical stabilizers but no tail per se. It first entered the fleet in 1952. The F7U-3 version was 44 feet long, wing span of 39 feet, gross weight of 31,642 pounds, and top speed of 680 miles per hour. It had four fixed forward-firing 20-millimeter guns and provision for four Sparrow missiles.
[†] Lieutenant Commander James S. Brown, USN.
[‡] Lieutenant Walter M. Schirra, Jr., USN; Lieutenant Doniphan B. Shelton, USN; Lieutenant Burton H. Shepherd, USN. Schirra was one of the nation's first seven astronauts.

Again, the first thing that I had to do, as far as I was concerned, was to prove my value in night fighters, which, as you know, is not my bag at all. But I certainly wanted to be night qualified and be reasonably competent so that when I talked to a pilot that he at least knew that I was interested in the profession. I couldn't get night qualified immediately on the coast. The West Coast of the United States is the worst possible place to train. The weather is bad almost all the time. There's always fog out there, and at that time we really were a VFR Navy. So I made arrangements with Commander Spin Epes, who had Air Group 15 that was deploying right then on the Yorktown.* We would fly out to Pearl, do night car quals on the Yorktown, and then I would proceed out to WestPac and visit the various detachments on the ships that were out there. They had never had that, as far as I know, before, and were quite pleased when I showed up, somebody that really was interested. So I made I think it was six night car quals on the Yorktown. It was just a piece of cake, and I had a lot of fun doing it.

I came back from that tour to WestPac to find that Sickel had the transitional training unit or Project Checkout pretty well under control, and we not only had the F7Us aboard, but we were getting FJ-3s, and, of course, we had some F9F-6s, which really had been the problem that brought this whole situation to the attention of higher-ups.† We simply weren't ready to start operating these aircraft aboard ship.

I'll get into the Cutlass problem. I checked out in the first class. It wasn't a bad plane to fly, as long as everything worked. I can recall that one of the requirements was to go through Mach 1 with it. The only way you could do it was to point it straight down in after burner. I can recall that Wally Schirra followed me through this thing, and as I was going straight down in after burner, I was looking at the Mach meter, which was wavering. I don't think I ever got through Mach 1, but I told Wally that I got through it to make him happy, but it was a real problem to try to get that thing through Mach, unlike the FJ. You could put that through easy, but, of course, you still had to go straight down. The only

---

* Commander Horace H. Epes, USN.
† The FJ-1 Fury, built by North American Aviation, was the first jet fighter to go to sea operationally. The FJ-3 version was 38 feet long, wing span of 37 feet, gross weight of 18,000 pounds, and top speed of 650 miles per hour. It had four 20-millimeter guns. The Grumman F9F-6 Cougar was first delivered to operational units in November 1952. The F9F-5 model was 42 feet long; wing span of 36 feet; gross weight of 20,000 pounds; and top speed of 690 miles per hour. It was armed with four 20-millimeter guns.

problem with the FJ-3 was that it had wing warp, not going through Mach, but coming back out. As you pulled on out, you were going to roll one way or the other. You weren't really sure which way, but you had to stand by because you were going to do a couple of rolls before you could get yourself squared away. I don't know if the F-86 had that or not.[*] We sure had it in the FJ-3.

The thing that really brought the F7U-3 problem to our attention, so far as safety is concerned, was a young pilot who was in the program. He pulled it a little tight, somewhere up around 29,000, 30,000 feet. He got into a maneuver that just couldn't happen. To begin with, the handbook of the F7U-3 said that this plane will not spin. He had ridden it for maybe a few thousand feet, and he punched out, which Sickel didn't like at all. He said, "Goddamn it, you should have stayed with it longer." When they checked the regime he was operating in on the V/G diagram, Sickel decided that this just shouldn't happen.[†] So Bud decided to go up and check it himself.

He got Bob Baldwin, who ran the FJ-3 school for us, to follow him.[‡] So Bud was up there plotting points at about 30,000 feet. All of a sudden, the F7U let loose on him. He rode the thing down to 12,000 feet, and finally bailed out. It was kind of a bad bail-out, because he couldn't get rid of the seat right away, and he ripped a panel in the chute, and it was a rather hairy landing for him. When the best pilot, at least in my opinion, in the United States Navy couldn't get the goddamned thing out of this maneuver, that meant trouble.

So I sent a message immediately to AirPac, wanting Chance-Vought to come on out, including a test pilot, and tell us about this thing. He came out and we talked about the

. . .

Q: Who was the test pilot?

Admiral Ramage: I think Konrad. I'm not sure.

---

[*] F-86 was the designation of the Air Force version of the FJ.
[†] V/G—velocity/gravity, the velocity of the aircraft plotted against the centrifugal force in terms of gravity units
[‡] Lieutenant Robert B. Baldwin, USN, who eventually became a vice admiral, serving as ComNavAirPac and Chief of BuPers in the 1970s.

Q: John Konrad.

Admiral Ramage: Yes. He came out and we asked him about this maneuver. I said, "Look, your handbook says that this aircraft will not spin."

And he said, "That's right."

And I said, "Well, what do you call this?"

And he said, "We call that the post-stall gyration."

I said, "Did you ever get in it?"

He said, "Yes, I was in it once."

I said, "What did you do?"

He said, "I bailed out."

That didn't give us any great feeling, so immediately after this briefing, I went to AirPac and suggested that they ask Chance-Vought to continue the spin tests. Apparently the aircraft had never gone through a complete test. All that I can say about the F7U is that everything that was mentioned in the Patuxent report was true, and yet the airplane continued to be accepted. I couldn't figure out why this was allowed to happen in the United States Navy.

Q: You know, it's curious that this comes up, because Jerry Miller's interview over here says almost exactly the same thing about the A-7, which, of course, was a much more successful airplane, that apparently it had not been spin-tested before it entered fleet service.[*]

Admiral Ramage: Well, let's say that certain companies seem to have an ability to do this. I don't know enough about the airplane business to get into discussing it.

---

[*] The oral history of Vice Admiral Gerald E. Miller, USN (Ret.), is in the Naval Institute collection. The A-7 was a Vought light attack plane developed in the 1960s.

In any event, the chief of staff, Rear Admiral Hobbs, came up from ComAirNavPac.* He wasn't much of an aviator. We gave him a presentation on our problems with the F7U, and this was a total shock to him. I'm sure Admiral Martin knew about it. Hobbs said, "How would you like to give this presentation down at AirPac?"

I said, "We're ready any time."

Sickel put together about an hour's discussion of the failings of the F7U, which were so long that you couldn't list all of them. The final item was the safety problem, which was terrible.

In the meantime, they'd had problems at various places with the airplane. This was nothing new, but I decided to try to kill the program once and for all. We flew down to AirPac for our presentation. Admiral Martin was there, and Commander Bud Brown had been asked to testify, to put on a rebuttal on how good the Cutlass was. Bud Sickel gave his presentation, and after he was finished, Martin got up and left the room and said, "Come see me when this is over." Then Bud Brown got up and told what a beautiful airplane the F7U was. Of course, he was talking to no one because the only guy that could make a decision had left the room.

So Brown was pretty unhappy about this. I always figure that he got his loyalty to the aircraft confused with loyalty to his squadron. It really wasn't of any value.

After it was over, Rear Admiral Jack Pearson, the AEDO on the staff, came over to me and he said, "You have just done the Navy a disservice. I know that Admiral Martin is going to take the F7U-3 out of the fleet, and it's your fault. The F7U is just another F4U. You know we had trouble getting the F4U into the fleet."†

I said, "Admiral, you know, the F4U never was the airplane the F6F was to begin with." And that dropped like a lead balloon. A lot of these people seemed to have a great loyalty to Vought, and I could never figure out why.

Sure enough, when I went in to see Admiral Martin, he thanked me for the presentation, and he said, "For your information, I'll take two squadrons out of F7Us this afternoon and we'll give them F9F-8s." That was an improved F9F-6. And he explained,

---

* Rear Admiral Ira E. Hobbs, USN.
† Rear Admiral John B. Pearson, Jr., USN.

"I'm going to have to deploy an F7U squadron, but I'm sure they won't operate aboard ship." As I recall, they didn't. I think they shore-based them in Japan when they went out.

Q: For some reason, VX-4 made the deployment with it.

Admiral Ramage: Yes, VX-4 had them because they had a special missile capability with them, and that was the F7U-3M.

Q: With the Sparrow.*

Admiral Ramage: Yes. I don't know if they deployed, but they retained them for a while.

Q: Yes, they did deploy. It was very unusual, because it was an experiment with the developmental squadron.

Admiral Ramage: As far as I recall, by that time the night fighter teams were beginning to look better. The transitional training unit was keeping everybody pretty happy, and with the exception of my immediate boss up in ComFAir Alameda, everything was fine. I think that probably Captain Jones, who was filling in for Admiral Ewen, who was ill, thought that I was pretty fancy, and took an intense dislike to me.† The people around Alameda used to call him "P-boat Jones" because of his background in seaplanes, and he knew nothing about carrier aviation.

I didn't help the matter any, because I had direct communications with not only the staff at NavAirPac, but also with Admiral Martin. He would call me up from time to time and ask me how things were going on, and I'll admit that I probably should have kept Captain Jones much better informed on what was going on, but I didn't, and it bit me later. That is why I'm telling this.

---

* Since the late 1950s the Sparrow has been the U.S. Navy's major long-range air defense missile. The Sparrow I version entered fleet service in 1956 on board F3H Demons and F7U Cutlasses.
† Captain Carroll B. Jones, USN, was chief of staff to Commander Fleet Air Alameda, 1953-56. For a time he was acting commander.

Towards the end of my cruise at VC-3, I took another tour of WestPac to visit the night fighter detachments. We had a very interesting exercise going on over in the desert. It was called Operation Teapot. Teapot was to let aviators be in the air in the vicinity of an air burst nuclear weapon in order to feel just what happen. They sent, I think, four planes from VC-3. There must have been 50 aircraft involved in this thing, flying at various levels above the detonation. The idea was to be heading away from the bomb at the time it went off, and, of course, we had a reasonably high altitude. They had one group, and I think they were from VX-5, who were actually supposed to simulate a loft bombing attack. They were at 5,000 feet rather than ground level, and supposed to be pulling back and turning away at the time this thing went off. I, of course, wanted to be one of the pilots and was.

We went over and operated out of NOTS Inyokern. All of these were pre-dawn operations because they liked to light off these bombs just before daylight. I guess it was because of instrumentation. Anyway, I was over there for about ten straight days flying about every day, but the weather conditions were not correct. Finally, after sitting over there and getting up every morning, I went back to Moffett.

The reason Operation Teapot is so interesting today is that the idea of, first of all, torching off a nuclear weapon air burst within the United States is now totally impossible, and also the idea of flying pilots into the vicinity of a blast just wouldn't sell anymore.

As I got ready to leave VC-3, I thought I should list my experiences of back-to-back tours of command in AirPac. I did so with a recommendation on personnel. It harks all the way back to the time that I saw what SAC was doing in the way of personnel management. I felt that the Navy had to do something quite similar. So I wrote a letter to AirPac concerning the way I thought aviation personnel should be handled, which is the way they're being handled today, so far as tours of duty and selection for squadron command. So I was a little bit ahead of my time, maybe ten years.

ComNavAirPac thought so much of my letter that Admiral Martin sent it out to CinCPacFlt. Rear Admiral Putt Storrs was chief of staff at that time at CinCPacFlt, and he concurred fully and sent it to OpNav.[*] He was one of the old-time test pilots. So I had

---

[*] Rear Admiral Aaron P. Storrs, USN.

unburdened myself on the way I thought that personnel management of naval aviation should go. When I got back to Washington, I got it on my desk for comment.

So after my year in VC-3--and that's what they promised me--I went back to Washington to fulfill the same orders that I would have fulfilled the year before.

Q: This is 1955.

Admiral Ramage: This was July of 1955. OP-05W was a fine place to be if you had to be in Washington. It was the remains of Arleigh Burke's OP-23, which had to do with preserving the aircraft carrier, and we had all of those files. It was founded by Rear Admiral Roy Johnson, and my old friend Don Griffin was up in the shipbuilding study group on the floor above.* These two were hand in hand on carrier requirements. 05W had some very fine people in it: Turner Caldwell, Hy Massey, Dave Richardson, A. B. Connor, Mickey Weisner, and Slim Russell.† That's the younger Russell; he's no longer slim.

Our job was political. The sharpshooting was still going on so far as the aircraft carrier was concerned, not only from the outside but oftentimes within the Navy. And we were supposed to be analyzing various things. We did studies, but basically we were trying to guarantee the future of naval aviation--the same as OP-23 had been doing before it was decommissioned, I think, at the demand of President Harry Truman. It was a fine spot to be in, and it was right across from OP-54, which was where all the aviation detailing was done, so I kept my nose in the detailing business. Whenever they'd pull a real bad one, I'd go in and say, "Well, you've done it again. You've sent the best pilot to some damn catapult school. Let's keep the good guys in the air." It oftentimes really got their goat, I'm sure, because they were trying to career plan people in the system at that time, which was ships first and aviation second. They really looking out for the welfare of the people, because under the system a full career in aviation could wreck a Navy career.

---

* Rear Admiral Roy L. Johnson, USN. The oral history of Johnson, who retired as a four-star admiral, is in the Naval Institute collection.
† Captain Turner F. Caldwell, USN; Captain Forsyth Massey, USN; Commander David C. Richardson, USN; Commander Andrew B. Conner, USN; Commander Maurice F. Weisner, USN; Commander Allard G. Russell, USN. The oral history of Richardson, who retired as a vice admiral, is in the Naval Institute collection.

One of the first things I found out when I went in to look at my fitness reports in BuPers was that my old friend Captain "P-boat" Jones in Alameda had bagged me. In spite of the fact that I thought I'd done a pretty good job at VC-3, he gave me a very, very mediocre report card. As a matter of fact, one that would have been sufficient to get me passed over for captain.

By that time Bob Elder had gone down to the staff of ComNavAirPac, so I sent a letter to Admiral Martin, pointing out that I thought that I had done a good job in VC-3, and that I had not been, in my opinion, correctly rewarded by ComFAir Alameda.*

Q: In these days you didn't see your fitness report?

Admiral Ramage: No, you didn't see them.

Q: In the present system the officer sees them.

Admiral Ramage: Yes. I don't know whether that's good or bad. But I sent this letter pointing out what I had done over the year and asking if he saw fit to please submit a concurrent fitness report on me. He turned the job over to Bob Elder, so Bob wrote a fitness report which Admiral Martin signed, which was so glowing that I ultimately got picked up a year early for captain rather than getting passed over.

Q: Sort of a conspiracy.

Admiral Ramage: But that's the fortunes of naval air, you know. I stayed interested in the personnel business, and I was convinced that we had to change it. Although I had various other jobs, I always stayed very close to personnel planning. By that time, Commander Jim Daniels was over in Pers-A, which is policy and plans in BuPers, and he agreed completely with me, although BuPers didn't have a lot to do with aviation personnel.† Jim, wherever

---

* Elder was by that time a commander.
† This is the same Daniels who had been in an <u>Enterprise</u> fighter squadron during World War II when Ramage was part of ship's company.

possible, tried to push along the idea of a better career for naval aviators, one which would keep them flying without getting passed over. Jim was a big help in this.

There were a couple of real boners going on when I got into OP-05W. I inherited the job on the nuclear-powered seaplane committee. I went to the first meeting, and my first thought was, "You've got to be kidding." The nuclear-powered seaplane, which was on the drawing board, was an enormous thing, as you might guess, and they had already gone so far as to at least analyze procuring land down in North or South Carolina to get this project going.

Q: Was there a manufacturer in mind?

Admiral Ramage: I don't think so, but it probably would have been Martin, because they were the seaplane people. Of course, the big problem was that without shielding for the reactor, you just couldn't fly it unless you wanted to radiate your crew. You would have to have enormous masses of material, whether it's lead or whatever, to keep the radiation from getting to the crew, and this would make this thing just enormously heavy. They even went so far as to recommend that the crews be made up of people that had completed their family because they probably would be sterile after they flew the airplane. It was just a ridiculous idea.

Q: The Air Force flew a B-36 with a nuclear reactor.*

Admiral Ramage: Did they? Well, I wonder how the people are doing. Well, of course, we were probably trying to keep up with the B-36. But the top speed of this thing would have been way down there. And yes, it could fly for a long distance, but you're talking about top speed of maybe 150, 200 knots. It was absolutely ridiculous. So I spent quite a bit of time on this thing. I went back to another meeting. I don't recall who was chairing it, but after we were through, I said, "This thing is absolutely ridiculous, and I intend to write a

---

* The Convair NB-36H Peacemaker made 47 flights between 1955 and 1957 as a nuclear reactor test bed aircraft. The plane was powered by conventional means, six propeller-driven engines. The reactor was operated over uninhabited areas to test radiation effects on instruments and other parts of the plane.

letter to OpNav-05 [at that time it was Vice Admiral Combs] and tell him that I think we ought to get out of this program right now. It's just a waste of money."* I did this, and Combs obviously had been looking at it also. He put a note on my letter and sent it forward to Arleigh Burke.† Arleigh always wrote in brown ink, for some reason or other, and he wrote, "I think that Commander Ramage is right. Cancel this thing as soon as possible."

So this came back through the Assistant Secretary of the Navy for Air. Appended to Admiral Burke's comments on it was a note signed by Tom Moorer, which said, "This is an example of some of the thinking in the younger aviators' minds. This is a good project and it is wrong to cancel it."

Q: Our Tom Moorer?

Admiral Ramage: Our Tom Moorer.‡

Q: Well, he's all PBY, hard-core VP all the way.§

Admiral Ramage: So that was canceled forthwith. There were some wounded people around, I don't know exactly, a lot of people over in BuAer that had a vested interest, but I'm sure there were a lot of people other than Jig Dog Ramage that wanted to cancel it.** In any event, I wrote the letter that caused Burke to get rid of it.

Shortly thereafter, I had the same problem with another project. It went under the name of exotic aircraft fuel. They wanted to get more power out of the regular aircraft engines that we had. The recommendation was that we use a boron derivative that would give maybe 20% or 30% more power per weight of fuel. The problem with this was that it was a toxic compound and that anybody in close proximity to it would be poisoned. The

---

* Vice Admiral Thomas S. Combs, USN, served as Deputy Chief of Naval Operations (Air) from 11 April 1955 to 1 August 1956.
† Admiral Arleigh A. Burke, USN, served as Chief of Naval Operations from 17 August 1955 to 1 August 1961. His oral history is in the Naval Institute collection.
‡ Captain Thomas H. Moorer, USN, a naval aviator who later served as Chief of Naval Operations and Chairman of the Joint Chiefs of Staff.
§ During World War II Moorer flew the PBY patrol plane.
** BuAer--Bureau of Aeronautics.

exhaust gas out of the jet would be a deadly poison. On top of that, we'd have to redo all of the storage tanks and the carriers, we'd have to button up the carrier to be able to land and launch aircraft. It was another thing I looked at, and I said, "You've got to be kidding." The head of this thing happened to be a Marine colonel, and I said, "Colonel, this is the dumbest thing I've ever heard of."

And he said, "I agree with you. Let's get it."

So I again wrote a letter to him saying that I thought this was absolutely absurd. The colonel carried the letter forward and got it canceled. Here I was in Washington--I hadn't been there two months and I'd already canceled two projects that were near and dear to people's hearts. So I was really making my mark.

Q: Did you ever find out who was behind either of these ideas?

Admiral Ramage: I knew at the time. I knew there was a lot of emphasis on it over at BuAer, because they really were both technical studies. We seemed to have money to burn on things like that that were really not worth it.

Q: I can recall about that same time having a shortage of money for fuel for airplanes to fly in the fleet, isn't that true?

Admiral Ramage: Yes, that's right. Of course, that was out of a different pocket.

Q: Maybe we were just putting our money in the wrong pockets.

Admiral Ramage: That's right. My letter from VC-3 on personnel management had come in by that time and was being sent around BuPers and various places in Washington. I was called various things by people, because it caused them a lot of work to try to staff this thing sent via a fleet commander. So I took it upon myself to continue the project. We're talking now about 1956. I used my experiences in the fleet from 1952 to 1955 concerning the introduction of the new high-performance aircraft to the fleet, and I wrote a study about

"Can the Navy meet the Mach two era." It was an in-depth study of the training costs, pilot personnel management problems, and it charted a path of the naval aviator for 20 years.

It was pretty well received by Admiral Combs, again, and it went forward with a note by him saying, "This makes sense to me. I think it needs more staffing. Let's send it out around BuPers and the Pentagon to see how we can make this so." His problem was that he didn't want to see us damage any naval aviators by specializing them in an aviation career. Under the circumstances at that time, I certainly agree with him. His comment was that the idea was excellent but that it would need further investigation. An endeavor should be made to find and eliminate objections in BuPers and OpNav while the program was still in the formative stage. The endorsement was good, but it didn't really have any horsepower behind it. He agreed, but he didn't really want to take the issue on. My opinion, at that time, was that we would have to sink lower in capabilities before we finally remedied the problem of aviation personnel career planning.

Q: It had to get worse before it got better.

Admiral Ramage: That's right. Shortly thereafter, we had an indication of the situation getting worse. The A3D was coming into the fleet. This is now '57. Do you recall when it first came in? Anyway, on the Bon Homme Richard they had a ramp strike by the squadron commander, and it was a terrible catastrophe.* Not only that, the A3Ds were having terrible problems in their introduction to the fleet. I didn't know anything about the A3D, but it seemed to me that any aircraft that Ed Heinemann had built ought to be easy to handle.

Q: Did you know Ed at this time?

Admiral Ramage: I just knew of him. I knew that he built the SBD. I think I had probably met him. Oh, yes, I had met him because he came out to the Oriskany in '53 and told us

---

* USS Bon Homme Richard (CVA-31) was an attack carrier of the period.

about the A4D and how he was building it.* He was interested in making sure that we get the Mark 7 nuclear weapon on the A4D. So yes, I had met him and was impressed. So what I did in this case was to send out to ComNavAirLant and ComNavAirPac a request for the background information on the three senior people in each heavy attack squadron. There were six of them at the time. I wanted the background on the three senior people.

As I recall it, I've got the figures somewhere, only a handful, like four or five, had come up the carrier route, and none of them had ever made a jet carrier landing before. So we've got the same old thing that I fought all the time, untrained people training untrained people. The speculation was that anybody can handle a Navy aircraft. Hell, I later flew the A3D, and it was no problem at all. As a matter of fact, it was a beauty. But here we had this project which was considered to be extremely important, which was being ruined by poor personnel assignment.

Q: With very little tailhook experience.

Admiral Ramage: Very little. Very little. I think the standard senior guy had far less than 100, maybe 50 landings. They had come up the VP or the VR route, and when we really decided that these planes would be permanently carrier-based instead of being a VC squadron sending detachments out, where the skipper never went, it became a problem.† So I again got into the personnel thing heavy, and sent this information to Admiral Combs. He in turn sent it around saying, "This makes sense. Let's do something about it." So again I was about to become mess treasurer in another operation. When I say mess treasurer, that means when you complain about the food, you ultimately are elected mess treasurer.

The most interesting thing that happened to me in the summer of '56 was that I was assigned to a special evaluation group. I believe it was attached to the Net Evaluation Subcommittee of the Joint Chiefs of Staff to evaluate an all-out nuclear exchange with the Soviet Union. As usual, the Navy sent a boy to do a man's job, in my particular case. The boy certainly wasn't Rear Admiral Parker, who was a black shoe rear admiral who was sent

---

* The Douglas-built A4D Skyhawk was a jet bomber used at the time in Navy and Marine Corps light attack squadrons. It was designed for nuclear weapons delivery.
† VR refers to transport aircraft rather than combatant types.

over to run it.* He was a very agreeable guy, but they gave me the job of running all of carrier aviation for three fleets, the Second, Sixth, and Seventh fleets.

In the meantime, SAC sent their entire planning group from Omaha, headed by a brigadier general. I think they must have had 50 people. It became pretty apparent to me that I not only needed help, I needed it in a hurry, so I sent a note to Butch Parker stating that we were overwhelmed, and I'd like to go to the Pentagon and get some help. Admiral Davis was then OP-05; he had relieved Combs.† Anyway, I told him that this was really about to be a catastrophe. If we wanted to save the carriers, we sure didn't want to look bad in this war game.

I got a firm handshake and everybody agreed that I needed help, but they couldn't afford to spare the people. So I went into OP-05 and I got Commanders Roy Isaman and Wiley Howell to come over to the National War College in their off hours and help me plan these strikes.‡ I knew one thing, having been acquainted with this thing before, that if any aircraft was going to penetrate the Russian defenses, we had to go in low. We had to go in under the radar. What I needed was somebody to make sure that I wasn't running my A4Ds and A3Ds out of fuel. We actually even played some P6Ms in this thing because it was supposed to be five years ahead.§ This was '56, so the action was supposed to take place in '61.

Q: Did ADs still figure in the ...

Admiral Ramage: ADs were not involved. By that time only A3Ds and A4Ds, with in-flight refueling were used. And our fleet air defenses were very interesting because we planned the haystack, which had been exercised at that time, that is, a random grouping of ships. They played out the total number of ships that would be in the Med on any given

---

* Rear Admiral Edward N. Parker, USN. The oral history of Parker, who retired as a vice admiral, is in the Naval Institute collection.
† Vice Admiral William V. Davis, Jr., USN, served as Deputy Chief of Naval Operations (Air) from 1 August 1956 to 22 May 1958.
‡ Commander Roy M. Isaman, USN; Commander Wiley B. Howell, USN.
§ The Martin P6M Seamaster was a swept-wing seaplane powered by four J-71 engines. It was designed for minelaying and reconnaissance flights. It made its first flight in July 1955. Plagued by technical problems and competing priorities, the plane was limited to prototypes. It never went into production or fleet service.

day, which is, I think, 2,000. We had the carriers interspersed among all the merchant ships, so the Soviet aircraft had to positively identify the carriers before they launched missiles against them. It was a great time for the Navy to look good. We started the play in July, and the original strikes were all pre-scheduled.

Q: Where did this take place?

Admiral Ramage: At the National War College in Washington, D.C., Fort McNair. I had only really one full-time helper, a guy named Dick Nicholson, who was a blackshoe from CinCPacFlt.* Commander Hal Shear, a submariner, was helping the other side, I mean the red side.† I was getting the original plans done and using the paper capabilities of the Navy aircraft.

It was an enormous project for SAC. After about three or four days when SAC penetrated the Russian defenses, it became apparent that they couldn't penetrate at altitude. And General LeMay stopped the war because he could see exactly what was happening. Our Navy strikes were getting in, they were damn few, but we were penetrating in at low level with in-flight refueling. As a matter of fact, the first plane on target was a P6M operating off a seaplane tender someplace in the Med. It was a big bomb. I can remember the thing appearing on the board. "Where in Christ's name did that thing come from?" The Navy, up to its capabilities, was getting its aircraft into the assigned target area.

Q: Were the Navy targets as deep inland?

Admiral Ramage: No, no, we couldn't go deep enough. Our targets were generally in the bloc countries, and into the northern areas. The Second Fleet was up there too. But we had very few losses, and to the surprise of absolutely everybody, when the Red Air Force sent their enormous strike group against the carriers in the Med, they ultimately only got

---

* Captain Richard P. Nicholson, USN.
† Commander Harold E. Shear, USN. The Naval Institute oral history of Shear, who retired as a four-star admiral, contains his description of this war game.

one carrier, and that was a CVS.* We only had the two CVAs in the Med, but they got all their strikes off and were unscathed. This got everybody's attention.

When we got through, Admiral Parker told me to prepare a brief for the senior people in the Navy. We presented it to Admiral Burke and all the op deps, the senior guys. I was quite nervous about briefing that kind of horsepower. I remember that Al Vito, who was kind of a PR type, was talking to me about it, and I said, "God, I'm nervous as hell."†

He said, "I'll tell you what you do, is what I always do. Just think of all those people sitting in front of you stark naked, and you'll laugh so hard you'll think it's funny and you'll get over it." And that's exactly what I did.

Admiral Burke received this presentation very well. He thought it was just great. Here it was; here was the carriers' reason to be. Not only had we gotten all weapons on target, as we were scheduled to, but also all the attack carriers were still in existence when the nuclear exchange was over. I don't think the other side planned it right, but on the other hand, I wasn't there to try to tell them how to sink a carrier. So it was quite an operation. And Admiral Burke told Admiral Parker, "I want you to take this presentation out to CinCPacFlt and give it to them out there," which we did, and also to CinCLantFlt.

Q: Not to belabor the point, but how were the nuts and bolts of this decided? For instance, how did you determine whether an aircraft had been spotted on radar or whether missiles ...

Admiral Ramage: They played out the probabilities, and if it came down to a choice, it was the roll of the die. But they did the thing within the advertised capabilities of 1961 equipment. Remember this is five years in advance, so we're talking dream capabilities in many cases.

Q: Right.

---

* CVS--antisubmarine carrier. CVA--attack carrier.
† Lieutenant Commander Albert H. Vito, Jr., USN.

Admiral Ramage: Then when it came down to a question, it would be the roll of the die. The roll of the die got the CVS versus the CVAs, for example.

Q: Do you feel that the whole program was realistic?

Admiral Ramage: Yes, I do. I think that the Air Force and many people have always felt that the aircraft carrier was a lot more vulnerable than it really is. We were using electronic countermeasures to try to make all ships in the fleet appear on radar with the same blip so that they couldn't tell a carrier from a destroyer or an oiler, and also by putting these 2,000 ships in the Med gave a definite identification problem to the Red Air Force. They were using air-to-surface missiles, and they couldn't identify the targets properly. I think they probably shot at a lot of merchant ships. I think at that time it was realistic. I can't say that it is now. But it certainly got everybody's attention.

I reported back to my office at OP-05W in time to find out that, believe it or not, I was pre-selected for captain. This was the summer of '56. It was an amazing thing to have gone through being afraid I was going to get passed over at VC-3 to early selection. This was 1956 that the war game was held, and I was selected in '56 for captain. That was at a time when only 1% or 2% were pre-selected. Things are a lot different now. Perhaps I had some friends around after all. I went to the National War College the fall of '57. I found that the time in OP-05W was very, very interesting.

We participated in lots of political things, including the Symington investigations of air power.[*] I was the carrier guy for Admiral Combs. I didn't know Admiral Combs very well. I knew Admiral Rees, who was the number-two guy, quite well, but I didn't know Combs.[†] Combs had the failing of answering all questions himself when he had somebody like me or two or three other people there that were experts. He misconstrued the questions and gave terrible answers.

---

[*] In the mid-1950s Stuart Symington (Democrat-Missouri) was a U.S. Senator. He had been the first Secretary of the Air Force, from 1947 to 1950, when it was formed as a separate service.
[†] Rear Admiral William L. Rees, USN.

At the same time, Admiral Jim Russell, over at BuAer, would come over and he would answer questions correctly.[*] Russell was just smarter than hell, and Symington, the whole group, just loved him. The committee got off on the subject one time of the A4D, and Russell said, "You know, talking about the A4D, the A4D is a poor man's airplane. It's a cheap man's airplane. We in naval air never get enough money."

Symington said, "Okay, Jim, you can sit down now. I get your point."

The purpose of that committee, of course, was to try to embarrass President Eisenhower for not providing enough money for air power. It fell through. One afternoon, after Admiral Combs's really poor performance, Rear Admiral Don Griffin, who was Radford's assistant on the Joint Chiefs of Staff, called me and gave me hell.[†] He said, "Damn it, you've got to do something about your boss over there."

I said, "Admiral, I can't answer for him unless he asks me to. I can't butt in. He persists in answering these damn questions."

And he said, "Well, you've got to correct it some way."

I said, "I'll do the best I can."

Well, we found a way to correct it. They sent his testimony back to us for correction of minor errors. We in OP-05W took out almost all of these errors and corrected them so the finished report looked pretty good.

That kind of finishes OP-05W. I got to meet a lot of people, I spent a lot of time in the E-ring, and in spite of the fact that it was in Washington, it was a good place for me to be.[‡]

---

[*] Rear Admiral James S. Russell, USN, served as Chief of the Bureau of Aeronautics from 4 March 1955 to 15 July 1957. The oral history of Russell, who retired as a four-star admiral, is in the Naval Institute collection.
[†] Admiral Arthur W. Radford, USN, served as Chairman of the Joint Chiefs of Staff from 15 August 1953 to 14 August 1957.
[‡] The Pentagon has lettered corridors, going from A at the innermost to E at the outermost. E-ring offices, which go around the perimeter of the building, are considered the most prestigious.

I might make a comment on duty in Washington. It's a pain in the neck, and unfortunately, probably 90% of the jobs that are there are of absolutely no value at all. You can't do anything. And even in the important 10%, there's darn little you can do. I think Beauty Martin expressed it the best way when he kept me from going to Washington the previous year. He said, "The Pentagon's like a log with 10,000 ants on it, each of whom thinks he's steering the log." On the other hand, what I learned in OP-05W was the system. I made a lot of acquaintances, and I realized how things were to be done if you could get them done. I think on balance it was definitely a plus for me. However, these other 90% jobs in Washington are nothing. You might as well be a clerk. I don't think an aviator should go there before he's a senior commander. You're at kind of a disadvantage at that time because the blackshoes have all gone at various times before, so you must learn the system faster. You just have to presume that you're smarter than they are.

Q: Now we're up to the time where you entered the National War College. What was the date?

Admiral Ramage: The date of the entry was August of 1957. By that time my pre-selection to captain had taken effect, so I was now a captain and very happy about it.

Q: How large was the class?

Admiral Ramage: The class, if I recall, was about 120 people, and it was split between the three armed services, including the Marines, a few Coast Guard people, maybe one or two, and then about 30 civilians from State Department, CIA, FBI, and other agencies that were involved with national security.[*] The college was started by General Eisenhower because he thought that military people should be much more aware of the economic and political aspects of a war and governing a country. He felt that the military officers were too one-sided, and I think that's so.

---

[*] CIA--Central Intelligence Agency; FBI--Federal Bureau of Investigation.

Q: Did the Army and Navy War colleges deal with any of those subjects previously?

Admiral Ramage: They did. They had a nice series of lectures, but nothing compared to what we got at the National War College. We would listen to the President of the United States, the Secretary of State, Secretary of Defense, the head of CIA, NSA, and others.[*] So during that year we were exposed to a lot of very fine lectures by the real policy-makers of the country. It was a very, very productive year. One of the problems that I couldn't help but note later on was that after educating people to do these various things, particularly when the Kennedy group came in, it was kind of, "Back in your cage, dogs. We don't want you involved with any of the policy decisions."[†] Of course, since Reagan has come back, it's more or less back kind of where it used to be under Eisenhower.[‡] Eisenhower was a great political-military leader.

What the school was doing was prepping people to be a Secretary of State and Chairman of the Joint Chiefs of Staff. They wanted people to look at things at that level. It was a very mind-broadening thing, particularly for those of us who had spent a lot of time in the cockpit.

Q: Who were some of the other naval aviators from that class?

Admiral Ramage: Harvey Lanham was there, Eddie Outlaw, Smoke Strean.[§] I think Al Burgess was in that class.[**] That's about it for the aviators. The services were supposed to be very selective in whom they sent. They used to call it "Admirals' Prep." The Army sent a tremendous group of people; Freddie Weyand, Haines, and Zais all made four stars in that group.[††] The Army is great on schools, as you know, and they didn't send anybody to that

---

[*] NSA--National Security Agency.
[†] John F. Kennedy served as President of the United States from 20 January 1960 until he was assassinated on 22 November 1963.
[‡] Ronald W. Reagan, who served as President from 20 January 1981 to 20 January 1989, was in office during the time of this interview.
[§] Captain Harvey P. Lanham, USN; Captain Edward C. Outlaw, USN; Captain Bernard M. Strean, USN. The oral history of Strean, who retired as a vice admiral, is in the Naval Institute collection.
[**] Commander Andrew L. Burgess, USN.
[††] Colonel Frederick C. Weyand, USA; Colonel Melvin Zais, USA; Colonel Ralph E. Haines, Jr., USA.

school unless he was not only going to be a general officer but probably a pretty high one. They were particularly good students because most of the Army people had been to school practically all their lives, and they were good at writing.

The Navy people were quite good too. They were about on a par with the various civilian elements. The Air Force officers were way down the line. They simply didn't have the quality of people that the other armed services did, I guess understandably, they were still a fairly new service and just hadn't had enough time to get the experience.[*]

Q: Not much institutional experience.

Admiral Ramage: No. That's right. Maybe they didn't consider the importance of the school as great as the other armed services did. In any event, the Air Force people, I think, were a cut under the rest of the school, with the Army being way out in front.

Q: You had to produce a dissertation, didn't you?

Admiral Ramage: Yes. Mine, as you might guess, was on nuclear weapons, which was the nth power getting the nuclear weapons. All I did was move it right over from what I'd been doing in the Pentagon, so it was a very simple thing for me to do. It was a very, very profitable year. The president was Vice Admiral Tyler Wooldridge.[†]

The instructors were good, the subjects were very interesting. They picked six or seven world areas where they would set up a problem, and you would try to solve the problem in committee, which was like a staff, and come on up with a solution. Invariably, when military force came into play, they always sent for the aircraft carriers, and the civilians, particularly the State Department people, always would look upon them as their ace in the hole because, of course, they didn't cause any international problems landing on somebody else's territory.

---

[*] The U.S. Air Force was officially established on 26 July 1947 as part of the defense reorganization embodied in the National Security Act of 1947.
[†] Vice Admiral Edmund Tyler Wooldridge, USN.

I might say that we got into a little bit of an argument one day, much to the amusement of the class, between, of all people, two naval aviators, Eddie Outlaw and Jig Dog Ramage. And it had to do with an area--I believe it was down in the Persian Gulf. The staff solution was to get the carriers there in a hurry, just like it was in real life. And Eddie, who was on that committee, tried to put in an objection. He pointed out that the carriers definitely couldn't be used in that manner because they were dedicated to nuclear war and had to remain in their launch positions. I was sitting next to Smoke Strean at the time, I recall very clearly, and I said, "Smoke, do you want to take him on, or do you want me to?"

Smoke, of course, said, "You go ahead."

So I stood up and pointed out that whereas the carriers had a nuclear capability, the big point that they had was flexibility. They could be called into action anyplace else in the world. I think this amused the various people, the students, because here they had the two most vocal--if not the most dedicated--carrier people, having an argument amongst themselves on the use of aircraft carriers. Well, it wasn't that funny. After it was over, Eddie was kind of mad at me. He knew he was wrong.

But a day or two later he came into my room. He said, "Come on down." They had a little coffee shop below. "I want to talk to you."

What had happened was that Vice Admiral Wooldridge had agreed with me, and he took it upon himself to call the CNO, who was Admiral Arleigh Burke at that time, and tell him how far off base Outlaw was. Wooldridge called Outlaw in and had a piece of him. And Eddie blamed me.

I finally said, "Well, Eddie, you know you were wrong."

He said, "Goddamn it, I know I was wrong, but you didn't have to make a point of it."

About March of every year, the people at any of the war colleges begin to shuffle around to find out where they were going when they get through school in June. I let Ralph Cousins, the detailer, know that I still would like to get another flying job if I could.* Ralph

---

* Captain Ralph W. Cousins, USN. Cousins eventually became a four-star admiral, serving in the 1970s as Vice Chief of Naval Operations and SACLant/CinCLant/CinCLantFlt.

gave me a little lecture. He said, "A squadron command is all you really need, and anything after that is a bonus." And he said, "I notice that you had VB-10 in 1944, and then you had VB-98 in 1945-46, then you had Air Group 19, which is another bonus, and then you went right across the field and had VC-3, which is also a bonus. I think you'd better forget about this flying business and do something else."

And I said, "Well, I don't know if there are any flying commands around or anyplace I can keep flying, but I'd sure like to do it."

He called me shortly thereafter and said, "Keep this under your hat, but I think I've got just what you want. They're going to go back into the replacement air group training business, and we know that you were in Air Group 98 and also you had this transitional training in VC-3. You've been nominated to head up the West Coast replacement air group."

I was, of course, just delighted, and he said at the same time that Bob Dosé had been nominated to be the CAG on the East Coast.[*] I was very flattered to be considered to be at the same level as Bob Dosé, because he was one of the people that I really admired. So I waited and waited, and everybody was beginning to get their orders, and I wasn't getting any. I've always been very reticent to call the detailers because I just think it's better to leave them alone. Also, my orders were so good, I didn't want there to be any chance of them being changed.

I finally called Ralph and he said, "How well do you know Admiral Pride out at ComNavAirPac?"[†]

I said, "Well, I really don't know him at all. I've never met him, I've never worked for him."

And he said, "Well, he doesn't want you."

I said, "What's the trouble?"

He said, "Well, he thinks that you're a throttle jock and he wants an administrator."

---

[*] Captain Robert G. Dosé, USN.
[†] Vice Admiral Alfred M. Pride, USN, served as Commander Air Force Pacific Fleet/Commander Naval Air Force Pacific Fleet from 1 February 1956 to 30 September 1959. The name of the command was changed 30 July 1957. His oral history is in the Naval Institute collection.

I said, "I'm not a throttle jock. I've been very fortunate to stay flying, but if you'll look in my record, I've had jobs in Washington and in administration."

He said, "I know it, but that's his impression of you, and on top of that he's got a very special guy that he wants to put in there named Brute Dale." Well, I'd run into Brute Dale.[*] I don't think he'd ever flown a jet. I remember he was in TBFs during World War II, but as far as being qualified in any way to set up a training syllabus for this type of an operation was absolutely ridiculous.

I said, "Gee, I'd like to appeal it."

He said, "Don't worry about it. It's been appealed. The Deputy Chief of Naval Operations for Air called Pride directly, and when he got turned down, the Vice Chief [who was Admiral Don Felt] called Admiral Pride, and Pride is adamant. He doesn't want you out here."[†]

This kind of shocked me a little bit. I had never been, to my knowledge, turned down for a job. He said, "Well, we haven't got anything for you. What do you think you'd like?"

I said, "Do you have any else that's flying?"

He said, "Yes. It's not anywhere near the jobs that you've had in the past, but how would you like VX-3?" It had just moved down from Atlantic City to Norfolk. This was the fighter operational development squadron.

I said, "Well, I'd be delighted. I think that would be a nice job." Of course, by that time VX-3 had really pulled in its horns, and I don't think they had over 12, 15 planes, and gradually their mission was phasing out, but I was glad to get it.

We prepared to move down to Norfolk and take over VX-3. I got a call from Ralph. He said, "We're thinking of sending you down to Sanford."

I said, "That doesn't appeal to me very much." I had no idea that he meant to be the wing commander.

What had happened was that about that time Admiral Cat Brown, Commander Sixth Fleet, had observed the A3D squadron that was deployed, I believe it was on the

---

[*] Captain Roland H. Dale, USN.
[†] Admiral Harry D. Felt, USN, served as Vice Chief of Naval Operations from 1 September 1956 to 28 July 1958. His oral history is in the Naval Institute collection.

Roosevelt.* They'd been thrown off the ship and shore-based over there for poor performance. He wrote a scathing dispatch, sending info copies to practically everybody in the world that pointed out that the A3D squadrons were simply not ready for sea. And the last sentence was a terrible indictment. It said that two A3D pilots were actually seen to congratulate each other after a successful carrier landing. So what they were going to do was to send me down there and see if I couldn't do something about getting the squadrons carrier-ready.

Q: This is the home of the heavy attack wing?

Admiral Ramage: Yes, this is Heavy Attack Wing 1, which was a fine command.† At one time it was a flag command that Admiral Goldthwaite had as a rear admiral, and it was a very senior command for a captain.‡ Jim Reedy was the commander at this time, out of the class of '33, and here I was out of '39.§ I think it shocked some of the heavy attackers of the past that I'd been associated with because they presumed that I was anti-heavy attack. I really wasn't. I was just pro-getting the lighter aircraft a nuclear capability.

So I was detached. When I was over at the Gun Factory in Washington getting my household effects squared away, Rear Admiral George Anderson was there. He was going to be a carrier division commander in the Atlantic Fleet, and he asked me where I was going.** I said down to Sanford to take over Heavy Attack Wing 1. He immediately had a piece of me. He said, "I hope you get down there and do something about that outfit. It's a disgrace to naval aviation." I think he presumed that I'd been part of the heavy attack program in the past, and I assured him that whatever I was going to do down there, I would

---

* Vice Admiral Charles R. Brown, USN, commanded the Sixth Fleet from August 1956 to September 1958.
† Admiral Ramage wrote an account of this tour of duty for publication. See "Heavy Attack Aviation 1958-60," The Hook (published by the Tailhook Association), Winter 1989, pages 50-52. Much of that issue of the magazine deals with the heavy attack program.
‡ Rear Admiral Robert Goldthwaite, USN.
§ Captain James R. Reedy, USN.
** Rear Admiral George W. Anderson, Jr., USN, served as Commander Carrier Division Six from July 1958 to August 1959. He served subsequently as Commander Sixth Fleet and Chief of Naval Operations. His oral history is in the Naval Institute collection.

try to improve it, but I was not one of the professional heavy attack guys. I was a carrier man all the way.

Then on the way down to Sanford, I dropped in to see Admiral Rees, who was ComNavAirLant, and he straightened me out in a hurry too.* He said, "We've got a real problem down there." He had a copy of the Cat Brown dispatch, and I told him that I'd read it. He said, "We're thinking of completely disbanding the heavy attack wing and sending the A3D squadrons to train with the parent air groups in order to try to get them more carrier conscious." He said, "They simply are not thinking carrier down there." I assured him that I would try to change it.

So I drove on down to Sanford and reported in with a charge by practically everybody to get in there and try to do something about heavy attack.

Q: This is still 1957?

Admiral Ramage: This is '58. I graduated from National War College in '58, summer of '58.

Q: What about the experience level of the squadron commanders and the A3D pilots? Apparently there was very little tailhook experience there.

Admiral Ramage: I can quote to you from my letter concerning that experience that I'd done when I was in OP-05W the previous year. I ended my letter with this quote. "I strongly recommend that the heavy attack squadrons be assigned more pilots with operational background in jet carrier aviation. Training untrained pilots by untrained pilots can lead to disaster." I think you've heard that before.

Q: That seems to be a recurring theme.

---

* Vice Admiral William L. Rees, USN, served as Commander Naval Air Force Atlantic Fleet from 29 May 1956 to 30 September 1960. Prior to 30 July 1957 the title was Air Force, Atlantic Fleet.

Admiral Ramage: So we can take a look at this sheet that I acquired from both ComNavAirLant and ComNavAirPac at that time, which I based the letter on. I notice in the Atlantic Fleet the three senior people in six heavy attack squadrons, that's 18 people, that's the commanding officer, the executive officer, and the operations officer, none of them had previous jet operational experience. And in the Pacific Fleet, the same thing is true, although they only had the four squadrons over there. None of them had had any jet operational experience.

In the recapitulation down here, I notice that in the Atlantic Fleet of the 18, 12 came from VP-VR background, and six had had a carrier squadron background; five of those actually were in heavy attack. So they really were a little bit different. None had carrier landing experience in jets prior to reporting. And in the Pacific Fleet, we had seven with VP-VR background, and two with carrier squadron experience, and none had made carrier landings in jets prior to reporting aboard. So what we had in the heavy attack program, again, was a personnel problem. There was nothing the matter with the aircraft. So certainly my intention was to go after the personnel input right away.

Q: Had you flown the A3D yet?

Admiral Ramage: I'd never seen an A3D when I went down there.

Q: How about LSOs? Do you have any idea what kind of background your LSOs had?

Admiral Ramage: I didn't have any idea. I was satisfied with the LSOs when I got down there.

Q: How many of them did we put in mental institutions?

Admiral Ramage: I don't know about that. So you asked the right question. You knew what I was going to hit when I first got down there. I went to work right away. I gave the Cat Brown dispatch very wide distribution among the squadrons, and then also made it required reading for any new pilot that reported in, and I made them report in through me. At the same time, I hung an F9F tailhook over my office door to indicate that heavy attack was going to be a carrier outfit and they'd better get ready for it, because that was the way it was going to be.

One of the things that was rather sad was that I considered this a problem of detailing, of administration that had been mishandled in Washington, and unfortunately I was forced to get rid of quite of a number of senior people down there. The only way they'd let me get rid of them was via the disposition board. They wouldn't let me transfer them out. They simply didn't have the background to make it. This had come from the idea that the VC squadrons in the past had been shore-based, and they sent the detachments out, so that the senior people stayed on the beach. It was presumed that here was a good way for a non-carrier guy to get a carrier reputation as skipper of a carrier squadron, but I don't think a lot of them ever really carrier qualified.

Q: Were the detailers at this time necessarily aviators for aviators, or did it matter?

Admiral Ramage: Well, I still think that we hadn't arrived at the point that I was driving at all the time here, that we had to look into a better career pattern to guarantee that people that really wanted to fly and could fly remain in the business. The big problem, as was pointed out by Admiral Theda Combs when I turned that study in to him, was that he was afraid that the pilots that were professional aviators would be hurt in the selection process.

Q: I have a friend who put a tour in a VC squadron. He was at least a lieutenant commander and he has six traps, which totalled his naval career.

Admiral Ramage: I went up shortly thereafter to call on Admiral Rees after I'd looked the place over, and I told him that I thought that the problem was really personnel. I would need all the help that I could get to get the personnel spigot pointed our way, and that I would identify some people--who wouldn't like it--but I would identify some carrier people who would be coming up for assignment. He said, "Fine."

The people that were let go, I felt very sorry for, because, in my opinion, this was not their fault. They had to go through the agony of disposition board. It is pathetic at the rank of commander. I might add at that time that I got a call from Captain Fuller Brush, who was in BuPers, and he asked me if I had anything against patrol plane pilots.[*] I said, no, I would be very willing to take some younger people who didn't get too set in their ways, but I didn't want any lieutenant commanders and full commanders coming down to Sanford with no carrier operational experience. It was just a disaster. And he said, "I want you to come up and talk to me."

So on one of my numerous visits up to Admiral Rees, I mentioned that I was on my way to see Captain Brush, and I told him what the subject was, and he said, "You go back to Sanford. I'll take care of Captain Brush." So that was the end of that subject. But it was not a happy time down in Sanford for a lot of very senior people.

Commander Joe Frossard was head of the Aviation Evaluation Board, and after about two or three months he said, "I'd like to get off this board." He said, "They're called me the executioner around here."[†]

I said, "Well, I think we've probably gotten the point across and you won't have very many more," and we didn't.

Another thing that I thought was entirely wrong was that the A3Ds' tactics were still based on high-altitude penetration and high-altitude delivery of nuclear weapons.

Q: This was the Air Force strategy that you had already proven was wrong.

Admiral Ramage: Well, that's right, and it just wasn't right, but nevertheless, we had this airplane, which was a good bird, incidentally, and we had to make it work. I learned that out at NOTS Inyokern, at VX-5, Commander Dick Beveridge was doing something about low-angle penetration and delivery of nuclear weapons in the A3D.[‡] So I flew out there just as soon as I could and discussed it with him. He was quite surprised. He said, "We've been

---

[*] Captain Frederick J. Brush, USN.
[†] Commander Clarence F. Frossard, USN.
[‡] Commander Richard A. Beveridge, USN.

talking about this thing now for four or five months, and you're the first one that has come out here and shown any interest."

I said, "Well, let's get into a maneuver and see what it is." It was a simple loft maneuver, except they didn't go over the top, as the A4Ds and other planes did. They pitched it off at a relatively high angle, like maybe 60 degrees, and then went into a high wing-over and through a 180-degree turn. It was probably as accurate as the other types of loft delivery.

After I checked out in the maneuver, I told Admiral Rees about it, and he was very interested. He understood completely that the A3Ds couldn't go in at high altitude. So he came down and we checked him out in a maneuver, and he thought it was quite simple.

Q: How far can you loft the weapon?

Admiral Ramage: I think the thing went out maybe a couple of miles. I don't have the figures in my head now, but it was accurate within 1,500 or 2,000 feet, which was comparable with a lot of the high-level bombing that was done. Of course, this was a makeshift proposition.

While I was there, Beveridge brought in some engineers from Douglas because he and I, too, were a little bit concerned about the strength of the wing on the A3D to withstand this maneuver. The A3D only had a two-and-a-half G wing, which certainly was awfully weak to go into this type of operation. Douglas, however, had already tested a wing to destruction, and they found out that we had far more than two-and-a-half G's in strength. So we put that problem to rest.

I'm very thankful that I had Admiral Rees's support and also had demonstrated the maneuver to him because, sure enough, within a reasonably short time, we had an A3D go in doing this maneuver. And some of the doubters in AirLant staff, namely Mike Hanley, who was the training officer, was ready with, "I told you so."[*] He said, "You're trying to make an A3D into an A4D." He didn't understand at all why we were doing it. He thought that I was just doing this because I wanted to get into the loft maneuver. I didn't want to

---

[*] Commander Michael J. Hanley, USN.

get into the loft maneuver at all. It was simply the only way that we could continue to penetrate with that airplane. And having been through that war game there at the National War College a couple of years before, I knew darn well that the high-altitude aircraft was doomed in the future because of missiles.

Q: What was Hanley's background?

Admiral Ramage: He'd been a blimp pilot.

Q: Okay.

Admiral Ramage: Don't laugh. It became apparent, of course, at that time that we must go in low. As a matter of fact, I set up a new slogan, "If you want to go, go in low." Next I had to get myself carqualed in the A3D just as soon as possible. I checked out just as soon as I could in the airplane, much to the shock of everybody. They wanted me to go through all the ground school and weapons training. I said, "Well, I'll go through the ground school, but I'll do it later. I've got to get my carquals in first."

And they said, "Carquals? You're not even a PC."

And I said, "What is a PC?"

And they said, "That's a plane commander."

I said, "Well, that designation is hereby rescinded. We have no plane commanders here. That sounds too much like VP."

So I went out and started bouncing, and I found the plane to be just a beautiful airplane. Because of its length, it had a little pitch instability, but as far as flying it, it was just a great airplane, and particularly in the landing configuration. I couldn't understand why anybody would have any trouble bringing it aboard.

So fairly soon I went out with a flight of four pilots. The other three were Johnny Miller, who was my chief staff officer, who had had a cruise in A3Ds, and a successful one; Hal Lang, who was one of the carrier pilots that we captured; he was going to be skipper of VAH-7, and then the famous Don Runyon, who had been one of our first aces in World

War II and had been in the famous Fighting Two.* Down at Sanford, they didn't even know who Don Runyon was. When I saw him there, I said, "My God, what are you doing here?"

He said, "I don't know. What are you doing?"

I said, "Well, it's going to change." So I said, "How about the airplane?"

He said, "They won't even let me check out."

Knowing how good Runyon was, I said, "Well, I'm going out within a week, and I want you to go out too and get qualified." I think it took eight landings to be considered qualified.

So out we went to the FDR, and I think we set an all-time record for carrier operations for the A3D.† We made a total of 64 touch-and-gos and carrier landings. We had no bolters and no wave-offs.‡ As we left the ship, Ralph Shifley, the skipper, sent his congratulations.§ The plane was a beauty.

When I left the carrier, I flew up to see Admiral Rees. He wanted to see me about something. He had said, "When you come up, you come on in in your flight gear and let's talk."

When I arrived, he said, "Where did you come from?"

I said, "I've been down on the Roosevelt to qualify in the A3D."

He said, "Could you get aboard?"

I said, "Was there any doubt?"

He kind of laughed. I didn't realize until later the reason he was laughing was because my predecessor had some severe problems with carrier landings.

So I was carqualed. All that I really wanted to do, was to get across to the people that I was a carrier guy, that I expected them to be carrier guys.

Q: And that the plane was a carrier airplane.

---

* Commander John M. Miller, USN; Commander Harold F. Lang, USN; Commander Donald E. Runyon, USN.
† FDR--USS Franklin D. Roosevelt (CVA-42).
‡ A bolter occurs when a jet aircraft misses the arresting wires on a carrier's deck and then puts on power to climb out and make another landing attempt.
§ Captain Ralph L. Shifley, USN, commanded the USS Franklin D. Roosevelt (CVA-42) from July 1958 to August 1959.

Admiral Ramage: And that the plane was a carrier airplane. Not only that, it was probably the easiest carrier airplane I ever took aboard, except maybe the F2H-3, which was a dream too. It was just a rocking chair in the groove; there was just no problem to it.

My next big thing to try to do for the heavy attack wing was increase morale. After they had been battered by the famous Cat Brown, and somewhat by me, I wanted to do something to bring them up and make them proud of being in heavy attack. They in the past had what they called a bombing derby, which was just an internal affair and not much noise was made about it. I had a good PIO officer, and we decided that we would really make this an all-out show.[*] We were going to tie it in with the PGA Open Golf Tournament that was being played in the golf course adjacent to Sanford. We would get the city fathers behind the bombing derby, and they really liked the Navy. We were their livelihood, and it was a real love-in as far as the Navy and Sanford. There was a chap named Braley Odom, who was particularly helpful. He was a good money-raiser.

Then, of course, we got Douglas involved with some of their money. They were really hurting at the time and wanted to see the A3D program go too. So we decided that we would have a bombing derby with high-altitude radar bombing on the SAC bombing sites around the country. In addition to that, we would start a new series of competitions. I challenged the A4D RAG up in Cecil Field to produce an A4D pilot to complete in a loft bomb contest with an A3D pilot.[†]

And speaking of stacking the decks, it was to be a one-bomb run, using a Mark 7 shape. I wasn't really thinking that the A3D might win, but I wanted to make everybody well aware of the fact that we were in the low-altitude penetration business. If we lost, we still would get the point across that we were in it to stay. And if we won, my God, I could really shoot my mouth off. So it was pretty well stacked, as far as I was concerned.

I also got another new program in, which was called the carrier landing competition. This was to have the squadrons, and we had probably about 40 or 50 airplanes there by that time, get into a formation and be called down into the landing pattern. I had Bob Dosé and

---

[*] PIO--public information officer.
[†] Cecil Field is part of Naval Air Station Jacksonville, Florida.

Bob Elder down there judging our ability to operate as carrier squadrons, right down to the touchdown. They came in by an LSO, and there was a trophy given for the best carrier operational squadron from the landing standpoint. So that got attention too!

In the meantime, Heavy 1, under Commander Sid Baney, had a stunt team, and the first time I saw them they scared me.[*] Obviously they couldn't go over the top, but they flew a nice formation and it was tight. It was a real pretty thing to see. As far as flying the formations were concerned, they were as good as the Blues.[†] Of course, they didn't do all the intricate maneuvers, but if you saw those four big horses up there being operated like that, you couldn't help but be impressed.

I invited everybody in the world down, starting with the DCNO for Air, who was at that time "the beard," Bob Pirie; Vice Admiral Wallace Beakley, who was OP-03, DCNO for Operations; the Chief of BuOrd, who was P.D. Stroop; my friend Don Griffin, who was still on the Joint staff; and AirLant, of course.[‡] Practically every aviation flag officer that I could get ahold of on the East Coast came down for this show. It was in early December. The night before, I was really concerned because the planes were out on this night high-altitude bombing mission, and the weather was just terrible. I was afraid that I was going to end up the big show part of it with aircraft at fields all over the South. It was miserable. It had been snowing up there in the north, where they were bombing, but they got back.

As I said before, I'm always lucky. This show went off just perfect. And when you saw this flight line of 40 or so A3Ds swing out into formation, it was impressive.

Q: The noise alone.

---

[*] Commander Sidney N. Baney, USN.
[†] Blue Angels is the name of the Navy's flight demonstration team, which has done close formation flying for air shows and other events since 1946.
[‡] Vice Admiral Robert B. Pirie, Jr., USN, served as Deputy Chief of Naval Operations (Air) from 26 May 1958 to 1 November 1962. His oral history is in the Naval Institute collection. Vice Admiral Wallace M. Beakley, USN; Rear Admiral Paul D. Stroop, USN, served as Chief of the Bureau of Ordnance from March 1958 to September 1959. The oral history of Stroop, who retired as a vice admiral, is in the Naval Institute collection.

Admiral Ramage: It was something. I might add that not only was it impressive, it impressed everybody there, particularly Sid Baney's stunt team. It just completely infused everybody. Bill Barrow, the A4D pilot, beat our A3D loft bomber, but that was all right.[*] We congratulated him and gave him a trophy and sent him back home. We were really on the way. Afterwards we had a debriefing of the program, and as you might know, a big party that evening at the local hotel, which was sponsored by a combination of Douglas Aircraft and the city fathers. The wheels all played golf, so they had a pretty big day. It was pretty apparent that Bob Pirie was impressed.

It was noteworthy that Vice Admiral Bill Rees, who was ComNavAirLant, did not come, and at the time I think he begged off because of being out of town or something, but I think he did that purposely. I think he wanted me to put on my show and let these people from Washington know that we were alive and well. Because by this time Rees was convinced that they shouldn't break up the wing, that they should retain everything at Sanford. So here we were in the matter of about four or five months beginning to look pretty good. On top of that, earlier in the fall, Heavy 9 got an attaboy from Cat Brown, saying that he was eating crow, and that the heavy attack squadrons were looking good. He said words to the effect that, "When crow tastes like filet mignon, it's easy to take." I can't claim any credit for this. This was before my time as far as having an impact. Heavy 9 had turned the corner and really had pretty much made Cat Brown realize that we did have something going at Sanford.

Q: Cat Brown was Sixth Fleet.

Admiral Ramage: He was Sixth Fleet. So from then on at Sanford, we were just on the rise. People began wanting to come down there, and we had excellent living conditions. The arrangement with the city was great. As a matter of fact, I'll tell a story. The field was right in the town. All we had was just temporary World War II buildings plus a few Butler buildings. I think we ran that whole base on $1.6 million a year or something like that,

---

[*] Commander William B. Barrow, Jr., USN.

which pleased Admiral Rees. We used to call him "bony finger" because he was so tight with his resources.

One night I got a telephone call. We didn't live on the base; we were out about four or five miles. The caller was not too unhappy. We were having night bounce drill, and it was really terrible under the runway. He held the phone out and he said, "Captain, can you hear this?" And I could hear this thing going right through his room.

I said, "Well, you know, we're getting these people ready to go aboard ship and it won't last much longer. You'll just have to bear with us."

Then he turned kind of nasty about it. I said, "Well, if you feel that way about it, why don't you call Mayor Higginbotham," who was a dear friend of mine.

He said, "I already did, and he told me to go screw myself." So that was the relationship with Sanford. As a matter of fact, the Episcopal Church was right under the flight pattern. When we were flying on Sunday, they would stop everything during the time a plane went over, and have a silent prayer for the pilot. We really had it made there. The little town was, I guess, maybe 10,000 or 12,000 people, but they really loved us and we loved them.

I was at Sanford two very pleasant years and was able to keep flying all the time. I was such a flight hog that I personally took every newcoming pilot for his original familiarization flight around the area. It gave me a good look at who was coming in. The A3D is a single-piloted aircraft, and while we were up there, I would change seats and let the new guy take the controls. I could tell right away whether the guy was good or bad. The big problem, of course, with the A3D, as far as I was concerned, was that it had a yoke rather than a stick, which made it a little difficult for a real carrier guy to get used to, and the throttles were not in the right place. They were on the right hand rather than the left. But the plane itself was a very good airplane to fly.

Q: This sounds like more of the VP influence.

Admiral Ramage: Well, I asked about that at the time, and it may be the VP influence. I think I asked Ed Heinemann about it, and he said that without the yoke there was not enough leverage in case the boost went out in the ailerons to control them. You could handle it with a yoke and the wheel because you could get leverage, but with a stick you might not be able to do it. That was the reason that was given to me.

Q: How about the throttle quadrant arrangement?

Admiral Ramage: Well, it was awkward, two throttles on the right-hand side, so in coming aboard ship, you had your hand on the throttle with your right hand, and you had just the one hand on the . . .

Q: Did Ed say why they chose that arrangement instead of a port hand?

Admiral Ramage: No. I didn't ever ask that. It just seems, I guess, when you have a yoke, that's where it goes.

Q: Your bombardier-navigator, did he ever back you up on throttles or anything?

Admiral Ramage: No, he was just not in any position. I'd like to talk about the bombardier-navigators in the heavy program because they were quite important. When I got down there, they did have pilot personnel problems, and they had bombardier-navigator problems too, but there was a nucleus of well-trained bombardier-navigators. They were all ex-enlisted or still enlisted.

Q: This was on a relatively brand-new program too.

Admiral Ramage: I don't know how long they'd been in there, but when they got a pilot in the past, he would be a bombardier-navigator for X number of years, and then he would fleet up to go into the left hand seat and be the pilot. Well, it was bad for two reasons. First of all, the pilot wanted to fly, because he was an aviator. Secondly, it was damn ineffective because training a bombardier-navigator is really harder than training a pilot in that particular configuration of an aircraft. So about the time that the bombardier-navigator, who was a pilot, was ready to transition over to the left hand seat, you lose all that skill and you start out with another nugget BN.

We found down in Sanford that there was a lot of talent already there. They were enlisted bombardier-navigators. I don't know where they came from. But what we would do would be to take a likely guy and put him into the A3D as a third crewman, and then send him through the various courses and qualify him as a BN. I liked this so well that I told Admiral Rees that I didn't want to have any more pilots sent down to be bombardier-navigators. I felt that I could fill all the requirements with enlisted.

Just before I left Sanford, I did a study on the effectiveness of this program of the enlisted bombardiers versus the pilot bombardiers that we'd had in the past, and the difference between them was day and night in their abilities, their bomb miss distances and so forth. So when I left, as far as I was concerned, there would be no more officers in the right-hand seat unless they came on up through as enlisted men. There were quite a number of them that made LDO because the bombardier-navigator course was very complicated and was a very hard course.[*]

I think it took more smarts to pass the BN course than it did to pass the pilot course. I had any number of them that fleeted up and became ensigns and became professional BNs. It was quite awkward because they were not in a rated category. There was no way to get them automatic flight skins like you can for NFOs now.[†] I think I was able to get flight skins for everybody, but it was quite a management problem to take care of these guys.

Q: Do you think that holds lessons for today? Could we do with fewer commissioned air crew?

Admiral Ramage: I think so. I think that the NFO program, although it has been successful, was kind of "to keep up with the Joneses." The Air Force, of course, always

---

[*] LDO--limited duty officer, a former enlisted man whose duties are related to his enlisted specialty.
[†] NFOs--naval flight officers. Flight skins is a slang term for flight pay that is in addition to an individual's regular base pay.

used commissioned officers for their bombardiers. When this study came on that actually set up our NFO program, they were looking at some of the problems of enlisted/officer camaraderie and all that bull, which didn't make a damn bit of a problem to me.

I think there is still an excellent source of both pilot and bombardier-navigator or RIO within the enlisted ranks of the Navy, and I really encourage personnel management to look into that source.* If they feel they must commission them, fine, but I was very satisfied with it the way it went down at Sanford. The people that didn't become LDOs generally were too old. I forget what the . . .

Q: It was 35 at that time.

Admiral Ramage: I don't know, but we had some BNs that were approaching 40, and so they were real experts. I might add, a little bit later, when they set up the NFO program, I was skipper of the Independence. I heard it was going on, and I wrote quite a treatise on what my experience had been in the multi-seated aircraft of heavy attack, and outlined my preference to use at least some enlisted. You might know what happened. I don't think they even read the letter. They probably were very interested to see whether NFOs were going to be eligible for command of a carrier or something like that.

Q: I suppose the majority of today's naval aviators are unaware that we ever had noncommissioned pilots.

Admiral Ramage: I suppose so.

When we were doing this radar bombing using SAC's system, we'd have the bombardier in the bomber stream at night--they always bombed at night--report in to the controller on the ground. You'd have Lieutenant Colonel Jones, of such and such a bomb wing, and then you'd have Ordnanceman First Class O'Leary, Heavy Attack Wing One.

Q: In Heavy Attack 1.

---
* RIO--radar intercept officer.

Admiral Ramage: In Heavy Attack 1 from Sanford, Florida. It kind of got their attention, and I always liked it. I think that's all for Sanford. You can see that I liked it, and although the original time was rather painful, I'm afraid, for some people, I think that the heavy attack program benefited.

I might add, at that time, also, that the A3J was coming along.[*] It was unbelievable that it was.

Q: The Vigilante.

Admiral Ramage: The Vigilante, another high-altitude penetrator. It was faster, of course, had after burners, but it excreted the weapon from the tail of the aircraft somehow, and it simply was not the aircraft that we needed. I had opposed it previously in OP-05W to no avail, and we were beginning to get ready to take it down at Sanford. None had been received down there when I left, but my relief, who was Captain Lou Edwards, got the job of introducing the Vigilante to heavy attack.[†] It simply was not the way to go, but I had my say on it. I wrote a letter to the effect that I thought that we should get out of the program.

At that time, Douglas had said that they could build another hundred A3Ds for less than $1 million a copy. My reason at that time for supporting more A3Ds didn't go very well with the people in heavy attack, because I foresaw it as an in-flight refueler. The cambered leading edge birds that came out with the in-flight package available. I've always said in-flight fuel was the most expensive fuel there is in the world, but when you need it, you've got to have it, and we were approaching the time that we had to get into a big in-flight refueling program.

Q: Do you know who proposed the A3D for the tanker?

Admiral Ramage: No, I don't. I think Moorer was behind it, though.

---

[*] The North American A3J Vigilante first entered fleet squadrons in 1961 as a carrier-based heavy bomber. It was reclassified A-5 in 1962. The photo reconnaissance version, RA-5C, entered the fleet in 1964.
[†] Captain Frank G. Edwards, USN.

Q: Had they talked about that at all while you were there?

Admiral Ramage: No. And in the battle problem the only in-flight tanking that we had was A4D to A4D, the buddy store system, which was quite good.

Q: That started in the mid-'50?

Admiral Ramage: Yes. I'm quite sure that Moorer was definitely behind that, but quite obviously the pilots in the A3Ds took a look at that tanker package. They didn't like it, and I didn't blame them. I didn't tell them that this was really the way to go, and that perhaps the A3D might be of great value to the fleet later on. Incidentally, today's the 23rd of February, 1985, and I just saw an A-3 go by into NAS North Island. Now that's just about 30 years of use. So it was a very effective plane, even if not used for what it was designed.

Q: It's been SLEPed to almost the end of the century, hasn't it?*

Admiral Ramage: I guess so.

Q: They're talking mid-'90s.

Admiral Ramage: Yes. It's a beauty. I think that Ed Heinemann looks upon that as his real masterpiece.

Q: Yes, he does.

Admiral Ramage: He's talked about it at length, how he came in way under cost and time, and it's a beauty.

---

* SLEP--service life extension program.

Q: I once asked Ed what was his favorite design, the one of which he was most proud, figuring he would answer the A3D, and he said, "Well, to tell you the truth, it's my blimp."

Admiral Ramage: Yeah.

Q: It was never built, but he bid Goodyear out of it.

Admiral Ramage: Well, now he's in the boat business, so he's a talented guy. But I think if he was serious, he'd tell you the A3D, certainly over the A4D.

Q: Back to this in-flight refueling thing just for a moment, I'd like to regress back to the Air Group 19. Was there any discussion? Fuel certainly had become a factor with jets by that time in carrier aviation. Was it in discussion at that time while you guys were out there in WestPac, "Gee, wouldn't it be nice if we could gas up here and do something?"

Admiral Ramage: I think at that time we were so concerned with trying to do the job we had, that those of us that were operating just didn't even look that far. We had all we could do. Obviously we needed it, particularly the F9F-6, which we were operating on a one-and-a-half hour cycle time at that time. The F9F-6 was really a problem because it didn't have the auxiliary tanks the F9F-5 did, nor the fuel capacity of the F2H-3. So the F9F-6 was always just a little scoshee. I don't think that any of those pilots ever landed aboard without seeing the red light. They got used to it.

Q: And that's down from what, about four-hour cycle times in World War II?

Admiral Ramage: Yes, that was the standard during World War II. A lot of carriers in Korea went to an hour and 15 minute-cycle time, which meant you could do nothing. Captain Griffin kept us right on the hour and a half. He made us work at it, and it could be done. But there was no room for error in the flying out there in the Sea of Japan. You couldn't plug into anything, except you could bingo over to Kimpo, the airfield in Korea.

We did always operate in groups of two carriers, and one carrier had the ready deck while the other carrier was operating, so they staggered the flight schedule.

Q: So a foul deck ...

Admiral Ramage: You generally had a ready deck all day long, or you could get one.

Q: What do you feel about the Navy's priority today on in-flight refueling? Do you think they're doing enough?

Admiral Ramage: Well, I hope so, and I will get into in-flight refueling a little bit later when we get into the Gulf of Tonkin. But it's a way of life, and we've just got to do it.

Incidentally, the Navy's first night in-flight refueling that I know of was done in VC-3 when I was skipper there. They had installed the probe into the F2H-3 and Ray Fernandez, who was skipper of Heavy 11, had arranged to plug in at night to an Air Force tanker over Japan while they were deployed.[*] We made a lot of noise about that. As far as I know, at least in an operational squadron, that was the first time there was ever a night in-flight refueling.

I'd like to go back to the A3J again and my feeling about it. I discussed it at length with Admiral Rees, and he agreed with me. He said, "You can go up and talk to Admiral Bob Pirie [who was DCNO (Air)] about it," and I did.

Admiral Pirie said, "It's just too far down the line. You may be right about it, but it's too late. We've got to take the thing. It's coming, so you'd better get down to Sanford and get ready to take it." So I did.

Q: Did you fly the airplane?

---

[*] Commander Caesar Fernandez, Jr., USN.

Admiral Ramage: I've never flown it, never been in it. I left before the first airplane came in. But there was quite a bit of construction that was required to support it, which was going on at NAS Sanford when I left.

Q: This gets a little sensitive, but what you're really saying there is that, yeah, we buy weapons in this country that we know aren't going to be any good, but politically we lose too much face to cancel the program.

Admiral Ramage: I can't talk to that. I've never been in the procurement business. I know when an airplane that's coming along isn't what we want. I'm fully aware of that because of my operational experience, but the footwork that goes on in Washington in plane procurement has always been a notch above me.

We had a group of people in OP-55 that set requirements about the time I was in OP-05W. That shop was headed by Noel Gayler, who I always claimed was Mach-happy.[*] He had been skipper of VX-3, but he had never commanded an operational jet squadron aboard ship, with the type of pilots that we had to use. When I had Air Group 19, we were just trying to keep these guys looking pretty good around the ship, and hopefully be able to do something, because we simply weren't ready for the aircraft. Noel, on the other hand, had VX-3, which was loaded with talent, and he used to come up with statements about jet operations that showed that he was just talking through his hat. He didn't know what the general pilot quality was in the fleet.

From the Heavy Attack Wing in 1960, that's in July, I went to the West Coast to take command of the Salisbury Sound, which was AV-13, a large seaplane tender.[†] I think that they gave me a seaplane tender at that time rather than an oiler or other logistic ship that most of the pilots were assigned to, because I'd opposed sending pilots to the service force so emphatically when I was in OP-05W. At least somebody took mercy on me and let

---

[*] Captain Noel A. M. Gayler, USN. The oral history of Gayler, who retired as a four-star admiral, is in the Naval Institute collection.
[†] USS Salisbury Sound (AV-13), a Currituck-class seaplane tender, was commissioned 26 November 1945. She was 540 feet long, 69 feet in the beam, had a draft of 22 feet, and displaced 13,635 tons. She remained in service until her decommissioning in March 1967.

me work for an aviator. I guess maybe they were afraid I might do something drastic. Anyway, I was very delighted to get a seaplane tender, because it kept me in the naval aviation organization.

The seaplane tender was a nice, large, comfortable hotel. It was a sabbatical year for me.

Q: She was the station ship out of Hong Kong, wasn't she?

Admiral Ramage: No. After I'd been aboard for about three months, that would be in--no, I was aboard longer than that, it was after Christmas, I deployed with the Sally Maru to WestPac to be the flagship for Taiwan Patrol Force, which was aboard a seaplane tender. I think previously that she'd been a tender in Hong Kong but not on my watch. It certainly was not a demanding job, and I enjoyed it. I learned a little bit about seamanship. We certainly didn't ever operate with anything. We were in the Navy yard shortly after I took over. We had a few problems as far as one shaft was concerned. I got so mad about the fact that they couldn't line up the main propeller shaft.

There were two engines in the seaplane tender. I finally got the Navy yard and the chief engineer together, and I said, "Look, we haven't got any more horsepower in that engine than we've got in a small jet engine in an aircraft. Why don't you go over to the O&R over at Alameda and find out how you line up a jet shaft? This looks simple."* I thought it was, but we continued to wipe bearings, and I just couldn't figure out why they couldn't fix it. I got through the cruise without any great problem, but it was always one of those things you were concerned about, because she had wiped bearings several times previously.

Out in WestPac we spent most of the time in Okinawa, at White Beach and Buckner Bay. We had a big crew, over 800 people. The crewmen spent a good part of their time having fights with the Third Marines over on the beach. It was a pretty good melee from time to time. We managed to keep people out of the hospital, but barely. There was a Marine colonel that had the logistics command, and we decided we'd set up a series of

---

* O&R--overhaul and repair.

home-and-home softball games. I had an excellent softball team on the Sally Maru. These were good games, but unfortunately the program worked fine for a while, but after the game was over and people got beered up a little and the fights went on again.

I've got a couple of anecdotes about Sally Maru. One of them was when I first went aboard--the first time I went to chapel on the ship. They held services down in the hangar deck, which was pretty good sized. I always encouraged people to go, pointing out that I sinned as much as anybody else, and they might just as well come along with me. I guess you don't do that anymore--not sin, but telling people they should go to church. When I entered the hangar deck, the new parson, who was a commander named Lindner, called out, "Attention on deck," as I came into the church service.[*]

I said, "Padre, you remember that Jesus said, 'Render unto Caesar what is Caesar's, and render unto the Lord what is the Lord's.' And today this hangar deck belongs to the Lord, not to Caesar. Let's not have any 'attention on deck' during chapel services."

Q: What was his reaction?

Admiral Ramage: Well, he was very quiet. It never happened again. I guess he figured himself very chastised.

Another really funny story--my navigator was a guy named Ort Rudd, who'd been a P5M pilot.[†] He was a good navigator, he took very good care of me. I might add that he took very good care of Jim Holloway later on.[‡] When we were coming into Okinawa the first time, we'd been warned about VD all over the place. So I got on the horn. I always felt we'd better have a little bit of direct contact with the crew on this thing. I said, "Now, you've got to remember that every girl over there has VD, and conduct yourself accordingly."

Ort said that there were only two women on the dock, his wife and mine. He didn't tell me that until last year. He kept that pretty quiet. It gave the crew a few laughs.

---

[*] Commander Newell D. Lindner, CHC, USN.
[†] Lieutenant Commander Richard Orten Rudd, USN. The Martin P5M Marlin was the U.S. Navy's last operational flying boat. It entered fleet service in 1948 and was last used in 1966.
[‡] Admiral James L. Holloway III, USN, was Chief of Naval Operations, 1974-78.

James D. Ramage #1 - 230

We were out there about six months, and we did operate with the seaplanes a couple of times. It was certainly a comedown. They were getting ready for one big operation, and the operation was to start at midnight, so I got up to see how the crews were being briefed. The operation went off with a bang. They launched one P5M, and that was the operation. I said, "Well, what else happens now?"

And they said, "Oh, at 6:00 o'clock we're going to launch another one."

"Oh, my Lord, I don't know if I can take the heat here."

We carried Johnny Gannon around, who was Commander Taiwan Patrol Force.[*] He was a very nice guy and we got along fine. He was relieved later by Smoke Strean.[†] He had been the CAG at Air Group 98 for a while when I was there.

We returned to Alameda, and I was relieved the following August. That would be the summer of '61, to proceed to OP-604, which was in the plans division of Policies and Plans branch under Ulysses S. Grant Sharp.[‡] Admiral Sharp really ran that OP-06 bunch of his like a martinet. He was very selective in the people that came to work for him. He had complete control over BuPers assignments, and once he put the finger on you, you were there. Once you got in there, you'd better perform. He was difficult to work for in that he was very demanding, but on the other hand, if you did your job right, he took very good care of you.

OP-604 was the nuclear weapons shop, as you might guess. We were responsible for the Navy nuclear war plans and pretty much oversaw the developments in weapons that were coming along, to make sure the fleet was kept aware of joint planning. It was an excellent job for me since I'd been in the nuke weapon business for so long.

About that time was the advent of McNamara, and I was, I think, the first one in the Navy Department to really get the treatment.[§] He attacked the nuclear capabilities first, because he could quantify them easily. The general-purpose forces would take longer. But I went in at the request of one of McNamara's whiz kids, to discuss the nuclear weapons

---

[*] Rear Admiral John W. Gannon, USN.
[†] Rear Admiral Bernard M. Strean, USN.
[‡] Vice Admiral U. S. Grant Sharp, USN, served as Deputy Chief of Naval Operations (Plans and Policy) from August 1960 to August 1963. His oral history is in the Naval Institute collection.
[§] Robert S. McNamara served as Secretary of Defense from 21 January 1961 to 29 February 1968.

capabilities of the fleet, and he promptly gave me a damn good hazing.* He was about 28 years old, didn't know a goddamn thing about anything, and indicated that if I were any good at all, I wouldn't be in the Navy anyway.

I later mentioned that to the CNO, who was George Anderson at the time, and he said, "You don't have to take that from any of those people, remember."† He advised all the people who briefed him for the Joint Chiefs of Staff daily actions, as follows: "You heard what happened here. Remember this. Unless a man is appointed with the advice and consent of the Senate of the United States, you don't have to take that." Was he ever wrong! As a matter of fact, ultimately that was the thing that did in Bob Pirie, when he was going to become CinCUSNavEur.‡ One of the whiz kids, I think his name was Rosenzweig, did in Bob Pirie. He went back and told his boss that Bob Pirie was not cooperating in any way, and Bob was retired out of OP-05 when he was definitely going to get his fourth star.

Q: At what point did it become widely known in the Navy that a new era was at hand and the professional military people were being essentially reduced to a communications channel?

Admiral Ramage: Well, darn soon, because the first thing we got, I think, was a list of 100 questions, and those were questions like, "Why do we need a Navy?" They were things that were absolutely self-evident, and, of course, one of them was, "Why don't we do away with aircraft carriers?" That was a nice big-ticket item that you could discuss. These things were passed around among all the armed services, and it kept the pros who were trying to staff these things so darn busy they couldn't do their jobs. You were always getting some kind of a special project that was just plain silly. You could be called to go to the upper regions to brief some whiz kid on something that really wasn't his business. It was just a

---

* "Whiz Kids" was the nickname for the group of young civilian officials whom McNamara appointed to key positions in the Department of Defense hierarchy.
† Admiral George W. Anderson, Jr., USN, served as Chief of Naval Operations from 1 August 1961 to 1 August 1963. His oral history, including an account of his being relieved of duty as CNO, is in the Naval Institute collection.
‡ CinCUSNavEur--Commander in Chief U.S. Naval Forces Europe.

terrible comeuppance for the professional military officers in all branches.

Q: This must have come as a particular shock and surprise in the Navy, considering Kennedy's background.

Admiral Ramage: Yeah, well, his background in the Navy was pretty limited, to be a PT skipper and not a very good one at that, I guess.[*] You're not very smart when you get run into by a destroyer at night when you're a PT skipper. I'll drop it there.

Q: His bravery is in question, his talent was a little shaky.

Admiral Ramage: Again, getting back to Admiral Sharp, whom I admire very much, as I pointed out, he was a very difficult man to work for. However, I learned a lot from Admiral Sharp about the specifics of writing. Be damned sure that you're exactly correct in what you say; don't be redundant; be sure you follow the Navy policy to the best of your ability. He wanted you to go down to the Joint Staff and put forth the Navy view, and you were expected to know what was good for the Navy.

Very shortly after I got there, we had the first indication of a joint planning group, which was to be established in Omaha. That was the JSTPS.[†] It had to do with coordinating all of the nuclear capabilities of the armed services. I might add that it was long overdue, and ultimately ended up with the publishing of the SIOP, which was the Single Integrated Operational Plan, to integrate not only the nuclear capability of the United States, but also to coordinate that capability with those other countries that had a nuclear capability.

Q: This was to avoid duplication.

---

[*] Lieutenant John F. Kennedy, USNR, was in command of the PT-109 the night of 2 August 1943 when she was rammed and sunk by the Japanese destroyer Amagiri while operating in Blackett Strait in the Solomon Islands.
[†] JSTPS--Joint Strategic Target Planning Staff, which is discussed in the Naval Institute oral histories of several officers who were assigned there: Admiral John J. Hyland, USN (Ret.); Vice Admiral Gerald E. Miller, USN (Ret.); Vice Admiral Kent L. Lee, USN (Ret.); Vice Admiral Edward N. Parker, USN (Ret.).

Admiral Ramage: Duplication, yes. When it came up for discussion, we didn't even have a paper on it. It was up for discussion in the joint arena the next day. We didn't even have any indication of what it was. I got a call from Admiral Anderson's office saying, "You've got to get so and so because it's going to be discussed the following day at the joint level, and Mr. McNamara's going to be in there."

So I went around and tried to swipe a copy of what this discussion was going to be in order to staff it for the CNO. I think I finally was able to steal one someplace, I don't know exactly where. At the briefing the night before, I briefed it as best I could, pointing out that it was going to be politically very heavy, and it was something that we had better watch out for. I really couldn't get the details, and we didn't get them for about a week. But in general, it was to coordinate all of the nuclear attack capabilities under one planning staff.

The problem, as far as the Navy was concerned, was that it was going to be in Omaha, and the director of the joint staff was also commanding general of the Strategic Air Command. So as the thing went downstream, it was apparent that the Navy was in a hell of a weak position. We didn't have any input at all.

In setting up the organization that joint staff, we did send out Vice Admiral Butch Parker; he was the first deputy for the Navy out there. We had maybe a handful of 10 or 12 people out there, I don't think many more than that. On the other side of the fence was SAC, with that enormous staff of, I'll say thousands. I think there must be certainly more than 1,000, maybe 2,000. And further, the SAC people were double-hatted. The director of operations of SAC was also the director of operations of the joint staff, so they not only worked out of their own pocket over there, but when they went over into the joint side, they had complete control. And at the time that it came about, we had no Navy man that headed any of the divisions on the joint staff; they were all SAC people. So it got to be a real problem, and it was my job in OP-604 to try to watch out for the Navy's situation wherever possible. Some of the things were pretty brutal.

For the original briefing, we went out to Omaha. I was Admiral Anderson's briefcase-carrier and the guy that sat behind him at the conference to come up with detailed proposals. Jerry Miller had been ordered out to JSTPS, and Jerry gave a very fine briefing on what the setup was going to be.

Q: This is Vice Admiral Jerry Miller now.

Admiral Ramage: Yes. He was a captain at the time. During this briefing, George Anderson turned to me and he said, "Who the hell is this guy? He's got on the wrong suit." Jerry is a very smart and personable guy, and he'd thrown himself completely into his joint job. He had certainly disturbed Admiral Anderson to the point that he wondered who the hell Jerry Miller was.

I can think of several interesting things that came up during that time. One was Skybolt, which was a Douglas missile, which was to be launched from the B-52, and I think that the McNamara whiz kids correctly attacked it when they said that it combined the two worst capabilities of two good systems. It combined the ground vulnerability of the fixed-base aircraft, which was the B-52, with the inaccuracies of the missile. Of course, this is before we got the ground-contoured maps. It was bound to be a relatively inaccurate weapon, because you would have to program the flight for the thing without any in-flight guidance.

Q: A cruise missile type weapon.

Admiral Ramage: Yes. I think it was supersonic. I'm not sure. I don't remember the details, but in any event, we in the Navy opposed Skybolt. It was very simple for me to go down and attack it, but I came back the first day and was called in to see Admiral Anderson, and he asked about what was going on with Skybolt. I said, "The Navy position is . . ."

He said, "The Navy position was." He said, "Change everything and support General LeMay on that."* I think that they negotiated something, and I don't know what it was. The program was canceled anyway.

One of the reasons that it was kept in being was that the British were going to buy Skybolt, and the Air Force and Douglas were saying, "Look, you can't go back on a contract."

The U.S. Government's position was that ultimately that the Polaris submarine would be a much better weapon for the British, and they were correct, and it ultimately went that way. Of course, that was years later, but that's the way it went.

Another thing that was kind of interesting was one about geodesy. I'm sure it's all corrected now. As a matter of fact, it was corrected after this incident. It was discovered that the North American plate, the grid plate, was based on a different set of coordinates than the European grid plate, so consequently, our ballistic missiles were not correctly targeted. You can imagine the consternation when that came up. I had a spy down in JSTPS there in Omaha that advised me of this thing. It was such a hush-hush thing, that I didn't have the clearance for geodesy matters. Geodesy is a science; it's the study of the earth. This was before we had a lot of satellites to pinpoint where everything is.

Q: Do you remember what would have been a typical error?

Admiral Ramage: I'd say at least five miles or more, maybe 10 or 12. It would be enough to certainly get the counter-weapon capability nullified.

The OP-604 job was a good thing for me. I gained a lot of visibility in the E-ring. For me it was a relatively easy job, because Admiral Sharp didn't know much about nuclear weapons and nuclear war plans. He knew everything about everything else that was going on in the OP-06 organization, so I was spared quite a bit of the hazing that went on. He was tough.

---

* General Curtis E. LeMay, USAF, served as Air Force Chief of Staff from 30 June 1961 to 31 January 1965.

About that time I found out that a postgraduate degree was really something I'd better strive for if I wanted to be selected for flag rank. They'd gone big for this thing. Of course, any time that there was an opportunity to go to postgraduate school, I wasn't eligible. And probably they wouldn't have taken me anyway because I stood so low in my class. I had the two war colleges, but I thought I'd better get a postgraduate degree. I did it at night school, which was run by George Washington University and held in the Pentagon. It was pretty rough.

The last year I was there, a typical day would be to be at work by 6:30, because I had to be there when Admiral Sharp got there. There were oftentimes things that the Joint Chiefs were going to take up that you had to be prepared to get to Admiral Sharp early. He was, as he called it, the conscience of the CNO. They'd have their meeting on most days, at least three or four days a week, and they generally wouldn't be through until 5:30 or 6:00 o'clock that night. Then you would have to wait for Sharp to come back and debrief what action had been taken on the items that the Joint staff worked on that day. So oftentimes you were very late, and although Admiral Anderson was very, very nice about things and he'd always say, "Gee, I hate to do this." And he'd then add, "If there's any way you can go home, don't wait for me."

But after you get called back two or three times, you think, "I better wait till the guy comes back because I'm going to come back anyway." The same thing was true with working on Saturday. After you'd been called in two or three times on Saturday, you automatically show up at 8:00 o'clock, because you know you're going to have to go in anyway. All jobs in Washington aren't this way. It just happens that I was in a particularly demanding job. The jobs are difficult, they're demanding, but the rewards are good. If you do a good job, they're going to take care of you.

Q: It must have been awfully difficult to fit in night school.

Admiral Ramage: Well, I generally would be a little late. School was right in the Pentagon, and I think the first class started about 7:00 or 7:30, and I'd attend school to about 10:30

and then go home. It was a course in international relations from George Washington University.

Q: Was this how many times a week?

Admiral Ramage: Three or four. I carried the full 16 hours, whatever was required, 12, I think, because they allowed a certain number of hours for my time I'd been at the National War College, and I was lucky enough to have my National War College paper, which was the nth nuclear power. I really knew it, having been in OP-604. And that became my thesis for my master's, so I was kind of double-dipping there.

I will say that my time at the George Washington night school probably cost me my marriage. Right after I left Washington, my wife Ty and I decided that we'd call it a day. And I don't blame her. I was a pretty selfish guy and in a lot of the things that I did, I realize. I certainly didn't consider the family--volunteering to go to sea and volunteering to do this and that. Many of the other people spent a lot more time around home. That wasn't the only reason, there were a lot of other reasons, but . . .

Q: You just had the one daughter?

Admiral Ramage: I had two daughters. I had a second daughter who was born just before I left VC-3. So we separated amicably, except she did make quite a bit of noise about it. I think it probably worked against me as far as selection later on. I can't say that, but as far as the divorce is concerned, I'd say that it was 90% my fault, and for putting up with me for 21 years, she should have a halo.

When I was detached from OP-604, I paid my respects to Admiral Sharp, and he was most friendly.

Q: What month and year was this?

Admiral Ramage: This would have been July of 1963. As you can see, I'm quite an admirer of Admiral Sharp. I wouldn't particularly like to work for him again, but at the same time, I admire him. He's such a feisty little guy. At that time, however, he hadn't learned what he learned later as CinCPac during the Vietnam War.[*] He definitely had a bias against aviation. Right now he's one of the greatest supporters of aircraft carriers, but at that time he was pretty much in the blackshoe line.

Q: What was he advocating, the Polaris submarine?[†]

Admiral Ramage: No, no. This Polaris thing was advocated by everybody. I might go on that while we're here. We had a little program called the M^2 program while I was there. One M was Johnny Miller, who had been my chief staff officer down at the HAT wing, and the other M was Mike Michaelis, who was in one of the other OP-60 branches.[‡] But they were the chief salesmen for Polaris. It's kind of strange, but two naval aviators were the chief salesmen. We did quite a bit of studying and planning to come up with the numbers of Polaris subs. We were really looking forward to Polaris at the time; everybody was. As far as an aircraft carrier guy was concerned, I felt very strongly that if we could get the Polaris into the fleet, it would more or less take over the strategic picture. Then the carriers could be free to do more of what they do so well. So there was complete support for the Polaris program throughout the Navy.

Q: What would you consider the blackshoe line on aircraft carriers?

Admiral Ramage: There was always a feeling that the airdales still got extra flight pay, kind of fancy Dans. I hope that's over now, but there was always some of the kidding--kind

---

[*] Admiral Ulysses S. Grant Sharp, USN, served as Commander in Chief Pacific from 30 June 1964 to 31 July 1968. His oral history is in the Naval Institute collection.
[†] USS George Washington (SSBN-598), the first submarine armed with Polaris ballistic missiles, went into commission on 30 December 1959. Her first patrol began in November 1960.
[‡] Captain Frederick H. Michaelis, USN. The oral history of Michaelis, who retired as a four-star admiral, is in the Naval Institute collection.

of funny, but some of it was rather biting. I hope we're over that, but we weren't by that time.

So I received my orders to command Independence, which was just great. I proceeded singly down to Norfolk, to undergo the fire-fighting school and all this stuff that a prospective commanding officer goes through. Independence had not deployed yet. She was to leave shortly, probably about late July.

Q: This would be her initial deployment?

Admiral Ramage: No, the Independence was commissioned in '59.[*] A strange incident occurred while I was there in Norfolk. It's a story on what goes on for a new captain of a carrier. At the BOQ where I was staying, the Filipino steward told me that a man had been there to see me one day when I was gone. I said, "Well, did he leave his name or leave a card or anything?"[†]

"No. He'll come back and see you." Well, this thing went on about three days.

I said, "Did he look like a policeman? A lawyer or something?" With the various problems I was having, particularly with a divorce in process, I couldn't figure out what it was.

Finally he caught me, and it turned out that he was a clothing salesman. He was a guy that worked out of Germany and sold to various military agencies all through Europe. I guess the reason that the steward thought he was so important was that he had a huge diamond ring. It may have been glass, I don't know, but anyway, when the steward told me he was very important, I couldn't figure out who it would be. He wanted permission to sell clothes on the Independence.

I said, "First of all, I'm not commanding officer of the Independence now, and I don't have any idea what the regulations are. If that is the common practice over there,

---

[*] USS Independence (CVA-62), a Forrestal-class aircraft carrier, was commissioned 10 January 1959. She had a standard displacement of 56,300 tons, was 1,046 feet long, 130 feet in the beam, and had an extreme width of 252 feet. Her top speed was 34 knots. She was originally armed with eight 5-inch guns and could accommodate approximately 70-90 aircraft.
[†] BOQ--bachelor officers' quarters.

come and see me when I get over there and I'll discuss it, but I'm not prepared to make any promises right yet." And I said, "However, I do need a suit of clothes and I'll give you an order." He measured me, and off he went. And I'll leave that there because I want to be reminded of it later on when we get to Cannes.

I left from New York, flew commercially over to Madrid, and ended up at the submarine base in Rota, Spain. I guess the Navy must have picked me up some way, because I don't think commercial planes fly into Rota. I was quite surprised that when I landed at Rota, there was a Willy Fudd aircraft ready to take me immediately to the ship. This was about maybe 4:30 in the afternoon, and we flew right out to the ship, which was just entering the Strait of Gibraltar, and they landed me aboard about 6:00 o'clock.

Q: It wasn't a Willy Victor, I hope.

Admiral Ramage: What is that?

Q: An EA-3 probably would have picked you up, wouldn't it?

Admiral Ramage: No, it was a Grumman. Willy Fudd, E-1.*

Q: I don't think we've taken any Willy Victors aboard a carrier ship.

Admiral Ramage: Well, anyway, it had the same function. So when I landed on board, I was met by Roy Swanson, who was the skipper, and he was in mess dress.† God, I couldn't figure out what was going on. I'd never seen a mess dress aboard ship in any carrier I'd been aboard under way. He said that the wardroom was having a farewell dinner for him. I thought, "Well, that's very interesting."

---

* The Grumman E-1 Tracer was a propeller-driven carrier-based airborne early warning aircraft that was originally known as the WF, nicknamed the "Willy Fudd" because of its initials. It resulted from a modification of the S2F antisubmarine aircraft by placing a large radome atop the aircraft. Delivery of the Tracers to the fleet began in 1958.
† Captain Leroy V. Swanson, USN, commanded the USS Independence (CVA-62) from 1 September 1962 to 23 August 1963.

He said, "Yes, I'm leaving tomorrow morning."

So I went down. I guess I washed my hands. I was still in khakis; everybody else was in mess dress. I met Admiral Shinn, who told me that he expected me to relieve in the morning, that he didn't believe in these long turnovers.[*]

I said, "Aye, aye, sir." I had never served on a big ship like that. I'd only seen one before, which was the Forrestal, and I really would have liked to have had a chance to take a look at the ship. But apparently Admiral Shinn wanted Swanson out right away. I don't know exactly what the reason was. I later talked to Swanson, and I said, "This is pretty sudden. I'd sure like to get checked out in general drills and see how you go alongside and a few things like that."

He said, "I'm leaving right away." And he said, "Good luck." He said, "I've been harassed so much that I'm constipated. The sooner I get off this ship, the better off I'll be."

I said, "Well, what's the trouble?"

He said, "Al Shinn is a real hard guy to work for."

I said, "He can't be that bad."

So we had the relieving ceremony on the 23rd of August, the following morning, and he left on the first aircraft launch, which I think was probably at 11:00 o'clock. So I was soon up in the pope's chair on the bridge as captain of the ship. I didn't even know where the hangar deck was. It was a real hurry-up operation. So we started operating on the 23rd, and I thought that the pilots were a little ragged.

Q: What air wing was this?

Admiral Ramage: This was Seven, Dutch Nearman.[†] We went right into our night operations, and on the first night cycle, we had a ramp crash with an A-4. That got my attention, as you might guess. It became apparent to me later on, as the days went by, that I was in command of a carrier that wasn't ready for sea. I began to look into the details of what had happened. Independence had come out of a long overhaul, had gone through

---

[*] Rear Admiral Allen M. Shinn, USN, served as Commander Carrier Division Six from 1964 to 1966.
[†] Commander Leonard M. Nearman, USN, Commander Carrier Air Wing Seven.

under way training, had hardly any operations at all and deployed to a NATO exercise in the Bay of Biscay. In the Bay of Biscay they had had an almost-catastrophe. I don't know how many airplanes they lost, three to five, due to launching the aircraft into a bad weather area in France, the target area. That was, I guess, one of the reasons that Al Shinn was interested in moving the skipper out. However, the people that make those decisions on scheduled operations are the staff, the admiral, and not the captain of the ship. The air group was pretty shaky after having gone through that, and that had been just two or three days previously. Here I was in the situation of trying to build up the ship and get this air group ready for sea.

I talked to Dutch Nearman, the CAG, about the situation, and he advised me that there were any number of pilots that hadn't made a night landing on the cruise. They had been expedited in their training, and that he realized that they were weak. I said, "Well, we'll just have to work it out the best way we can."

About the first thing that happened, the following Sunday, was my first confrontation with Shinn. It was my first Sunday at sea. We were operating under an op plan which was written by the preceding carrier division we were just relieving. The schedule was put out by the preceding carrier division commander. It was Sunday morning, and I started flying at 8:00 o'clock, in accordance with the schedule. About 8:30 I got a call from the flag bridge, and it was Admiral Shinn. He said, "Aren't you a Christian?"

I was pretty much nonplussed. I didn't know that was a subject for discussion. I said, "Yes, I am. Why, sir?"

And he said, "Well, what are you doing flying this morning?"

I said, "Well, it's on the flight schedule."

He said, "Oh." So he apparently took a look around and said, "Come down and talk to me."

So I went down. He said, "I want you to cancel all flight operations."

I said, "Well, I can't very well. We've got a launch going and that launch is involved with the Fleet Air Defense exercise with the Sixth Fleet flagship," which was the Little Rock. "They've got a TOT of 10:00 o'clock."[*]

---

[*] TOT--time over target.

He said, "All right, then cancel out all of the aircraft that aren't part of the air defense exercise."

I said, "Admiral, I just can't do that. The pilots are manning their planes, and I can't separate these people out at this time. We're going to have to go with a full launch."

He said, "Well, that's all right then, go with a full launch." He said, "However, when you get those planes down, that's all."

So we conducted the exercise and I got all the planes down about 11:30, 12:00 o'clock. I secured from flight operations. Then I began to kind of smell things. I had this premonition. About 2:30 Admiral Shinn called me down to the bridge again and he said, "Are you going to fly tonight?"

I said, "No, sir."

He said, "Why not?"

I said, "In accordance with your desires, I've canceled the flight operations and I've secured from flight quarters, and it isn't my intention to shake the ship up again by going to flight quarters after having secured them once."

And he said, "I'd like you to fly tonight."

I said, "Do you order me to fly tonight?"

He said, "I'd like you to fly tonight."

I said, "I'm not going to fly, Admiral, unless you order me."

And we looked at each other for about 15 or 20 seconds, it seemed like four or five minutes. The people around there, particularly the flag operations officer, Si Johnson, looked aghast.[*] I finally said, "Admiral, can I have permission to leave your bridge?"

And he said, "Yes, sir." And off I went. We didn't fly.

So here we had this direct confrontation for really no reason at all, except I guess I'm stubborn. There wasn't any way that I was going to shake the hell out of that ship by calling them back to flight quarters and getting flight quarters going again. Admiral Shinn had been skipper of a carrier before, and I think he knew what that meant to get the operation going again. It isn't something you do just by pushing a button. It shakes all the way down to the bottom of the ship.

---

[*] Captain Silas R. Johnson, USN.

So in a little while, Si Johnson came up on my bridge. I said, "Well, Si, I guess I've done it. I sure didn't mean that confrontation, but damn it, I just couldn't bring myself to looking shabby before the crew. They'd think I'd lost my mind."

And he said, "I wouldn't worry about it."

I said, "Why?"

He said, "Admiral Shinn knows he was wrong, and if I were you, I wouldn't worry about it."

I said, "Well, I'm still going to worry about it." But that's the way it turned out.

Q: Had you heard of anything comparable to this ever happening?

Admiral Ramage: Never in my life. I flew on Sunday morning, Sunday afternoon every time I'd ever been to sea. I don't know where it came from.

Q: It seems like a little whimsy.

Admiral Ramage: I don't know.

Q: Could he have been trying you out?

Admiral Ramage: I don't think so. Another very strange incident occurred on the 28th of August. One morning I was going through the dispatch board and I noticed a dispatch from ComCarDiv 6, CTF 60, to Carrier Division Six and USS Saratoga.[*] Saratoga was the other CVA in the Med, being commanded by Captain Fred Moore.[†] It was info-ed to Com6thFlt, ComNavAirLant, all the Commander Fleet Airs back in the States, Commander Second Fleet, and CinCUSNavEur, the four-star admiral up in London, and the title was "Charthouse Movies."

---

[*] CTF 60--Commander Task Force 60.
[†] Captain Frederick T. Moore, Jr., USN, commanded the USS Saratoga (CVA-60) from 3 November 1962 to 28 September 1963.

It read as follows: "It has come to my attention that in some carriers it has become the custom to show movies in the charthouse, and these movies are shown even while steaming in formation or while night flying is in progress. Facility spaces and personnel at the bridge level are provided and should be employed for operations only. The charthouse is not a rec hall, and to so use it inevitably diverts attention and facilities from operational use. The practice of showing charthouse movies at sea injects needless hazards into our operations. It is forbidden in carriers of this division/task force."

I looked at this message in complete amazement because I'd only been aboard 13 days, but I had never shown movies in the charthouse. I'd never heard of it. I was able to get a back-channel message over to Fred Moore on the Sara, and asked him what goes on with these movies in the charthouse that he obviously was running, because we were only the two carriers in the Med. He said he'd never done it.

So I then got hold of the chief of staff, Max Berns, who was a classmate of mine, and I said, "What is this stuff about movies in the charthouse?"[*]

And Max said, "I haven't the slightest idea."

I noticed at the end of the message that it was originated by Admiral Shinn and released by Admiral Shinn, and that nobody had seen it. I didn't pay any attention to it, because as far as I was concerned, it didn't apply to me. But it certainly had quite an impact on Admiral Gentner, who was Commander Sixth Fleet at the time.[†]

When we finally got into Polenza Bay for the turnover of carrier divisions and also a meeting with Commander Sixth Fleet, Admiral Gentner came aboard and he got ahold of Admiral Shinn, and he said, "Come down to the cabin below. I want to talk to you." It was my cabin. He turned to me and said, "Jig, what in the hell is this movies in the charthouse at sea about?"

I said, "Admiral Gentner, I haven't the slightest idea. I've never done it."

And he turned to Al Shinn, and he said, "If you have a minor local problem, handle it yourself and keep your mouth shut."

---

[*] Captain Max A. Berns, Jr., USN.
[†] Vice Admiral William E. Gentner, Jr., USN, commanded the Sixth Fleet from March 1963 to June 1964.

That was end of subject, and that was it, and I still to this day don't know what the message was all about, but it made me wonder what kind of a madhouse we had there.

The operations continued, and it became more and more apparent to me that I had really taken over a carrier that wasn't ready for sea. The ship was in fair shape, but the air group really was floundering. It wasn't their fault. They simply hadn't the right buildup time, and if you want to point fingers, you'd have to point them at ComNavAirLant to begin with, letting them go into this NATO exercise as unprepared as they were.[*]

So we found ourselves over in the Med, deployed, in a very, very low state of readiness.

Q: Could part of this problem have been our commitment to have two carriers there regardless of . . .

Admiral Ramage: Absolutely. I don't condemn the people that put me in this position, but I think that part of the responsibility certainly was the carrier division commander's too, which apparently he was sweating out because he had been aboard when these various problems arose in the Bay of Biscay just before I took over.

But the worst night, I think, that a carrier skipper ever had occurred to me shortly thereafter, and I'll try to picture it. They were having, I think, three night cycles that evening, and this would have been the second cycle, which would have been a takeoff probably about 8:30 or 9:00 o'clock.

The first plane aboard was an F-4, flown by one of the best pilots and one of the best guys I know, Obie Oberg, who was skipper of VF-41.[†] He broke a wheel and it took a while to get the F-4 off to the side, and we continued taking aircraft aboard.[‡] Either the next or the following F-4 landed. The pilot apparently, when he went into full power,

---

[*] NATO--North Atlantic Treaty Organization.
[†] Commander Owen H. Oberg, USN, commanding officer of Fighter Squadron 41.
[‡] The McDonnell Douglas F-4 Phantom II first entered fleet squadrons in 1961 as the F4H; it was redesignated F-4 in 1962. It was a two-seat airplane with the pilot in the front and the radar intercept officer (RIO) behind him. The F-4B version had the following characteristics: length, 58 feet; wing span, 38 feet; gross weight, 54,600 pounds; top speed, 1,485 miles per hour. It was armed as a fighter with either Sparrow or Sidewinder missiles and also could carry bombs. It had a maximum external stores capacity of 16,000 pounds.

which you're supposed to do when you engage a wire, went into afterburner. I later found out the flame that came out made him think he was on fire, so he pulled on up about 300 feet and ejected both himself and the RIO. So I had two people in the water. At that time we had the UH-1 aboard and they were down, as they were down the entire cruise, so I had ...

Q: UH-2, correct?

Admiral Ramage: This is the one with only the one engine.

Q: Yes, UH-2.

Admiral Ramage: Yes. When they put the second engine on it, they changed the nomenclature.

Q: The first one was UH-2A.[*]

Admiral Ramage: Okay. UH-2A, it was down, so I had no helo recovery. There were two destroyers with us, and I detached one destroyer to pick up these two guys who were in the water. We continued to bring the aircraft down, and about that time the first A-5 made a high pass, dove for the deck, and blew up. Flames 300 feet in the air were coming up the flight deck, and the plane went over the side. It didn't do the deck any harm, but it certainly got our attention. Therefore I had two more people in the water, very probably dead, because it was such a tremendous explosion. Nevertheless, I had to detach the other destroyer to look for those two people.

By this time the conversation between operations below and the planes up above had gotten hectic. I later gave air ops hell for unnecessarily disturbing the people up there, but it got loud. By this time Admiral Shinn, on the flag bridge, had gone crit, and he was

---

[*] The Kaman UH-2A Seasprite was a utility helicopter that entered fleet squadrons in 1962.

buzzing me every 13 seconds. "What are you doing now, Captain?" "Captain, what's going to happen now."

Well, I got Newt Foss, who was my exec and a damn fine one, up there, and I said, "Newt, you take care of the admiral. Let me work myself out of this thing."[*]

In the meantime, CIC had noted a crossing situation, a large ship coming from the right, and pointed out that I was on a collision course with this large object.[†] This didn't bother me too much, because I knew that I could change course five or ten degrees. Wind over the deck has never been a great problem for me. LSOs bitch about it, but pilots can handle a hell of a lot more wind, that is, variation from down the deck than they think they can. So I was gradually easing the thing to the right in order to pass astern.

By that time, Admiral Shinn had broken loose from Foss, and he wanted to talk to me directly. It turned out to be a tanker that we were heading into. I said, "Admiral, don't worry about it. I've got it in sight. We're going to pass at least 500 yards astern of it. We've got it in sight, we know where it is, and we're going to make it." So that finally calmed him down.

So we had four men in the water, the fire on the flight deck was out, and we had six or eight planes up in the air with no tankers, no bingo, no nothing.[‡] So they started coming down, and they were wild. We finally worked down to two, one A-5 and one A-4. Both of them were so low that they were on fumes. Finally the admiral broke through the barrier again and got me and said, "What are you going to do now, Captain?"

I said, "Well, if I can land one, I'll net the other one. I'll get them, don't worry about it."

And I think it was the A-4 came around, he was under 300 pounds, and he boltered. The A-5 came around and he made it, and he got clear. The A-4 by then was down to zero. Ops wanted him to punch out, but I said, "No, let's bring him on. Just let him make up his own mind on what he wants to do." I didn't rig the barrier, he landed aboard, and the crisis was over.

---

[*] Captain Newton P. Foss, USN.
[†] CIC--combat information center.
[‡] "Bingo" is a slang term for an alternate landing field ashore in the event the planes can't get aboard the carrier.

So as we finally began to sort out the whole thing, it became obvious that we had a real disaster, you know, a real sad situation in the air wing.

Q: Were the four people in the water found?

Admiral Ramage: Two of them were picked up. The F-4 pilot and RIO were picked up, but the other two were cinders.

Q: Do you suppose that there was liquor found aboard a naval vessel?

Admiral Ramage: I wouldn't know about that. I'll tell you, there was none found in my cabin. We finally got things squared away about 11:30 or 12:00 o'clock, and I knew that the admiral wanted to talk to me about that time. He was back in the flag spaces, sitting in the far corner, just very dejected. He said, "Jig, what are we going to do?"

I said, "Admiral, I've been on these carriers now for about 24 years, and this is my big command, and I can guarantee you that we're going to work our way out of this thing. I'll get the CAG and the operations people together tomorrow, and we'll come up with some recommendations. The ship and the air group are simply not ready for sea, but we're going to make it so." So that was the end of that thing. But I don't know of any carrier skipper that had a worse night. I might also add that adding to it the actions of the admiral were not helpful.

So the next morning I got the CAG and squadron skippers together, and we went through our problems. I asked whether we had any unqualified people, and if so, should we get rid of them? But it appeared that the biggest problem was that they simply didn't have enough recent flight time. They weren't current in carrier operations, and they needed a lot of training. At the same time I couldn't help but note that VAH-1 was the worst.[*] Before I had reported to the ship, while I was still in OP-60, I had written a letter to Joe Tully, who was then the heavy attack wing commander, and said that I'd taken a look at the roster.[†] I

---

[*] VAH-1--Heavy Attack Squadron One.
[†] Captain Joseph M. Tully, Jr., USN.

told him I'd noticed that the skipper, Reinhart, was strictly a VP guy.[*] And I noticed two or three other guys that were in Heavy 1 were people that I had kicked out of the heavy attack program when I was down there when we flew A-3s.

Q: This is the Vigilante squadron.

Admiral Ramage: This is the Vigilante squadron, yes. It appeared to me that whereas they might have some strength further on down, I know they had a guy named O'Gara, who was a good pilot, and two or three others, but they simply had gone back to where they were in '58 when I went down to HAtWing 1, and it was very disconcerting.[†]

We decided then, all of us, that we'd take a good look at our pilots to make darn sure that we weren't wasting time, money, and airplanes on somebody that wasn't worthy. They came up with three recommendations. The first one and the simplest was to take the Sparrow missiles off the F-4s and fly only with Sidewinders, which would lighten them so that they could do more touch and gos and conduct more carrier operations for a longer period of time.[‡]

Secondly, we recommended that we stand down from our nuclear readiness posture. The carriers were required to keep, I believe, eight aircraft in a ready status, and I believe we had probably four A-5s and four A-4s. Of course, that tied up a huge part of the deck, which really was a problem. That we be permitted to stand down was a very reasonable thing because SAC did it all the time, and I knew they did because I just came from our nuke plans shop. When they'd get a problem, they'd stand down an entire wing and then, in turn, targets would be assigned to somebody else, no problem. And the third one was that we move over towards Sicily. What's that base?

Q: Sigonella.

---

[*] Commander Leonard J. Reinhart, USN, commanding officer of Heavy Attack Squadron One.
[†] Lieutenant Commander Patrick E. O'Gara, USN.
[‡] Sidewinder is an air-to-air infrared-homing missile with a speed of approximately Mach 2.5. It has been operational, in various forms, since 1956.

Admiral Ramage: Sigonella. That we move half the air group ashore and we begin to conduct car quals both day and night and get this air group up to where it should have been when it left the States. I thought it was a very good program. I then went up to see the admiral. I said, "This is what we'd like to do. We'd like to take the Sparrows off the F-4s."

He said, "That's simple. Make it so."

And I said, "We'd like to stand down from our nuclear readiness posture."

And he said, "In no way."

I said, "Well, Admiral, it's entirely feasible. I just came from OP-60, war plans, and the Air Force does it at times. There's no problems, there's no reflection at all on the unit."

He said, "Just forget it."

Then I said, "Now, the other thing is to go on over toward Sigonella and put half the group ashore and conduct car quals."

He said, "You will not put any aircraft on the beach as long as I'm the carrier division commander. It's against Navy policy."

Well, we were stuck. Here we had a whole load of jet aircraft, no tankers except the A-4 buddy stores, 12 A-5s, which were a load of junk, and a green air group. I got together with Dutch Nearman again, and we figured out a way that we could do it. It was going to be painful, but we could do it. At about sunset, we would launch about 40 aircraft. We would have half the A-4s loaded without using aux tanks, then we would have a group of A-4s with loaded aux tanks, and we would have the F-8s, the F-4s, and the A-5s stacked up on top.

We would start as soon as possible after the sun went down, pulling the A-4s down that were light-loaded, doing first touch and gos, then arrested landings until they ran out of fuel, and then the next group would come down, then the next groups would come down in order. Finally they'd all come on down, and we would have made quite a number of touch and gos and arrested landings. Of course, the carrier was through for the night. It had been absolutely uncocked, and there was nothing you could do with it.

So I ran this through the admiral, and he said, "Well, that seems to be a way to do it." So we started doing that. This was probably in about late September. We did it for four or five days, and we rang up over 100 night landings a night doing this. It was painful, but we did it. And at the end of that time, we had everybody current in both day and night operations.

Q: Did you have any more accidents?

Admiral Ramage: No. No, we had no more accidents the rest of the cruise.

Q: How proficient were the Marine A-4s in comparison to the two Navy Skyhawk squadrons?

Admiral Ramage: VMA-324 was a good Marine squadron. The skipper's name was Chuck Hiett.* They had one basic problem in that they had A-4Bs, and the two Navy squadrons had A-4Cs, and, of course, there's a world of difference between those two aircraft. It's mainly in the engine, but it's just a better aircraft all the way around. So they were at a disadvantage with an inferior plane to begin with. Also, I don't think any of them had ever operated aboard ship before, and when you have to put a Marine squadron into a carrier, it's like putting a quart in a pint bottle. The carrier squadrons are used to jamming up and going aboard, but Marines, if they haven't operated aboard ship, take a long time to shake down.

I take it back on the loss of life. We did have another Marine A-4 aircraft that just disappeared one night. He just disappeared in the vicinity of Sardinia, and I don't think to this day we know what happened. But other than that, we began to really make this team work.

Q: Why did you have a Marine squadron on board?

Admiral Ramage: The Navy squadron, VA-75, was transitioning into A-6s.† That was

---

* Major Charles O. Hiett, USMC, was commanding officer of Marine Attack Squadron 324.
† On 14 November 1963 Attack Squadron 75 became the first operational fleet squadron to be assigned the A-6A Intruder.

Swoose Snead's squadron.*

Q: Were they the first Intruder squadron?

Admiral Ramage: I'm not sure. I don't know.

Q: That's the Sunday Punchers.

Admiral Ramage: So they didn't make the cruise with us. But we had come around by the first of November to the point that the Independence and the air group were ready for sea. It was a superhuman effort. As a matter of fact, at one time Admiral Shinn told me that he thought I was paying too much attention to my air group and working them too hard and too little attention to the ship. I said, "Well, Admiral, that's where the problem is. We've got to do it." He said he understood. So much for those operations at that time. It was a challenge, and I like to think that I was helpful.

The squadron commanders, with one exception, and that was Reinhart, VAH-1, were good. We high-nooned Reinhart and the three or four senior people in the A-5 outfit. High-noon is when you don't let them fly at night. We were able to make do. But at the same time, I asked if I couldn't get Leroy Heath, who'd been skipper of the A-5 squadron on the Enterprise, to relieve Reinhart.† My request was not granted by BuPers.

We'll get into some of the other parts of the ship's operations now. I want to talk about the ports. The first port we went into was Cannes, and that was at the height of the tourist season.

Q: This is when your friend with the big ring showed up?

Admiral Ramage: Yes, he showed up in Cannes. When I got into Cannes, the first thing I was bombarded with was requests for people to come aboard the ship and sell clothes and

---

* Commander Leonard A. Snead, USN, commanded VA-75 in 1964-65.
† Commander Leroy A. Heath, USN.

you name it. It surprised me, but I got lots of requests from admirals, like, "Please let David Sun aboard to sell clothes."

Q: Active duty U.S. Navy admirals?

Admiral Ramage: Active duty U.S. Navy admirals. I'd made up my mind at that time that I was not going to have my hangar deck become a bazaar, regardless of what the other carriers had done. I considered that it was not a security plus to have all these people wandering around the ship. So there weren't to be any. Finally my friend with the big ring showed up and came aboard, and brought with him a very beautiful blonde gal, a real knock-out, and he said, "I have your suit."

I said, "Fine." He came in the cabin. I tried on the suit.

He measured it for some alterations. Then he said, "I also brought this out. I'd like to give it to you." It was one of these very fine Italian silk suits. It was a beautiful thing.

I said, "I didn't order that."

He said, "Yes, but I'd like to have you take it."

I said, "I don't do business that way. Take it back."

He was very upset about that, and I said, "I'll be in in the afternoon to pick up my suit." He was redoing the cuffs or something on the one that I had ordered.

So I went ashore that afternoon and went over to his establishment, and the good-looking blonde was there. She had a gold watch, it was a much more expensive watch than I've ever owned in my life or ever hoped to, one of those with a gold band, probably a Rolex. This good-looking tamale handed me the watch, and she said, "A fine-looking officer like you ought to have a fine-looking watch like this."

And I said, "That's the end." I said, "You take that watch." I turned to the guy and I said, "If we ever do permit people to sell clothes on USS Independence, it won't be you." And so I left with my suit that I'd bought and paid for and went on up toward the Martinez Hotel.

I was with Bill Elliott, who was skipper of the Nantahala, the oiler that was with us.[*] We were sitting out on one of those sidewalk cafes, and Bill got up to do something. No sooner had he left than here was the blonde right beside me. She said, "You were very mean to my boss today."

I said, "Well, I meant to be. After all, he was trying to bribe me, and I just don't like that sort of thing."

She said, "Well, I've been told to be very, very nice to you, and my apartment is right up here." She pointed up to the apartment.

Q: A little bribe, perhaps.

Admiral Ramage: I said, "Get out, lady. You come closer than the gold watch and neither one of you are going to make it." Anyway, that was the story on that. But just to go on a little bit further, I got so much pressure from external sources in the Navy that I ultimately let people come aboard and sell clothes on the ship.

Q: Including your friend?

Admiral Ramage: I did not let him ever come aboard, no. He was forbidden, but I ended up with the damndest bazaar on the ship that you've ever seen. It wasn't to my liking, but the pressure was intense.

Q: Would you care to comment on why you think this pressure was brought on?

Admiral Ramage: Well, I don't know. People, particularly over there, make friends with these merchants. I don't know whether there were freebies passed around or not. I would hate to think so. All I know is that I wasn't going to be involved in it.

Later on, about November, the ship was beginning to look pretty good, everything was coming along fine, and we went in Palermo. I used to be able to make every party,

---

[*] Captain August William Elliott, Jr., USN.

every division party. Being a bachelor over there had some advantages. Whereas most of the senior officers had wives over there that took up their time, I spent almost all the time that I could with the crew. I'd go to five or six division parties in one day, and I guarantee you, when I got through, I wasn't really fit to look at. But I enjoyed it and I gave them a lot of tender, loving care.

This Palermo incident is funny because VA-86, the skipper was Fred Koch, was an A-4 outfit, and the VF-41 skipper was Obie Oberg.[*] They were my two favorite squadrons on there. The reason they were is because they were not only good squadrons, but they had a lot of pizzazz. I ended up at a nightclub called Mirage, and it had a flamenco troupe, three gals that were knockouts. The brother of one of them played the guitar. They were pretty good.

Obie Oberg showed up, and he had about 500 bucks that he just won off of Freddie Koch, shooting craps someplace. He had all this money crumpled up, and he said, "Captain, let's have a hell of a big party." Of course, I'm always one to help somebody enjoy himself. It's all part of morale. So in due course, we had the flamenco troupe over. The main singer's name was Maria Rodriguez. I remember her very well. She knew my favorite song, which was "La Noche de Ronda," the perfect night, and she would sing this to me. In the meanwhile, Obie would be putting out his money, and we were popular! Soon, we picked up two sailors, both of them were third class petty officers; one was a Puerto Rican and the other one Cubano. The Cuban was a pretty high-pressure guy, you could see; he was a pretty smooth operator.

Q: This is from the Cuban Navy?

Admiral Ramage: No, from our Navy. Both of these were firemen, by the way, firing our boilers.

Q: It's turning into a real democratic evening.

---

[*] Commander Ferdinand B. Koch, USN, commanded Attack Squadron 86.

Admiral Ramage: So, of course, these guys were bilingual, and the gals couldn't speak English. So in due course everything was going fine. I indicated to Maria that I thought they ought to come out to the ship the following day to entertain the crew. Of course, her brother, the leader of the troupe, said he thought that would be just great. I heard one of the two firemen say to the other, "I bet five bucks the old man won't do it." That stuck in my mind.

Around 10:00 o'clock the next morning, I began to think about that gal there and the troupe. I became interested in flamenco music. I thought that maybe we ought to have them out. I also remembered about this bet. I couldn't remember the fireman's name, so I got hold of the chief engineer, and I said, "You've got a couple of Latinos down there. Do you know them?"

He said, "Oh, yeah, that's Garcia and somebody. Garcia's Cuban."

I said, "That's right." I said, "You send him up here."

Garcia reported in, and I guess he thought he was going to be horsewhipped. I said, "Now, Garcia, I think you owe your buddy five bucks because here's your next job. You get my gig, and you go to the landing, and you get my car, and you go out to where those gals are, wherever they are, I don't know, and you bring them out to entertain here on the ship."

Well, he was very relieved. Sure enough, later in that afternoon he showed up. Here they were--really beautiful gals. So we set up a concert in the captain's cabin. The Independence had the most sumptuous quarters I've ever seen. Always follow a guy that spends money. Pete Aurand had been skipper, once removed, before Leroy Swanson, and he'd had some interior decorator do that cabin.* It was out of this world. So I got a lot of people, maybe 30 or 40 in there, and we had the concert by the flamenco troupe. Numerous people were overwhelmed by the artistry of these people.

So in due course, we owned a flamenco troupe. There wasn't any way around it. As a matter of fact, the admiral was going to give a reception the following night. They gave sundown reviews on those carriers over there, a beautiful thing, Marines and the

---

* Captain Evan P. Aurand, USN, commanded the Independence from September 1961 to September 1962.

whole ceremony at sunset. It was a beautiful thing. He invited the consul general of Palermo and the various Mafioso, which all of them were, for this review. So I thought it would be pretty nice if I asked the flamenco troupe to come aboard. So I was in the receiving line with Mrs. Shinn, Sevilla, who's a charming gal, and by that time the word was around. She said, "Jig, I understand have got a flamenco troupe."

I said, "Yes."

And she said, "I'd sure like to hear them."

I said, "Well, that's rather a coincidence, because they're coming aboard tonight, and I think we can get them to play." She'd asked me to a dinner party they were having in the admiral's cabin, and I had to refuse because I was entertaining with the flamenco troupe.

So she said, "Well, how will I know them when they come through here?"

I said, "Sevilla, there will be no doubt when this group comes through who they are."

Q: How many were there in the troupe?

Admiral Ramage: Just the three girls and the one brother. Sure enough, they came down the line, and Sevilla said, "My, I can see what you mean." The review was fine, and I had a few guests there. About that time Sevilla came around the bend out of the admiral's cabin, and she said, "Do you think the troupe would play for my guests?"

I said, "Well, you'll have to ask them. They don't work for me, after all." Of course, they were delighted. As you know, those flamenco people are loud. They went in the admiral's cabin and put on a nice show. I did notice that over in the corner Admiral Shinn was very dour. He didn't think this was very funny at all.

Well, to carry this thing further, our friendship with the flamenco troupe continued on through our time in Palermo. A night or so later, our group was going over to spend some more of Oberg's money at the Mirage. By that time the air group is gathered around, and the flamenco team was paying attention only to us. Finally the owner of the nightclub came over and said, "You see that man at the end of the bar sitting over there?"

I said, "Yes."

He said, "He said he's going to kill you."

I said, "My God, what have I done?"

He said, "Maria is his girlfriend."

I said, "Oh, God. Maria?" My ardor evaporated. There wasn't any one way that I was going to be killed by a Mafioso in the streets of Palermo. I said, "Well, tell the guy that I'm not serious about this thing. As a matter of fact, I can leave right away."

And he said, "Well, take my advice and don't you leave this nightclub until daylight has come." So Oberg and the rest of us spent the night there until about 5:00 o'clock in the morning, whooping it up. I can assure you that when I left that nightclub, that was the end of my association with Spanish music.

Operations at sea had now proceeded to the point where it was a real pleasure to operate with <u>Independence</u>. She never did come up to what I considered a West Coast carrier could do, but at least they were operating, and they'd improved. We were getting ready for the Christmas holidays, but in the meantime, we'd gone into Beirut, Lebanon, which turned out to be just a great port for us. The American community had been very kind, and the crew just loved it. They just bent over backwards. I was very wary of going back to Cannes because we'd gone there before, and I didn't think the crew was well-treated, the prices were too high. I had asked if we couldn't go into Barcelona instead, but I'd been turned down. So we were due to go back into Cannes for Christmas.

In Beirut there was one of these salesmen that follow the fleet--he'd been a Navy pilot--named Pleas Campbell. I guess it was short for Pleasant. I had talked with him about what we were going to do with the crew and the officers over the holidays in Cannes, because I didn't want it to be the way it was before. It was expensive, and I didn't think people had a good time, except maybe the old-timers who had something stashed away over there.

He said, "Well, I think we can have a good time in Cannes." He said, "I'll work on something over there."

I said, "I want something for the crew, and I want something for the officers."

Q: What was this fellow's position?

Admiral Ramage: He was a salesman. He had been a Navy pilot and resigned. I think he was selling Fords or something. They followed the fleet all over the Med, these vultures. But he was a nice guy, so I said, "Well, let me know what you can dig up, and I'd be willing to consider anything."

So by the time we got into Cannes for Christmas, Campbell had lined up two things, and they sounded very good to me. One of them was the Martinez Hotel Ballroom. The Martinez Hotel is a huge place; it's owned by the government. I think they had to take it over. But the ballroom would easily take care of 2,000 people. It's a huge operation. The agreement that he had been negotiating was that we could rent the ballroom for $10,000 for ten days, and we could bring our own food, we could bring our own music.

Q: No flamenco dancers?

Admiral Ramage: No. They in turn would sell wine and beer, nothing very strong. It sounded like a real good deal. My exec, Newt Foss, said, "That's really neat. Nobody's ever done that for a crew in the Mediterranean. It'll set a new first."

So I said, "Let's go with that."

The other one was a chateau, the only one in the area. It was called the Louis XVI Chateau, and it was an elegant place. There was a guy there that owned it named Teddy Cole, and I think that he was willing to let us have that for $5,000. It was a large place; it probably had the equivalent of about 12 to 14 apartments in it, large entry hall, bar, swimming pool. It's an elegant place. It's one of the show places of Southern France. So I said, "Well, let's go for that, too. The crew will have the Martinez Ballroom every night, and the officers can set up their admins up there in the chateau." I said, "There's only one thing. We're going to have a Mother Superior over there. I don't want to run a brothel. I don't care what people do, but I don't want them to do it in that place." The Mother Superior was Scotty Lamoreaux.* You know Scotty? He was the exec of VF-41. He said

---

* Commander Lewis Scott Lamoreaux, USN.

that he'd be willing to take on this charge. It was going to be quite a problem, but he'd take it on.

So when we got into Cannes, we had everything pretty well lined up for everybody. I did get one warning, and that was from the admiral. He said, "I hope you know what you're doing with all of your men up there on the croisette," the fashionable area where the hotel was located.

I said, "I understand. I can assure you that we won't have any problems." And we didn't, because I know how to handle those things. That is, you get quite a number of petty officers who are not on shore patrol, but who are conveniently around the area, and you just kept everything under control. That didn't worry me a bit.

The chateau, on the other hand, turned out to be a real boomer, because most of the neighbors around the chateau had never been in it. They call them villas around there, and they were all Brits, mostly Jewish people, and they wanted to come in. They didn't want to meet the notorious Teddy Cole. Apparently he had quite a reputation in London, but they would like to come into his house. So we picked up quite a few friends at that time, and it worked out fine.

Included in that group was the richest man in England, Sir Isaac Wolfson. I think he's still alive. He owned land all over the world, and he entertained me one night. I said, "Well, Sir Isaac, I'd sure like to repay you. Can you and Lady Edith have lunch with me on the ship?"

She interrupted and said, "You have to understand that we are very orthodox Jews, and it's quite a problem to feed us."

I, not knowing exactly what I was getting into, said, "Lady Edith, this will be no problem at all. We can handle it." Well, it turned out to be not much of a problem because amongst the hangers-on of the Wolfsons, there were a lot of people who were just eager to get invited to this luncheon. A couple of the gals took on the job of procuring the proper food and making sure that things were done correctly. So it didn't really turn out to be the logistics problem that it could have been.

So I planned this luncheon for 12. I think it grew to 30, because everybody had to be with Wolfson. I can recall after the lunch, which was nice, I was walking up and down the flight deck with the guests, including Sir Isaac and a friend of his named Weisgal. They were all part of the international Jewish set. They were really nice people and extremely funny.

One of the first questions that Sir Isaac asked was, "Captain, about how much does a carrier like this cost?"

I said, "Well, I think this went for $250 million. It would probably cost at least five times that right now, but that's what it cost."

And Weisgal said, "Sir Isaac, if you don't stop talking money, the captain's going to think we're a couple of Jews."

So we then took a look at the F-4, and they were extremely interested in the F-4. I think really that was one of the reasons that Weisgal, in particular, came out. They hadn't procured the F-4 yet.

Q: Israel?

Admiral Ramage: Israel. And they asked me about it, and I said, "As far as I'm concerned, this is the finest fighter in the world."

Q: I think the Israelis accepted their first F-4s in about 1965 or 1966.

Admiral Ramage: This was 1963-64. So then Sir Isaac said, "How about letting me borrow one?"

And Weisgal said, "Make it two. One might not work."

We continued to have a wonderful time ashore with that particular group. They entertained us, and we in turn had a lot of fun with them.

One of the other funnies of that time is something I think it bears a little storytelling. During that time we were in port there, I went up on the flight deck, and the catapult and arresting gear crew were up there working, as usual. You know, they work in port and at sea, and they just never get a chance to do anything. I was talking to the division officer, his name was Hoch, and I said, "These guys are having a hell of a time. Have they been ashore?"*

He said, "No, sir, we've got to overhaul these catapults before we go to sea."

I said, "Well, they're going ashore and I'm going to arrange it." So I got Newt, the exec, and I said, "What I want to do is to give a party for the catapult and arresting gear crew. I'm going to set the rules, and the rules are that it's going to start in the early afternoon, anybody can go in, but nobody can come out. It's going to be free booze and whatever activities that go on wherever we go, but I'm not going to have these kids getting out and getting in trouble with the police and shore patrol."

So they chose a place called the Green Dolphin; the chiefs knew where to go. I went in there about 2:00 o'clock in the afternoon, and people were just beginning to arrive. The ship's shore patrol was on the outside, and nobody could get out. Soon a few gals began to show up, and everything was pretty quiet. I went back about 5:00 o'clock to see how that damn thing was going, and I'll tell you, it was swinging. By that time they had a whole raft of gals, the guys were really enjoying it, the music was loud, everything was just great. The gal that ran the thing said, "Are you going to come back again?"

I said, "No, this is your problem. There's only one point I'd like to make. Whatever damage there is, let me know. Don't make any reports. Whatever damage there is, I'll cover, so don't worry about it." The following morning, I went up on the flight deck to see how things were going. There wasn't a soul up there. They had had it, but they had their night on the town, and I always found that something like that is a good way to take care of people and let them blow off steam.

We went out to sea for one day. The admiral wanted to get us out to just get us out of town, and I agreed with it 100%. People were just having a hell of a good time. They were living it up pretty hard. There weren't any problems at all. And it turned out that Admiral Shinn was very pleased with our operation for the enlisted men at the croisette. The consul general came over from Nice. The thing was going great guns.

---

* Lieutenant James E. Hoch, USNR.

But when we came back into port the following morning, the notorious Teddy Cole met me. He had a Rolls-Royce, of course. He said, "Captain, I understand you're planning on having a New Year's Eve party at the chateau."

I said, "That's our intention."

He said, "You have every right to have it there; I can't stop you. You've leased it and there's nothing I can do about it. But that is a national treasure, it's been registered. The furniture is all true Louis XV or XIV time. I would appreciate it very much if you could arrange not to have that party there on New Year's Eve."

I said, "Teddy, there's no problem at all. I'll move the whole operation down to the Martinez Hotel." You'd think that I had hung the moon. I got back up to the chateau, and there was a case of champagne up in my room. Boy, he was relieved. And it turned out that he really didn't own the chateau; his wife owned it, and his wife didn't know that he had leased it out to us. If anything much had been broken up there, he'd have been in deep trouble.

Another one of the oddities that occurred during this wonderful time we had in Cannes this time involved Admiral Shinn. He put out a message to Independence and Shangri-La, which had at that time relieved Saratoga.* Fred Moore had come over from being skipper of Sara to relieve Max Berns as chief of staff to Al Shinn. This message was dated, I guess, the 14th of December and titled "Musical Groups." "In a large crew such as CVA/CVG, it is not unusual to find volunteer groups of amateur musicians, especially of the jazz combo variety. Such groups are useful and tolerable, if the music activities do not interfere with the performance of regularly assigned duties. They can be good morale builders for controlled entertainment aboard ship. Hangar decks, smokers, and so forth. Further, such groups may be permitted to play at affairs on shore which are officially sponsored U.S. Navy affairs for CVA/CVG crew, but not for other organizations."

He had his ComCarDiv 6 band, and they were available. So it ended up, "Musical groups will not, repeat not, be allowed to exist as representatives of any command in CarDiv 6 except as above. They will not be offered as part of the people-to-people program. The official Navy band embarked in CVA or authorized subdivisions thereof are

---

* USS Shangri-La (CVA-38) was an Essex-class attack carrier.

the appropriate musical organizations authorized to represent CarDiv Six commands ashore and afloat." What he was shooting at was that we had two combos, one was the Sidewinders and the other was the Snakes. I didn't like them, and they were terrible. But the people ashore loved them, and they'd much rather hear them than the ComCarDiv 6 band.

Q: Playing "Semper Fidelis."

Admiral Ramage: Yeah. So I took a look at this message and asked Freddy Moore, "What's this?" And I noticed in the message is was drafted by Rear Admiral Shinn and signed by Rear Admiral Shinn, and nobody had seen it. So I said, "Fred, do you realize that tonight I've got the Voices of <u>Independence</u>, which is our choir, going over to entertain at the Catholic church? They're not a part of the ComCarDiv 6 musical organization. Do you want me to cancel it?"

He said, "Oh, God, no. I know the admiral didn't mean that, and he didn't clear the message through anybody."

I said, "Well, you'd better get me some kind of a cancellation because under the present circumstances, I'm not going to send them in to the church tonight for midnight Mass. It just would be wrong to do."

He said, "Well, let me tell you something else that happened. The consul general's daughter had lined up the jazz combo, the Snakes [or whatever the name of it was] to play at her dinner party tonight that she's giving. We're going to have to cancel that unless Admiral Shinn cancels his message."

I said, "Well, I will expect a cancellation any minute," which I got. But again, I don't know where these things came from. They'd seem to float up from the bottom, and nobody on the staff would know anything about it.

I guess I'm being a little hard on Admiral Shinn, because he was not a bad guy at all. Our personal relationship was quite pleasant, in spite of these little things that went on and these confrontations. He was just a very difficult man to work with. He would go down below decks and wander around on the third deck, alone. He'd even break away from my

Shinn-watcher, who was Newt Foss. I'd get a report that the admiral was down inspecting the compartments.

But he was a very busy individual, concerning himself entirely with details which I didn't think an admiral should be concerned with. It had quite an effect upon me because when I got to be a flag officer, I was exactly the opposite. I never was on the bridge during operations except just to say hello. If I ever went up on the navigation bridge where the captain was, I always requested permission to come aboard, and I never gave him any orders to do anything. That's the way the admirals that I knew in the past had conducted themselves.

Q: It sounds like Admiral Shinn simply didn't want to delegate authority.

Admiral Ramage: I would say that's it. By this time, one of my stewards, John Page, said, "We've really got a swinging ship, Captain." And we really did. It only took about three or four months of damned hard work to get the ship up to where it was operating, and the crew, I think, was happy. It was a good cruise. We completed the cruise with "attaboys" from all over. I had a real problem. I had taken over a carrier not ready for combat. I worked the hell out of them and felt that the crew should get some kind of repayment.

We had one rather hairy incident. Admiral Gentner came aboard during an operation that we were doing with the Spaniards. We were just inside the Strait of Gibraltar, and he wanted me to get the carrier in close enough so the Spanish people could see the carrier launching aircraft, which was all right. I didn't know the area, but that's where he wanted to go, so that's where we went. During the daytime the wind was pretty much down the slot there, in the straits, which are just busy as hell, and the one thing I didn't know is in the evening time, the winds change and you get this convection from the land, and all of a sudden the winds started going north and south in the vicinity of the straits. So in operating aircraft, I was cutting across that main ocean thoroughfare.

Q: And would cause traffic for everybody else.

Admiral Ramage: Oh, it was hairy. I had quite a few airplanes up there that night. That's the night I learned that wind doesn't make much difference where it's coming from as long as the pilots don't know it. I took aircraft aboard with the wind at least 20 degrees on the starboard side. Portside, never, because if they have an error, they're going to go over the side as they correct for the wind. I always tried to keep the wind right down the crotch, not down the angle but down the crotch between the straight deck and the angled deck.

We got away with it that night. It was not a very bright thing to do, but I didn't know any better at the time. If I'd have known the winds in the Straits of Gibraltar at night, you can rest assured I would have complained about it, and I'm sure that if Admiral Gentner, Com6thFlt, had known it, he wouldn't have directed me to do it either.

Q: These were the days when the Med was an American lake. Was there much Soviet activity there at all?

Admiral Ramage: Very little. One thing that I missed a little earlier and I think it's a good story, was when we were in Beirut, which was, as I pointed out, a wonderful port for us. Admiral Shinn had me put the ship right in the harbor, which was very small, just as close as we could get, so that when the ship swung--we always anchored out in the Med--the fantail looked like it couldn't have been 200 or 300 yards from the beach. I think it was more than that, but you were looking right down on the people on shore.

About that time, Khrushchev's son-in-law, who was a newspaperman, had come into Beirut with some kind of a spitkit, with about 300 journalists aboard.[*] It happened about that time that the Propeller Club there, which was an American club, had asked Khrushchev's son-in-law to be a guest at the same time I was invited. It was a very pleasant lunch. The son-in-law couldn't speak English, but he had an interpreter. He got up, and he said that here he brought his press group into this friendly neutral port, and he was greeted by a giant American aircraft carrier sitting right in the middle of it. He didn't think that was

---

[*] Nikita S. Khrushchev was Soviet chief of state from 1958 to 1964. His son-in-law was Alexei Adzhubei, editor of the Communist Party newspaper Izvestia.

very proper. The mayor of the town stood up and said, "Any time the Soviets would like to bring a giant Soviet aircraft carrier in here, we would like to have it, too."

I thereupon stood up and said to the mayor, "You now have a carrier of your own. It's called the USS Independence."

Q: There's been a lot of discussion between the blackshoes and the airdales about we've got some hot-rodders, as they put it, carrier skippers that are not qualified to run ships at sea, and they keep wanting to run their carriers into the small boys and make erratic maneuvering. What are your comments on this?

Admiral Ramage: You're talking about me.

Q: Well, the reason I ask is it seems like you were really ill-prepared to command a carrier as far as ship handling. Do you feel that there's any validity to this, that there should be more training for carrier skippers?

Admiral Ramage: I didn't need any.

Q: So you don't feel there's any validity to the claim?

Admiral Ramage: It's been going on ever since--I think it was around 1927 when Captain Whiting pushed the law in Congress that a carrier had to be commanded by a naval aviator.[*] The complaint has been there since then, and it will always be there. I claim, on the other hand, that these limited duty officers are not qualified in any way to command a carrier.

---

[*] On 24 June 1926 Congress enacted a law implementing the provisions of the Morrow Board that had examined naval aviation. Among its provisions, the law directed that command of aviation stations, schools, and tactical flight units be assigned to naval aviators and that command of aircraft carriers and tenders be assigned to either naval aviators or naval aviation observers. Captain Kenneth Whiting, USN, was designated naval aviator number 16 and had a distinguished career that included being the initial executive officer of the Navy's first carrier, the Langley (CV-1).

Q: I'm not questioning the validity of an aviator commanding a carrier, but do you think there should be some more . . .

Admiral Ramage: I think the actual shipboard maneuvering of an aircraft carrier is the simplest thing that there is. I think that it's a mystique, which is another name for bullshit. There's nothing difficult about it. After making the first two or three approaches with the Independence, I always let somebody else do it, unless it was a particularly hairy night. I let the CAG and the squadron commanders and other middle-level aviators make approaches with the Independence.

Q: What about transferring allegiance from airplanes to ships? Did you enjoy driving a boat as much as flying an airplane?

Admiral Ramage: Never. I don't believe you asked that.

Q: I've heard of some CV skippers who claim they did.

Admiral Ramage: Well, I think it's one of these things, you know, when you get older, you forget.

One more point that I'd like to say, and I think it's my anti-Shinn day, but it's true, so I'm going to tell it. We were getting towards the end of our cruise in the Med, and I looked back at it with a lot of happiness. I'd had a good time. I think that we had a very demanding situation on the ship and the air group, and all of us had overcome it, and we were a good operating ship. This was about, I guess, May of 1964 now. So we were scheduled to return to Norfolk. The plan was that we would make the southern crossing at a speed of advance of 25 knots, which is awfully fast when you've got destroyers with you. The idea was that we would try to see if we could evade the Russian searches that dogged all the carriers going across.

As we were about to leave, we were to stop in Gibraltar just for the day, and this would provide an opportunity for the crew to go ashore, one half at a time, for about four hours to pick up whatever last-minute shopping, including their booze, which, of course, was put under lock and key. So we anchored about two miles off the port of Gibraltar. The three destroyers that were to accompany us went on in and tied up inside the little harbor there. We granted liberty half and half, port and starboard, with about half going in the morning and half in the afternoon. It was a nice day, there was no bad weather around, although as you might know, in the Mediterranean squalls come up in a hurry there. It's kind of like Lake Michigan; it's a small spot and squalls arrive and they disappear just that fast.

I sent the first liberty party ashore, and about 11:00 o'clock we began to get a fairly brisk wind and some rain. I went up and took a look around and told the exec I'd like to have somebody on the bridge so we can see how the boats were running back and forth. I also told the officer of the deck to be sure that the boat officers were well checked out and be prepared to go to reduced numbers in the liberty boats in case the squall got any worse.

I went in for lunch in my cabin, and I was sitting there at about 12:00 o'clock. Admiral Shinn came bursting in to my cabin and said, "What are you going to do?"

I said, "What am I going to do about what?"

He said, "Well, this squall that we've got down here."

I said, "Well, I've been watching it. I've got the bridge manned, and the boat officers are fully checked out. If things continue the way they are, we'll just have to cancel this afternoon's liberty party and get these people that are on the beach back slowly because I don't want to take a chance of being late for departure." It was scheduled for about 6:00 o'clock.

He left the cabin and went down on the hangar deck. I went down to the hangar deck, because I wanted to see how the boats were unloading back on the fantail. These big carriers have an accommodation ladder on the fantail, not on the side. It's a very handy thing because you don't get anywhere near the weather and waves. So I went back there and asked the officer of the deck how he was doing. He said, "Well, we're coming along pretty well. I've gone down to only half-loads in the boats, and things seem to be riding pretty well."

About that time, the new exec, who was Commander Dick Fowler, came up to me and he said, "I'm hoisting all boats aboard."[*]

I said, "You're hoisting all boats aboard? What for?"

He said, "The admiral ordered me to."

I said, "Dick, who is the captain of this ship?"

He said, "I know, sir." He apologized. "You'd better see the admiral."

About that time the admiral came hotfooting it down. He said, "I've directed that you hoist all your boats aboard." He said, "What we're going to do is tell all the people that you've got ashore to get on those three destroyers, and we'll transfer them by highline on the way back across."

And I said, "Admiral, we've got at least 1,500 men ashore at the present time, and that just isn't right. On top of that, with the speed of advance that's scheduled, we'd never do it." I also knew that they were my people, and if I left 1,500 people on the beach, that Paul Ramsey over in AirLant would know that they were my people, not Al Shinn's people.[†] So we talked back and forth about the thing. I said, "Well, I intend to continue to get these people back. It isn't that bad, and I'll be up on the bridge where I can watch what's going on. We'll see if we've got any problems, but I don't think it's that serious."

In the meantime, the boats continued to run. By about 1:00 o'clock the weather cleared up, and the boats were back. As a matter of fact, the weather was so clear we sent a couple of boats back to make a round of the whole harbor, to make sure we hadn't missed anybody. So everybody was back aboard, but unfortunately the rest of the people couldn't go in for their shopping tour--just not time to do it.

About that time, Admiral Shinn came up on the bridge, and he said, "Why didn't you carry out my orders?"

I guess I kind of looked out into space, shuffled my feet, and walked around. He said, "I asked you a question."

I finally said, "I didn't think it was a good decision." And I didn't have to say that.

---

[*] Commander Richard E. Fowler, USN.
[†] Vice Admiral Paul H. Ramsey, USN, served as Commander Naval Air Force Atlantic Fleet from 30 September 1963 to 31 March 1965.

Admiral Shinn then left the bridge, and I didn't see him the whole rest of the cruise till we got back to Norfolk.

Q: How come you've never had an assignment to the diplomatic corps?

Admiral Ramage: Well, what would you have said? He wanted an answer. I didn't say "stupid."

Q: Really, "Are you sure you want me to answer that question?

Q: "Would you like to rephrase the question?"

Admiral Ramage: Well, let's go on. So we continued our trip across the pond there, and at 25 knots, such an exchange of 1,500 personnel would have been, of course, completely impossible. As I recall, we did evade the Bears.* They didn't fly over us.

One thing that was in the op plan from Com2ndFlt specified that <u>Independence</u> was not to refuel before it entered port in Norfolk. So on the day before we were about to enter port in Norfolk, the chief of staff, Fred Moore, told me that the admiral wanted me to refuel.

I said, "Fred, the op order here says specifically that <u>Independence</u> is not to refuel before entering port." I don't know what the Com2ndFlt's idea was. I think he wanted to get over the idea that you don't have to go plugging in every time you get under one-third full, because we had plenty of fuel, of course. It was always custom to refuel before you entered port. I said, "That's against the op order."

And he said, "I know, but do it."

Well, we entered port the next morning. It was one of the worst days I've ever seen as far as fog is concerned.

---

* "Bear" is the Allied designation for the Soviet Tu-95 strategic bomber, a missile platform and maritime reconnaissance aircraft.

Q: You did refuel?

Admiral Ramage: We refueled. As we entered port, it was zero-zero. We were in direct communications with the port authorities inside, and we got a pretty good lead on what was coming out, and I was pretty sure of my radar gang. I also put Les Lampman, the operations officer, down in the bow of the ship on a sound-powered phone, just in case something came up, to let me know.*

Q: This has to be a very scary maneuver for any skipper.

Admiral Ramage: So we're coming along--fine, no question about where we were. We were in the harbor, there was nothing coming this way, when all of a sudden Lampman said, "Goddamn it!" And about that time, the biggest tanker I've ever seen disappeared right under the side of the ship. Of course, at that time we didn't have close-in radar like they have now. Immediately after that they installed this Raytheon radar, which is what small boats have, but our radar didn't pick up this monstrous thing that went by. It was one of these things that you say, "There but for the grace of God," and it would have been a complete shock to me. Of course, it was my fault. Just chalk one up to the man up topside.

In any event, about the time we got into the basin there, it cleared up. We got the docking pilot aboard, and we came in on time. But I made up my mind at that time that I would never enter port again under circumstances like that. I think maybe I felt that because of all the dependents out there on the dock that I didn't want to be late. And to hazard a ship, which I was doing to make that dock on time, just wasn't worth it. I was lucky.†

As soon as we had docked and everything was squared away, the staff left the ship and went back down to their home port, which was down in Jacksonville, so I did not have a flag aboard. I went in to pay my courtesy calls on Com2ndFlt, who was Vice Admiral

---

* Commander Lester B. Lampman, USN.
† The Independence's return to her homeport of Norfolk was on 4 March 1964.

Martell, and the first thing he asked me was, "Why did you refuel before you came into port?"*

I said, "I was directed to by the admiral."

He said, "Okay." Well, that was the end of that subject, but I know that he was very unhappy about it. And the unhappiness showed up about a month later. We got 30 days alongside, and we were about to go into a large fleet exercise. I went over to the planning conference for the large fleet exercise, which consisted of carrier strikes and ended up with an amphibious landing down in the Carolinas, which is pretty standard. There was Independence, plus we would operate three notional carriers. At the end of the planning session, I indicated that I would get hold of the admiral and let him know what had transpired, and Com2ndFlt said to me, "You're the admiral."

I said, "I beg your pardon, sir?"

And he said, "You are going to operate the carrier forces for this exercise."

When the exercise finally took place, it was a great flattery to me to take the striking force to sea and operate not only the carrier force but the notional carriers at the same time. I had a darn good operations division on the ship. It was really no problem at all. Let's say it was my first command, but it was really rather embarrassing for me because I sure as hell didn't want to have Al Shinn think that I did this thing to him. I don't know really what happened. I don't know why ComNavAirLant didn't put on another staff. I never did question the whole operation, but I felt very flattered that they gave me that responsibility to run that operation as skipper of Independence.

Here I would like to interject some discussion about Al Shinn. He was an excellent officer, very dedicated to naval aviation. He was a very fine materiel man and an outstanding administrator. On the other hand, my forte was operating aircraft. I have included these anecdotes on the friction between the commander and his flag captain because they highlight the built-in problem when a commanding officer is stubbornly clinging to his point of view. Our association was not unfriendly. As I'll describe later on, Al had a lot to do with my selection to flag rank. We are good friends today.

---

* Vice Admiral Charles B. Martell, USN, commanded the Second Fleet from August 1963 to April 1964.

Q: You've referred a couple of times to the various large staffs which the Army and the Air Force use. In your experience from World War II on, do you think that the Navy did as much work with fewer people?

Admiral Ramage: Well, they certainly did, but we're succumbing to the growing trend. Everything is expanding to the point that you've got a lot of these people that I call feather merchants. It's a growing concern, I think.

Q: Fewer staffs and fewer people on them?

Admiral Ramage: I think so. I've always felt so. Work them harder and try to clean out the nonessentials that people have to do.

After that exercise, there wasn't much more before I was relieved. I was relieved in July, I believe it was July 15, 1964, and it was rather an interesting thing because I didn't have any orders. The reason was that you're right in the spot, having been skipper of a carrier, where you're up for flag rank. I had been asked by Paul Ramsey, ComNavAirLant, if I would like to be his chief of staff, which is a damn fine job. It still is a flag billet, but they never fill it with a flag officer. It's one of those jobs that you get kind of a hold on a couple of stars at the time you move in there, because you're in a preferred position. Of course, I was delighted.

What happened was that Harvey Lanham, who was the chief of staff and they expected to get promoted by that selection board, didn't get selected.[*] So I was redundant. And in the meantime, I was asked if I'd like to be a cardiv chief of staff, which I didn't want. It was for Admiral Smoke Strean, and it wasn't a personal thing particularly; I'd rather work for other people, but he wasn't a bad guy.[†] I just didn't think that a chief of staff in a carrier division would do me any good. It was just a waste of time. I thought I was qualified far above that.

---

[*] Captain Harvey P. Lanham, USN.
[†] Rear Admiral Bernard M. Strean, USN, commanded Carrier Division Two, 1964-65.

So I asked Paul if he couldn't use me someplace else on his staff, and he said, "Yes, I'm going to fill you in as training officer," which is the number-three job, and that's a big job on the AirLant staff, it was at that time, at least. I was delighted with that. But in the meantime, I got this advance information that I was going to go to Joint Task Force Two, which I didn't know anything about. I went to Paul Ramsey one night, and we had a couple of martinis, and I said, "I don't know about this Joint Task Force Two business, but I'd sure like to stay around here and work for you, because I think that Harvey will certainly make it next year, and I'll fleet up to chief of staff, and I'd like that job."

And he said, "Okay, we'll call Joe Cobb."[*] Joe was the rear admiral in charge of detailing officers at the time. He got Joe on the phone, they talked for two minutes, and Paul came back and he said, "There is absolutely no way that you're not going to go to Joint Task Force Two. Admiral McDonald considers this the most politically important job that there is for a Navy captain at this time, and you are going to do it."[†]

It turned out that Joint Task Force Two was to study a problem that was brought about by General Everest of TAC.[‡] The TAC command insisted that in penetrating at low altitude, you had to have the capability of going supersonic. The Navy, on the other hand, indicated that they would like to stick with something subsonic like the A-6. We did not feel that supersonic speed was that important. And what Mr. McNamara wanted to do--and this was his project--was a series of tests which would examine this problem.

Q: Is this leading up to the Navy F-111?[§]

Admiral Ramage: The F-111 is part of it, that's correct. The Navy had a lot of experience in low-altitude penetration. We were not speed happy. What can you do past Mach 1 at 50 feet, you know? Is it even a reasonable thing to do? So Rear Admiral Brick Blackburn was

---

[*] Rear Admiral James O. Cobb, USN.
[†] Admiral David L. McDonald, USN, served as Chief of Naval Operations from 1 August 1963 to 1 August 1967. His oral history is in the Naval Institute collection.
[‡] Brigadier General Frank K. Everest, USAF. TAC--Tactical Air Command.
[§] The F-111--originally designated TFX--was a controversial fighter plane that Secretary of Defense Robert McNamara tried to develop in the 1960s for use by both the Air Force and the Navy.

James D. Ramage #1 - 277

to head this test.* It got to be a political argument in which the Air Force demanded that the thing be headed up by an Air Force officer, and it turned out to be Major General George Brown, whom I got to know very well and admired very much.† The project was to be an extensive one, and it was to cost a considerable amount of money over a prolonged period of time.

Q: Where was this JTF 2, in Washington?

Admiral Ramage: At this time it was located in Washington, but they were supposed to select a base outside of Washington in order to conduct these exercises and get on with this program. As far as I know, there isn't a soul, including General Brown, who was involved with this thing who thought it was worthwhile. But I went on up to Washington and reported in. There was no way that I wasn't going to go to JTF 2.

---

* Rear Admiral Paul P. Blackburn, Jr., USN.
† Major General George S. Brown, USAF, who later served as Chairman of the Joint Chiefs of Staff from 1974 to 1978.

Interview Number 2 with Rear Admiral James D. Ramage, U.S. Navy (Retired)

Place: Admiral Ramage's home, Bonita, California

Date: Saturday, 30 March 1985

Interviewers: Robert L. Lawson and Barrett Tillman

Admiral Ramage: Before reporting in to Joint Task Force Two in Washington, I was married for the second time. My new wife was Ginger Keesling Cordes. We were married in Rome on August 14, 1964. I reported in to Washington, D.C., in early September. Among the letters that I opened when I reported in was one from ComNavAirLant, advising me that Independence had been recommended for the Arleigh Burke Award for the past year. The Arleigh Burke Award is made to that ship or unit that has shown the most improvement during the preceding year. It went on to point out that Independence had been taken from the very bottom of the list and had arrived at number two during my stewardship. It pointed out that Enterprise was number one and that we were pushing Enterprise real hard for that position. This was quite pleasing to me because Enterprise was still being favored with priority manning, whereas Independence was just taking the run-of-the-mill personnel.

To get back to Joint Task Force Two, it had been directed by Secretary of Defense McNamara, and its task was to test whether it was essential to have a supersonic low-altitude dash while penetrating an enemy defense. General Everest, of the Tactical Air Command, had said that it was absolutely essential. The Navy, on the other hand, had said, no, that it wasn't required. The point is that if you're going to build an aircraft that goes supersonic at low altitude, you practically have to build a snowplow. The price of such an aircraft is much higher than it would be otherwise. In other words, we're talking about something like the F-111, which the Air Force is flying today, and the A-6, which we have flown for about 15 years, and I think we'll fly for many years to come.

It was considered a political hot potato, and the first indication was that Rear Admiral Brick Blackburn was to head it up. However, I was told that General Curtis LeMay had figured that it was so important to the Air Force that he wanted an Air Force commander. He negotiated with Admiral McDonald, the Chief of Naval Operations, to permit Major General George Brown to head up the operation. George Brown, in my opinion, is one of the finest officers of any service that I've ever worked for. However, we in the Navy were warned against him when the task force was set up. He had been Secretary McNamara's executive assistant, and was known to be a very political general.

The first job was to organize. It was organized with a commander, who was General George Brown. He had two assistants, Rear Admiral Tom Walker, a recent selectee, and Brigadier General Howard Michelet, of the Army.[*] They were to lend balance to the operation. It was rather difficult to figure out exactly why they were there, because there was certainly nothing for them to do.

Q: I was going to ask, what was the Army involvement?

Admiral Ramage: Well, it turned out that they were to get into later tests, and they did head up the support directorate, which was a logistic directorate, which I will describe later.

In organizing the staff, it was decided that we would have three directorates. The first would be operations, which would actually conduct the tests, the second would be the logistics and support directorate, and the third would be analysis and reports. General Brown asked me which of the three I would like to have, and I said, "I would like to be the director of analysis and reports."

He smiled and said, "You would?"

After organizing, our first job then was to find a place to exist outside of Washington, and we settled at Sandia base near Albuquerque, New Mexico. It was adjacent to Kirtland Air Force Base, so air support was available. There was plenty of space down there because the weapons programs had been diminished markedly. There was quarters, office space, and also available was the Sandia Corporation, which was a contractor to the Atomic Energy Commission, and it was a very well-qualified technical

---

[*] Rear Admiral Thomas J. Walker III, USN, was a Naval Academy classmate of Ramage; Brigadier General Howard E. Michelet, USA.

corporation which had a lot of experience in test procedure. They became the contractor to develop the technical support for conducting the tests.

We moved down to Albuquerque in early 1965. The first test was a very simple one, although it was very expensive. We were to select three types of terrain: one was flat, one was rolling, and the other was hilly or mountainous. We were to lay out 50-mile courses over which aircraft would fly as closely as they safely could in order to find out just how close to the nap of the earth a person could fly. Those of us who had had experience in Korea didn't think much of the test because we knew that the biggest problem, when you get down that low, is small arms fire and semi-automatic and automatic fire, and that we wouldn't be flying down there anyway if we could help it. But nevertheless, we were directed to do the test.

We selected an area in Nevada, which is between Nellis Air Force Base and Naval Air Station Fallon.* That area is government property and is part of the Tonopah Test Range, where atomic weapons testing is done. The three courses were marked by flame orange painted barrels about every 200 or 300 yards apart along the course. You can imagine how hard it was to place these barrels in the hilly and mountainous terrain. It had to be done by helicopter, and it was really quite an expensive project.

Q: That would have been an awful lot of barrels.

Admiral Ramage: It was a lot of barrels, 50 miles times three, each 300 yards. In order to prove out what we were trying to do, we were to fly at varying speeds and the low speed was 120 knots, the high speed was Mach 1.1.

Q: What type aircraft?

Admiral Ramage: The aircraft involved were the OV-1, which was to be flown by the Army; the A-1, which was to be flown by the Tactical Air Force, which was unusual; the

---

* Nellis Air Force Base is in the extreme southeast corner of the state, near the Arizona border. Fallon is 100 miles due east of Reno.

A-4 and A-6 were to be flown by the Navy.* Part of the A-6 flights had to be done by the Marine Corps because there were not enough Navy A-6s available to do the job. The F-4 and F-105 were to be flown by the Tactical Air Force, and the B-52 and B-58 to be flown by the Strategic Air Command.† In addition, the Air Force was forced to provide three C-130s for instrumentation.‡ The instrumentation belonged to the Atomic Energy Commission, and it was part of that which was required to be on short notice in case we wanted to commence nuclear testing in the atmosphere in a hurry.

Before the tests started, General Brown called me in and designated me to be the test director for the first test. I told him that I thought that it was incorrect for the person that was responsible to analyze the results of the test to conduct the test. Also, I pointed out that I felt that it would certainly cause Colonel Joe Kelly, an Air Force officer who was the boss of the operations directorate, a lot of unhappiness and gas pains to have me up there running his test.

He said, "That very well may be, but I'm going to have no problems with the Navy on this thing, and if I designate you as test director, you and I are going to take the flak when all of it comes out."

I might point out that there was plenty of flak that resulted too. The reason was that the test was really not necessary, and it was rather an absurd thing to begin with. Brown was catching quite a bit of flak from my friend Rear Admiral Fred Bardshar, who was in J-5, which was that section of the Joint Staff which was responsible for overseeing this thing.§ Fred didn't like the test, nor did we, and he seemed to presume that somehow George Brown was responsible for setting it up, which he wasn't. George told me one time to go and see my friend Freddie Bardshar and tell him to get off his back. He mentioned

---

* Grumman's OV-1 Mohawk was a battlefield surveillance aircraft developed for the Army to provide ground commanders with all-weather observation and reconnaissance capability. It was a two-seat twin-turboprop aircraft.

† The Fairchild Republic F-105 Thunderchief was designed as a tactical nuclear strike aircraft with an internal weapons bay for carrying nuclear weapons. The Boeing B-52 Stratofortress is an eight-engine jet-propelled heavy bomber flown by the U.S. Air Force. Convair's delta-wing B-58 Hustler was the Air Force's first supersonic bomber.

‡ The Lockheed C-130 Hercules is a cargo aircraft powered by four turboprops. It was developed for the Air Force in the 1950s and has since been adapted for use as well by the Navy, Marine Corps, and Coast Guard. The plane has a maximum cruising speed of 357 miles per hour and a maximum takeoff weight of 135,000 pounds.

§ Rear Admiral Frederic A. Bardshar, USN, a naval aviator.

that he wasn't going to be a major general forever. I guess the Air Force has ways of knowing far in advance how high one is going to go. I told Freddie, but I'm not sure that it did any good.

George Brown and I went around to brief the various commands on the requirements for the tests, and, as you might guess, we weren't very well-received by any of the commands. The Air Force, in particular, really was unhappy, because I think when it comes down to a question of money, support, and so forth, they probably picked up 90% of the tab.

I caught a large amount of flak from General Sweeney, the TAC commander, when I briefed the test to him.[*] He seemed to presume that I was the guy responsible, and let me know that he thought that the test was pretty dumb, and therefore I was kind of dumb for even being a part of it.

When George and I walked out of the briefing room, George turned to me and he said, "That man is not a son-of-a-bitch," which indicated exactly what he thought he was.

So we had the courses laid out, and I moved up to Nellis in March of 1965. I selected Colonel Jim Mason of the Air Force to be my assistant, to run the Nellis part of the operation, and Commander Jack Herman to set up our operation in Fallon, Nevada.[†] In conducting such a test, in order to make the test meaningful, the briefing that is given to each pilot must be exactly the same, and it must be standard. Otherwise, the basic data will not be worthwhile. In order to make sure that we had it exactly correct, we recorded it and it served the purpose, except in one case, which I'll get around to later on.

About that time, what I choose to call the Great SAM Hunt occurred out in Vietnam. There were the surface-to-air missile installations being built in North Vietnam, and, of course, the Air Force and the Navy wanted to go after the missile sites while they were being constructed.[‡] In all its wisdom, the government policy at that time was not to hit the SAM sites until they were completed and the missiles were in place. That's not very

---

[*] General Walter C. Sweeney, Jr., USAF, served as Commander Tactical Air Command from 1 October 1961 to 31 July 1965.
[†] Colonel James E. Mason, USAF; Commander John S. Herman, USN.
[‡] On 5 April 1965 an RF-8A Crusader photo reconnaissance plane returned to the carrier Coral Sea (CVA-43) with the first pictures of a surface-to-air missile site under construction; it was about 15 miles southeast of Hanoi, North Vietnam.

bright, but nevertheless, that's the rules that we were operating under. Finally, the missiles were in place and the Navy was given the job of going on into an area south of Hanoi to find the missiles and to destroy them. We didn't have adequate intelligence, and it was an absolute bust. I don't know how many planes we lost in that operation, it's something like four to six, and it was just a terrible waste of life.

Q: It's my understanding the first Ironhands were flown like in August or thereabouts, and the first SAM killed wasn't until October of well up into the year.

Admiral Ramage: Well, that could be true. The Navy after this catastrophe commissioned a board to go out there to investigate really what happened, and the board was headed up by Rear Admiral John Hyland, who was in Strategic Plans, and Captain Mickey Weisner, who was probably in BuPers or OP-05 at the time.* Their findings were, of course, very clear. They said that the rules that were given to fly by were absolutely inflexible, that there was no latitude given to the strike commanders. And at that time, I thought that if there was any opportunity for me to get out to Vietnam, in some way I perhaps could stop something as stupid as that from happening.

Also at about the same time, Eddie Outlaw came through Albuquerque and gave us a briefing on what had been going on so far as Task Force 77 was concerned.† He was absolutely irate, and had let the seniors up the line know that this was not the way to win a war. Eddie is very direct, and when he comes out on something, he doesn't spare the horses.

We did a total of 500 runs over these three courses. We completed the flat course runs by August. We were very much afraid that we would kill somebody. That's quite a challenge. We did have three mishaps. An A-1 flown by the Air Force hit one of the barrels with the prop and, of course, that big prop just cut the barrel to bits. An A-4 flown by the Navy pranged a barrel with some part of it, probably a wing tank. A Navy A-6 hit it,

---

* Rear Admiral John J. Hyland, USN; Captain Maurice F. Weisner, USN. The oral history of Hyland, who retired as a four-star admiral, is in the Naval Institute collection.
† In the spring of 1965 Rear Admiral Edward C. Outlaw, USN, was Commander Task Force 77, the Seventh Fleet carrier striking force. He was between jobs at the time of this briefing.

I think, with the instrument pod that he carried to record all the data. There was no damage in any of the three cases.

Q: These are 55-gallon barrels?

Admiral Ramage: That's right.

Q: At three feet off the ground?

Admiral Ramage: Yes. While we're talking about the instrumentation, which was absolutely great, we had to have the three terrains digitized, which was done by the Army Map Service. We had a special altimeter which went in all the planes, accurate to about six inches. Then the three C-130s flying above could place the aircraft in space to about one foot accuracy, so the instrumentation far outclassed the requirements for the test. It was beautiful instrumentation. We got far too much information at 16 bytes a second than we could possibly use.

Again, getting back to the standard briefing, which I mentioned before, it was absolutely essential that each pilot be briefed with the same information. For some reason or other, the A-6 officer in charge of the Marine detachment saw fit to lay an additional briefing on his crews, and consequently their flying was absolutely atrocious. Unlike the cooperation which we normally expect from the Marines, it was the worst information that we gathered. Apparently he added his own safety coefficient, and the performance of the Marine A-6s was worse than the B-52s and the B-58s. As this was occurring, it became obvious, and I advised General Brown about it, and he said, "Well, we'll just have to face that when the information comes out. I'll have to go to the Marine Corps and tell them that they were not satisfactory."

I'd like to tell you a little bit about Chief Butterfield. Chief Butterfield was an Air Force chief warrant officer, but he liked to be called "The Chief." He was the Mr. Everything to the C-130s that were provided by the Tactical Air Command. He was topnotch, and his people were some of the best personnel I've ever worked with. He had the three C-130s. None of them ever missed a flight. He took such excellent care of his troops that they were always invited out in the evenings to various shows up in Las Vegas where they were based. He just ran a perfect operation, as far as I was concerned.

However, he got himself in a little hot water. One day I was sitting over in my office at Nellis Air Force Base. It was in the same hangar as the Thunderbirds.* One day the lieutenant colonel who was skipper of the Thunderbirds came in and said, "Captain, you have a warrant officer working for you who I want you to tell to stay away from my outfit."

I asked, "What's the problem?"

And he said, "Well, he's over there bracing my men, straightening them out, and telling them how they should behave, and I don't appreciate it."

So I got hold of Chief Butterfield when he came in, and I said, "Chief, have you been over talking to the Thunderbirds?"

And he said, "Yes, sir." He said, "They're a disgrace to the Air Force."

And I said, "Well, be that as it may, I think it's probably a little bit more proper that you pay attention to your own unit, which is great, incidentally, and stay away from the Thunderbirds because their skipper has been over and said that you're bothering them."

Butterfield said, "Captain, I would be derelict in my duty if I didn't go over there and straighten out that horseshit outfit."

I said, "Okay, Chief, I agree with you, but please stay away," which he did.

I was able to get him a special award after the tests were over because he was really an outstanding guy.

We completed all the tests and got all the data together in time to brief the JCS on the outcome in 1965.† The presentation was very dramatic because we had mounted cameras with color film during all the runs, and the Joint Chiefs, when they observed them, were constantly gasping at how close these runs were to the ground. On a flat course, they were within three feet of the ground most of the time.

The ones who probably got the biggest kick out of the whole thing were the SAC pilots in the B-52s and B-58s, because they'd never been permitted to flathat, and they really

---

* The Thunderbirds are the Air Force's flight demonstration team, comparable to the Navy's Blue Angels.
† JCS--Joint Chiefs of Staff.

had a good time making their runs. They did a damn good job at it, I might add. I was quite amazed to see that enormous B-52 flying down the course at about 50 feet. If they made a turn, you know, they'd dip a wing and roll it up in a ball, but they loved it and they did a good job.

So as far as I was concerned, my job was done. I was still looking around to see if there wasn't something else available. I had done my duty as far as the Navy was concerned. What the Navy was concerned about--the unfairness of George Brown--simply didn't materialize. As I've mentioned previously, he's one of the finest and fairest officers that I've ever worked for.

So I dropped by my friendly detailer at the Bureau of Personnel, asked them if there wasn't anything more demanding for me than running planes over the desert. And Spin Epes was the chief detailer at the time.[*] He handed me a list of ten captains and asked what I thought of them. I said, "Well, not much. What's it all about?" My name was at the very bottom of the list with a big NA--not available--after it.

He explained that George Mahler had been designated to be chief of staff of CTF 77, and the day before he was supposed to leave, he turned in his suit.[†] He had been skipper of Constellation, and Constellation was in overhaul up in Bremerton, Washington, and somebody had prevailed upon him to try to run for Congress. I told Spin that I didn't think that the people that were included on that list looked like they would be very competent to be CTF 77 chief of staff, and I'd like the job. I said, "I know that General Brown will let me go if I can contact him right away."

So I called Albuquerque. He wasn't in Albuquerque, but he was in Tucson playing golf. I was able to get him on the telephone, I guess, at the ninth hole as he came in. I told George that I had an opportunity to take over the job of chief of staff at CTF 77 if he'd let me go immediately.

He said, "Not only will I let you go, but see if you can't get me a job out there too. I've just about had enough of this."

---

[*] Captain Horace H. Epes, USN.
[†] Captain George H. Mahler III, USN, retired in April 1966.

Q: Incidentally, we should probably note for the benefit of the typist, CTF 77 is Commander Task Force 77 in the Tonkin Gulf.

Admiral Ramage: Yes, they ran the five carriers that were operating in and out of there at that time. So I told Spin I'd be delighted to take the job, and he said, "Well, I can type up your orders right now, or I can send them down by dispatch."

I said, "Well, I can't wait for you. I've got to leave, but send them on down."

So I went down to my bride of not quite a year in Albuquerque and told her that I was heading for Vietnam. I had three bottles of Canadian Club Whiskey that I'd picked up in Washington. I said, "This will stand you in good stead during my absence." She and the two kids, Randy and Karen, were in government quarters there, and the situation during that war was that if you were ordered out under those circumstances, you could remain in the quarters until you could make other arrangements.

Q: Randy and Karen were young children?

Admiral Ramage: Yes, Randy and Karen Cordes. Randy was about 14 and Karen about 10 at the time.

So just as soon as I could pack my bags, I headed on out to Vietnam to relieve John Lacouture as chief of staff.[*] I arrived there in late January of 1966. I, of course, stopped by CinCPacFlt on the way and talked with Admiral Roy Johnson, the commander, and also Rear Admiral Bush Bringle, who had operations and plans.[†] I was quite excited about getting the chance to go out to Vietnam.

I reported aboard Kitty Hawk and was greeted by Rear Admiral Jim Reedy, known as "Sunshine Jim."[‡] Sunshine is a fine officer. He was trying very hard to fight the war under the same wraps that everybody else was under out there. Sunshine hadn't had a lot of experience in carrier operations, and I thought that I'd be able to be of some benefit to him.

---

[*] Captain John E. Lacouture, USN.
[†] Admiral Roy L. Johnson, USN, served as Commander in Chief Pacific Fleet, 30 March 1965 to 30 November 1967. Rear Admiral William F. Bringle, USN.
[‡] Rear Admiral James R. Reedy, USN.

I also learned before I left that Rear Admiral Dave Richardson was to relieve him within about two or three months, and I, of course, was very delighted to work for Dave.* I'd known him for many years. Dave also was an excellent naval officer but hadn't had much experience in jet aviation. He had mentioned that he wanted me to come out there, and I was very glad to be able to make it.

Q: Jim Reedy is the officer you relieved in HAtWing 1.

Admiral Ramage: That's right. Jim was a very gung-ho guy, as we'll see later here, and Dave was equally gung-ho. I enjoyed working for both of them because as chief of staff they let me pretty much run the operation, which is the way I operated when I was a carrier division commander.

After about two weeks aboard ship there, I began to get the swing of things and could see that things were pretty tight as far as restraints, but in the armed reconnaissance or armed recce part of the program . . .

Q: The Rolling Thunder.†

Admiral Ramage: Well, it was part of Rolling Thunder, but it was the armed recce that went on in connection with it. Rolling Thunder was the actual targets that were called out. The armed recce had certain very strict rules, but you could also bend the rules fairly easily.

Q: As we know from Cam Pha.

Admiral Ramage: Yes. You couldn't play around too much in the northern area around Hanoi and Haiphong. Anything down in the southern reaches below about latitude 20, you could do about anything you wanted within reason.

---

* Rear Admiral David C. Richardson, USN. The oral history of Richardson, who later served as Com6thFlt and Deputy CinCPacFlt, is in the Naval Institute collection. He retired as a vice admiral.
† Operation Rolling Thunder was the designation for U.S. Air operations over North Vietnam.

Q: That would have been route packages one, two, and maybe, what, part of three?

Admiral Ramage: One, two, three, and four. It wasn't until you got on up towards the north that the North Vietnamese got very sensitive.

One of the first events that happened was that I went into Saigon to meet General Meyers, who was Commander Seventh Air Force at that time; he had three stars then.[*] I also went to meet the various people that I would be dealing with on the Air Force side of the Rolling Thunder operation. It was very touchy in Saigon because Admiral Sharp had just assigned the route packages to the Air Force and the Navy.[†]

His assignments were very reasonable, we thought. The Navy would take those targets which were closest to the maritime area, which, of course, were the best. The Air Force would be farther back inland. Route Package One, which was the closest one to South Vietnam, was to be considered part of the internal area of South Vietnam and hence was under control of General Westmoreland.[‡] Two, Three, and Four went on up to the north, plus 6B, which was the one farthest to the northeast, was to go to the Seventh Fleet or Task Force 77, with the Air Force aircraft operating out of Thailand, operating in Package 5 and 6A. 6A included Hanoi, and 6B included Haiphong.

The Air Force really didn't like this because it precluded them from a lot of the best target areas, and as the first naval officer into Saigon after this was promulgated, I took quite a bit of heat. Admiral Sharp did it for one good reason. Unless you have somebody definitely in control of an area, it's very hard to keep current on the intelligence that goes on in there, and since the carriers were the closest to 2, 3, 4, and 6B, it was obvious that they should be assigned those packages. And, likewise, the Thailand squadrons of the Air Force would be assigned 5 and 6A. It was, I think, a reasonable thing to do, but quite obviously the Air Force didn't like it.

---

[*] Lieutenant General Gilbert L. Meyers, USAF.
[†] Admiral Ulysses S. Grant Sharp, USN, served as Commander in Chief Pacific from 30 June 1964 to 31 July 1968. His oral history is in the Naval Institute collection.
[‡] General William C. Westmoreland, USA, served as Commander U.S. Military Assistance Command Vietnam from 20 June 1964 to 2 July 1968.

One of the other things that I, as the Navy Rolling Thunder coordinator, realized immediately was that I was certainly outranked by everyone in the Air Force. I had to deal with a general officer for in-country operations, a general officer who handled the Rolling Thunder part of the operations, and a general officer who took care of Steel Tiger and Barrel Roll, which was the operations in Laos, and also a general officer in intelligence, and a general officer in air defense.* So by the time I made the rounds as a captain, with probably a lieutenant commander or commander with me, I was exposed to a lot of Air Force generals.

I might talk a little bit about the Cam Pha operation that you mentioned previously. This was while Sunshine Jim was still there, so it was in the spring of 1966. Big Red Carmody, who was skipper of the Kitty Hawk, was a task group commander in his own right, because Commander Task Force 77 had split the force in such a manner that the flagship itself was a task group.† Big Red had command of his own group plus its escorts. Big Red had been a fighter in the previous two wars, and he was trying in every way to really get something done.

One day Big Red came in with two messages. The first one was from Commander Seventh Air Force, asking for an interpretation of a target up in the Package 5, which was northwest of Hanoi. It was within the prescribed distance of a major line of communication, which I think was 100 meters, and was a target that could be considered an armed recce legal target, if you interpreted it in that manner. The interpretation came back--I presume it was cleared through Washington; at least it was cleared through CinCPac--that this filled the requirements for an armed recce mission. I believe it was an installation, it wasn't a moving target. So Big Red came in with this, plus the response saying that it was cleared. He said, "This is the way we're going to do it. Have you taken a look at Cam Pha?" Well, Cam Pha was a major coaling port in North Vietnam, and it was the port out of which went a particularly high quality hard coal.

---

* Operation Barrel Roll, begun in December 1964, and Steel Tiger, begun in April 1965, were limited air campaigns against enemy troops and supplies in Laos.
† Captain Martin D. Carmody, USN, commanded the USS Kitty Hawk (CVA-63) from 29 May 1965 to 18 July 1966.

Q: Anthracite.

Admiral Ramage: Anthracite. It had the coal washing plants, the docks, loading docks, and it also filled the armed recce bill because it was adjacent to a major highway and a major rail line. So if the Air Force target was okay, so was the coaling area at Cam Pha. So Red recommended that we send in an op rep, I believe it was three, which was the one which proposed an immediate lucrative target strike. Normally the nominating op rep went in about the night before, and it would give the various commands up the chain a time to say yes or no. They normally did not say no. But this one was for lucrative and immediate targets. It was really bending the rules.

Both Red and I went in to see Jim Reedy, and he looked at it and said, "Well, my ass is out, but I think we ought to go for it." So Red immediately loaded up and launched about 24 aircraft for the coaling area of Cam Pha. It was a real fine strike made up of A-4s and A-6s, plus F-4s. And they were loaded for bear. They got up there and just raised hell. They knocked out the coaling plant, and they threw rail cars all over the place, and they got a real lot of damage done on that whole port.

Q: I recall in your Hook article, you said that he issued the warning order as they launched.[*]

Admiral Ramage: That's correct.

Q: He requested permission, then he launched.

Admiral Ramage: Big Red nominated the targets as the aircraft went off and there was no way we could be stopped. Well, in addition to the damage to the North Vietnamese that they had done, there was a Polish freighter in port. I don't think we hit the freighter, but we certainly got their attention. By the time the aircraft landed back aboard and we were ready

---

[*] Rear Admiral James D. Ramage, USN (Ret.), "The Cam Pha Strike of 1966," The Hook (published by the Tailhook Association), Fall 1984, page 10. The article indicates that the strike was on 19 April 1966.

to get a second strike off, a direct flash from Washington ordered cease and desist. All hell had broken loose. The Commies, as usual, had immediately brought pressure to bear, and the pussycats in Washington saw fit to cancel the second strike. I won't say that we didn't expect it, but on the other hand, you've got to do the best you can.

I got a personal call on the command net from the ops officer up in CinCPacFlt, who was a blackfoot, incidentally, and he said, "Well, "Jig Dog," now you've done it. You've only been down there about two months, and you're about to get your boss fired."

I said, "Well, this wasn't entirely my idea, you know."

And he said, "Well, stand by."

So I went in to see "Sunshine" and I said, "I guess we can expect some high priority stuff from above."

Big Jim said, "Well, so be it." So we waited, and nothing happened. There was no news from Sharp in CinCPac, or Roy Johnson in CinCPacFlt, or Johnny Hyland, who was then Commander Seventh Fleet.[*] There was just total silence, which would indicate that they kind of thought that it was a pretty good operation, too. So finally it must have been about a day or maybe two days later, we got a message from CinCPac, which pointed out that CTF 77 had exceeded his authority, among other things, but it ended up with a little paragraph which said, "However, it appears to have had a very salutary effect upon the enemy." So it was obvious that Sharp thought it was a pretty damn neat job, too.

Q: Do you know, was Cam Pha ever struck after that?

Admiral Ramage: I think they got permission later, but I heard later from intelligence that that coal processing plant was out of business for six months. So it was a good day for the good guys.

In May of 1966, Rear Admiral Dave Richardson relieved Rear Admiral Jim Reedy as CTF 77, and there was pretty much no change in the procedures. Both of them were very easy to work with and, in my opinion, fine officers.

---

[*] Vice Admiral John J. Hyland, USN, served as Commander Seventh Fleet from 13 December 1965 to 6 November 1967. The oral history of Hyland, who retired as a four-star admiral, is in the Naval Institute collection.

I'll now go into the strikes on the oil storage plants in Haiphong and Hanoi, which occurred during late June in 1966. We would read in Time magazine and various newspaper arguments about an air strike on the oil storage facilities in Haiphong and Hanoi. This, of course, permitted the North Vietnamese to disperse their storage tanks throughout the northern area, so that by the time we got around to hitting them, the effects certainly weren't what they would have been if we could have hit them at the proper time.

We got ready to hit them in early June, but the strikes were canceled two or three times by the President, who was Lyndon Johnson.[*] Finally, when the day came, it appeared that it was just going to be another cancellation. We got ready to go, and the Air Force was assigned the storage areas in Hanoi. The Navy got the larger installation, which was right in the port of Haiphong. It was a very well executed operation, both by the Air Force and the Navy. We put the carriers up to within about 100 miles of Haiphong. By doing this, we were able to fly the A-4s without aux tanks, which would give them a lot more maneuverability, because going into that area, we knew after all the warning that had been given that the Commies would certainly be ready with everything they had, and they were.

The Navy targets were completely annihilated. It did take two strikes, however. The Air Force targets in Hanoi were completely knocked out, too. They only required the one strike. Both outfits did just an excellent job. It was a great credit to the people that were involved in the strikes that it was done so neatly, without any collateral damage to speak of. It was always a great requirement, "Be sure you don't hurt anybody." Incidentally, I think we only lost one aircraft, which was an A-4, and we recovered the pilot at sea outside of Haiphong. So it was another good day for the good guys, and those were hard to come by with the restrictions we operated under. That was in June of 1966.

Q: I wanted to ask you, do you have an opinion on what Johnson and McNamara and these people in charge, what were they thinking? What did they think we were trying to accomplish?

Admiral Ramage: It would be hard for me to figure out because . . .

---

[*] Lyndon B. Johnson served as President of the United States from 22 November 1963 to 20 January 1969.

Q: They didn't really define the objective.

Admiral Ramage: Well, the objective, as far as it was defined, was that we were trying to coerce the North Vietnamese into not causing trouble down south. We were trying to do it with air power. But you can't coerce anybody that won't be coerced. And if they know that you are restricting your forces to the point that they can't be hurt, they're not going to pay too much attention to it.

Q: There's no incentive.

Admiral Ramage: Plus, as you know, we had already guaranteed them that we would not invade North Vietnam, and the President had also indicated that he didn't want to change the government in North Vietnam. Well, if you're operating under those type of rules, the people in the north had nothing to lose. They could just keep going and going and going, and they did. They were prepared, apparently, to go for 20 or 30 years in this case.

To get back into CTF 77 operations, we had two operations in September that were particularly good. By this time we had a pretty good hold on just what was going on in the way of traffic down the rail lines and down the highways in North Vietnam. While it's true that the Ho Chi Minh Trail in Laos was open and there wasn't a hell of a lot we could do about it, they would prefer to use the major transportation and lines of communications in North Vietnam.

We conceived an idea of finding choke points. A choke point was an area where three types of communications crossed, the highway, the rail, and the waterways. There were two such places that we concentrated on. The first was Ninh Binh, and the second one was Thanh Hoa. The Ninh Binh operation started on the 14th of September. In one of the early morning armed recce operations, a pilot noticed a lot of rolling stock and ultimately three trains that were in the vicinity of Ninh Binh, which was in upper package three. That flight of four cut the rail line to the south and called in immediately that they had cut the rail line, and there was a lot of rolling stock. We immediately sent in another already airborne flight, and they cut the rail line to the north. So we had these trains stuck right in that general area, and there was nothing they could do about it.

About that time we really loaded up for bear and diverted all the strength of three aircraft carriers into that area. You can do easily from the task force, but it is pretty hard to do from the beach. You can schedule them in there and also divert those in the air. We really brought immediate pressure to bear on those trains.

I recall that the first strike leaders that went in reported that a lot of the rolling stock was in the town of Ninh Binh. You may recall that cities and towns, you couldn't hit. So I reported to Dave Richardson that a lot of this stuff was in the town, and he said, "The target is the trains."

I went back into the operations room and told the talker to say, "Tell them to get them all."

Dave was just like Sunshine Jim. Anything that you could do to get after these guys was fine, and if you got canned, why, that was your problem.

We worked in that area for about two days and later had a similar operation at the choke point at Thanh Hoa. The results were quite good, and we received a request from Westmoreland's office to come on down and put on a presentation of these results in front of the press corps down in Saigon. I think it was probably instigated by Captain Buddy Yates, who was the Navy liaison officer in Saigon at the time.[*] This thing, which went on at 5:00 o'clock every day, had become known as the 5:00 o'clock follies, because the press thought that the briefings that they normally received were pretty damn dumb, and I might say that I don't blame them. So Dave told me to put a presentation together on these two operations and get on in there.

I went in on the 25th of September. I'd been able to get a lot of very fine pictures of both of these operations and appeared before the group down there in the theater. I pointed out that in the first instance, which was Ninh Binh, that the trains had been isolated, and showed them the results by picture. These included two locomotives destroyed, 144

---

[*] Captain Earl P. Yates, USN, a naval aviator who shortly afterward became the prospective commanding officer of the John F. Kennedy (CVA-67) and first skipper when she went into commission in September 1968.

railroad cars damaged, two bridges dropped, 10 to 15 major explosions, including ammunition and numerous other fires. We had pictures of the North Vietnamese actually trying to off-load all this gear from the railroad cars before they were blown up. They tried to off-load them into the karst caves along the side. It was a nice operation. It was direct control of an interdiction campaign as it should be done.

I went to the Thanh Hoa area from there and pointed out that a similar operation was done on the 21st of September, where a three-day treatment was given to the North Vietnamese with even more damage. I pointed out the damage in this case was two locomotives, 121 railroad cars, a thermal power plant destroyed, plus a lot of supporting buildings around the plant, two petroleum processing plants, and at least 22 major secondary explosions. So it was a great day, and General Westmoreland had thanked CTF 77 and the air crews for such a fine operation. He said that it couldn't help but be of great use to him down south, because we certainly had destroyed a lot of the stuff that was on the way down.

My talk was very well received, and the press in particular was quite friendly. One of the reporters told me that it was the best briefing that they'd ever had. The fact that I had the pictures of the actual operation was good, because there was no way to refute the fact that we had done this.

After it was all over, I received some glowing messages, one from Westmoreland himself, and, of course, when Westmoreland did it, it was picked up by the various commands all the way down the chain. Even The New York Times, which was never very friendly to the war, wrote a very nice article on it, stating, "U.S. using in-depth interdiction to disrupt North's rail lines." And gave a complete description of my talk. Of course, the press didn't really turn against the war until 1968, so this was not unusual at that time.

Q: Don't you think that one of the reasons that the press turned against the war was the 5:00 o'clock follies?

Admiral Ramage: Well, I believe so.

James D. Ramage #2 - 297

Q: They'd been lied to so many times and deceived, how can you be sympathetic to the people you're dealing with?

Admiral Ramage: I believe that's so. I was in there another time, I forget exactly what the case was, but it was after one of Lyndon Johnson's famous standdowns. As you know, Johnson always hoped that after one of these standdowns that the North Vietnamese would see the error of their ways and get out of the war. Harry Truman did the same thing in Korea, you know. Of course, the North Vietnamese were not going to do anything like that. But this question came, I believe, from a reporter from Baltimore, which was, "Are you striking in the north now, Captain?"

And I said, "No." And later on I said, "That's kind of a silly question."

And he said, "Well, you know that we've been given the information in a handout just before this meeting that they couldn't discuss that."

And I said to the reporter, I said, "You know we're not striking in the north."

And he said, "Yes, I know that, the North Vietnamese know it, and I don't know why in the hell these people here in Saigon don't tell us. You're the first honest guy we've had in here for about six months."

So I think probably there is not much to be said about the 5:00 o'clock follies, because they were kind of a routine dance.

Shortly after that, a Rolling Thunder conference was to be held out on board the Constellation, the CTF 77 flagship. So the Air Force generals came out, and they enjoyed being on the carrier. They couldn't understand how we could run a war with the four or five people that were actually doing the job. Of course, we delegated on down to the task group commanders, and we didn't tell each strike leader how to fly his flight. They were just amazed that I would sit there at my desk, and people would come in once in a while, report what was happening, and ask for direction. They appreciated the fact that we had direct control over our forces over North Vietnam, which they couldn't have.

This conference was called aboard ship, and it was to be concerned with a message that we had received from CinCPac, which was to ask us to review some of the areas in the package assignments with an end to getting the Air Force more active in some of the western sections of the Navy armed recce packages. The chief negotiator for the Seventh Air Force was a brigadier general. In due course, it became apparent to me that I could "pants" him. We wrote up a very innocuous agreement, and I gave it to him, and I said, "Will that fill the bill?"

He said, "Looks good to me."

So he signed it and I signed it, and I took it in to Dave Richardson, who was not in the meeting, and he said, "No kidding! Did he sign that?"

I said, "Yes, let's get it on the wire up to CinCPac immediately."

Well, this, I thought, was pretty good, till the next day I got a personal message from Roy Johnson, Commander in Chief, Pacific Fleet. It was a real zap. He told me that I was intransigent, and that there would be no further actions of this type to be done in the Rolling Thunder negotiations. I thought, my God, here I am doing exactly what I know Roy Johnson wants me to do, I just can't understand it.

But Dave Richardson looked at me, said, "Don't worry about it. I think this will all come out in the end."

Well, it did, about two or three weeks later. We were up in Yokosuka, and I was standing in the pissoir next to Admiral Johnson, and I said, "Admiral, I got that nastygram from you. That was quite a zapping."

And he said, "You know I didn't mean that. You're doing exactly what I wanted you to do." He said, "Oley [referring to Admiral Sharp] had heard this complaint from the Pacific Air Force commander that you had been extremely unfair to them down there, and he told me to give you a zapping, and I did it. But forget it." So that was the end of that one.

Just before I left Task Force 77, we were advised that we were going to get the use of the battleship New Jersey some time within a year or so, and the Cruiser-Destroyer Force commander sent a captain down to tell us how we were going to use it.[*] So far as we could see in CTF 77, there wasn't any requirement for it in North Vietnam. They were talking

---

[*] The USS New Jersey was recommissioned on 6 April 1968 for shore bombardment duty. She arrived on station and began bombarding North Vietnam on 30 September 1968. A bombing halt at the end of October put the rest of North Vietnam off-limits to bombing and shelling. She completed her Vietnam tour in March 1969 and was decommissioned later that year.

about such things as hitting the Thanh Hoa bridge and various targets that were very heavily defended, but we were going to have to put a spotter plane up over the target anyway if you were going to try to hit it. If you're going to put a spotter plane up there, you better send some other escort planes, and if you're going to send these other planes, they'd better be loaded for bear and they'd better hit the target themselves. So it didn't make much sense. In addition to that, the 2,000- or 2,800-pound shell of the New Jersey carries a very small amount of high explosives compared to what a bomb carries, and the impact wouldn't be very large anyway.

We studied what could be done up and down the coast, and really it appeared that there was very little that the battleship could do. We faced that problem a year or two later and still didn't know what to do with it.

I had another interesting thing happen to me while I was chief of staff of CTF 77. Just after the first of the year, that's 1967, Captain George Talley, who was skipper of the Franklin D. Roosevelt, had a heart attack, and they couldn't get anybody immediately available to relieve him.[*] So I was designated by John Hyland, who was Com7thFlt, to go over and take over the FDR for a short period.[†] We were en route to Hong Kong for a good time, and I was able to help the crew enjoy that.

I might tell a little anecdote about that trip up to Hong Kong because it's the most uncomfortable time that I've ever had aboard ship. That is, mentally uncomfortable. We had to do a little flying as we left Subic Bay in order to exercise the flight deck and keep the pilots current. So we spent one day in the lee of Luzon flying, and the weather was good. But I knew very well that as we headed on up towards Hong Kong that the seas that come down through the Bashi Channel, which is between Formosa and Luzon, would be very rough. These big rollers come down out of the North Pacific and sweep through there, particularly during the wintertime. If there had been a storm, they could be very high. We finished flying about 1800, and I told the air boss to rig for heavy weather, as I knew that we were going to be in for some pretty rough stuff. The FDR had a very low freeboard; it had been loaded up so much since it was built that it sat very low in the water. And so it

---

[*] Captain George C. Talley, Jr., USN.
[†] Captain Ramage commanded the ship from 7 January to 15 January 1967.

was about 6:00 o'clock, and I'd probably had a hard night the night before, I don't recall, but anyway, I went in to take a nap.

About 8:00 or 9:00 o'clock, I could begin to feel the old bucket begin to roll a little bit, so I thought I'd go up and take a look around and see what was going on. I was in absolute consternation when I saw that the aircraft on the flight deck were tied down athwartship with their tails pointing over the sides. This is the normal procedure, but on every carrier that I'd been on before, when you'd rig for heavy weather, you put the aircraft fore and aft. So I got ahold of the air boss right away, and I said, "Is this your heavy weather tie-down?"

And he said, "That's our heavy weather bill."

I said, "Jesus, that's not right. They should be fore and aft."

And he said, "Well, we've never had any problems."

I said, "Well, I'll tell you what you do. You put on triple tie-downs and I want you to increase the security watch, because I don't want one of those aircraft to break loose and roll across the deck and maybe knock one or two of the other aircraft into the water.

He said, "We'll do that."

Well, hindsight is always the best. About 4:00 or 5:00 o'clock in the morning I began to get really uncomfortable, and I began to curse myself for not heading back in the lee of Luzon and telling them to respot the flight deck fore and aft. But I was kind of committed, and so we went on. We had about maybe 36 hours of this weather, which was not good, and every roll of that ship made me think of one of those planes getting loose. They didn't get loose, but it sure taught me a lesson. If there's ever a question, never take a chance. We finally ended up in Hong Kong with no problems whatsoever, but it was an extremely disconcerting thing for me.

The day that I took over the ship, I asked the exec what he'd done for the crew in getting ready to go into Hong Kong. He said, "Nothing." FDR, of course, was an East Coast ship, and they didn't know how you did various things in Hong Kong. You had to go in early, get your big money out, and make reservations for hotels and entertainment. So I was able to get the COD off during that day we were exercising, with a group of five or six people to go on in there and make some preparations to let these guys have a good Hong Kong liberty.* Otherwise, I don't think they'd have known what the heck to do.

I stayed on in TF 77 an extra month. The tour of duty out there was 12 months, and I wanted to be darn sure I got a good relief. There were several people nominated, and finally Tex Conatser was nominated, and I told Dave Richardson, who knew Tex already, that I thought that he'd be a good relief.† He said, "Well, it's going to take a little longer to get him out there."

I said, "I don't mind staying out here. My wife may mind it, but I don't. I'll just stay out a month or two." So I was finally relieved in late March of 1967.

On the way back I stopped through Pearl, of course, and discussed the operations. It was quite apparent in talking to Admiral Johnson that he was very pleased with my performance, and he wished me good luck in the coming selection for flag officer. I was to be sent back to ComNavAirPac to stand by for the selection process.

Just before I left Task Force 77, ComNavAirPac had been relieved, and Vice Admiral Al Shinn was to be the new ComAirPac. When he came out to visit the flagship, I was in Saigon, but I left him a note which stated that I had been advised by at least one member of the previous selection board that the reason that I wasn't the flag officer was because of the fitness report that I had received from him when I was the skipper of Independence. He wrote me a note which said, "If this is the case, I will correct it," which he did.

Q: That's a pretty rare occurrence, isn't it?

Admiral Ramage: Yes, it is, and I think perhaps that, as I said previously, I could have been a little more diplomatic in getting along with him. On the other hand, you only get to be a captain of a big carrier once, and if you're captain, you want to run the ship. That is a problem which is inherent in the relationship between a flag officer and a flag captain. If the flag officer decides he wants to run the ship and the flag captain is very docile, it goes fine.

---

* COD--carrier on-board delivery, an aircraft configured for carrier takeoffs and landings, dedicated to transporting personnel and cargo between ship and shore.
† Captain Charlie N. Conatser, USN.

But if the flag captain's rather stubborn, oftentimes this dissension occurs between the two, and mine was a beauty!

By the time I reported in to ComNavAirPac, Al had written a letter to the selection board, and more than that, had asked BuPers to detail me to be ComFAir Whidbey, which was just about to become the Medium Attack Wing Pacific. He further said that he wanted me to have that job whether I was a captain or a flag officer. In other words, he was trying to force the selection, and certainly that didn't do me any harm. The response that he got from Washington was, of course, that I would be assigned up there in the event that I was selected. But I think that my selection finally--and it was three or four years later than my peers--was kind of a foregone conclusion, particularly when Tom Moorer became the CNO.* I do know that he was most helpful in making damn sure that I made the grade.

About that time I had been offered a job up at the Rand Corporation up in Santa Monica, and considered very seriously taking it, because I was actually in the selection zone and most flag officers are selected two to three years prior to the time they get in the zone. I was in the zone early because I had been selected for captain early, and if I had been passed over that first time in the zone, there really wasn't any chance of making it. So I was beginning to look around for something else to do.

I, of course, didn't take the job up at the Rand Corporation and told them the morning that I was selected, "Please hold the job open for a few years, because I do have another job that's been offered, and I think I'll make the Navy my career."

Q: You one time told me that to make flag you had to have a sponsor.

Admiral Ramage: I think you do. My problem, as was told to me by several people, was, "You have absolutely no blackshoe support. You get all the aviation votes on the board every time, and you don't do very well with the surface people." And I guess I kind of generated that feeling. I considered myself to be an expert in carrier operations, and I

---

* Admiral Thomas H. Moorer, USN, served as Chief of Naval Operations from 1 August 1967 to 1 July 1970.

thought that was the way to go. I perhaps should have been a little more diplomatic, but that's not my way.

So I was selected, as I say, much to the surprise of my classmates. It didn't surprise me a bit, but it did surprise a lot of them. I relieved Rear Admiral Joe Jaap up at Whidbey the first of July of 1967.* I was particularly interested in the job because it was the coming thing. I thought the A-6 would be a fine airplane. We had been using them very sparingly out in WestPac. It was to be a big job with eight or so squadrons of A-6s, plus we still had the remains of the A-3s up there.

Q: You were in WestPac when the first A-6s came out there.

Admiral Ramage: Yes, that's right.

Q: Did you get involved with the bomb problem?

Admiral Ramage: Yes. I'll go into that here a little bit later, because I took up that problem as I moved in there. The first thing I did, as I do in every situation, was to take a look at the pilots. I had been warned that probably the problem up in Whidbey was quite similar to what had existed in the A-3 wing when I took it over, that is, that there was an improper personnel input.

The A-6 was actually replacing the A-1 or AD, and it was much easier to move the AD pilots into the A-6s than to look around and try to get a good mix of jet-experienced pilots. When I looked at the squadrons up there, particularly VA-196, which was about to deploy, I concluded that it didn't have sufficient jet experience. This was a sad thing, because we had thousands of jet-qualified people by this time. It wasn't like the previous situation. BuPers just hadn't paid attention to past experiences. And certainly having been through it twice, first in the night fighters and then in the heavy attack, I was prepared to do something about it right away. I went down to see Admiral Shinn and told him that I

---

* Rear Admiral Joseph A. Jaap, USN, who retired from active duty on 1 July 1967.

thought we were standing into trouble with the squadrons up there. We certainly were not getting our fair share of jet-qualified people into the A-6 program.

He said, "What do you propose?"

I said, "I propose that I go in to BuPers and tell them about it."

So I had prepared a presentation on the background of the pilots. What we needed was a large input of A-4 drivers. We would take fighter pilots who would probably fight like hell, and the A-4 pilots, a lot of them didn't want to go to multi-engine, but I thought that the people, particularly the experienced people that were coming in, should be at least two-thirds jet-qualified carrier pilots.

By that time Rear Admiral Walt Curtis, was the head of the personnel detailing section when I gave the presentation, and there was no problem whatsoever in improving the situation.[*] I might add that it was quite different going in to BuPers as a flag officer than it was a captain. I was just absolutely surprised at how well I was treated.

Up in Whidbey, I ran into some rather strange things. Joe Jaap, the guy that I relieved, was a very strict constructionalist on many items. One of them was wearing flight jackets. He didn't like them worn anywhere but on the flight line, and he didn't like any of them with a lot of insignia on them. Apparently he'd had some duty with the Air Force, and I think the Air Force still only allows one insignia, which is the major command. Well, I had flight jackets which were completely loaded with everything I'd ever done. So after I'd been aboard about two weeks, I put on the gaudiest flight jacket that I had and went down to the PX and looked around, swaggering around in this flight jacket.[†] I didn't have to say a thing. The flight jackets began to appear, and the insignia began to appear, and within about three or four months I had everybody looking like a naval aviator should.

There were a few other things that he was really kind of funny about, he and also the skipper of the base, who was Beecher Snipes.[‡] One was on clamming. There was an area where they had gooey ducks, and it was a particularly lucrative area. But in order to get there, you had to go through a restricted area, which was a gasoline farm. The skipper of the base had closed the clamming area. In order to get to it, you had to walk about a mile

---

[*] Rear Admiral Walter L. Curtis, USN.
[†] PX--post exchange.
[‡] Captain Beecher Snipes, USN.

up the beach, and it was a rough beach. So with no problem at all, I was able to open the gooey duck clamming area, and you'd think that I ran for God up there just by saying, "All we'll do is make the keys available. You guys, if you go on in, draw a key and be damned sure you lock the gate when you're through." It was a very simple thing.

I had a leading chief nominated from one of the squadrons, they hadn't had one, to sit in on my weekly conferences. After a week or two, I asked the chief if there were any complaints that he knew about that we could correct on the base. He said, "Yes, the EM Club would like to be able to sell a beer between 12:00 and 1:00."[*]

And I said, "Well, I don't see any great problem with that." And I turned to Beecher Snipes, who was the skipper, and said, "Let's give it a try and see if we have any problems with it."

He immediately said, "Oh, this is a very bad precedent to set. The kids will drink beer and then they won't be able to do their jobs."

And I said, "Well, that's command problem. That's not one that you run from the top. Let's just see what happens."

So the following week at the meeting I asked Beecher how the beer situation was going, and he said, "I didn't open it yet."

I said, "Beecher, tomorrow I will be down at the EM Club at noon, and I will have a beer." Again, a very simple thing. You always wonder why people get themselves into things that become problems. It turned out there was absolutely zero trouble. Certain people seem to think that there is a better reason to say "no" to anything than just to say "yes."

One of the things that I wanted to get to right away was an evaluation of the A-6's bombing accuracy. We were having a lot of trouble with track radar, among other things. We couldn't seem to really figure out what kind of hits we were getting and what kind of intelligence was required to do the job. In other words, the system was new, and typical of the Navy, they had tossed it right into operation without really any planning. So I asked for a little help from WSEG in Washington.[†] They sent a guy out, and I told him that I wanted

---

[*] EM club--enlsited men's club.
[†] Weapons Systems Evaluation Group.

to try to find out what the kill probability was when operating with various levels of air crew, training, experience, and also intelligence.

I wanted to get the radar bombing accuracy against various types of targets, because we figured on using the A-6 basically at night. We, of course, also used them in the daytime. And I wanted to find the minimum time that was required for a bombardier to acquire and track on a target. This was particularly important in the North Vietnam area, where there was a hell of a lot of opposition from SAMs. So I wanted to see really how long these aircraft had to be in a good level bombing run in order to get the bomb on the target. This was not completed until after I left. They did turn out a pretty good study, which was distributed around the fleet and also in Washington. I think it was the first effort that was ever made to find out really what the A-6 and the bombing system could do.

Q: Did you have an opportunity to fly an A-6?

Admiral Ramage: Yes, I had the opportunity and availed myself of it. I did not carqual, though. I only stayed there for about two or three months, and I had so damn many problems to get to that I didn't really get a chance to get bounced and get on the boat, but it certainly was my intention.

What occurred was that Roger Mehle had relieved Rear Admiral Dave Richardson as CTF 77.[*] When I heard that these orders were being issued, I knew that there were going to be problems out there. Furthermore, I had a gut feeling that the problem somehow would affect me, and I was right. Roger didn't last over a couple of months.[†] He was fired. And so I entered into the daisy chain, as they call it, as a result of his being fired. They had to get a carrier task force qualified rear admiral out there immediately. The only one available was Rear Admiral Ralph Cousins, who was in the plans job at CinCPac. Now, the plans job is a dead end. Everybody that's ever been there has not been continued as a rear

---

[*] Rear Admiral Roger W. Mehle, USN.
[†] The relief of Admiral Mehle is discussed in the Naval Institute's oral histories of Vice Admiral David C. Richardson, Vice Admiral Kent L. Lee, and Admiral John J. Hyland.

admiral, so Ralph can thank Roger Mehle for all his future success, which was great.* So that left that job open.

At the same time, Rear Admiral Bush Bringle, who was operations and plans at CinCPacFlt, was to relieve John Hyland as Com7thFlt, and John Hyland in turn was to become CinCPacFlt.† The officer that was to relieve Bush Bringle in CinCPacFlt was Rear Admiral Walt Curtis. Walt had had his carrier division, which was the requirement to take over that ops and plans job at fleet, so the easiest thing to do was, since Ralph had to leave immediately, was to send Walt Curtis to Cousins's job at CinCPac. Roy Johnson asked for me to relieve Bush Bringle as ops and plans at CinCPacFlt. This was certainly a boost for me, because the job had always been given to a flag officer who had completed his carrier division tour. So I was very flattered, although I did hate to leave Whidbey Island after only three months.

Q: Why was Mehle relieved?

Admiral Ramage: Incompetence.

Q: That's pretty forthright.

Admiral Ramage: The job of Deputy Chief of Staff for Operations and Plans at Commander in Chief Pacific Fleet was just a great job for me, because I was current in the main operation that was going on, and also the people on the staff were just great people. First, Roy Johnson, who was very soon relieved by John Hyland, Vice Admiral Red Baumberger, known as "Bombo," was just a fine guy, and the people on the staff were just as friendly as they could be.‡

It was an operating staff, and I fit into it perfectly. It was a hard job because it was a seven-day-a-week operation, but if you're busy doing what you like and in a place where

---

* Cousins became a four-star admiral, later serving as VCNO and SACLant-CinCLant-CinCLantFlt.
† Admiral John H. Hyland, USN, served as Commander in Chief Pacific Fleet, 30 November 1967 to 5 December 1970.
‡ Deputy CinCPacFlt was Vice Admiral Walter H. Baumberger, USN, a surface officer.

you think you're worthwhile, you're much happier. Whereas I enjoyed the job up in Whidbey Island, I felt that with the past experience that I had, that it was quite a waste of the Navy's talent to have me sit in that position up there. I'd really been pretty much running the task force operations out there for the previous year plus, and some use should be made of this experience.

Q: The Navy doesn't do a good job of that, do they?

Admiral Ramage: Well, occasionally you run into some terrible things, but this wasn't planned from Washington. It was planned by Roy Johnson, with Johnny Hyland's concurrence.

Q: I mean, like you going to Whidbey Island, being current with what's going on in the war, to be sent back to Whidbey Island to take care of . . .

Admiral Ramage: Well, there just wasn't anyplace open. At that time they never gave a fresh-caught flag officer a carrier division. They usually hit him on the second tour, and probably there wasn't anything else available. After all, Shinn had asked for me to go on up to Whidbey. It was a good assignment for me with my background, particularly with recent experience off Vietnam, plus the A-3 experience, which had pretty much the same type of requirement. So it was a good assignment. I was just in a lucky position, and I really enjoyed the three years that I spent out in Pearl working for Hyland.

There isn't too much that I can say about the job there. I liked it. I think I was helpful. I was certainly able to intercede a little bit for Admiral Hyland with Admiral Sharp in various problems because I had worked for Admiral Sharp before.

I might just divert a little bit to point out that there is a built-in trap in the CinCPac-CinCPacFlt arrangement. CinCPac really commanded nothing. The Army in the Pacific at that time was pretty much being run directly from Saigon. Although Westmoreland had to report to Admiral Sharp, there was an awful lot of direct communications going on between Westmoreland and Washington. Admiral Sharp said it never bothered him, because Westmoreland kept him advised, but nevertheless, there wasn't much direct control over the Army. Plus, the Army command, that's the commander of the Army Pacific, Commander in Chief, Army Pacific, which was at Fort Shafter, was basically a logistics command. It had very little to do with operations. PacAF, on the other hand, over at Hickam Field, did have some operational responsibilities.* However, there's always a tendency not to interfere into something you're not particularly familiar with, so that left CinCPacFlt to be directly monitored by CinCPac. It's been a problem over many, many years, and is just kind of a built-in situation.

Q: How did CinCPac become an exclusively Navy job?

Admiral Ramage: Well, by law it isn't. It's simply that we had the predominant forces in the Pacific. As a matter of fact, at one time there was a chance that it might become an Army job when there were more than a half a million troops in Vietnam.

Q: Do you know to what extent that was discussed?

Admiral Ramage: I'm not sure. When McCain came in, I understand that it was a matter of discussion.†

I am now talking about March of 1968. The Chief of Naval Operations, Admiral Moorer, felt that it might be a good idea to have Admiral Hyland come in to Washington to brief the Washington retired flag and general officers on what was actually going on in Vietnam, because they really weren't getting much information that was good. Johnny Hyland immediately gave me the job of putting the thing together and said that since he was so busy, that he knew that I'd be delighted to go and do it. So I was to present a view from the fleet to these elder statesmen. I might say that I've never faced such a load of brass in my life. There must have been 300 or so of these people. They came from all up and down the East Coast.

---

* PacAF--Pacific Air Force.
† Admiral John S. McCain, Jr., USN, served as Commander in Chief Pacific from 31 July 1968 to 1 September 1972.

Q: These were not just Navy?

Admiral Ramage: Marines were there, but none outside the Navy. But I felt that I could take off the gloves on this presentation, since it was to be in-house, and I outlined the war as it was being fought, the problems that CTF 77 and the Seventh Air Force faced in trying to do something. It ended up to be a very damning accusation against the Johnson Administration. The questions afterwards were directly pointed at these problems, and I let it all hang out, in that I told the people very exactly what the problems were out there.

Moorer, in particular, enjoyed this. He said that these guys really can't comprehend how it is to try to fight a war under these circumstances because most of these people were in World War II, where you could do about anything you wanted as long as you took the war to the enemy. I went through the Kennedy-McNamara philosophy of graduated response, and I told them that I couldn't understand the war out there any better than they could.

So my time there on the staff was very good. I was out of town when both the Pueblo and the EC-121 incidents by the North Koreans occurred, so I won't dwell too much on them.* I've got something a little bit later that I think might be of interest because I don't think it's recorded anywhere.

In the summer of 1969, Admiral Hyland came to me and said, "You should be moving fairly soon." He gave me a list of three names. He said, "These people have been nominated for your job."

I took a look at them. Incidentally, all three of them became vice admirals. I said, "I just wouldn't feel good about any one of these three people relieving me."

He said, "I'm glad you said it, because I don't either." He said, "Would you be willing to stay on for an additional year?" He pointed out that when I was out there as chief of staff of CTF 77, that certainly was the equivalent of carrier division command, and he

---

* USS Pueblo (AGER-2), an electronic intelligence ship, was seized on 23 January 1968 in the Sea of Japan by North Korean naval forces. The ship's crew members were held as prisoners until 23 December of that year. Of the 83 officers and men on board, 28 were intelligence specialists. A U.S. Navy EC-121 electronic reconnaissance aircraft with 31 crewmen on board was short down 14 April 1969 by North Korean aircraft. The incident took place approximately 90 miles off the coast of North Korea. The entire U.S. crew was lost.

said, "I don't think you need it." He said, "I think we have a little bit better job in mind for you if you'll stick around the additional year."

I didn't say, "What?" But I presumed that it was Com7thFlt, and I said, "Well, I'd be delighted to stay on," particularly since I liked the job so well. So I stayed on for an additional year.

I'd like to discuss an incident that occurred in March of 1970 while I was still on the staff of CinCPacFlt, that I don't think is recorded anywhere unless it might be in Admiral John Hyland's personal history.[*] But it has to do with a merchant ship called the Columbia Eagle.[†] The Columbia Eagle was a contract ship to MSTS, and it was loaded with ammunition which was to go to Thailand.[‡]

Q: That would be the seagoing equivalent of the airlift command.

Admiral Ramage: Seagoing equivalent to MAC.

Q: Military Airlift Command.

Admiral Ramage: Anyway, they're contract ships generally, and it's a cheap way to do it. The Navy uses it more and more. What had happened was that on the 14th of March, we began to get messages from the Columbia Eagle which were very confusing. There had been a bomb scare aboard, and 24 members of its crew got into lifeboats and were picked up by another merchant ship called the Rappahannock.

Q: Where was the ship at the time?

---

[*] This incident is covered in Admiral Hyland's Naval Institute oral history.
[†] The U.S.-flag merchant ship Columbia Eagle was delivering ammuntion to Thailand when she was seized by two armed crewmen on 14 March 1970. The two set 24 of the crew of 39 adrift in lifeboats and then ordered the ship to Sihanoukville, Cambodia, where they claimed political asylum. The U.S. Government viewed it as an anti-war protest rather than mutiny.
[‡] MSTS--Military Sea Transportation Service, which has since been renamed Military Sealift Command.

Admiral Ramage: This is just south of Cambodia en route to Thailand. Other than that, we didn't know much about it. The radios on the Columbia Eagle were dead, and it was obvious that we were in the midst of probably a hijacking. At 7:00 o'clock that evening the U.S. Coast Guard cutter Mellon, which was in the area, was attempting to contact Columbia Eagle, and they couldn't contact them either, but Mellon was fairly close. The Columbia Eagle was ultimately sighted by a P-3 aircraft in the area and there didn't seem to be any great problem, but she seemed to be heading into Cambodia, Sihanoukville.* There were no visual signs of distress, and everything seemed to be all right. Of course, CinCPac and Washington was being advised of all these things.

Shortly thereafter we finally did get a message from the Columbia Eagle, it was an SOS, "Columbia Eagle hijacked by two armed seamen, and proceeding along the central coast of Cambodia." So we immediately had the problem.

The question then came up, "What are we going to do about it?"

As I mentioned previously, I hadn't been in Honolulu when the Pueblo and the EC-121 incidents had occurred, but we were in a position to do something about this one. Brian McCauley, who was the ops officer, immediately went down to our opcon center and began trying to figure out what had happened. I'll read from his memorandum at the present time.

I quote from the memorandum for the record submitted by Captain Brian McCauley, who was the CinCPacFlt operations officer. He states, "At about 2130 I was called and informed that the ship had been taken over by two armed seamen. I directed that this be passed up the line." Which, of course, was to me and to Admiral John Hyland. "At about 2230 I was called and told that the Coast Guard cutter Mellon had radio contact and was closing SS Columbia Eagle with an ETA of some time after midnight. At 2310, we received word the ship had anchored in Cambodian waters. Then followed a series of phone calls between me and Rear Admiral Ramage and Admiral Hyland." It was decided that we should give the Coast Guard cutter some guidance when she arrived on the scene. Admiral Hyland and I immediately headed for the command center. In the meantime, Brian McCauley had gotten ahold of our attorney, who was an expert on international law,

---

* The Navy's P-3 Orion is a land-based turbo-prop patrol aircraft with antisubmarine capability.

Commander Rogers, and he in turn got hold of the fleet legal officer, Commander McHugh.* What we wanted was a definition of piracy and what to do about it.

"At that time, at 2345, I drafted up a message. Admiral Ramage called Major General Peterson up at CinCPac [he was the operations and plans, my opposite number] to tell him of the action we were taking. General Peterson said that he would set up a call between Admiral McCain, who was in Washington at that time, and Admiral Hyland. Our message was for the Coast Guard cutter to approach the Columbia Eagle and stand by to retake the ship." Which I might point out, in my opinion, was the correct thing to do. It was about 16 miles from Sihanoukville. It was not in port; it was at anchor pretty far out to sea, so we didn't see any international repercussions.

About that time we designated who was to be the operational officer in control of this; it would be Rear Admiral Draper Kauffman, who was ComNavPhil.† That was his area of responsibility. At the same time I advised Admiral Zumwalt, who was down in Vietnam, that this was taking place.‡ At that time I told Zumwalt that we were in the process of taking some action, and he made two points. First, that it was politically sensitive, which, of course, we sure as hell knew, and second, that he thought that he, not ComNavPhil, Admiral Kauffman, should have opcon of the Mellon. I advised Admiral Hyland of these reservations, who was by this time on the line with Admiral McCain in Washington. Admiral McCain told Hyland to call off any operation and make damn sure that the Mellon did not enter into Cambodian waters."

So that was the Columbia Eagle episode. I point it out because the following week, it caused a great rift between Admiral McCain and Admiral Hyland. McCain either didn't know or chose not to believe that we were in constant contact with his staff for the entire time this was going on, and when he scolded Admiral Hyland, which he did in public in the meeting there, it was as though CinCPacFlt was running around in circles screaming and shouting and taking action that nobody knew about. He was dead wrong in it. Johnny was

---

* Commander Richard J. Rogers, JAGC, USN; Commander James J. McHugh, JAGC, USN.
† Rear Admiral Draper L. Kauffman, USN, Commander U.S. Naval Forces Philippines. His oral history is in the Naval Institute collection.
‡ Vice Admiral Elmo R. Zumwalt, Jr., USN, served as Commander Naval Forces Vietnam/Chief of Naval Advisory Group Vietnam from 30 September 1968 to 14 May 1970.

James D. Ramage #2 - 314

very unhappy and very upset about this thing, but this was a public scolding in front of Air Force, Army, and Navy personnel at the command center.

At a later time, I was talking to Admiral Moorer in Washington about the <u>Columbia Eagle</u> incident, and he knew about it. He said, "Why the hell didn't you do it?"

I told him that McCain had directed Johnny Hyland not to take action.

He said, "Well, "I'll be damned."

I think it was the correct action to be taken at that time, and I think that it would have at least shown that the Navy was on the ball and capable of doing something. McCain, of course, was a political animal to begin with and didn't want to have anything like that happening in his bailiwick. Whatever his contact was in Washington, I don't know. He very possibly advised the State Department and so forth, who, of course, would be expected not to take any action whatsoever.

Q: What was the ultimate outcome of this whole thing?

Admiral Ramage: Other than Johnny Hyland getting badly treated by McCain, there was nothing.

Q: I mean, about the ship.

Admiral Ramage: The ship was quarantined for the remainder of the war. The two people that hijacked it went on into Cambodia, and as far as I know, nothing happened.

Q: Were they Americans?

Admiral Ramage: Yes, they were dope-popping, anti-war people that decided this was going to be their operation. They were going to stop those bombs going into Thailand.

Q: Did they?

Admiral Ramage: They did. And we did absolutely nothing about it.

Q: On a similar basis, what do you recall as the professional discussion as to what should have followed the Pueblo seizure?

Admiral Ramage: That's a little beyond me. I can only point out what the finding was of the court, which was that Bucher should not have ever given up his ship, but I don't propose to get into that at this time.[*] The skipper's performance was very, very poor, but his performance as a POW was exemplary.[†] Let's not discuss that.

I think before I leave the CinCPacFlt duty, I might start out a little bit about our associations with Admiral Zumwalt, who went down to South Vietnam in 1969 in the spring. This is the first time I'd ever heard of him. He passed through Pearl as a two-star admiral, which was to be upgraded to three when he got to ComNavFor Vietnam. He would be working for U.S. MACV down there, that is, Westmoreland or later Abrams.[‡] And other than providing his logistic support, he was not in the chain of command of the fleet. However, we were definitely interested in it because it was our money that was being spent.

After he'd been down there about two weeks, the chief of staff, Red Baumberger, came in and asked me if Admiral Zumwalt had told me anything about pending ideas or things that he was about to do down there.

I said, "He didn't clear a thing with me." As a matter of fact, I don't think that we even saw each other. My wife later tells me that I saw him, because I always entertained visiting flag officers that came through, and I guess he was over at our house for cocktails, but he was just a very insignificant item.

However, after he got down there, we began to be bombarded with great gobs of fecal matter on how important the war was in the riverine forces. In a recent discussion

---

[*] Commander Lloyd M. Bucher, USN, was commanding officer of the Pueblo at the time of her seizure. A court of inquiry in 1969 recommended that he be court-martialed for loss of the ship, but Secretary of the Navy John Chafee decided not to carry out the recommendation, saying that Bucher had suffered enough.
[†] POW--prisoner of war.
[‡] General Creighton W. Abrams, Jr., USA, served as Commander U.S. Military Assistance Command Vietnam from 1968 to 1972.

which I set up for Will Morrison, who is writing a book called The Elephant and the Tiger, Admiral Sharp told Will that he didn't think that the riverine operations were of any value. Morrison does not include the subject. Apparently Admiral Baumberger was quite upset about certain things that were going on down there, and I was well aware of the fact that Zumwalt was operating out of the chain of command. He was doing things in the way of Vietnamization and giving away stuff, that had never been cleared with us, and since we were the supporters of the funding, why, it was quite a problem.*

Finally one day, we're talking about the spring of 1969 now, about June, the ops officer, Brian McCauley, came down with a message to Admiral Zumwalt, and it was a son-of-a-bitch. It was to be released, of course, by Admiral Hyland, because it accused Zumwalt of operating beyond his authority and doing various other things. So we took it in to Baumberger first because this would certainly be something he'd be interested in. He said, "Let's go in and see Johnny."

Johnny Hyland took one look at it and he pointed to me and he said, "Do you think this is true?"

And I said, "You're damned right."

He took his pen, he didn't look at the thing 15 seconds, and released it. That was the start of the Hyland-Zumwalt feud, which ultimately resulted in Hyland getting some very cavalier treatment later on the part of Zumwalt.

It was a very scalding message, and it infoed the CNO, Admiral Moorer. Later on it became apparent to me that very probably Moorer and Hyland had discussed this previously, because otherwise Hyland wouldn't sign off a message in about 15 or 20 seconds that was really a very, very derogatory message.

So about the following day, we got Zumwalt's response, which was one of the most mealy-mouthed things I've ever seen. It started out by saying, "I regret that I have not served you well," and so forth. But it was an indication of what was about to happen as far as Zumwalt was concerned. He was not operating within the Navy's chain of command in any way.

---

* Vietnamization was a process that began during Zumwalt's tenure to turn the fighting of the war over to the South Vietnamese. This involved U.S. personnel training Vietnamese crews for naval vessels and other military equipment, then turning the equipment over to them.

Relative to my finding a relief, I recommended to Admiral Hyland that either Rear Admiral Spin Epes or Roy Isaman would be ideal to relieve me, and he concurred.* So he asked for Roy Isaman to relieve me, and we actually just changed jobs, he was Commander Carrier Division Seven, in June of 1970, while I was out there at CinCPacFlt. When he came through in <u>Oriskany</u>, we simply just swapped jobs, and I went out with the flagship and its escorts to Vietnam.

By the time we got around to the summer of 1970, a lot had happened. We were not any longer striking in the north. We were dropping DST-36s, and I'll define those. DST-36 was a mechanism that was attached to a 500- or 1,000-pound bomb, which would change it into a mine, which was exploded electronically. It was a magnetic mine. It was useful both on the beach and at sea, and was about the only thing we could do since we weren't doing anything on up in the north. Lyndon Johnson, as you know, before he left, foreclosed on practically all of Nixon's options by stopping the bombing in the north, and we were no longer doing it.† So about all we could do was try to interdict over in the Ho Chi Minh Trail, which was useless. We sowed these DST-36s in the southern part of North Vietnam, to try to impede the traffic as it came down. It was a very terrible waste of equipment.

Q: Isn't this a carry-over from the thing that started clear back in Italy in World War II, Operation Strangle, and it was carried through Korea, trying to interdict supply lines in this type of work in any war we've ever fought?

Admiral Ramage: I guess so. It certainly didn't work in Korea, and I'm familiar with that.

Q: It didn't work in Italy either, did it?

---

* Rear Admiral Roy M. Isaman, USN.
† Richard M. Nixon served as President of the United States from 20 January 1969 until his resignation on 9 August 1974.

Q: To a certain extent, but it reflects the Air Force doctrine as opposed to Navy. It's my impression the Air Force approach worked reasonably well in World War II, so we'll apply it in these other fracases.

We did about as much good as we could under the circumstances out there during that cruise. We didn't have any problems. We didn't lose any people. It was a successful cruise, but we simply weren't permitted to do the job that we should have done. We still had five carriers in the force, usually three on station, sometimes two. But it was even worse than it was before, because in the past, at least, you could bring some pressure to bear, but now there was nothing we could do.

I will dwell a little bit on the Son Tay operation because it is kind of interesting.[*] CTF 77 at this time, in November of 1970, was Vice Admiral Freddy Bardshar. They'd given him the third star because it was about time. With five aircraft carriers, you sure should have more than two stars. He was the first one to get it, I think.

I first heard about the operation when Fred came out to the ship. I was the officer in tactical command at the time. He got me aside and said, "We're going to have a big operation tonight." This was about 1:00 o'clock in the afternoon. He told me it was to be the attempt to rescue our people from the Son Tay prison camp up in North Vietnam, and Task Force 77's job was to provide air cover. We were to raise as much hell around the eastern area as we could, to try to divert the North Vietnamese from the action that was going on to the west where the prison delivery was to take place.

In getting briefed, the first point I made was it looked like a really big operation at night. We were to launch at midnight. I had a new carrier out there on the line, the Hancock, which was not very ready. I pointed out that I would need extra fuel, and Freddy had already taken care of that. He'd gotten the use of a KC-135, 100,000 pounds of giveaway fuel over the force.[†] So as far as I was concerned, it was no great problem. The

---

[*] On 20 November 1970 a U.S. commando force landed at the Son Tay prison, 23 miles west of Hanoi, North Vietnam, in an attempt to free U.S. prisoners of war reported to be held there. The commandos did not recover any POWs, because they had been moved to another location shortly before. For details, see Benjamin F. Schemmer, The Raid (New York: Harper & Row, 1976).
[†] The Boeing KC-135 Stratotanker, an Air Force plane used for air-to-air refueling of jet aircraft.

question now was to brief the pilots on what we wanted. Freddy said, "You can't do it. This is by word of mouth only. There is nothing written on it."

I said, "Freddy, I can't launch this number of planes," which was to be an all-out effort and probably the biggest night effort that had ever been launched from Task Force 77, "without explaining to them what they're going to do."

Freddy thought for about 15 seconds. He said, "Oh, hell, go ahead and tell them."

So we put the word out to the pilots that this is what it was, and, of course, the pilots were just delighted at the opportunity to participate in this attempt to get these prisoners out.

The prison break was to be made in Son Tay, which was to the west of Hanoi. It was rather an isolated prison camp.

Q: It's almost on the Laotian border, isn't it?

Admiral Ramage: I don't think it's that far over. It was isolated, though, and it was to be done by the Army. They had practiced it at length, and it was to be a complex operation. The results were, as you know, that apparently the North Vietnamese somehow found out that it was going to happen and when the Army guys landed there, they landed on an empty camp. But the prisoners that were in North Vietnam at that time said that it had a decided impact upon their treatment. It indicated to the North Vietnamese that they'd better pull all the prisoners on in to Hanoi, where they could be more carefully watched and we couldn't get to them. That stopped the isolation for many of the people who were in solitary. There just wasn't room to keep them all separated. Jim Stockdale, in particular, thought this was a very worthwhile operation.[*] It's just a damn shame that we didn't get them out, because it was well-planned. How the leak went, I don't know.

Q: Did they actually find out about it? I was under the impression that it was just a coincidence.

---

[*] Captain James B. Stockdale, USN, was one of the leaders of the POW community in the Vietnam War. He was awarded the Medal of Honor after his release by the North Vietnamese in 1973.

Admiral Ramage: I have no idea. At least they were moved.

Q: It was roughly two weeks before, I think.

Admiral Ramage: Yes.

Q: I thought it was just dumb luck.

Admiral Ramage: I felt at the time a great amount of respect for President Nixon. I had been used to Lyndon Johnson farting around on things like this, and I thought that as we got down towards the end, that somehow this exercise would be canceled just like had gone on many times before. I'm talking about the petroleum storage raids three years before. But no, we got down towards about 10:00 o'clock, and the crews were all briefed and ready to go. As it got down towards about 11:00, I felt, well, we're going anyway. And we were loaded to do all the damage that we could. Any time after 11:00 o'clock was too late as far as holding it back. And, sure enough, there wasn't any cancellation at all. We went for it. It's just a damn shame that we didn't do better.

We did get some real beautiful messages on the performance of Task Force 77 after that. I'll read only the one, because it came from CinCPac, who at that time was McCain, saying, "I am extremely proud of your forces that so effectively conducted the diversionary and strike operation against North Vietnam last week. To have flown the largest night sortie level of the war and to have conducted the strike operations all without incident was indeed an exceptional achievement, particularly considering the fact that two F-8 squadrons were new arrivals, was particularly noteworthy. Please accept and convey my sincerest well-done to all concerned."

It was a fine operation, and it was a good way to end up a rather quiet cruise at that time. We at least had done something, and we were quite pleased with it.

Q: I always have difficulty keeping track of the bombing halts. Did this operation take place during a bombing halt?

Admiral Ramage: This operation took place when we were not bombing to the north. There had been a bombing halt really since 1968, when Lyndon Johnson closed off everything to the north. So, yeah, you could say it was during the bombing halt because there wasn't much going on.

Q: So what did these guys do after they launched?

Admiral Ramage: They were loaded with bomblets. What do you call those?

Q: CBUs.*

Admiral Ramage: CBUs. We loaded out with a lot of Shrike missiles and Mark 82s and 83s, which are 500- and 1,000-pound bombs.† They knew that whatever fired back at them was fair game, so the pilots enjoyed the opportunity to take a crack at them, and we got some pretty licks in. Again, one of these things of having to cheat to be able to do the job that you should be able to do.

That was our last major operation before Oriskany and group returned to the coast. We had the privilege of hosting Admiral John Hyland's retirement ceremony aboard ship. He was relieved by Admiral Clarey in December of 1970.‡

I went back to the coast and immediately was requested to come in to Washington to discuss with various people what was going on in Task Force 77. When I got into town, I dropped by Admiral Zumwalt's office to let him know that if he wanted to see me, I was available as a recent returnee in charge of the operations in the Gulf of Tonkin. However, I

---

* CBUs--cluster bomb units, which are anti-personnel weapons.
† Shrike was the Navy's first specialized tactical antiradar missile. It was essentially a Sparrow airframe with an enlarged blast-fragmentation warhead. It had a speed of about Mach 2 and range of up to 25 miles. Shrike entered fleet service in 1965 and combat in 1966.
‡ Admiral Bernard A. Clarey, USN, served as Commander in Chief Pacific Fleet, 5 December 1970 to 30 September 1973.

was advised by his executive assistant that the admiral very rarely saw his commanders from the field, which is probably about the dumbest thing I ever heard. Because if you don't talk to your commanders from the field, I don't know what the hell you know is going on. It was pretty obvious that Zumwalt didn't want to see me.

Q: He was too busy taking care of haircuts.

Admiral Ramage: Well, he was very busy taking care of his racial programs and all these beautiful things, you know. Any seaman that wanted to complain could get in the office, but not a task force commander, particularly an aviator.

So I then went down to Joint Chiefs of Staff to see Admiral Moorer, and he was just the opposite.* I got in to see him, and he immediately began asking questions. After about 30 or 40 minutes, I knew that there were people waiting on the outside, and I said, "Admiral, I'm taking up too much of your time."

And he said, "When you are, I'll tell you. Now sit down there, and let's keep this thing going." He said, "You're the first guy that's been back in about three or four months directly from out there." And then he, incidentally, congratulated us on this Son Tay operation. But it was kind of an unusual thing, the chief of my service wasn't interested in knowing what was going on in the Gulf of Tonkin, but the Chairman of the Joint Chiefs of Staff was.

The Oriskany was a direct turn-around ship, that is, she spent about five months back on the coast in Alameda and I was to ride her on back out for a repeat cruise, which was just fine with me. However, Bardshar was about to be relieved, and the question came up of who was to relieve him. I was obviously the logical candidate.

Q: What job did he have there?

---

* Admiral Thomas H. Moorer, USN, served as Chairman of the Joint Chiefs of Staff from 3 July 1970 to 30 June 1974. His oral history is in the Naval Institute collection.

Admiral Ramage: He was CTF 77. It was to drop to a two-star job. He was three stars. But I then heard that Hutch Cooper was going to take it.[*] Now, Hutch is an old friend of mine, but Hutch had no experience out there except as a ship commander many years previously. Of course, he was in BuPers; he was the detail officer.

Q: Well, Hutch helped start the whole thing.

Admiral Ramage: Hutch was a pretty good guy, but he nominated himself, and he was one number senior to me. He later apologized, and I said, "Well, so be it. That's not my problem."

But I'll read here from a letter that Mickey Weisner, who was Com7thFlt, wrote to me at the time.[†] He said, "For a two-star, I had wanted someone for the job with more experience in the ways of the Gulf than Hutch. To be specific, I had submitted your name as one of those, cited you as the one with the greatest experience. Obviously my recommendations were not bought. The reason given was the seniority problem. I had even agreed to accept an inversion. I am sorry you will not be in the job."

When I talked to Hutch, he was embarrassed about the whole thing. I told him to forget it, and I thought, "Well, hell, I'll be out here, and I'll have operational control of Task Force 77 at least half the time." But it did kind of gripe me that I didn't actually get the title of CTF 77, although I did have the force for two cruises, and was in command at least half of those two cruises. So that was one of life's little problems, but certainly didn't do any lasting damage to me. I was very thankful to be able to get in three complete cruises in Task Force 77.

When we returned to the Gulf in the summer or spring of 1971, things had not changed very much. We were still making toothpicks in Laos, and we were dropping DST-36s and really not doing much. There would be an occasional opportunity to do some damage, but it was always a reactive situation which could occur if you were doing a photo

---

[*] Rear Admiral Damon W. Cooper, USN.
[†] Vice Admiral Maurice F. Weisner, USN, served as Commander Seventh Fleet from 10 March 1970 to 18 June 1971.

recce of the area. They were always escorted, and if you would claim that you were being shot at, you could drop on them. But it was a very unsatisfactory situation.

We were actually charged to conduct so many photo recces up in the northern area. This was pretty damn dumb, because first of all, what we were going to do with the information we obtained? Secondly, they were very well armed up in the northern areas. I told our recce pilots not to do anything dumb. You've got to go into Package 3, but there's no requirement for you to fly over Thanh Hoa, as an example. All you're required to do is make a presentation. This is a hell of a way to fight a war, but I didn't want anybody to get killed unnecessarily. I told Frank Haak, the skipper of the Oriskany at that time, if there was any way that we could drive this goddamn carrier right up to Hanoi, I'd do it.* But I didn't want to see anybody killed unless we can really bring a lot of pressure on these guys. And there really wasn't much we could do.

Towards the end of this second cruise, a very interesting operation did develop, which was known as Operation Prize Bull. This was conceived by the Seventh Air Force and had approval in Washington. Apparently it was tied in with some kind of a political move that was taking place in Paris at the peace conference. In any event, they wanted to have some pressure brought against North Vietnam at that particular time. The big problem was that we weren't offered any targets, and this was to be done regardless of weather, at a specified time. The targets were nothing; they were way down in Package 1 and 2, that is, in the southern part of North Vietnam. To make it worse, because of the time element, Seventh Air Force had conceived the idea that we would drop on signal in straight and level flight, using Loran guidance.† That is, the Air Force Loran-equipped F-4s would lead the formations. We were to jettison on signal. This was just throwing ordnance in the general direction of the enemy.

Q: The F-4s were the pathfinders.

---

* Captain Frank S. Haak, USN.
† Loran (long-range aid to navigation) is a system of electronic navigation that involves the reception of pulse signals transmitted simultaneously by paired stations ashore.

Admiral Ramage: Pathfinders. That's right. On top of that, because there was no pressure on Hanoi, we were beginning to get cuts on SAM movement to the south. We could follow them electronically. There were SAMs going into the southern area. We didn't know exactly where because we couldn't locate them, but we did have indications that there was a probability of SAMs down in the southern area. This didn't make much sense to me. First of all, the targets were useless. Secondly, there was a possibility that we could be zapped by SAMs while flying above an overcast. It just wasn't a worthwhile use of my forces. On top of that, the area that the Navy would fly in was close to the coast, and the weather would probably be CAVU, that is, visual flight.* So my planes would be flying straight and level in a possible SAM area on the wing of these Air Force F-4s, where they could be easily fired on by guns and possibly by missiles. And if they were over an overcast, they were really vulnerable. One thing that we had learned previously was never fly in or above an overcast in a possible SAM area.

This situation that I found myself in reminded me of the response that Admiral Mitscher had given Black Jack Reeves, that I referred to earlier. Reeves had recommended that Task Group 58.3 be detached from Task Force 58 for another Truk raid in 1944. Mitscher's reply was, "I will not be badgered into an unwise decision." And after having been associated with this war for six years, I certainly wasn't going to do anything that would possibly cost lives unless we could get something for them. In my opinion, there was no way that this operation made any sense at all.

So when this thing was conceived, I sent a message on the 20th of September of 1971. It was highly classified, and it was to General Lavelle, who was the Commander Seventh Air Force in Saigon at the time.† I infoed CinCPacFlt, Admiral Clarey, Admiral Mack, the first blackshoe to have the Seventh Fleet in a long time, and Rear Admiral Hutch Cooper, who at that time was in Singapore.‡ Hutch had sent Captain Ed McKellar, his

---

* CAVU--ceiling and visibility unlimited.
† General John D. Lavelle, USAF, Commander Seventh Air Force until March 1972, when he was recalled to the United States. He was soon retired with the reduced rank of lieutenant general. In subsequent congressional hearings, Lavelle admitted that he had ordered repeated unauthorized bombing strikes against targets in North Vietnam between November 1971 and March 1972, and he had falsified reports of those strikes.
‡ Vice Admiral William P. Mack, USN, served as Commander Seventh Fleet from 18 June 1971 to 23 May 1972. His oral history is in the Naval Institute collection.

operations officer, into Saigon to support this special operation, whatever it was going to be.*

My response was, "I feel that there are two basic weaknesses in Reference A [this was the one which called on us to do this thing] which should be given careful consideration. In my judgment, both violate the intent of Reference B [which is the JCS message]. A, there is no provision in the plan which calls for Navy participation during the first target period in the event of VFR weather. Potential for max effort is therefore not realized. Request you attempt to get a VFR option for CTG 77.6 for the first wave. And B, I have very strong reservations about the scheduled Navy IFR involvement. I feel that this type of weapon delivery over an overcast involves an unwarranted risk, even in a relatively permissive environment. Also damage expectancy would be negligible.

I do not intend to meet the IFR options in Reference A unless I receive recommendations to the contrary."†

So I had stated my position. I knew Hutch Cooper would back me up, because he wouldn't do it either. And I knew that the people up at CinCPacFlt would concur. Mack, who was the blackshoe Com7thFlt, I knew didn't know enough to know what the hell I was talking about. So as Ed McKellar will tell you--he was in the Saigon op center when my "bomb" hit--Lavelle was very happy, because he felt that this proved again that the Navy was uncooperative and that he should have control of the carrier force. So it was a political problem too.

The next thing that happened was that I got a back-channel call from Com7thFlt asking me to reconsider my decision. I responded, "Put it in writing."

We did get a written message back, but it didn't say anything about reconsidering my option. It ended up by saying the "MACV op order represents unmistakably clear direct ordering of Navy participation in the 21 September Prize Bull execution. Because of high up level interest in Operation Prize Bull, believe conditions over North Vietnam should be examined by 2400 Zulu, by flight leader for an on-scene decision made on his best judgment [which, of course, I was going to do anyway]. Do not desire that Navy sorties be held

---

* Captain Edwin D. McKellar, USN.
† VFR--visual flight rules; IFR--instrument flight rules.

aboard Oriskany as our marching orders are clear. However, Jig, you have the conn, and if the strike represents an unwarranted risk, then you'll be fully supported by Com7thFlt."

In other words, I sure wish you'd reconsider it, but he wasn't going to direct me to reconsider it. A real candy ass.

Of course, I got a nice backup from CinCPacFlt which said, "Concur with your [so-and-so]," which was my message. It said, "I will likewise support your decision." So I knew that I had the support of Cooper and Clarey, and Mack did not put it in any real objection. It did cause a lot of gas pains in Washington, but I repeat that I didn't go out there to be dumb, and that's the way I felt about it.

What happened in the actual operations was that as expected, the Navy area was VFR. I sent the CAG in, Sam Hubbard, to take a good look at the area, and he incidentally was loaded.* As long as you've got permission to go on in there, you might as well drop something. He and his wingman bombed something in there, and he said, "Send them on in. The area is clear. Let's go."

So I launched aircraft and advised Lavelle in Saigon that the area was clear, and we intended to launch a VFR strike against the assigned targets. He hit the ceiling at that time. He said, "Under no circumstances will your aircraft enter into that area. Divert them to Laos." So we spilled some more ordnance into the Steel Tiger area in Laos. That was the last operation of the second cruise. I hated to see it end under these conditions, but I still felt and feel today that I had the right dope on the thing.

I'll read from another message, which is in January, and it's from the Electronic Intelligence Analysis Group, which is in San Antonio, Texas. It points out that near Vinh, 30 December, they tried to do the same thing. I don't know why somebody didn't cancel it, but you apparently have to have a set of balls to do it. But the point is that two U.S. aircraft, an F-4B and an A-6A, were downed near Vinh on 30 December: "The F-4B was ahead of the strike group and was evading six missiles. One detonated behind in close proximity. The A-6A was lead aircraft approaching its target. A single SAM was heard to make a direct hit. Although the loss rate during Proud Deep [which is the code name for the second Prize Bull] is not considered statistically significant when compared with

---

* Commander Samuel W. Hubbard, USN, Commander Carrier Air Wing 19.

previous experiences, it is the observation of the on-scene commander that discipline and the sophistication of North Vietnam countermeasures have increased since the bombing halt." It ends with, "Although SAM firings may first be directed electronically, timely visual acquisition is also required to provide for adequate defense. The emergence of SAMs from top of the undercast gave too little time for evasion." There were four killed, and if I'd been out there, they'd have lived! I would have again refused.

I went back by way of CinCPacFlt and called on Admiral Clarey and thanked him very much for his support in that particular operation. He said, "Well, you were absolutely right. You don't have to thank me for that support. I thank you for making the right decision."

I went in to see Dave Richardson about it.* He was then deputy to Clarey. He said that Admiral Zumwalt had called Clarey and told him that he always had reservations about my capability to be a task force commander and that I had proved it in this case. Richardson said that Clarey had responded by saying that, "Ramage is the best man we have out there." So I felt vindicated.

My discussions at this time seem to be going back again and again at the Chief of Naval Operations. I don't mean for this whole thing to be an indictment of Admiral Zumwalt. His career will have to stand or fall on its own merits. I cannot help but note his impact upon the Navy. Perhaps the arrogance of this man can be understood by this memorandum dated 9 June 1971 to all COs, which says, "After almost a year as Chief of Naval Operations, I am convinced that our Navy is now moving with the times." I can't help but wonder how Tom Moorer, who had been his predecessor, felt when he read this revelation.

Q: I'd say the times were drugs, racial dissension, sabotage.

Admiral Ramage: What was happening was that the morale and discipline in the Navy was eroding. At a time when the country was in ferment, Zumwalt joined the crowd. Through his Z-grams, he relaxed grooming standards, he set up vertical lines of communication by

---

* Richardson was then a vice admiral.

bypassing the chain of command, particularly the chief petty officers.[*] Ships and stations were directed to set up hot lines where a seaman could contact the commanding officer direct, or even the commanding officer's boss. Zumwalt's hair hung down over his ears and bushed out and back like a haystack. Admiral George Anderson, a former CNO, told me that he had even seen the broken peace cross sign on the yard in CNO's quarters in Washington.[†]

He mentioned that the CNO's quarters were often filled with various types of people, activists and various groups. So I don't know really what this guy was after, but it certainly was the wrong way. He used to have these rap sessions, where he'd get in a room with 300 or 400 sailors who had to attend, and then he would talk to them and they would ask him questions. But the only sailors who would ever respond would be people that would ask such questions as, "My wife and I are both in the Navy. Can we both get BAQ?"[‡] These various things would go on.

Any of the people that really had anything to say wouldn't think of standing up and asking him a question. It was just the show-offs. If this guy really wanted to find out what was going on in the Navy, he could have gone over to the chiefs' club any Friday night during happy hour, and he could find out exactly what was going on in the Navy. That was, of course, the way most of us that had been in the Navy before did our business. We went direct to the source and let the chiefs tell us what the hell was going on, and we tried to do something about it.

In brief, Zumwalt did not know the Navy and in particular he did not know the U.S. sailor. He was very willing to listen to any recruit or anything tell what was wrong with the Navy, and he would put in these various things which were certainly to the detriment of the Navy.

I guess I can't help but point out that after I returned from my second command cruise, it would have been December of 1971, I again returned to Washington to be

---

[*] Z-grams were consecutively numbered policy directives from Chief of Naval Operations Zumwalt that attempted to deal with such issues as enlisted rights and privileges, equal opportunity, and Navy families. Junior personnel viewed them much more favorably than did their seniors. See U.S. Naval Institute Proceedings, May 1971, pages 291-298.
[†] Anderson was Chief of Naval Operations, 1961-63.
[‡] BAQ--basic allowance for quarters.

debriefed by the Deputy CNO for Air. I again left my card in Admiral Zumwalt's office, and he again had no desire to see this task force commander. And again, I had another hour with Tom Moorer down in the JCS office.

It was quite apparent that after two cruises as flag officer in the Gulf of Tonkin, I would be moved. Freddy Bardshar told me the reason I was still there was because I was unassignable, and he was probably right. They didn't know what the hell to do with me. So I dropped by to see Tex Guinn, who was Chief of Naval Personnel, and I said, "I can't stay there forever. I'd like to. I'm ready to go for number-four cruise if you'll let me go."

He said, "No, those jobs are hard to come by, and you've had it longer than anybody else to date. We've got to move you."

I said, "Well, what have you got to offer?"

And Tex responded, "What did you ever do to Bud Zumwalt?"

And I said, "I hardly know the guy."

And he said, "Well, he knows you, and he's told me that I can offer you three jobs: Commander Naval Forces Korea, Commander Naval Forces Japan, and Commander Naval Forces Marianas."

Q: A long way from home.

Admiral Ramage: All of them are boneyards. And I said, "Tex, a guy with my performance in three wars, in particular, the job I know I've done out in the Gulf of Tonkin, I think I deserve better than that."

And he says, "You know that doesn't mean a thing. You can be the best fleet commander we've ever had, and that doesn't mean anything nowadays. You're either on Bud's team or you're not. And take it from me, you're not."

I said, "Well, doesn't he want me closer than 10,000 miles from Washington?"

And he said, "That's about it."

So I didn't know quite what to do. I went back to Alameda, and I began to hear rumors about the chance of being Commander Naval Air Reserve Force, which I thought would be a pretty neat job as long as I couldn't get anything else. Apparently it was in the works. Howard Greer, who was then the Naval Air Reserve admiral, was going to get a carrier division, and he told me about the job.[*] He said, "I think you'll like it. The force has improved immensely due to this reorganization." He said, "I want to warn you about a couple of things, though."

So he talked to me about an hour or two on the individuals involved. He said that it was very, very political, which I knew. He said, "However, there's an awful lot of horsepower that goes with the job in the way of political influence if you use it right." And then he told me about the reorganization that was going on, where both the surface reserve command, which was in Omaha, Nebraska, and the Naval Air Reserve Command at Glenview, Illinois, would both be moved to New Orleans and merged.

This could cause a problem because Naval Air Reserve at that time had begun to be a very effective force. He was afraid that if there were a true merger, it would certainly hurt naval aviation. Then he pointed out the big problem, which was the "gaining command principle," which was that the Naval Air Reserve Force would be divided between ComNavAirLant and ComNavAirPac, and the Naval Air Reserve Force as a command would cease to exist. The Naval Reserve Aviation Command would become just like the surface command which commands nothing, with no forces, no control. In other words, we'd have a bunch of school houses around, and maybe I could get to run some reserve air stations. At that time he said, "This has been discussed." And I'd presumed, of course, that he'd been in Washington and made his views known. He didn't tell me that he didn't oppose it openly. That was left to me.

So I went back to Washington and talked to Tex Guinn, who said, "Okay, you can have this job if you want it. These two commands are moving down to New Orleans, but there's no way that you'll ever keep the job because it is going to go up to three stars, and Zumwalt will not give you a third star under any circumstance."

I'd always liked the reserves and certainly used plenty of them in the three wars, so I looked forward to the job. As I departed, I told Tex, "This is probably the last time you and I will be friendly, because if I take over that command, I'm going to fight for the Naval Air

---

[*] Rear Admiral Howard E. Greer, USN, served as Chief of Naval Air Reserve Training from December 1969 to April 1972.

Reserves, and there are many, many times when you and I will be on the opposite sides of the fence."

He said, "I understand that completely, and I think that you will be a good Commander Naval Air Reserve Force."

In leaving Commander Carrier Division Seven, I felt that it would be better to have the change of command down at Lemoore, where the squadrons that I had been with for so long were based, rather than up in Alameda.[*] As I recall, all three of my carriers in my division, which were the Enterprise, Ranger and Oriskany, were in port there at that time. I felt that I owed it to the pilots to say goodbye to them at their home base, because they'd done such a good job. I was relieved by Rear Admiral Jack Christiansen, who is another one of the real doers.[†] I was very, very pleased that he would be the man relieving me, because I knew that he didn't hesitate to do what he thought was right.[‡]

Q: Should we insert for the record that that's Rear Admiral Jack "Big Coolie" Christiansen?

Admiral Ramage: If you desire. So I got together my farewell speech, which was rather scathing, and I'll read parts of it: "I guess someone could write a book entitled How to Fight a War Without Really Winning during the 1966-68 period. We were often assigned targets in highly defended areas whose value in the opinion of many was not worth the risk. I can assure you that the higher echelons in the Navy up through the fleet commander in chief, the Commander in Chief Pacific, and Chief of Naval Operations were constantly trying to obtain better targets, but this is not to be. The risk-target value relationship is one that was always uppermost in my mind. It is a problem, however, beyond military controls. We often found ourselves in the position of driving a tack with a sledgehammer."

And it goes on. "Our political leaders even set up sanctuaries in North Vietnam where great quantities of war materials were safe from attack. We advised the enemy of

---

[*] The Lemoore Naval Air Station, site of a master jet base, is in the San Joaquin Valley, ten miles west of Lemoore, California, and about 45 miles southwest of Fresno. Alameda was one of two principal carrier homeports on the West Coast at the time, the other being at North Island Naval Air Station, Coronado, California.
[†] Rear Admiral John S. Christiansen, USN.
[‡] The ceremony took place on 30 April 1972.

things that we would not do, in my opinion the worst thing possible. And for the time being, I'd like to express my highest admiration for those of you here today who represent the thousands of air crewmen, including, those who made the great sacrifice and those who are still held by the enemy." There were a lot of families of POWs there. "We've asked for a lot, you have answered with superb skill and aggressiveness always. You are the greatest."

Apparently the people in the press in that general area didn't quite agree with me, and I'll read from the Fresno Bee of 1 March, which says, "A revived search for scapegoats. The echoes of old illusions were reverberating louder than sonic booms at a recent change of command ceremony at the Lemoore Naval Air Station. Rear Admiral James Ramage, who was yielding command of Carrier Division 7 to Rear Admiral John Christiansen said, 'We could have accomplished victory in Vietnam long ago except for the political decisions that prevented us from going to the proper targets.' Ramage apparently is one of those military men who finds it intolerable that the Navy did not bring North Vietnam to its knees by any means necessary, as the saying goes.

"This assumes proper targeting would have done the trick. If it had not, well, perhaps proper weapons would have. Down the road lay nuclear catastrophe. What the admiral said to the assembled officers and enlisted men is more than moot speculation, however, that political decisions, he decried, were made, of course, by politicians, in his words are an invitation to scapegoating. We will be hearing more of this all of the time in words almost identical to those which followed the Korean War stalemate. It will be a time of trial for the United States. The admiral, with his martial dreams of what might have been, is doing his bit to fan the flames." I consider that editorial to be one of the greatest accolades that I ever received.

That evening I was listening on the TV to see what would be said, because the affair was well-covered, particularly for something so far out in the country. We had a big fly-by and all these things that people don't do anymore. And when it came time to my speech, the TV announcer said that the admiral's speech was so inflammatory that it was not considered proper to air it.

Q: They knew who you were by then.

Admiral Ramage: Not only that, but apparently the people out on the staff of CinCPacFlt were interested, because they called Joe Tully, who was Commander Fleet Air in Lemoore, and asked him what the local reaction to Ramage's change of command speech was.[*] Tully answered that there was no local adverse reaction, and Tully sent these two comments to me.

After that I went to Glenview, Illinois, where I assumed command; I didn't relieve anyone. One of the first things I found was a real 4.0 officer as the TAR man there.[†] That was Captain Dick Altmann, who later became an admiral.[‡] He's the only TAR I know that ever had any guts.

The first item that I was going to have to face was the merger and move to New Orleans. Behind it was the idea that Congressman Hebert, the big New Orleans guy, wanted some more naval representation down there.[§]

Q: This is in the era when we were going to get everything out of Washington.

Admiral Ramage: Basically it had to do with Eddie Hebert's demand for more Navy presence in New Orleans, and it had a great impact because Eddie Hebert was the chairman of the House Armed Services Committee.

After about three weeks there, I went to Washington for a meeting of the reserve flag officers. It was to be a briefing by a classmate of mine named Vice Admiral Means Johnston, who was the inspector general.[**] He was one of Zumwalt's sycophants, and as such was doing his bidding. I had never really seen the reorganization plan. Greer had told me about it, but I hadn't seen the plan, and I had never been asked whether or not I

---

[*] Captain Joseph M. Tully, Jr., USN.
[†] TAR--training and administration of reservists. Those individuals designated as TARs are reservists on active duty. Most of their duty involves the reserve program rather than the active-duty Navy.
[‡] Captain Richard G. Altmann, USNR.
[§] Representative F. Edward Hebert (Democrat-Louisiana).
[**] Vice Admiral Means Johnston, Jr., USN, Naval Inspector General.

concurred. Whether Greer had seen it or not, I don't know, but it apparently was a total surprise when I opposed it.

Previously, I had contacted Tom Walker, ComNavAirPac, on the "gaining command" idea.[*] He answered with a strong letter in opposition. I also knew from conversation with Mike Michaelis, who was ComNavAirLant, that he opposed it.[†] So when Means Johnston got up and briefed the plan, I didn't oppose the move to New Orleans. I strongly opposed the losing of the reserve squadrons to ComNavAirLant and ComNavAirPac. This gaining command was a real big thing so far as the reserves were concerned. They wanted to have a reserve command, and they wanted the Naval Air Reserve Force to be commanded by reserves, reserve squadron commanders, and so forth down the line.

Q: What would the force structure have involved? How many squadrons or wings?

Admiral Ramage: Well, we had the four carrier air wings and I think 12 VP squadrons, and we had the 30 C-118s, then we had a lot of cats and dogs.[‡] It was a big force, as a matter of fact, as an RAF officer reminded me at the time, "Your Naval Air Reserve Force is larger than the RAF."[§] And it's much larger now. It was getting good, it had been reorganized, and they were all Vietnam veterans. It was a fine force.

At this briefing, which Means Johnston gave, I'll have to admit I sandbagged him. I was completely ready for him.

When the presentation was completed, the Secretary of the Navy, John Warner, asked, "Are there any comments?"[**]

I stood up, and I said, "Yes, Mr. Secretary. I have strong objections." And I pointed out that moving any naval activities, particularly flags, out of the Midwest, I

---

[*] Vice Admiral Thomas J. Walker III, USN, served as Commander Naval Air Force Pacific Fleet from 28 May 1971 to 31 May 1973.
[†] Vice Admiral Frederick H. Michaelis, USN, served as Commander Naval Air Force Atlantic Fleet from 29 February 1972 to 14 February 1975. Admiral Michaelis's oral history is in the Naval Institute collection.
[‡] C-118 was a four-engine propeller-driven Navy and Air Force transport built by Douglas as the military counterpart to the DC-6 civilian passenger plane. The Navy designation prior to 1962 was R6D Liftmaster.
[§] RAF--Royal Air Force.
[**] John W. Warner served as Secretary of the Navy from 4 May 1972 to 9 April 1974.

thought was a great error because that's where 35% of our sailors come from. The Midwest is very pro-Navy. But that wasn't my great heartburn. My heartburn really was this gaining command principle where the Chief of Naval Air Reserve Force would lose command of his forces. I mentioned that both ComNavAirLant and ComNavAirPac agreed with me. Warner immediately turned to Means Johnston, who was flabbergasted, and said, "Has Ramage been asked for comments on this?"

And Johnston said, "No."

And he said, "What about these comments about ComNavAirLant and ComNavAirPac?"

I read the letter from Tom Walker, in which said he was very satisfied with the improvements that had occurred in the force since the recent reorganization, and I mentioned that I knew that Michaelis agreed and would come up and so state if the Secretary wanted him to.

Well, Johnston was really in a bad way; he simply hadn't done his staff work. I guess he was surprised that I would get up and oppose this thing, because Zumwalt had approved it. Several of the reserve flag officers got up and made comments. They were all on my side, of course; some of them were way off base, but it didn't make much difference. There was a lot more heat than light. The one that really did have telling effect, however, was a reserve rear admiral, who was a vice president of Chase Manhattan Bank, States Mead.* When he got up, you could see that Warner paid particular attention to him.

So the Secretary said, "Well, this throws a different light on the whole thing. I would like to talk to Admiral Michaelis in the morning if you can get him up here."

The following morning, Mike Michaelis did come up from Norfolk and supported my position completely. This then became a real problem. The Secretary took me into this office, and he said, "You've won your point. You are not going to oppose the move down to New Orleans?"

And I said, "No, sir. I know that Chairman Hebert wants more Navy presence down there, and although I think it's a great error, that certainly isn't anything I'm going to oppose. If I win my point about the gaining command, I'll support the move."

---

* Rear Admiral States M. Mead, USNR.

He said, "Well, you've won that point."

And then I said, "Mr. Secretary, you're going to have to be very careful of another item. This study that we're to follow points out that it's only going to cost about $2.8 million to move these two commands and rehab that old government building where Chairman Hebert wants us to move into. My engineer says that we're off by many millions of dollars. He says that it's going to cost at least $50 million. So don't try to sell this to anybody with the idea that it's going to save money. It's going to be expensive."

Johnston's study had stated that it was going to save a lot of money. It wasn't going to save a damn cent. The old building we were moving into down there was a World War I concrete structure, an enormous old thing known as the Green Monster. At that time it was painted green. I don't think you could knock it down with an A-bomb. It's just an enormous old structure and built to stand. And it did ultimately take about $60 million or $70 million to make this move.

The Secretary thanked me very much. He said, "I want to commend you for making your views known. I don't know exactly how I'm going to make this up to the CNO, but it's going to work out just about the way that you want."

So as far as I was concerned, the major battle had been won, and I went back to try to see if I couldn't do something constructive as far as the Naval Air Reserve Force was concerned. I found the force in good shape. It had been reorganized about one or two years previously, and they'd done away with a lot of deadwood.

One of the interesting things that I ran into right away was that we were going to upgrade into DC-9s.[*] It became apparent to me that if the Navy bought any DC-9s, that the place for them would be the reserve squadrons, certainly not in the regular Navy. So I had a study made concerning the number of qualified DC-9 pilots and Boeing 737 pilots that were available in the reserves. There were over 1,000. In other words, there would be no transition required. I made the recommendation, and I'll admit that it probably was a little brutal, because I pointed out that there really was no future in the regular Navy for a transport pilot, whereas in the Naval Reserve it could be a career, plus the fact that many of these people were flying this type of plane for a living.

---

[*] DC-9 is a commercial airliner built by McDonnell Douglas.

I wrote a letter to Mickey Weisner, who was DCNO (Air), after I got this study done.* It said, "By the time this reaches you, I will have completed the survey to identify and locate the qualified airline certified pilots who could be useful in the introduction of the C-9 to the Navy inventory. The attractiveness of turning all CONUS operations to Naval Air Reserve Force is apparent. Attached is a paper by one of our selected air reservists which touches on many aspects of this subject. You may want to give it to your planners for study."† I also pointed out that this would be a great savings in cost and time.

I got a response fairly soon from Mickey, who said, "I have had my staff review your proposal of assigning CONUS VR operations to the Naval Air Reserve. It appears that only minimal saving could be realized from implementing this concept and the capability of the reserves to maintain the required tempo of operations is uncertain. However, I have instructed my staff to investigate the possibility of utilizing reserve flight crews in the active VR squadrons in an associate concept. In this manner we will be able to benefit from the airline expertise embodied within the reserve personnel and be able to better evaluate the capability of the Naval Air Reserve to assume a larger proportion of the CONUS VR mission."‡ And he enclosed the staff paper which, of course, completely ignored fact. At that time we were only talking about nine DC-9s. If we couldn't keep them operating with 1,000 transport pilots from our civil population, we were in deep trouble. Well, of course, the transfer has taken place, and all the VR CONUS is now handled by reserves.

Q: Wasn't that also one of the things that saved the VR for the Navy? The Air Force would have taken it over.

Admiral Ramage: Well, this was my point, that for the regular Navy, it was a problem. But the VR in the Naval Air Reserve would not only support the reserve operation but they were ready for support of the fleet, and, of course, that transpired.

---

* Vice Admiral Maurice F. Weisner, USN, served as Deputy Chief of Naval Operations (Air Warfare) from 1 September 1971 to 4 August 1972.
† CONUS--continental United States. The C-9 Skytrain II is the Navy version of the commercial DC-9.
‡ VR is the designation for the Navy transport function.

The Naval Air Reserve had a very, very active PR program, and I gave probably two television performances a month all around the country, and I used it first to sell the Naval Air Reserve program, but second, since I was just a recent returnee from Vietnam, I would strike the gong wherever possible about what was wrong about the war in Vietnam. I began to hit some very severe snags in Washington, and I had quite a run-in with our Chief of Information, who was a guy named Thompson.* Perhaps I was overstepping my bounds, but I was still so damn unhappy about that war out there, that I just couldn't be quiet. My speeches were pretty well canned, but there was a question period afterwards, and it was during the question period that I could really let go.

---

* Rear Admiral William Thompson, USN, served as the Navy's Chief of Information from July 1971 to February 1975.

Interview Number 3 with Rear Admiral James D. Ramage, U.S. Navy (Retired)

Place: Admiral Ramage's home, Bonita, California

Date: Sunday, 31 March 1985

Interviewers: Robert L. Lawson and Barrett Tillman

Admiral Ramage: Sometime during the summer of 1972, after I'd taken over as Chief of Naval Air Reserve, I got a call from Mickey Weisner in Washington asking me to attend a testimonial dinner for Walter Cronkite.* It was to be given by an American Legion post in New York at the Lotus Club. This wasn't your normal American Legion post; it was made up of very important people. It wasn't one which people just joined; it was a very special post. Cronkite had been very helpful in the space program, by doing the various broadcasts, and he was to be the honored guest. Mickey said that Admiral Tom Moorer had asked him to ask me to fill in for Tom at this particular affair, because he felt that perhaps in talking to Cronkite I might be able to get some points across that he hadn't been able to get across in the past. Mickey further said, "You will be sitting right next to Walter at the head table on this dinner."

    Everything transpired as planned, except that they did somehow insert an Air Force colonel in between me and Cronkite, but I did have a chance to talk to him during the dinner. The testimonial was very fine, and he was presented an award for helping the space program, and everyone was very happy. However, I told Mr. Cronkite that I thought he'd done a great disservice to the armed forces of the United States in some of the work he'd done on television. That got his attention right away. He said, "I'd like to talk to you about it afterwards down in the bar."

    We retired to the bar after the dinner was over and had a couple of brandies. I told him that I thought that the press corps and that he, in particular, had been very, very hard on the military, whereas lots of the problems that had been going on with the war were

---

* Walter Cronkite has had a long career in broadcast journalism, highlighted by his tenure from 1962 to 1981 as the managing editor of the CBS evening news.

politically generated. I told him I thought that he was doing a great disservice to a whole group of people that were doing a very, very fine job for their country.

He received these comments very seriously, and he said, "Maybe you're right. I won't be your flack," which apparently is a term which the newspaper people use and the media use, which I presume means, "I won't be your stooge."

Q: Public relations.

Admiral Ramage: He said, "But I will look very carefully at things that I say in the future along that line." I can't say that there was any change. I don't know. But at least when I called Mickey to report back he could tell Tom Moorer that the message was delivered and certainly received.

That fall, that's the fall of 1972, I was able to get Captain Dick Hanecak to be my chief of staff in Glenview.[*] Dick had been a fine pilot, had his deep-draft command, and had been given command of the naval air station at Cubi Point for his major command and hadn't been selected for flag rank.[†] I thought that he was certainly flag rank material compared to many that were selected, but he didn't make it. So knowing that he was an excellent guy, I sure wanted to have somebody there, because I knew that my job as Chief of Naval Air Reserve was basically one of public relations and I'd be gone all the time. Dick filled in very well in that position.

Chicago is a very strong Navy town, and the job of Chief of Naval Air Reserve there was a fine position if you like the social life, if you like golf, and so forth. I didn't play golf, but I think I had honorary memberships to five of the finest golf clubs on the North Shore.[‡] During the latter part of my tour, I also became commander of the Ninth Naval District, so I was double-hatted part of the time.[§]

---

[*] Captain Richard G. Hanecak, USN.
[†] Cubi Point is at Subic Bay in the Philippine Islands.
[‡] North Shore refers to the ritzy bedroom communities on the shore of Lake Michigan, north from Chicago.
[§] The headquarters for the Ninth Naval District, which has since been disestablished, was at Great Lakes, Illinois, part of the North Shore area.

Chicago was a fine area. A particularly strong family there was the Gallery family. You probably remember Dan Gallery, the author, who was a flag officer, and also his brother, Bill Gallery, who had a fine combat record, was also a flag officer.[*] There were three other Gallerys in Chicago, all of whom had served in the Navy, too, so they were a very dedicated family. Also Vice Admiral Dick Whitehead, retired, was there.[†] We used to do quite a bit of talking about the Navy, and these people would let me know in no uncertain terms that they were extremely unhappy with the way that the Navy was going under Admiral Zumwalt. I guess they presumed that I could do something about it. There wasn't much I could do about it, but we used to talk about it a lot.

Bill Gallery brought me a letter from his brother, Dan, and I'll make some quotes from it.[‡] He was talking about the riots, mutinies, whatever you want to call it, on two Pacific Fleet carriers, the Kitty Hawk and Constellation.[§] I think his feelings will be of interest to people in the future.

He said: "I just returned from a trip to the coast where I got aboard the Constellation and Kitty Hawk and I talked to the skippers and some of their people. It's a grim tale. On the KH they had what was a race riot--a one way riot of black and white. Bands of blacks ran amok on the lower decks after taps beating up whites at random and going into the bunk rooms and beating up people who were in their bunks."

Then he went on with some of the words that were used in the attacks, which I won't repeat. "There were 60 of them in the mob, all black, all first enlistment, and all of class 4 intelligence.

"They were incited to riot by about 8 or 10 black power types, they split into eight or ten groups and waged guerrilla warfare for three or four hours.

"The Skipper was in a hell of a spot. He says he figured he never lost control of his ship. He could always have gone to General Quarters and told the Marines to restore order.

---

[*] Rear Admiral Daniel V. Gallery, Jr., USN (Ret.); Rear Admiral William O. Gallery, USN. Both were naval aviators.
[†] Vice Admiral Richard F. Whitehead, USN (Ret.).
[‡] The letter was dated 20 December 1972.
[§] Racial disturbances broke out in the carrier Kitty Hawk (CVA-63) on 12 October 1972; in the oiler Hassayampa (AO-145) on 16 October 1972; and in the carrier Constellation (CVA-64) on 3 November 1972. See Captain Paul B. Ryan, USN (Ret.), "USS Constellation Flare-up: Was it Mutiny?" U.S. Naval Institute Proceedings, January 1976, pages 46-53.

He said he didn't want to do this until he felt control of the ship was in danger because he would have 4,000 whites--plus 300 non-mutinous blacks--confronting a mob. It would have been hard to distinguish the good blacks from the bad, the Marines would have had to use force, and some of the people might have been killed.

"He wanted to avoid this at all costs, so he and the exec went about the lower decks trying to restore order. The exec, incidentally, is half-black and half-Indian and a damned good man." You probably remember him as Ben Cloud up here, our neighbor, and he is a damned fine individual.* "After three to four hours, the riot petered out. It was after taps and most of the men were in their bunks. Forty white boys wound up in the sick bay with cuts, bruises, and fractured skulls. None of the rioters were injured. At least the skipper came through this ordeal without spilling any blood chargeable to the U.S. Government.

"But as evidence of how critical the situation was, the exec at one time heard a rumor that the skipper had been killed and he believed it! He then took command and issued some orders on the loud speaker--which the captain promptly countermanded. This has been widely publicized as a conflict of authority--but it wasn't. The exec supported the skipper loyally.

"The same sort of thing was brewing on the Constellation. The skipper, knowing about the KH riots, dumped all his mutineers ashore. They were the same sort of low intelligent blacks, first enlistment.

"Racial conditions on the ship had nothing to do with it. They had no legitimate complaints. Everyone had equal opportunity, but they weren't interested in that. They demand special consideration because they are black. They expected to get rated whether or not competent to do the job. When they don't get rated, it is a racial discrimination, and the black power types work them up into a frenzy of white hatred. This is only about 25% of the blacks on board. The other 75% are good, loyal sailors.

"A large part of this is chargeable to Zumwalt and his Z-grams. They have generated an air of permissiveness, led to the deterioration of smartness, and the denigration of the CO's authority. People now feel that if they don't like the way the skipper runs his ship, they can by-pass him, go over his head and find a sympathetic ear in Washington.

---

* Commander Benjamin W. Cloud, USN.

"I had an interview with Zumwalt yesterday and told him this. He listened respectfully, but I don't think it did a damn bit of good.

"I also had a session with Tom Moorer and told him the same thing. I think Tom sees eye to eye with me on this."

He concludes by saying, "I think Zumwalt has got to go--and the sooner the better." And that's from Dan Gallery, who really is a patriot in my book and always has been.

This was only one of the types of comments that I was getting from this group of people in Chicago. It was about this time that I was to go down to New Orleans and pay my first call on Chairman Hebert, because the command was going to move down there in six or eight months. When I got down there, I was ushered into his very pleasant quarters in the Federal Building. He had a group of hangers-on there, I would say nine or ten people, and I, of course, had two or three people with me.

The chairman or "the admiral," as he liked to be called, because he did love the Navy, liked to hold court, and he would make his comments and look around the room to see how people took them. I found him very pleasant. Partway through our conversation, he started talking about the Kitty Hawk and Constellation problems. He said that he had appointed a committee under Congressman Hicks to investigate the mutiny or whatever you want to call it, and that he expected a report on that fairly soon.[*] Then he looked at me and said, "I think that these Z-grams have been very harmful to the Navy." I'm not used to discussing my superiors in the Navy with civilians, even if they're congressmen. So I didn't respond. He kept on the subject, and finally he looked at me again and he said, "Admiral, I think that Admiral Zumwalt is doing the Navy a lot of harm."

I couldn't hold my tongue, and I said, "Mr. Chairman, that man is a catastrophe."

After the call and the luncheon, I returned back to Glenview, and by the time that I had gotten back up there, what I had said in New Orleans was already in Washington. It was quite apparent that Zumwalt was running a gestapo on the chairman, because he was scared stiff of Eddie Hebert. I got a call from Mickey Weisner again, warning me.[†] He

---

[*] Representative Floyd V. Hicks (Democrat-Washington), a member of the House Armed Services Committee.

[†] Weisner, who by this time was a four-star admiral, served as Vice Chief of Naval Operations from 1 September 1972 to 1 September 1973.

said, "I'd just like you to know that you were heard loud and clear down in New Orleans today." I couldn't figure out how it had gotten up there so fast.

I later talked to Hebert and told him what had happened, and he said, "Well, it wasn't one of my men." I later found out that it was one of his men who definitely reported to Admiral Zumwalt pretty much what the congressman was doing. That was, I guess, an indication of the method that Zumwalt used.

In addition, of course, he had completely bypassed the regular organization of the Navy and set up a staff within a staff, which he had up on the fifth deck in the E-ring. I ran into this when I asked the DCNO (Air), Bill Houser, about command structure and Zumwalt's methods.* I said, "What does the CNO think about this?"

And he said, "I don't know, I never see him. I haven't seen him for six weeks." He said, "All the decisions are made up in the fifth deck in this group of Zumwalt's cronies." That group consisted of the two Bagley brothers, Emmett Tidd, who had been with him down in Vietnam, and Stansfield Turner.† There may have been some other people who were involved up in the super cabinet, but that, according to Houser, was the makeup of the people who were running the Navy. This was bad, of course.

About the same time, I received a request for an input to a staff study that was being done by the Chief of Naval Personnel, who by this time was Dave Bagley.‡ He had replaced Tex Guinn. It was about the new fitness reports, which were to be goal oriented rather than performance oriented, which didn't make much sense to me. I always thought that fitness reports were a report on your performance of duty, but this was to be something else. It had very heavy racial inputs in it, very strong. I thought that these people in BuPers were interested in my views, so I responded thusly:

"It seems to me that you're trying to put leadership and effectiveness into a mold. As you know, there is no way of achieving these goals. I cannot help but think back over

---

* Vice Admiral William D. Houser, USN, served as Deputy Chief of Naval Operations (Air Warfare) from 5 August 1972 to 30 April 1976.
† Vice Admiral David H. Bagley, USN, Chief of Naval Personnel; Vice Admiral Worth H. Bagley, USN, Director of Navy Program Planning; Rear Admiral Emmett H. Tidd, USN, Commander Navy Recruiting Command; Rear Admiral Stansfield Turner, USN, Director Systems Analysis Division, OpNav.
‡ Vice Admiral David H. Bagley, USN, served as Chief of Naval Personnel from 1 February 1972 to 10 April 1975.

some of our great leaders in the past and can only comment that they would be woefully lacking in some of the elements which you are trying to appraise. First in my mind is Fleet Admiral Ernest J. King. History will show that he was probably the most difficult to work for during his entire career. He definitely defined his goals, but his methods of achieving those goals would get low marks in some of the other areas. Likewise, Admiral Raymond Spruance, who was probably the greatest strategic planner, had very little contact with those whom he commanded. He was extremely shy and very reticent to express his views in public. Admiral William F. Halsey was undoubtedly one of our greatest combat leaders, but he would flunk the course because of his personal behavior. So what am I getting at? My point is that we have to look at the complete man."

Then I went on to point out that performance must be the way you select your flag officers of the future. I ended up by saying, "I'm afraid that you've taken on an impossible task. I'm afraid that the new fitness reports tend towards increasing mediocrity. We have enough of that today."

I think they probably but that right into the circular file and said, "There's another one of these old bastards."

Q: Another Jig Dog crank letter.

Admiral Ramage: Well, about that time also, as I said, I was on the speech circuit, and because of my close contacts with the various people around the country, I was getting all of these inputs on the situation in the Navy, true concern by these people who had been in the Navy, particularly during World War II. I was down to a Navy League convention down in Scotsdale, Arizona, and I saw Stansfield Turner down there, who had some kind of a sinecure, I don't know what. He was carrying Zumwalt's briefcase from place to place, but he was part of the reigning group. So I thought I'd pull his chain a little bit, and I said, "Stan, I understand that Bud is kind of standing into trouble with various people around Washington."

And Turner said, "Not with anybody that really amounts to very much." He said, "George Anderson and Arleigh Burke and some of those old fogies are giving him a bad time, but he's going to come through; don't worry about it."

Q: If only we had more old fogies like Arleigh Burke.

Admiral Ramage: One item of interest, as I look through my letters here, has to do with the Blue Angels. They were operating F-4s at this time, which, in my opinion, was certainly not the way to go. There was a question of whether or not the Blue Angels were really worth the effort, and this, of course, comes up often. The point is that they are very expensive, and the question is whether they really do enough in the recruiting field, which is supposed to be their aim. I think we'd lost some F-4s at this time, and the question came up of whether or not we're heading in the right direction with them.

My recommendation was, "I am certain that the rising costs of operating the Blue Angels compares in every way with the manning and operating of a full combat F-4 fleet squadron. Whether we must keep up with the Joneses is the question. Perhaps the Air Force is asking the same questions. We might see if we could reduce our expenses by forming a joint demonstration unit [which I'm sure would go over like a lead balloon]. And in the event that this is not worth it, I recommend that you go into A-4s, which are a much cheaper plane to operate." I pointed out that reservists had an A-4 demonstration team that really cost us not a damn thing and seemed to get a lot of publicity at really no cost to speak of. As you know, that's what did happen. We retained the Blue Angels and we did go into A-4s. It's going to be interested to see what happens here when the A-4s go out. Some people are going to try to put them in F-18s.

Q: They're already talking about it.

Admiral Ramage: And they shouldn't go into that. What's that new trainer?

Q: T-45 Hawk.

Admiral Ramage: I hate to admit it, but it probably does. Oh, my God. You know, those F-18s cost $30 million a copy. It's just too expensive. I do think that the Blue Angels are worthwhile. However, I occasionally wonder whether people go to see the airmanship demonstrated, or whether they look to see if somebody's going to get killed and they want to be there. But that's just a feeling on my part.

I was very happy with what was happening within the Naval Air Reserve Force. They had won the CNO Safety Trophy for the first time ever. Bill Houser, who was OP-05, asked me where I wanted the trophy delivered, and I said, "Don't deliver it. Just put it outside your office there in the E-ring in the Pentagon," which he did. My purpose, of course, was to get across to the various people that the Naval Air Reserve had arrived and that they were a very effective force.

After about six weeks, Bill called me and said, "Okay, you've won your point. Where do you want it sent now?"

I said, "Well, we certainly don't want it in Glenview, Illinois. No one's going to see it there. How about putting it down in the Naval Air Facility waiting room there at Andrews Air Force Base?" So for the remainder of that year, that's where the CNO Safety Award was, demonstrating the fact that it was won by the Naval Air Reserve Force.

Another gimmick that I did was to enter the reserve attack squadrons into Joe Tully's bombing derby up in Lemoore. Of course, we had A-7s, but we had A's and B's and were going into E's. But I knew that my people in the squadrons were absolutely tops because they had no nuggets. They'd all had probably two or more combat tours in Vietnam, and they were real pros. Tully really wasn't very smart about it, because he didn't realize who made up the Naval Air Reserve Force. So I stuck these guys in the tournament and, of course, they won the individual best team, best everything. They carried off an awful lot of the silver at the tournament. After it was over, Joe let me know he knew that I'd sandbagged him. But that again was a way to build up the morale of the Naval Air Reserve Force, and they were really coming. They were getting on the carriers without incident; they were doing just a neat job.

Q: Were they entered in the derby as units or as one team representing the air reserves?

Admiral Ramage: They were representing the two West Coast squadrons we had, and they wiped everything. It was a fine show.

Just about after Christmas at that time, I got a call from Mr. Don Huemanns, from New Orleans, who was a personal friend of Chairman Hebert's. He mentioned that the chairman was getting very unhappy, that he knew that the move down to New Orleans had been directed but he didn't see anything going on in the Green Monster, the building that was to be improved, and he'd like to see at least some move down there right away.

So I called up Mickey Weisner, who at that time was the Vice Chief, and told him that I'd received this call, and I thought that we'd better respond to the chairman's desires. He said, "Okay. I don't know exactly what to do, because we haven't named the new Chief of Naval Reserve, so we'll have to send you down for temporary duty."

I said, "Well, there's no problem there."

So I went on down on the first of February to the ceremony, which set up the Chief of Naval Reserve down in New Orleans, with me as the acting chief. It was rather a strange situation because the Chief of Naval Reserve, and that applies only to the surface side, was also the Chief of Naval Personnel. So I was in a sense relieving Dave Bagley of his job of Chief of Naval Reserve and at the same time taking over the new command. So Dave came down to the ceremony. Chairman Hebert and I were sitting in the admiral's office in Com 8 when Bagley walked in.[*] Chairman Hebert said in a very loud voice, "Here comes that liar."

I looked at him, and I saw he was looking at Bagley, and he said, "There's that liar over there."

About that time Bagley turned around and walked out the door. I looked at the chairman and the chairman looked at me, and he said, "He's a goddamn liar." That was the end of conversation.

Then Hebert started addressing me as Vice Admiral Ramage during the ceremony, which I'm sure really endeared me to Bagley, who didn't like me to begin with. So I

---

[*] Com 8--Commandant of the Eighth Naval District.

relieved under pomp and circumstance, and we proceeded to put the staff together to ultimately make the move down south.

About that same time Secretary Warner came out to Milwaukee. He liked me, I'm very sure. He particularly liked the fact that I had a lot of medals on my chest, and he could carry me around. If he ran into a problem, he could turn to me and say, "Admiral, will you handle that?" But he wasn't about to try to propose me as the Chief of Naval Reserve and promote me to three stars over Zumwalt's objections. So while we were up there in Milwaukee, the Secretary said, "Jig, as you know, we're forming up that command down there, and it's coming along fine, thanks to the job that you're doing. We've got to find a commander." And he said, "What aviator do you know who already has three stars that you would recommend to have that assignment?"

I said, "Mr. Secretary, you don't have to hit me over the head with a club. I understand completely that I am not in the running to be Chief of Naval Reserve, and I understand exactly why, so you don't have to beat around the bush." I said, "The only person that I know that could really put that thing together is Mike Michaelis, who is ComNavAirLant, and I happen to know that he just wouldn't like that job at all because he's got a much better job. Other than that, I don't know any other three-star people that are particularly competent."

It turned out that the following week Zumwalt nominated my friend Hutch Cooper. Hutch was out in Vietnam; he'd completed his tour as CTF 77. They had raised the rank to three stars, so he already had them, and I know that he presented an assignment problem to Zumwalt, because he just didn't fit into the Zumwalt program. What better place to put him than down in New Orleans? The fact that getting along with people and glad-handing people, which the reserve job is, wasn't a strong point in Cooper, was beside the point. It was a way to move Cooper and possibly get him deep-sixed, and at the same time get rid of me into some spot that I would not any longer be a thorn in his side. So I proceeded to organize the staff and wrote to Hutch and told him by the time he got there, which would be about two more months, that he would find things in very good shape.

Well, we're getting down to the end of my career in the Naval Reserve. Hutch reported in, and on his first trip up to Washington, when he was making the rounds, Dave

Bagley, Chief of Naval Personnel, told him that he, Bagley, wanted to see me. So Hutch faithfully called when he got back to New Orleans--I was up in Glenview--and told me that the Chief of Naval Personnel wanted to see me. So I had my aide call his aide to see if this was an immediate thing or whether it could wait, because I got into Washington every two or three weeks. The response was, "Well, next time you're in Washington." So I didn't think too much about it.

About a week later, Hutch called me again. He said, "Did you ever see Bagley?"

And I said, "No, there didn't seem to be any urgency about it."

He said, "You'd better go in there."

So on 7 April 1973 I had a command performance before Dave Bagley, the Chief of Naval Personnel. When I went in, we sparred around a little bit and asked various nonessential questions of each other. He finally said, "When are you going to start supporting the Chief of Naval Operations?"

And I said, "Well, you must have some specifics."

He said, "Yes, I do." He said, "We have found out that you don't support his racial program."

I said, "Well, you know I am for equal opportunity, but this idea of affirmative action I think is wrong, and I don't think that the Navy should be so deeply involved in it as it is. I'd like to talk to Zumwalt about it if he'd ever let me talk to him, but I can never get to see him." I said, "Also, you know, we don't have very many blacks in the Naval Air Reserve Force, so really what program that there is really doesn't apply to us. For some reason or other, blacks just don't go in to the reserves. It's not their bag." I said, "Where do you get this information?"

And he said, "We have ways of finding out." So then he said, "We also hear that you don't show the CNO's sitreps within the Naval Air Reserve command."* These sitreps were about a quarterly movie that was put out, it was pure propaganda on what a great job Zumwalt was doing.

I replied to Dave, I said, "I haven't really paid much attention to them. I don't think they're very good, but I have never even stated within the command whether they should or

---

* Sitrep--situation report.

should not be shown. As far as I know, they're on automatic distribution. They're probably shown. Where do you get this information?"

He said, "Oh, we hear about it." So then he said, "You're overstating the case for the Naval Air Reserve to the detriment of the surface reserve."

I said, "I think that's very flattering. If I were in charge of the surface reserve, I'd be very happy to help them, too, but as it is, I am a major claimant. I have personally gone before the various committees both within the military and within the Congress, and I have lobbied very strongly for funds for new hangars for the Naval Air Reserve, and we're getting it." I said that, "I don't consider that to be something against me. I think that that's something that I should be congratulated for."

Then Bagley finally got around to what he wanted to talk about. These other three things were not important. This was. He said, "About two weeks ago you were in San Diego at a flag officers' conference."

I said, "Yes, I gave a talk on readiness of the Naval Air Reserve."

He said, "Well, that isn't what I'm talking about. That evening at a dinner given by the Navy League, you were overheard at your table when it was announced that Admiral Zumwalt would be unable to attend, but Admiral Clarey would speak in his place. You said, 'Now, ain't that too damn bad?'"

I said, "Dave, you mean you called me in to Washington to discuss this?"

And he said, "Yes, that's disloyalty."

And I said, "Well, as you know, I don't deny saying it. I don't recall it, but I very well could have, but I simply don't think that is a proper thing to call a flag officer in to Washington to talk about."

And he said, "Well, I just want to let you know, you're on notice." Notice for what, I didn't know.

The following month, or I guess it was probably in June of 1973, I found out what being put on notice was. I was in Washington, and walking down the E-ring where the newly-selected flag officers were being given a talk by the various senior officers on the future of the Navy, and new selectee Tom Russell came out and said, "Hey, Jig, I'm coming out to relieve you."[*]

And I said, "Have I been fired?"

And he said, "Haven't you heard?" He said, "Oh, God, I shouldn't have told you that, I guess."

And I said, "Well, I guess I'm about to find out later, but this is a heck of a way to find out."

So I went back down to Hutch Cooper's office, and I said, "Hutch, am I being transferred?" I was still commander of the Naval Air Reserve. I said, "Have I been fired?"

He said, "I haven't heard a thing about it."

I said, "Well, I want to go up to see Zumwalt. I want to ask him about this thing."

He said, "Steady now."

I said, "Well, I think the son-of-a-bitch ought to at least tell me."

So he said, "Steady now. I'll go up and see Mickey," who, of course, was the vice chief. "You sit here. Don't you come with me."

Q: Stay off the telephone.

Admiral Ramage: So after he'd been up to see Mickey, Hutch he came back and said, "Yep, that's right."

So I said, "Well, what's going to happen?"

He said, "I haven't the slightest idea. They didn't tell me that."

So I thought, "I'll make that son of a gun come to me and see what happens."

So I went back to Glenview, and the following Monday I got a call from Rear Admiral Beetle Forbes, who was the chief detail officer.[†] First he apologized, he said, "I understand that you heard last week that you were getting orders."

I said, "Yeah, Beetle, that's a hell of a way to find out."

---

[*] Rear Admiral Thomas B. Russell, Jr., USN, became Commander Naval Air Reserve; Commander Naval Air Reserve Force/Deputy Chief of Naval Reserve (Air).
[†] Rear Admiral Bernard B. Forbes, Jr., USN. The oral history of Forbes, who retired as a vice admiral, is in the Naval Institute collection.

He said, "Well, I apologize for that."

I said, "Where are you going to send me?"

He said, "Well, the boss wants to send you down to Puerto Rico to the Caribbean Sea Frontier."

And I said, "Beetle, I think if you'll look at my performance in three wars and general performance throughout a long Navy career, you'll have to admit that I don't deserve that."

And he said, "You know that I'm not doing this to you."

And I said, "Well, I'll have to think it over."

And he said, "I have been told to explain to you very carefully what the alternative is if you don't desire to carry out these orders."

And I said, "I understand that, too, but I can't reorder my whole life right away. When do you want to know about this?"

And he said, "I want an answer right now."

And I said, "Beetle, I can't reorder my whole life right today. Let me at least talk to my wife. I've got some things to think about."

And Beetle then said, "Well, please call me or I will call you the first thing tomorrow morning, because I've got to go with the Chief of Naval Personnel up and see the boss, Zumwalt, to see if you're going to carry out your orders."

So I went home and talked to Ginger about it. I said, "Jiminy Christmas, I can't really make up my mind right now. I don't think that that's a very good job for me, but on the other hand, it's certainly pleasant. If it was Adak or Argentia, he'd get my retirement papers right away, but I think I'll tell them that I'll go on down there."*

Well, the next morning, Beetle called and I said, "You tell them that I'm going to carry out my orders."

---

* Adak, Alaska; Argentia, Newfoundland.

So I had to be detached immediately, because what had happened was that Rear Admiral Bub Ward, who was down there, wanted to retire on the 30th of June, and they wanted to get me down there as soon as possible.*

Apparently they had decided to send one of the newly selected flag officers down there, but then it was decided that they wanted somebody with a little more maturity down there because it is quite a political problem. And I guess they probably figured that I could take the heat just about as well as anybody else.

Ginger and I left Glenview about the middle of June of 1973. We had enjoyed our time with the reserves very much. I liked the people, I liked the attitude of the reserves. In many cases they're certainly much more dedicated to the Navy than the regular Navy people are. The Naval Air Reserve Force couldn't be better, compared to the regular forces. They were superior in almost every respect. But as I pointed out, they should be. They don't have any nuggets, they're all fully trained people, so they should be far more ready than people just coming out of training command.

I relieved Bub Ward down there on the 30th of June. It was quite a big affair. It was held at Isla Grande, which was the base in San Juan. There were elegant quarters, and they had a small airport that had been built before the war. The flag officer's quarters had been built for Admiral Spruance, who was Com 10 shortly before World War II, and they were very fine.† The plan was, and it was correct, to move the staff out to Roosevelt Roads, where the Atlantic Fleet gunnery range was and weapons range, where all the operating ships and squadrons came. I agreed with the move. I think some of my predecessors didn't want to leave the social environment in San Juan, which is pretty hectic. It's a pretty pleasant life, and the quarters, which were right next to the Caribe Hilton, were elegant.

So we set about getting ready to move the whole operation, and I wanted to expedite it just as soon as I could move into temporary facilities out at Roosevelt Roads. I

---

* Rear Admiral Norvell G. Ward, USN, served from May 1970 to July 1973 as Commandant Tenth Naval District; Commander Caribbean Sea Frontier; and Commander Antilles Defense Command. He retired on 1 August 1973. His oral history is in the Naval Institute collection.
† In his first billet as a flag officer, Rear Admiral Raymond A. Spruance, USN, served as Commandant of the Tenth Naval District from February 1940 to July 1941.

soon found out that I was in an entirely different Navy than I'd ever seen before--that is, the overseas shore Navy. In many cases, people were sent down there because they were unassignable, as I was, and not only that, once getting down there, they were permitted to extend for a prolonged period of time. This made the Bureau of Personnel very happy, because they were trying to save money on travel orders. So we had people down there that had been down there six, eight, and ten years and were deeply rooted into the structure of the Puerto Rican economy in many ways.

I soon found out that I had some problems on my staff. Not only were the officers generally not up to the competency that I was used to even in the reserves, but some of them were of questionable integrity. It turned out that one of the first things I ran into was a chief legalman who was working for our judge advocate on the staff, and he was forging household effects shipping orders and getting the checks and cashing them. This was for many thousands of dollars. I immediately got a general court busy on him. I thought that the general court didn't do its job very well, in that they took his chief's hat, but I thought that he should have gotten a lot more. So when things went on further, I made damn sure that I got a president of the court who was a little bit tougher, because I knew that there were going to be quite a few more courts-martial.

Q: What were some of the early indications you had that these activities were being conducted?

Admiral Ramage: Well, in moving out of Isla Grande, it was very hard to put your finger on a lot of the Navy-owned material. It seemed to be moving around in the various areas. I had discovered that one lieutenant commander, in leaving, had shipped with him 12 refrigerators. He was going to the 12th Naval District for discharge, and I got to Red Carmody, who was Com 12 at the time, and told him to put a hold on him because I wanted to bring him to trial.* Sure enough, he was guilty. There was no problem.

---

* Rear Admiral Martin D. Carmody, USN; as a captain, Carmody had been commanding officer of the Task Force 77 flagship when Ramage was on board in 1966 as chief of staff.

Q: So that would, what, involve a general discharge, or what?

Admiral Ramage: I wanted him in prison, but no, he got away. He probably wasn't eligible for retired pay, but he was getting out, and I guess they figured that that was the way to do it.

One of the other things that was going on was that there was a chief quartermaster on the staff who was the prime mover in establishing a new bar outside the base at Roosevelt Roads. It turned out that my writer was involved in this bar, and a lieutenant commander and lieutenant on my staff were also involved. This immediately got my attention, because it just didn't smell right.

Sure enough, I began to get reports about tax-free whiskey going out the gate and being used in the bar out there. Also, I got a report that there was Navy furniture showing up at the bar. So I called in the NIS and I said, "I want you to investigate my staff. I want you to investigate everyone, including me, to find out who's on the take. I know that things are going on. I can't help but hear about it."[*]

And he said, "I've been hearing the same thing. You don't mind if I get the FBI in, too, because I think a lot of this stuff is involved with the civilian community."

I said, "Please be my guest, and don't hesitate to open the whole thing up. If it embarrasses me, that's my problem."

It turned out that the chief quartermaster was not only involved in appropriation of government money and selling tax-free booze that was illegal, but also he was involved with numerous other things, one of which was ripping off his fellow chiefs. He claimed that he had an in with the chief detail officer in Washington, and he would take 500 bucks from a chief to get a set of orders that the chief wanted. I had this investigated thoroughly.

I contacted Bagley at BuPers and told him that I had this investigation going on, and that there may be dishonesty in his detailing office. I didn't know, but there certainly was down here. It turned out that my chief was simply ripping off his fellows. He had no contact at all in Washington. He was simply taking their money, and if they didn't get the orders that they wanted, why, he'd say, "I'm sorry, I just couldn't do anything, but I tried."

---

[*] NIS--Naval Investigative Service.

And in case they got the orders, he took full credit. But he pocketed the money, anyway, at 500 bucks a crack. That was pretty good income.

Q: Some pretty dumb chiefs.

Admiral Ramage: As I said, boy, this was the bottom of the barrel. He also was involved with carrying firearms on the beach and shaking down various people. He was just a crook. Finally the NIS guy came in and he said, "Well, we've got enough to get him."

I said, "How much can you get him for?"

He said, "Well, I figure about 65 years at the present time."

And I said, "Can you really make it stick?"

He said, "Oh, there's no question about it on all of these charges."

I said, "I only want the charges brought up that are sure fire, because I don't want this guy to get away; he's a crook." This time I appointed the Marine colonel down there, Colonel Black, to be head of the court-martial. The results that I desired were obtained, and he was sent to prison and busted down to a seaman recruit and lost all his retired pay. Something like this is very pathetic because the guy was married, although he used to beat the hell out of his wife

Of course, she called and she said, "Well, you know, you're punishing me, too."

And I said, "I'm just sorry, but your husband's a crook."

And she said, "Well, he's that."

I said, "He's got to go," and that's where he went. He got ten years, and, of course, under the system he probably only served five, but at least he was out of the Navy and he'd lost all that retired pay, which was quite a kick in the tail.

You mentioned, Bob, about dumb chiefs. Yes, some were dumb and some were smart. And it was about this time that I was really unhappy about the situation on the base. The enlisted men looked terrible. It was a disgrace to the Navy. Officers and chiefs were using the excuse, "Well, that's what the CNO wants." In other words, they were not doing their job.

Q: I heard that an awful lot.

Admiral Ramage: Yeah. So I did something that I didn't think I would ever do. I got all the chief petty officers on the base, and there must have been 200 or 300 of them down there, and I got them in the chiefs' club, closed the bar, and closed the doors so that I was the only guy in there that was not a chief. I proceeded to chew their ass out. I started by saying, "As you know, I'm no admirer of the permissiveness that is attributed to Admiral Zumwalt. However, I am not letting down my requirements, and I don't think that you should let down your performance. The excuse that this is what the CNO wants simply won't wash with me. Now, I want you to get back and live up to your chiefs' oath and behave yourselves like chief petty officers should." There may have been a time in the Navy when something like this was done before. I don't know. But when I was through, you could hear nothing, just total silence. And then there was a group that started applauding, and then everybody started applauding, and then they all stood up, and it was quite apparent that they understood me and they understood what I was talking about, and that a great majority knew that they were goofing off. We immediately opened the bar and I went over and I had numerous chiefs come over and said, "Thank you very much, Admiral. We've needed something like this for years, and I think that maybe you'll get across what's going on."

Another attention getter that I did was in driving around the base, I would come upon some extremely disreputable sailor. I'd put him in the car with me, and I'd kidnap him. I'd take him up to my office and then I'd have my aide call the unit and say, "This is Admiral Ramage's aide. We have Seaman So-and-so up here, and the Admiral has picked him up as being one of the most disreputable-looking sailors on the base, and he wants you to come on up here and get him." Then the commanding officer, of course, would have to come up and see me, and that was enough. This immediately had quite an impact on what was going on. All that they needed was a little command attention and tender loving care. In general, I had a real nice time and a good rapport with people after they realized that this type of performance of duty and appearance just wasn't going to go around there. It's the same old story. If you communicate with people and tell them what you want, they're going to respond, but if you don't pay any attention to them, and they hadn't had any attention paid to them for years, they're going to goof off.

Q: Getting back to the thing about the chiefs, I feel that too much got blamed on Admiral Zumwalt for this. Little management and sound advice.

Admiral Ramage: I agree with you.

Q: They just sat down and said, "To hell with it."

Admiral Ramage: That's right.

Q: They were getting no direction from the top, they weren't really getting good direction from the commanding officers. But you really have to lay that on Zumwalt because he's still the ultimate senior man. But I know myself personally, I got so sick and tired of being the only bad ass on the base, I always felt like I was the only guy that was stopping one of these kids and saying, "Why are you walking around with your hands in your pockets? Where's your hat?" I just got tired of that. But nevertheless, the rules were still there. Nobody told this kid to walk around with his hands in his pockets, his hat off and his hair down over his shoulders. But the chiefs and the middle management officers had just said, "To hell with it."

Admiral Ramage: Well, I agree with you 100%.

Q: That's just my reaction.

Admiral Ramage: I agree with you 100% that what existed was that this was a perception of what Zumwalt wanted, and, of course, setting the example that he did with his hair down over his ears didn't do much good.

Q: No, that didn't help any.

Admiral Ramage: You can't chew a guy out for having long hair when the CNO is walking around looking like a haystack.

Q: I did.

Admiral Ramage: Well, I obviously did too. Okay. Shortly after arriving down in Puerto Rico, Admiral Chick Clarey had retired as CinCPacFlt, and I wrote him a letter thanking him for support. He responded to me in this manner. He said, "I hope I have made some small contribution and was perhaps successful at least some of the time. It's always great to go into a 'contest' when you know logic and good sense are on your side." And, of course, he was referring to our Prize Bull episode. That made me quite pleased, as you might guess, when the boss man still continued to stroke you by saying you did the right thing.

The rest of my career was involved mainly in political things down in Puerto Rico, and they may be interesting. I inherited the Vieques/Culebra problem. There had been an awful lot of pressure, which was initiated in Washington, by a so-called public--these attorneys that do things good for people.

Q: Public defender?

Admiral Ramage: No.

Q: Advocate?

Admiral Ramage: No. Public Interest. Anyway, the outfit was Covington and Burling, which is one of the big ones there, and they feel that they have to take on the establishment at various times, and their establishment was the Navy in this case, over Culebra and Vieques, which were target islands. So I got right into the middle of that, and it wasn't too unpleasant for me because I got along quite well with the governor. His name was

Hernandez Colon, and he's the governor now. The big problem that I had was with this Covington and Burling, their advocate was a guy named Copaken, and among other things, he was dishonest. Whereas he was supposedly helping the commonwealth, he was also relieving them of $250,000 in fees plus travel expenses. He was making all sorts of charges there against me which simply weren't true. This thing went on all during the time I was down there. We did move off Culebra, which wasn't particularly important, because Vieques is the key to the whole range system. Culebra was simply a redundant target area. I think the reason that the Navy was reticent to give it up in the past was the domino effect, that they felt that if they moved off Culebra, that then the pressure would go on to Vieques, which it has. So that may have been a good reason, but as far as I was concerned, the battle was over by the time I got down there. I didn't oppose it.

Q: Did anyone live on either one of these islands?

Admiral Ramage: Oh, yes, there were a few people on Culebra, maybe 500, but Vieques has a pretty good population in the center of the island, which is out of the government-owned area. They're all squatters.

About that same time, a rather interesting thing happened which Ward briefed me on before we left. He said, "This water contract for St. Thomas is coming up for renewal on the first of September."

I said, "What have we got there?"

He said, "Well, we've been furnishing water to St. Thomas for a period of about 11 years."

Q: St. Thomas, Virgin Islands.

Admiral Ramage: Yes. "They've had this emergency."

I said, "Well, what are we doing it for?"

And he said, "I don't know. We were doing it when I got here, and we're still doing it."

I said, "Well, I just don't think that's right. We shouldn't be in the water business." What the Navy was doing was drawing water from Puerto Rico, which is a scarce commodity there, out of our reserves and purifying it and selling it at our dock at 25 cents per 1,000 gallons to aid this shortage over in St. Thomas, which was perennial. The government of St. Thomas was in turn selling the water for $4.00 per 1,000 gallons, so it was a nice little take for them, and the civilian barge crews. They were large barges, of course, so they were making a nice cut on the thing, too.

Q: Where was that?

Admiral Ramage: It's about 15 to 20 miles. So I said, "Well, I think that's wrong." So one of the first things I did was write a letter to Governor Evans of St. Thomas and told him that as of the first of September, the Navy was not going to renew this contract.[*] He didn't respond, and I didn't think he would. Knowing the government of the Virgin Islands, I don't think they ever went to work. So in the meantime we closed the spigot. On the first of September I could see the barges down there; they'd begin to line up at the dock and no water was being poured into them. There were two or three of these big barges.

Then nothing happened, and I thought, "I know I'm going to get a blast; I'm not exactly sure from where." And I got it. It was direct from the White House, and it was from a very good friend of mine, a brigadier general reserve in the Air Force named Ted Marrs.[†] He'd been the Deputy for Reserve Affairs on SecDef's staff, and he'd been moved over to the White House. He got on the telephone and said, "What are you doing to the virgins down there?"

I explained to him what the problem was, that the Navy had somehow gotten itself into the water business and whereas if they had an emergency, we certainly were able to help them, but this was not an emergency, it'd been going on for 11 or 12 years.

And Ted said, "Well, Governor Mel Evans is a real fine guy, and I'll have him get in touch with you."

---

[*] Melvin H. Evans served as Governor of the Virgin Islands from July 1969 to January 1975.
[†] Theodore C. Marrs was then serving as Special Assistant to the President for Human Resources.

I said, "You know, there's been a letter on his desk for at least a month telling him this."

He said, "You know what goes on over there--not much."

So the governor called me and he said, "I want you and your wife to come on over and let's discuss this thing."

Q: On my private yacht.

Admiral Ramage: I went over and he turned out to be a real fine guy. He was black and had attended Howard University, in Washington--a very smart guy. He was the last of the appointed governors. He was a Nixon appointee. The rest of them that have been elected ever since are all Democrats. But he said, "We understand your problem, and as a matter of fact, we are just finishing a desalinization plant, and hopefully we'll have it on the line by next year. If you'll see fit to extend the contract for the year, I think I can guarantee that we'll be out of the barging business in a year." So I didn't have much alternative.

As far as I was concerned, Marrs pretty much told me to get on with it, so I told him we'd sign for a year and that we'd keep track of construction. Actually, we set up kind of a friendly group of people who would get together and talk over their problems from time to time, and they have plenty of them down there. You know, Virgin Islanders just don't work. Puerto Ricans don't work either, but compared to a Virgin Islander, a Puerto Rican is a flash. It's just a poor farm down there, supported by the federal government.

So that was taken care of, and I reported back to Ted Marrs, and told him that I thought we had this thing taken care of. Ted responded with this letter. He said, "Dear Jig, It is a real comfort to know the needs of the virgins are being met by such an experienced operator. If there is any help needed in this area, please call me. The higher levels here were most pleased with your response on this. Incidentally, when I get my punishment, I hope it can be meted in wonderful Puerto Rico or Governor Evans's island. Best, Ted." So we solved that, and actually the following year we did get them out of the water business. I understand they're back in it again, but I can't do everything. So that thing was dispensed with at least for a while.

One of the things that made life so pleasant for me down there was that I acquired an aide, Lieutenant Commander Malcolm Schantz.[*] He was a blackshoe. The reason he wasn't an aviator was because he couldn't see, but he had a private license and actually shamed me into getting a commercial license. We used to fly all over the place. He had a very light touch and a good sense of humor. I hope that I didn't ruin him for his future life in the Navy, because I let him write all of my personal reports on what was going on down there in Puerto Rico, and I said, "At least keep it light." He not only kept them light, he kept them funny. I used to get phone calls from Washington on this report that went on up there. They said, "Keep them coming. It's the only funny thing we get every two weeks."

I felt that Culebra was not worth a fight. The former Secretary of the Navy Chafee had made an agreement with the government of Puerto Rico that they would hire 60 people over there to do nothing as long as the government used the peninsula to bombard.[†] Being the tightwad that I am, I said, "We'll move off, and also the first thing we're going to do is fire those 60 people," which I did. There was a little heartburn on that in the newspapers about me being a little difficult to get along with, but so far as I was concerned, they hadn't lived up to their obligation to keep the heat off the Navy, and so consequently I didn't feel that when we moved off that we should in any way leave anything, including any material or any jobs.

Puerto Rico, when we moved off Culebra, was supposed to provide an alternate, and the Navy wanted them to continue to work on the alternate, knowing that there really wasn't one available, because they thought that would keep them from trying to get us off Vieques. The people in Vieques were then claiming, of course, that when we moved off Culebra, that they were getting the full charge of all the Navy operations, so they were complaining, but we really didn't need Culebra, so it made no difference.

So the negotiations started. Copaken was directly involved, and I in turn couldn't take this lying down. This operation was being handled by the Assistant Secretary of the Navy for Logistics, Jack Bowers, who's now chairman of Sanders, you know, the EW firm.[‡]

---

[*] Lieutenant Commander John Malcolm Schantz, USN.
[†] John H. Chafee served as Secretary of the Navy from 31 January 1969 to 4 May 1972.
[‡] Jack L. Bowers, Assistant Secretary of the Navy (Installations and Logistics), 1973-76; Sanders Associates, Nashua, New Hampshire; EW--electronic warfare.

He was most helpful, but, of course, he was trying to look out for the politics and decide with concern for the Republican Party, and I was trying to do the best for the government and the people down there. Occasionally we were at odds, but not really. He was much more patient with Copaken than I was. I guess he felt that he had to, since he lived in Washington and I didn't give a damn.

So it turned out they wanted to move the Culebra operation over to an island in the middle of the Mona Passage, which is the channel between Puerto Rico and the Dominican Republic. It's right in the middle of the major north-south traffic flow between Venezuela, on up to the East Coast, and the Gulf ports. It's just no place to put it at all. That was the proposal that they came up with, which I think they knew was totally impossible, but anyway, that was what their offer was.

So this thing was heating up, and I was getting pretty heated, too, at Copaken, and so I wrote a letter to Wally Gaddis, he was the 04, the logistics man for the CNO, a vice admiral.* I wrote him this memorandum entitled, "Copeken. I understand that Copaken has been named as the Puerto Rican negotiator for future Culebra-Monito-Desecheo problems." That's the area out in the Mona Passage, where the alternative was going to be. And I said, "Copaken directly attacked the integrity of the Navy and Assistant Secretary of the Navy Bowers as the signer of a letter which stated the Navy had intentions to return to Culebra. I personally will have nothing further to do with him. In future negotiations, I feel that if Copaken is the agent for the commonwealth, that the Assistant Secretary of the Navy would not be appropriate as the Navy representative, nor should a flag officer be so designated. This provides Copaken with undeserved status."

I thought that maybe the best thing to do at this time was to go after the source of the problem, maybe I should go after Copaken, and after all, I had nothing to lose. So I immediately went to see the governor and told him that I didn't feel that he needed a negotiator, that I felt that he was a man of integrity, and I certainly was, and that I felt that whatever could be done, that we could arrive at a conclusion without the help of Covington and Burling.

---

* Vice Admiral Walter D. Gaddis, USN, served as Deputy Chief of Naval Operations (Logistics), OP-04, from 11 April 1973 to 31 July 1975.

I further mentioned to one of the leading female politicians at that time on the island, Celeste Benitez, who was a part of the ruling group there, that I didn't think he was required and that I felt that we should negotiate directly. And in due course, I think I won my point. He was dropped about the time that I was relieved in Puerto Rico. These so-called public interest firms can be a real pain in the neck. They really were giving the Navy a bad time, and the Navy was accepting the abuse.

Concerning the Monita-Desecheo thing, which made use of the Mona Passage, it, of course, was very bad as far as international trade was concerned. When you close a major international passage, I think it's probably against international law. So I felt that the thing for the people in Washington to do was go to the Department of State right away and point out that this was going on, and we got immediate help from the Department of State. State immediately came back and told the commonwealth that this was not the solution.

It happened about that time that Kissinger came down to St. John, part of the Virgin Islands, on vacation.[*] He came back by way of Roosevelt Roads in order to refuel. He had an Air Force jet, and they had to refuel there because they can only refuel with government fuel, I guess, in these VIP planes. While he was there, he came on up to my quarters. It happened that we were giving a reception for the staff, and we were having a fine time, except when Kissinger walked in, all the gals that were there all gathered around him, and the rest of the men there, we kind of sat and talked to ourselves for the hour or so while he was there.

Incidentally, Kissinger is the smoothest thing I've seen. I went over to thank him for the work on the Mona Passage, and he was very familiar with it. He looked at me and said, "Admiral, is there anything else you want?" And he wrote a very, very nice letter when he got back. He did it to the right person, he wrote it to the Chief of Naval Operations, who at that time was Jim Holloway.[†] Jim sent me a nice note pointing out that Kissinger was very impressed with what we were doing down there, which was a lot of baloney, but at least it feels good.

---

[*] Henry A. Kissinger served as Secretary of State, 1973-77.
[†] Admiral James L. Holloway III, USN, served as Chief of Naval Operations from 29 June 1974 to 1 July 1978.

In my opinion, when Jim Holloway became the Chief of Naval Operations, he had an awful lot of work to do. I wrote him a congratulatory message and made two points. I stated, "Among the many problems which you will face are two which would appear to demand your attention. First is the perception by the chief petty officers that they no longer hold their time honored position within our Navy. While this may not be factual, they consider it so. And second, the officer corps of the Navy has been seriously fractured. Middle level officers are confused as to what to expect. Senior officers have experienced vindictiveness and even capriciousness in assignments. It appears that there has been an endeavor to place less capable flag officers in the most responsible positions, while several of our most highly qualified officers have been forced into early retirement."

I got an immediate response from Jim, and he said, "Your words of advice are perceptive and well-chosen, as I would expect from you. Let me assure you that I will try to do things the Navy way, but effecting policy from the top is a slow process, and I ask your continued understanding and support." And I think that Jim Holloway did try to turn back the clock. I talked to him at length on several occasions, telling him that I thought he was moving too slow, but as you look back at it, he had four years to try to correct, and two upheavals with two successive CNOs would have been just too much. So he probably went along at just about the right pace.

He did try to get rid of the troublemakers, and he did get rid of most of them. It is a long process, as he said, and it took him four years, and it really is not yet completed to date, and this is 1985. Zumwalt left in 1974. Dave McDonald, a former CNO, said it would take 20 years, and I think we're on the track now, though.

Q: We're fortunate to have some very strong CNOs.

Admiral Ramage: Yes. I think that Holloway and, in particular, Tom Hayward, did an excellent job.[*]

---

[*] Admiral Thomas B. Hayward, USN, served as Chief of Naval Operations from 1 July 1978 to 30 June 1982.

In Puerto Rico, I was generally surprised to discover things that were wrong that had been going on for quite a number of years. One of them was another water problem, which had to do with water for the island of Vieques, which is only about five miles east. It turned out that they, too, were in a constant problem with emergency water. But they had no contract, they just had a telephone line from the mayor of Vieques to a buddy of his over in our public works department. He'd call up and say, "I'd like some water sent over to Vieques," and it would appear over there.

So when I found this out, I said, "Well, that's not right. First of all, it's using Navy bottoms." It wasn't a contract like the other one. It used Navy fuel and Navy sailors' time. So I decided that maybe I ought to stop that too. I wrote a letter to the governor, who, of course, knew nothing about this and told him that this had been going on for many, many years, and that the Navy was very willing to help in an emergency, but this was a routine affair. I would like to initiate a system where his chief of water supplies would contact the skipper of our base, and the skipper of the base, who at that time was Bob Rasmussen, would make the water available as he saw fit.*

This, of course, was quite a surprise to the governor because he had no idea that the Navy had been supplying this water. He wrote a very nice letter saying that this seemed to be a workable solution, and designated the contact points. This immediately got the mayor of Vieques really mad. He said that I was trying to belittle him, that I was showing how poor the people of Vieques were because they didn't have enough water to even take care of themselves. And he got to the editor of the English newspaper, the Star, which wrote an editorial on my character, which pointed out that I was one of the those arrogant Yankees who came down there to belittle. I don't think he called me Yankee; a gringo. I was one of these arrogant gringos who tried to belittle the Puerto Rican people by making them beg for water over in Vieques.

This seemed to fill the bill, because when the governor found out that we were in fact providing this water, he came back and said, "Well, if this is the case, we'll try to do something about it." And they did. I think the Navy has continued to help them from time to time, but it wasn't done on a routine basis.

---

* Captain Robert L. Rasmussen, USN.

Anyway, I stopped that, but about that same time, the end of the line was coming up for the St. Thomas water. Their desalinization plant was beginning to work and produce a little water. I went to a party in Humacao, where I met a man who ran the barge line between Roosevelt Roads and St. Thomas. It, of course, had been a very lucrative business for him. He finally got me aside after dinner and he said, "You know, I could fix it so that you wouldn't have any financial worries for the rest of your life."

And my response was, "I'll bet you could." That was the end of the discussion.

But they ultimately got pretty well squared away in their water business. As I said, however, I understand that they're back in a problem and that perhaps the Navy is involved with furnishing water again, I don't know.

We're now getting towards the end of my active duty tour. I had been suffering from severe pains in my left arm for about seven years. I had been to see the neurosurgeons in Oak Knoll, and they had pinpointed the problem, a severe compaction of my spinal cord. Although one of the doctors wanted to operate at that time, the senior surgeon said, "Let's wait and just see what goes on."

I then saw a surgeon, Dr. Fred Jackson, who was a captain, one of the outstanding neurosurgeons in the business, at Camp Pendleton.[*] He took a look at me and said, "I think maybe we ought to go for it now." This would have been about 1975. I was back on a trip.

I said, "Well, it just isn't convenient to do it now. Is there any chance that it might correct itself?"

He said, "Well, slight, but I don't think so."

So as I was getting towards the end of the line, I thought if I was going to get something done, I'd better get it done while I was on active duty because it makes a big difference. So in about March of 1975, I went up to Bethesda and met Dr. Cal Early, their chief neurosurgeon.[†] He took one look at all of the X-rays and said, "I don't know how "Fearless Freddy" [that was Jackson's name] ever let you go last time. You'd better get operated on now. Your left arm has atrophied to the point that you're never going to regain much of it." He said, "Also I noticed you're dragging your left leg. I can only predict that

---

[*] Captain Frederick E. Jackson, MC, USN.
[†] Captain Calvin B. Early, MC, USN.

within four or five years, if you don't do something about it, that you could be a basket case."

So in May of 1975, I was operated in Bethesda for a laminectomy, which is a back operation where they remove the outer casing of your backbone segments, and they operated on the second, third, fourth, fifth, and sixth cervicals. So it was a pretty strenuous operation. Early hoped that that would do the job, but after about three or four weeks he indicated that he was going to have to go back in and fuse the cervicals. He obviously was an excellent surgeon. I was in pretty bad shape by that time. I'd gotten down to about 158 pounds from 190, so I was pretty weak and in a wheelchair and so forth.

About that time I put in my retirement papers, having no place to go. But I got to the point where I couldn't retire even if I wanted to, I was in that bad a shape. I was due to retire in the latter part of August in Puerto Rico. They sent me back to recover down in Puerto Rico, rather than stick around Bethesda. I was mobile, but barely. I was to be relieved by Rear Admiral Bill Flanagan.[*] I wanted to be able to walk when I saluted for the last time, so I did get myself in good enough shape so that I could get up and walk around if I wore a neck brace.

General Chardon, who was the commanding general of the National Guard, was my guest speaker.[†] Mike Michaelis came down from ComNavAirLant to see me over the side, and the governor came out, and the mayor, who later became governor. Chardon furnished the Puerto Rican National Guard band, which is about the best military band I've ever heard. It plays John Philip Sousa with a Latin beat, and, boy, you can't help but march to that music.

The general even furnished the saluting battery, which was a 105-millimeter battery. They were a little enthusiastic when they fired all the salutes--to the oncoming admiral, my retirement salute, Mike Michaelis's salute, and the governor's salute, and we never knew how many guns were being fired or what the timing was. When these guys get shooting, you'd never know what to expect. They'd say, "We're now going to honor Vice Admiral Michaelis," and he may get 23 or maybe 14 guns, but anyway, it was colorful, and

---

[*] Rear Admiral William R. Flanagan, USN.
[†] Major General Fernando Chardon. The change of command and retirement ceremony was on 31 August 1975.

everybody enjoyed it. I ended my active duty days there in Puerto Rico, and went up to Bethesda for one last checkup. The doctor said, "There's just no way you can retire in the condition you're in."

I said, "Well, I don't want to stay in Bethesda."

And he said that San Diego had a very fine neurosurgery department, so that they would transfer me as an ambulatory patient to Balboa Naval Hospital.

Q: What had caused this problem?

Admiral Ramage: I think maybe flying, to a certain extent, but they said that it probably was congenital to a certain extent. And of course, as you get older, whether you have severe arthritis or not, there is a certain amount of calcium that goes on in there.

Q: By flying, would that mean high G?

Admiral Ramage: I can recall I used to have a lot of problems flying fighter runs when pulling quite a few G's. Your head is not exactly down the line of your spine, so that it puts a stress at an angle. I used to be in severe pain. The doctor told me that if I had ever punched out of an airplane that I would have snapped my spinal cord. People would have never known what happened, probably, because they wouldn't have been able to find me unless I was on the beach, and they wouldn't know why I died. Apparently it was something that had been there for quite some time.

In any event, I finally got into such a condition that I could retire on the 31st of December, 1975, and I retired from one of my favorite ships, the Kitty Hawk. I had a lot of my old friends around me. Dave Richardson was kind enough to make the speech, and Freddy Bardshar was there, and Jim Stockdale, and quite a few people that I had served with over the years.* So I left the Navy in a good mood and very thankful for the 40 years that I'd been in it.

---

* Rear Admiral James B. Stockdale, USN. He was awarded the Medal of Honor for his heroism while a prisoner of war in North Vietnam from 1965 to 1973. He retired in 1979 as a vice admiral. Richardson and Bardshar were retired vice admirals at that point.

I continued treatment in Balboa after I retired, but I was getting along quite well. They gave me therapy and exercises and so forth, and I got to the point that I could even play tennis again. I could never play golf again, because I lost pretty much of the use of my left arm. With every retiree, there comes the question of what you're going to do. I had long ago made up my mind that I was never going to be in the position of trying to sell military hardware to my peers or people who used to work for me.

Q: Did you have a lot of offers from industry?

Admiral Ramage: Not really. To begin with, I was so sick at the time that I wasn't ready to do anything. I had an offer from an industrial security agency up in Los Angeles. They call it the National Industrial Security Council. It's a group of industry people who put on symposiums. I told them I would be interested if they'd move the job down to San Diego, because there was no way I was going to move to L.A., and that dropped through. But I never actively asked for anything, and I really wasn't well for about a year after these operations because they were quite a shock to my system. I think in retiring, you either select an area that you want to live in or you select an area where you can get a job. Most of the places that have good jobs are not places that are pleasant to live in. There are very few military jobs of any consequence in San Diego.

What I decided to do then was to try to repay some of the nice things that the Navy had done for me. By the Navy, I really mean naval aviation. The Association of Naval Aviation was being formed in the fall of 1976 in Norfolk. I went to the first convention and talked at length to Tom Moorer, who was responsible for ANA. I told him I'd be glad to help him, and became a vice president in charge of recruitment for the first two or three years. I spent quite a bit of time on the Association of Naval Aviation.

In the meantime, I began to get more interested and more active in the Tailhook Association, which is a very fine organization also. It had some rather difficult beginnings and had acquired a rather bad reputation for some of the things that had gone on previously, but it had become a very reputable association and has aims that are completely consistent with mine, which are the support and furtherance of carrier aviation. So I had become interested in and helped them to a certain extent, particularly in the publishing of the magazine, the Hook, which is a very fine magazine.

I also became involved with the Aerospace Museum in Balboa Park here. They're trying to recover from a serious fire that they had four or five years ago, and that's coming along fine.

I've been interested in politics, mainly in the Republican Party. It isn't the Republican Party as such; it's the party that helps the defense establishment, and at the present time the Republican Party is hands down the greater supporter of the military establishment. I wouldn't hesitate to support some of the Democrats that I've known in the past like Eddie Hebert or Senator John Stennis, and these people that are generally from the South.[*] But most of the Democrats that we run across are people that are anti-military and liberal to the point of being against practically everything I believe in.

I also have a folly, which is the Bohemian Club. I was able to get into that on--I call it a military scholarship, when I was a carrier division commander, and it's, I think, the finest men's club in the world. Not only is the membership very exclusive, mainly the business and professional and political leaders of the United States, but it's fun. It has no ax to grind. Its motto is "Weaving Spiders Come Not Here," which means that at the annual encampment up in the Redwoods, you're not supposed to talk business.

If you think that's so, you're very confused, and if you think that politics isn't talked about up there, you're quite wrong, too, because mainly all of the conservative politicians belong: President Reagan, Schultz, Weinberger, Ford, even old Governor Brown.[†] This is not "Moonbeam" but the older Governor Brown of California.[‡] Although he's a Democrat, he is a member and a good practicing member. Outstanding writers like Herman Wouk and numerous others, Cronkite, Buckley.[§] You can go on naming the various people.

---

[*] Senator John C. Stennis (Democrat-Mississippi). The aircraft carrier John C. Stennis (CVN-74) is named in his honor.
[†] Ronald W. Reagan was President, 1981-89; George P. Shultz was Secretary of State, 1982-89; Caspar W. Weinberger was Secretary of Defense, 1981-87; Gerald R. Ford was President, 1974-77; Edmund G. Brown, Governor of California, 1959-66. Reagan succeeded Brown as governor.
[‡] Edmund G. Brown, Jr., son of the former governor, became California's governor in 1975.
[§] Herman Wouk, who was a Naval Reserve officer in World War II, wrote one of the outstanding novels about that war, The Caine Mutiny, published by Doubleday & Company in 1951. William F. Buckley is a syndicated newspaper columnist known for his conservative stance.

I particularly enjoy Herman Wouk, because he loves the Navy and he likes to hike, which I do, too, and we talk about various things. I got into an all-night session one night about the Navy, and he kind of ticked me off in that he said that he thought that Stansfield Turner was a fine naval officer and a fine representative of the Navy.[*] I responded that you could be an intellectual without being intelligent. And Herman said, "Well, you know, it isn't every day that you get an officer in the Navy who's a Rhodes Scholar and has a reputation around the educational establishment."

And I said, "Well, that's fine, but he happens to be a naval officer and he hasn't done a damn thing for the United States Navy."

And we went on from there, but he made a point, which I was a little unhappy about at the time, but he's dead right. Wouk said, "During a war, we can get a lot of people like you that will fight and will do a good job in running the squadrons and ships. But during peacetime, there's an entirely different criterion. People look up to educated people. With that in mind, Stansfield Turner is a credit to the Navy."

My response to that was unprintable.

Q: As far as scholarship goes, what relationship, if any, do you see between academic standing at Annapolis and effective leadership years later?

Admiral Ramage: I would say not much. Only two people in my class made four stars, and both of them were at the very bottom of the class. That was Means Johnston and Blackie Weinel. They were noticeably low in aptitude for the service, or grease. So that would indicate perhaps that there's something wrong in how they judge people at the Naval Academy.

Q: Do you recall any instruction or even discussion of combat leadership at Annapolis? Was that subject ever addressed?

---

[*] Among other tours of duty, Turner was president of the Naval War College, 1972-74; Com2ndFlt, 1974-75; CinCSouth, 1975-77; and Director of the Central Intelligence Agency, 1977-81.

Admiral Ramage: None. I don't recall at any time where anybody got up and told us, "You know, the main thing you're here for is that some day we'll probably have a war and you're expected to be in it." That was not part of the program.

Q: I suppose that leads in large part to what you were saying about Turner and some of the others, the mind set, the different mentalities between warriors and managers. How do you think the Naval Academy and the Navy generally can produce more warriors?

Admiral Ramage: Well, this has been a subject of discussion between Jim Stockdale and me and various other people that I have a lot of respect for. Jim at the present time is on a board which is supposed to take a look at the curriculum at the Naval Academy and how that applies to the future. I get quite unhappy with the various things come out in our magazine called Shipmate, pointing out the scholastic ability of the classes as they come in.[*] As a matter of fact, the last plebe class is supposed to have the highest SAT scores of any freshman class in the country.[†] They're elated with that, but I'm not sure that's good.

I would ask two questions. The first is, will they fight? And secondly, will they stay in the Navy? That is, will they make it a career? I know that I sit on the opposite side, in that I have certainly no great academic background. I've been a good average student as far as the Navy's concerned, although later on in life I did a lot better. But at the Naval Academy I was certainly unexceptional. I had problems, just like Johnston and Weinel did, with aptitude for the service. I just don't know what can be done, but I don't think that we've been successful in the past.

Q: Taking that in the other direction, who are some of the officers whom you most admire, and what do you think made them particularly effective?

Admiral Ramage: The officers that I admired the most obviously were those that wouldn't hesitate to stand up and be counted. This takes a lot of courage, because the situation is

---

[*] Shipmate is a monthly magazine published by the Naval Academy Alumni Association.
[†] SAT--Scholastic Aptitude Test.

such that the Navy tries to mold everybody into a certain pattern, and the people that don't mold into that pattern just don't succeed. People that have been the most successful and the strongest advocates, as far as I'm concerned, were Freddy Bardshar and Dave Richardson at the three-star level. I'd have to search pretty far to come up with any more. At the two-star level you find a few more. You find Eddie Outlaw, Sam Brown, Roy Isaman, Red Carmody, but there really aren't very many people that I would expect to really challenge something that they thought was wrong.[*]

Q: I think you have missed one that I know that you admire very much, who I'm sure you feel falls in that category, Jim Stockdale.

Admiral Ramage: Well, Jim, of course, yes.

Q: He's so obvious that you forget.

Admiral Ramage: I am only talking about people that I directly worked with. Jim was a little bit later than I was, and he's a great man, I certainly would put him in the category.

Q: He certainly seems to refute Herman Wouk's opinion that you can't have an intellectual warrior.

Admiral Ramage: I guess so.

Q: What advice would you give a plebe entering the academy these days for being effective? In other words, is it going to be necessary to buck the system in order to be effective at some point?

Admiral Ramage: This is very difficult for me to answer, because perhaps I could have lived my life in a different way. Perhaps I could have followed right along the line in lock

---

[*] Rear Admiral Samuel R. Brown, USN.

step and done exactly as directed, and never argued with things that I thought were wrong. So when I express an opinion, it's so biased that it may not be worthwhile. When we became flag officers, we were addressed by Tom Moorer, who was the new CNO, and his advice was, "Call it as you see it." I had been doing that, and I did it all through the time that I was in the Navy. I'm not very sure that a lot of people do that. The penalty for not being a member of the club is quite great, and you simply don't get along with the group.

Q: Do you think that each individual has his own method of obtaining the goal he wants to achieve?

Admiral Ramage: That's correct.

Q: Some people have the ability, they don't have to buck the system per se, but they can figure a way to get around it.

Admiral Ramage: To get around it, yes.

Q: And still it accomplished the same goal.

Admiral Ramage: You're exactly right. I would pick in that category a very effective officer, Mike Michaelis. However, Mike was lucky enough to have sat out on a joint staff in Omaha a great deal of the Zumwalt era. I've talked to him about it. He said, "Well, maybe I was just fortunate." Because he was never in a position during those first two years when things were pretty hot. He just wasn't in a position to do anything about it. Whether he would have done something about it, I don't know.

Q: Do we have too many flag billets in the Navy? Could we get by with fewer admirals?

Admiral Ramage: Oh, I think so. I think that there's been grade creep. Again, you have to keep up with the Joneses, however, and the Air Force in particular has always been able to acquire a lot of general officer billets. I think that the tremendous amount of high-priced talent in Washington is just terrible, but that's the nature of the beast. It's an enormous bureaucracy, and if they could ever start cutting down in there, it'd be great. But you can't cut down the service establishments in Washington and let that enormous Secretary of Defense staff continue to be there. They are constantly assigning jobs to the services to produce studies and do various things.

What the services have done quite recently, however, is turn a lot of studies over to the Beltway Bandits, you know, the study groups.[*] That's expensive, but when the Office of the Secretary of Defense asks for a study on ASW or whatever you want, the service has to produce it, whether it's in-house or they hire it. It's extremely complicated. My feeling is if they'd cut the Secretary of Defense's staff by quite a number of people, they'd have fewer people asking for the studies, and then in turn the services could cut their staffs in Washington.

Q: You obviously look upon your naval career as successful, and you take quite a bit of pride. What do you attribute the success of your career to?

Admiral Ramage: I take a great pride in my career. I feel that the Navy was just the greatest thing that ever happened to me. I'd certainly do it all over again if I had the chance to do it. Strangely enough, I would say that probably one of the great items is luck. I'm a lucky man. Everything I do is lucky. Going back through the various things that happened to me in my career, you'll see that I was at the right place at the right time when important events occurred. On top of that, in the three ships that I commanded, I didn't ever scratch any paint. In the 5,000 hours or so that I logged in aviation, I never blew a tire. I don't think that takes any more skill; I think a lot of that is luck. So I'd say that was one of the first items that helps a naval career. As a matter of fact, I always think of Arleigh Burke's statement about carrier skippers. He said he hoped they were good, but he didn't want any

---

[*] "Beltway Bandits" is a derisive nickname for consulting organizations, many of which have their offices located near the Capital Beltway that circles Washington, D.C.

unlucky ones. And I've seen some people that were very unlucky that were damn fine officers. I have in mind Bob Elder, who's a real hero of mine.*

Q: Do you have any significant achievement of your career that you feel is the most significant one?

Admiral Ramage: I have several instances that I think of as being high points. Quite obviously the Battle of the Philippine Sea has to be one. I would say that in the nuclear weapons business, my fight for the light tactical weapons when I was at Sandia Base and almost got canned was certainly a high point. I think that I was correct in that instance. I would say that probably my opposition to General Lavelle's Prize Bull was a high point in my career. I think I was correct. With the exception of the Chief of Naval Operations at that time, I think everybody that knew anything about operating task forces agreed with me. But in general, my career was just a very pleasant series of nice jobs.

I think I probably had more commands than anybody that has been before me or perhaps ever will. I was a commanding officer from 1944 through practically the rest of my career, first as skipper of Bombing Ten on the Enterprise and then moving over to Bombing 98, which was the replacement air group on the West Coast after the war. My next real time at sea was in command of Carrier Air Group 19, and I went from there over to command VC-3, which was the night fighter squadron for the Pacific Fleet. The next time I went to sea was a commander of Heavy Attack Wing One down at Sanford, and then as skipper of the Salisbury Sound, then the Independence, some staff jobs and very briefly as commanding officer of the Franklin D. Roosevelt. Then after I made flag rank, after my time in CinCPacFlt as operations and plans, which was a fine job, I was in command constantly from then as commander of Fleet Air Whidbey or Medium Attack Wing, Commander Carrier Division Seven, commander of the Naval Air Reserves, and then ultimately commander of the naval forces in the Caribbean. So I was just very lucky.

---

* Captain Robert M. Elder, USN (Ret.). His career stumbled when he was commanding officer of the carrier Coral Sea (CVA-43). She ran aground in the fog off Alameda, California, in 1963; he retired later that year. For a detailed article on his career, see Barrett Tillman, "Where Are They Now? Bob Elder," The Hook, Fall 1989, pages 12-17.

People often asked how you get these jobs, and my response was, "I just asked for them." I'll admit I didn't ask for the last one.

Q: Did you ever consider leaving the Navy at any time before retirement?

Admiral Ramage: Oh, I think several times, specifically in the summer of 1946, when this chance to go into the Air Force was offered. I didn't really very seriously consider that. The time that was most important was after I had Air Group 19, in coming back through Pearl on the way back, I was offered a job with the Bishop Bank, which had been my father-in-law's bank in Honolulu. It was quite a flattering offer. He had retired by that time. And I thought that over for a few minutes. As a matter of fact, my father-in-law at that time told me that he thought I shouldn't do it. He said, "You're going to be a success at whatever you do, and if you like the Navy, why get out?"

But I always kept one foot in and one foot out, in that I felt that if the Navy stopped being fun for me, I might do something else. I was never concerned much about whether or not I could make a living, and perhaps that's one of the reasons why many of the officers are so conservative and won't oppose things. Maybe they aren't so sure of themselves that they can make it elsewhere. I've always been certain that I could make it anywhere. Every time that I considered leaving the Navy, they came up with a new airplane or a new job or a new something that I wanted to stay with. So it was always a fun thing for me.

Q: Let me ask what's maybe too obvious a question. Not just based upon your own experience, but naval aviators generally, what's the attraction of naval aviation?

Q: Besides girls.

Admiral Ramage: The main reason I went into it at the time I did was people. When I went to the Enterprise as a boot ensign there in 1939, it was so apparent to me that the people in the air group and the people in the air department were far superior to the blackshoe people, and they had so much more fun doing it. Then, of course, the duty itself is more fascinating. You've got a lot of independence there in flying around in the air, and then the challenge. Particularly on the carriers, there's a challenge every day. It keeps the old adrenaline going. It's just a fascinating life. I think because it is a fascinating life, you do get superior people in it. In general, they're pretty fine individuals.

Q: I guess I should ask you the standard question. What would you do differently if you could do it over again? Anything?

Admiral Ramage: And I guess I'll give you the standard answer. There isn't a thing I know of. No, I have nothing that I can think of. Things seemed to work out regardless of how badly I screwed it up.

Q: All in all, what would you say about the system? Does the system work?

Admiral Ramage: I think the system works, and I think probably the Navy system is superior to the other armed services' systems. I would say, of course, the fact that I made flag rank proves the system works. Because I couldn't work the system to get a little higher than I did, I guess indicates that probably I didn't know what the rules were. I was very stubborn.

Q: Did you ever have any secret aspirations of being the Chief of Naval Operations?

Admiral Ramage: No. I would have liked to have been ComNavAirPac or ComNavAirLant. I would have liked to have been Com7thFlt. But as I look back on it, I became aware of the fact that those upper jobs are made almost entirely politically, and I really didn't have any political support. I could have had some, I think, if Zumwalt had let me go down to New Orleans. I think that I would have had strong support from Eddie Hebert because I admired him, and I think he admired me.

James D. Ramage #3 - 383

Q: This concludes the Naval Institute interview with Rear Admiral James D. Ramage. The interview was concluded at Bonita, California, on 31 March 1985.

Addendum:

I have completed proofreading my oral history and had made no substantive major changes. It is now New Year's Day, 1998. I am adding some information about what has transpired during the intervening years since the original interviews.

Since the country has been very good to me, I feel that I owe much in return. I have been involved in local charities, including the chairmanship of the Red Cross, and served as a driver of the station wagon for hospital patients. I have run 20 annual tours of naval ships and installations, including Marine Corps, for influential winter visitors to Coronado. I used my influence to get the city of Waterloo, Iowa, to dedicate its new civic center to the memory of the five Sullivan brothers, who were killed when USS Juneau was sunk south of Guadalcanal in November 1942.

I recently founded and endowed the Enlisted Aircrew Roll of Honor, which is located aboard Yorktown in Charleston Harbor. I helped acquire and fund an F4F-3 for permanent display in O'Hare Airport in Chicago. This it the type fighter flown by Butch O'Hare when he won the Medal of Honor in 1942. I have spent a lot of time, along with Bill Houser, trying to correct the travesty imposed on innocent attendees at the Tailhook symposium held at Las Vegas, Nevada, in 1991.

I have been more than amply rewarded for my services in and out of the Navy. I have been inducted into the Carrier Aviation Hall of Fame aboard Yorktown. I am a member of the Golden Eagles. I was the first to win the Lifetime Achievement Award by the Tailhook Association. And--proudest of all--I am the first to be declared an Honorary Combat Aircrewman with the rate of Seaman (CA).

In reviewing my record, I realize that without the wars I may have reached the rank of commander. In today's "politically correct" Navy, I doubt that I would have gone that far.

Index to the Oral History of
Rear Admiral James D. Ramage,
U.S. Navy (Retired)

A-1 Skyraider
Transition in the late 1960s of A-1 pilots to fly the A-6 Intruder, 303-304

A3D/A-3 Skywarrior
Navy aircraft specifically designed in the early 1950s to carry large nuclear weapons, 143-144; difficulties getting into the fleet in the late 1950s because of poor personnel training, 195-196, 207-209; tactics for use in the low-altitude loft delivery of nuclear weapons, 212-214; carrier qualifications in the late 1950s for pilots new to the aircraft, 214-215; various competitions as part of HATWing 1 in the late 1950s, 216-219; cockpit design, 219-220; role of the bombardier-navigator, 220-221; proposal in the late 1950s to use the plane as a tanker, 223-224

A3J/A-5 Vigilante
Navy aircraft specifically designed in the late 1950s to carry large nuclear weapons, 223, 226-227; landing accident and fire on board the aircraft carrier Independence (CVA-62) in the early 1960s, 247-248; pilots' lack of carrier experience in the early 1960s, 249-250, 253

A4D/A-4 Skyhawk
Described by the Chief of the Bureau of Aeronautics in the mid-1950s as the poor man's airplane, 201; nuclear weapon delivery maneuvers, 213; involved in bombing competitions in the late 1950s, 216-218; difficult landing on board the aircraft carrier Independence (CVA-62) in the early 1960s, 248-249; Marine squadron VMA-324 operated A-4s off the Independence in the early 1960s, 252; used in April 1966 strike on Cam Pha, North Vietnam, 290-292; in strikes against Hanoi and Haiphong, North Vietnam, in June 1966, 293; in the 1970s replaced the F-4 Phantom as the aircraft flown by the Blue Angels, 347

A-6 Intruder
Navy attack plane used in the mid-1960s for bombing tests in Nevada, 278, 280-281, 284; used in April 1966 strike on Cam Pha, North Vietnam, 290-292; in the late 1960s several squadrons were based at Whidbey Island NAS, 303-304; concern in 1967 about bombing accuracy, 305-306; strikes in late 1971 against North Vietnam, 327-328

A6M Zero (Japanese Fighter Plane)
Used by the Japanese during the June 1944 battle for the Marianas, 116

A-7 Corsair II
Used by Naval Reserve pilots who won a bombing competition in the early 1970s at Lemoore, California, 348

AJ Savage
Special-mission aircraft developed for nuclear weapons delivery, 138; in 1950 Ramage investigated the crash of an AJ in New Mexico, 139-140; design deficiencies, 140-141; expedited for political reasons, 141; difficulties in 1953 during qualifications on board the aircraft carrier Oriskany (CVA-34), 168-170; background of pilots for the plane, 169

Accidents
In 1950 Ramage investigated the crash of an AJ Savage in New Mexico, 139-140; Lieutenant Frank Repp had a spectacular ramp strike on board the aircraft carrier Oriskany (CVA-34) in the mid-1950s, 172; landing accidents on board the aircraft carrier Independence (CVA-62) in the early 1960s, 246-248

Aircraft Carriers
Carriers did not figure strongly in the U.S. Navy's offensive planning prior to World War II, 33-35; a few carriers were built in the 1930s as part of Depression Relief measures, 36-36; contribution in the Pacific War of the light carriers (CVLs), 92-93; Ramage didn't believe carriers got the best personnel in the years right after World War II, 131-132; demonstrated their capability during a 1956 war game testing the usefulness of nuclear weapons, 196-200; late 1950s argument at the National War College over the role of nuclear-armed carriers, 205; concern about the experience and training of carrier skippers, 268-269

See also: Enterprise, USS (CV-6); Franklin D. Roosevelt, USS (CVA-42); Independence, USS (CVA-62); Kitty Hawk, US (CVA-63); Oriskany, USS (CVA-34)

Air Development Squadron Three
The squadron's top-notch pilots in the 1950s were not typical of those in the fleet, 227

Air Force Pacific Fleet (AirPac)
Management of enlisted personnel in the late 1940s, 134-137; headquarters moved from Hawaii to North Island in 1949, 135; shifted Ramage to command of VC-3 in 1954, 179-180; interest in the mid-1950s in problems with the F7U Cutlass, 187-188

Air Force, U.S.
The Strategic Air Command's role in nuclear weapons planning and development in the early 1950s, 142, 145-147; attempts in the late 1940s to recruit officers from the Navy, 148; flew a B-36 bomber with a nuclear reactor in the 1950s, 192; involved in a 1956 evaluation of the effects of an all-out nuclear exchange between the United States and Soviet Union, 196-200; in the early 1960s the United States had a short-lived program for the Skybolt missile, which was to be launched from the B-52 bomber, 234-235; in the mid-1960s Joint Task Force Two ran tests to determine the speed necessary for low-altitude bombing by Navy and Air Force aircraft, 276-286; in the mid-1960s an Air Force warrant officer sought to straighten out what he perceived to be sloppy performance by the Thunderbirds flight demonstration team, 285; contention with the Navy in the mid-1960s over the assignment of bombing target packages in Southeast Asia, 289-290; role

in strikes against North Vietnam, 293, 297-298, 324-328; has a large number of general officers, 379

Air Group Ten
See: Carrier Air Group Ten

Air Group 19
See: Carrier Air Group 19

Air Warfare
Attacks by Japanese Zeros on U.S. bombers during the battle for the Marianas in June 1944, 116-117

See also: Bombing

Air Wing Seven
See: Carrier Air Wing Seven

Alcohol
In 1967, as Commander Fleet Air Whidbey, Ramage responded to a request from chief petty officers for beer in the enlisted men's club at lunch, 305; tax-free whiskey was illegally used in the mid-1970s at a bar near the base in Roosevelt Roads, Puerto Rico, 357

Altmann, Captain Richard G., USNR
Did an admirable job in the early 1970s while serving in the Naval Air Reserve, 334

Amphibious Warfare
U.S. invasion of the Marshall Islands in February 1944, 81-85; U.S. invasion of the Marianas Islands in June 1944, 97

Anderson, Admiral George W., Jr., USN (USNA, 1927)
Gave Ramage a hard time in 1958 about the poor performance of heavy attack planes, 208-209; as CNO in the early 1960s was contemptuous about Secretary of Defense Robert McNamara and his Whiz Kids, 231; concern for nuclear weapons matters, 233-235; long working hours as CNO, 236; in the early 1970s observed a peace sign in yard of the CNO's quarters, 329

Andrews, Vice Admiral Adolphus, USN (USNA, 1901)
Was known as "Lord Plushbottom" while serving as commander of the fleet's Hawaiian Detachment in 1939-40, 31-32

Antiair Warfare
Gunnery training schools on board the Brooklyn (CL-40) and Utah (AG-16) shortly before World War II, 37-38

Antilles Defense Command
See Tenth Naval District

Armed Forces Special Weapons Project
Potential in the early 1950s for developing smaller weapons than previously, 138-139, 148-155; types of weapons in the early 1950s, 141-143, 149; role in the 1950s in supporting nuclear war plans, 145-147

Army, U.S.
Role in the invasion of the Marshall Islands in February 1944, 84; in the invasion of New Guinea in April 1944, 93-94; sent top-notch officers to the National War College in the late 1950s, 203-204; involved in the mid-1960s with bombing tests by Joint Task Force Two, 279-281; in the mid-1960s Admiral U.S. Grant Sharp as CinCPac was often out of the loop on Army matters, because communications went directly from Washington to Vietnam, 308-309

Army Air Forces, U.S.
Made exaggerated claims for credit in the victorious Battle of Midway in June 1942, 52-53

Arnold, Captain Murr E., USN (USNA, 1923)
Known as the "Coronado Cobra" while handling naval aviation assignments on the West Coast during World War II, 71

Atsugi, Japan, Naval Air Station
Base site in the early 1950s for AJ Savage nuclear-capable aircraft, 168-170

Aurand, Captain Evan P., USN (USNA, 1938)
Decorated the captain's cabin sumptuously when he commanded the aircraft carrier Independence (CVA-62) in the early 1960s, 257

Aviation Cadets
In 1940-41 former cadets were among the aviators in the air group of the aircraft carrier Enterprise (CV-6), 40-41

B-36 Peacemaker
Air Force plane that carried a nuclear reactor for some tests in the mid-1950s, 192

B-52 Stratofortress
In the early 1960s the United States had a short-lived program for the Skybolt missile, which was to be launched from the B-52 bomber, 234-235

Bagley, Vice Admiral David H., USN (USNA, 1944)
As Chief of Naval Personnel in the early 1970s, solicited inputs for a revised fitness report format, 345-346; was not well regarded by Congressman F. Edward Hebert, 349-350; called Ramage on the carpet in 1973 for not supporting CNO Elmo Zumwalt's

programs, 350-352; contacted about the possibility of BuPers detailers being on the take, 357

Bairoko, USS (CVE-115)
Supported Operation Sandstone nuclear weapons testing at Eniwetok in 1948, 133-134

Baldwin, Lieutenant Robert B., USN (USNA, 1945)
Bailed out of an F7U Cutlass while flying from Moffett Field in the mid-1950s, 185-186

Baney, Commander Sidney N., USN
As part of HATWing 1 in the late 1950s, led a flight demonstration team of A3Ds, 217-218

Bangs, Lieutenant Louis L., USNR
Commanded the strike group from the aircraft carrier Enterprise (CV-6) during a portion of the Marianas Islands operation in June 1944, 98-99, 108, 115-116, 119; served in 1944-45 in Bombing Squadron 98 on the West Coast, 126, 128

Bardshar, Vice Admiral Frederic A., USN (USNA, 1938)
While serving on the Joint Staff in the mid-1960s was unhappy about bombing tests being conducted by Joint Task Force Two, 281-282; was Commander Task Force 77 in November 1970 during the U.S. attempt to rescue prisoners of war from Son Tay prison in North Vietnam, 318-319; relief of as CTF 77 in the early 1970s, 322-323; in 1972 told Ramage that he was unassignable, 330; in December 1975 attended Ramage's retirement ceremony, 372

Baumberger, Vice Admiral Walter H., USN (USNA, 1934)
Fine officer who served in the late 1960s as Deputy CinCPacFlt, 307; concern about Vice Admiral Elmo Zumwalt's riverine initiatives in the late 1960s while commanding U.S. naval forces in Vietnam, 315-316

Beirut, Lebanon
The son-in-law of Soviet Premier Nikita Khrushchev complained about a visit the aircraft carrier Independence (CVA-62) made in the mid-1960s to Beirut, 267-268

Berns, Captain Max A., Jr., USN (USNA, 1939)
Served as chief of staff to ComCarDiv 6 in the early 1960s, 245, 264

Beveridge, Commander Richard A., USN
Development work in the late 1950s on low-altitude loft delivery of nuclear weapons by A3Ds, 212-213

Bitler, Commander Worthington S., USN (USNA, 1922)
Did not extend a warm welcome to aviators while serving as first lieutenant of the heavy cruiser Salt Lake City (CA-25) early in World War II, 51

Blackburn, Rear Admiral Paul P., Jr., USN (USNA, 1930)
Was temporarily designated in 1964 as head of Joint Task Force Two for conducting bombing tests, 276-178

Blesh, Commander Paul K., USN
Served as executive officer of the aircraft carrier Oriskany (CVA-34) in the early 1950s, 165, 172-173

Blue Angels
In the 1970s the Navy's flight demonstration team switched from the F-4 Phantom to the A-4 Skyhawk, 347

Bombing
Practice by the SBDs of Air Group Ten during training in 1943, 75-79; SBDs used in bombing operations in support of the invasion of the Marshall Islands in February 1944, 81-85; U.S. attacks on Truk in February and April 1944, 86-89, 94-97; New Guinea operation in April 1944, 93-94; SBDs used in bombing operations in support of the invasion of the Marianas Islands in June 1944, 97-115; methods of nuclear weapon delivery by Navy aircraft in the mid-1950s, 162; low-altitude loft delivery of nuclear weapons by A3Ds in the late 1950s, 212-214; Heavy Attack Wing One was involved in practice bombing derbies in the late 1950s, 216-218, 222-223; in the mid-1960s Joint Task Force Two ran tests to determine the speed necessary for low-altitude bombing by Navy and Air Force aircraft, 276-286; role of Task Force 77 in the mid-1960s in carrier bombing operations against Vietnam, 287-298; concern in 1967 about the bombing accuracy of the A-6 Intruder, 305-306; in support of November 1970 attempt to rescue POWs from Son Tay prison in North Vietnam, 321; Task Force 77 bombing of North Vietnam in the early 1970s, 323-328; in the early 1970s Naval Reserve A-7s won a bombing competition at Lemoore, California, 348

Bombing Squadron Ten
After service in the aircraft carrier Enterprise (CV-6) in the South Pacific, returned to the West Coast and then to Hawaii for retraining in 1943-44, 73-80; SBDs used in bombing operations in support of the invasion of the Marshall Islands in February 1944, 81-85; attacks on Truk in February and April 1944, 86-89, 94-97; New Guinea operation in April 1944, 93-94; in support of the invasion of the Marianas Islands in June 1944, 97-121; return to the States in the summer of 1944, 125-127

Bombing Squadron 98
Formation of in late 1944 as part of a replacement air group, 126-128

Bon Homme Richard, USS (CVA-31)
Had a ramp strike when an A3D Skywarrior was brought aboard by a squadron commander, 195

Bowers, Jack L.
As Assistant Secretary of the Navy in the mid-1970s, was involved in negotiations to get the Navy out of the island of Culebra, 365-366

Bringle, Admiral William F., USN (Ret.), (USNA, 1937)
Member of the secret Green Bowl society that consisted of Naval Academy graduates who looked out for each others' careers, 63; in 1967 took over command of the Seventh Fleet as part of a daisy chain of promotions, 307

Brown, Vice Admiral Charles R., USN (USNA, 1921)
As Commander Sixth Fleet in the late 1950s, complained about the poor performance of A3Ds, 208-211, 216

Brown, General George S., USAF (USMA, 1941)
Did a capable job of commanding Joint Task Force Two in the mid-1960s when it was running tests on low-level bombing, 276-277, 279, 281-282, 284, 286

Brown, Lieutenant Commander James S., USN
Introduced the F7U Cutlass to the fleet in the early 1950s, 183, 187

Brush, Captain Frederick J., USN (USNA, 1931)
While serving in the Bureau of Naval Personnel in the late 1950s, was concerned about the backgrounds of pilots going into the heavy attack community, 212

Bureau of Naval Personnel
Initiatives in the mid-1950s for better career planning for naval aviation personnel, 191-192, 194-195; response to a complaint in 1967 about pilots for the A-6 Intruder, 303-304; revision of the fitness report format in the early 1970s to reflect goal achievement, 345-346; in the mid-1970s a chief petty officer in Puerto Rico falsely claimed to have an inside track with BuPers detailers, 357

Burke, Admiral Arleigh A., USN (USNA, 1923)
As chief of staff to Admiral Marc Mitscher during the Marianas action in June 1944, 118; as CNO in the mid-1950s, concurred in the cancellation of a nuclear-powered seaplane, 193; reacted favorably to a briefing about a 1956 nuclear-weapons war game, 199

Burns, Captain Richard H., USN (USNA, 1935)
Commanded Fleet Composite Squadron Three at Moffett field in the early 1950s, 180-181

Byrd, Rear Admiral Richard E., USN (Ret.) (USNA, 1912)
Gave lectures around the country in the 1920s and 1930s about his trips to the South Pole, 6

C-9 Skytrain II
In the early 1970s the Navy added this transport plane to its inventory and subsequently transferred their operation to reserve pilots, 337-338

Cambodia
In March 1970 the U.S.-flag merchant ship Columbia Eagle was hijacked and taken to Cambodia, 311-315

Cam Pha, North Vietnam
Coaling port hit by Navy bombers of Task Force 77 in April of 1966, 288, 290-292

Cannes, France
In 1963 served as a liberty port for the crew of the aircraft carrier Independence (CVA-62), 253-255, 259-267

Caribbean Sea Frontier
See: Tenth Naval District

Carlsten, Midshipman Earl E., USN (USNA, 1939)
Bright individual who attended the Naval Academy in the late 1930s, 13

Carmody, Rear Admiral Martin D., USN
Served in 1944-45 in Bombing Squadron 98, 126, 128; was commanding officer of the aircraft carrier Kitty Hawk (CVA-63) and her task group in April of 1966 during strikes against North Vietnam, 290-292; served in the mid-1970s as Commandant 12th Naval District, 356

Caroline Islands
Truk was hit by air-sea attacks by U.S. naval forces in February and April 1944, 86-89, 94-97

Carr, Lieutenant Commander Charles H., USN (USNA, 1941)
Served in Fleet Airborne Electronics Unit Pacific in the early 1950s, 156-157

Carrier Air Group Ten
After service in the aircraft carrier Enterprise (CV-6) in the South Pacific, returned to the West Coast and then to Hawaii for retraining in 1943-44, 73-80; operations in support of the Central Pacific campaign in 1944, 81-121; shuffle of air group command in the spring of 1944, 93

Carrier Air Group 19
Based at Moffett Field, California, in the early 1950s, 158; transition to jet planes in the 1950s, 159-164, 166; addition of new personnel, 159-160, 162-163; capable of delivering nuclear weapons in the early 1950s, 160-162, 166, 168-169; workup for deployment in 1953, 163-166; deployment to the Western Pacific in 1953-54, 168-175; the group had

about 50% recalled reservists during its deployment, 177-178; difficult mix of aircraft types, 179; short cycle times because of limited fuel capacity in the aircraft, 225-226

Carrier Air Wing Seven
Needed training because of ragged performance on board the aircraft carrier Independence (CVA-62) in the early 1960s, 241-243, 246-253; landing accidents, 246-249

Cawley, Aviation Radioman First Class David J., USN
Served as rear seat man in Ramage's SBD during World War II, 74, 116, 120

Chafee, John H.
As Secretary of the Navy during the Nixon administration, made an arrangement to hire people on the island of Culebra, 365

Chance Vought Division of United Aircraft Corporation
Introduced the difficult F7U Cutlass into the fleet in the early 1950s, 183-188

Christiansen, Rear Admiral John S., USN
In April 1972 took command of Carrier Division Seven, 332 in a ceremony at Lemoore, California, 332-333

Clarey, Admiral Bernard A., USN (USNA, 1934)
Commanded the Pacific Fleet during strikes against North Vietnam in 1971, 325-328; response to a letter from Ramage at the time of Clarey retirement, 361

Clifton, Commander Joseph C., USN (USNA, 1930)
Lack of radio discipline while commanding Air Group 12 during the invasion of the Marshall Islands in February 1944, 83-84

Coast Guard, U.S.
The cutter Mellon (WHEC-717) was involved in the U.S. response to the seizure in March 1970 of the merchant ship Columbia Eagle, 312-313

Columbia Eagle, SS
U.S.-flag merchant ship that was hijacked in March 1970 and taken to Cambodia, 311-315

Combs, Vice Admiral Thomas S., USN (USNA, 1920)
While serving as OP-05 in the mid-1950s, concurred in cancellation of a proposed nuclear-powered seaplane, 192-193; views on aviation personnel policies, 194-196, 211; reluctant to rely on subordinates, 200; did poorly in testifying before Congress, 201

Commercial Ships
See: Merchant Ships

Communications
Radio discipline among aviators supporting the invasion of the Marshall Islands in February 1944, 83-84

Composite Squadron Five
See: Fleet Composite Squadron Five

Composite Squadron Three
See: Fleet Composite Squadron Three

Congress
Iowa congressmen were involved in Ramage's attempts to get an appointment to the Naval Academy in the 1930s, 9-11; as Chief of the Bureau of Aeronautics in the mid-1950s, Admiral James Russell testified to Congress about the A4D as a poor man's airplane, 201; OP-05, Vice Admiral Thomas Combs, did a poor job in testifying in the mid-1950s, 201; in the early 1970s Representative F. Edward Hebert arranged for the move of the Naval Reserve headquarters in to his district in New Orleans, 334-337, 344-345, 349-350

Constellation, USS (CVA-64)
Site of a Rolling Thunder conference in 1966 while serving as Task Force 77 flagship, 297-298; racial unrest on board in the early 1970s, 342-344

Cooke, Lieutenant (j.g.) Lemuel D., USN (1939)
After completing flight training in 1942, he was sent to floatplane service, though he wanted carrier duty, 45; left behind a list of Green Bowl members when he served in the aircraft carrier Ranger (CV-4), 63

Cooper, Vice Admiral Damon W., USN (USNA, 1941)
In the early 1970s became Commander Task Force 77 to run the air war against Vietnam, 323, 325-327; in 1973 became Chief of the Naval Reserve, 350-351, 353

Courts-Martial
Trials of individuals serving in the mid-1970s on the staff of Commander Tenth Naval District, 356-358

Cousins, Rear Admiral Ralph W., USN (USNA, 1937)
As the captain detailer in the late 1950s, was able to find a flying job for Ramage, 205-207; became Commander Task Force 77 in 1967 when Rear Admiral Ralph Mehle was relieved, 306-307

Crommelin, Captain John G., Jr., USN (USNA, 1923)
Shortly after World War II, he published a list of members of the Naval Academy's secret Green Bowl Society, 23, 63-64; qualities as executive officer of the aircraft carrier Enterprise (CV-6) in 1943, 58-64; survived when the aircraft carrier Liscome Bay (CVE-56) was sunk in November 1943, 77; in the Yorktown (CV-10) in June 1944, 120-

121; served as training officer in late 1944 for Commander Fleet Air West Coast, 125; role in trying to save naval aviation in the late 1940s, 146

Cronkite, Walter
CBS television news anchor who was honored by a testimonial dinner in 1972 and listened to Ramage's views on the Vietnam War, 340-341

Culebra Island
In the mid-1970s the Navy gave up its training facilities on the island as a result of continuing outside pressure, 361-366

Curtis, Rear Admiral Walter L., USN
In 1967 headed the detail section of the Bureau of Naval Personnel, 304; moved in 1967 to take over the plans job on the CinCPac staff, 307

Dale, Captain Roland H., USN (USNA, 1932)
Was the choice of ComAirPac, Vice Admiral Mel Pride, to command a replacement air group in the late 1950s, 207

Daniels, Commander James G. III, USN
Former aviation cadet who served in the aircraft carrier Enterprise (CV-6) in the early 1940s, 41, 65-66; role as landing signal officer in the Enterprise, 66, 68; initiatives in the mid-1950s for better career planning for naval aviation personnel, 191-192

David, Midshipman Edmonds, USN (USNA, 1939
Sneaked off the grounds while a midshipman at the Naval Academy in the late 1930s, 20

Defense Department
Difficulties in the early 1960s between Secretary Robert McNamara's Whiz Kids and uniformed naval personnel, 230-231

Discipline
Punishment of disciplinary infractions by Naval Academy midshipmen in the late 1930s, 18-21; Ramage and his roommate were stopped in Honolulu for driving without a license shortly before World War II, 30-32; courts-martial of individuals serving in the mid-1970s on the staff of Commander Tenth Naval District, 356-358; Ramage had a closed-door meeting with chief petty officers about perceived lapses in discipline as a result of initiatives by CNO Elmo Zumwalt, 358-360

Dufficy, Lieutenant Commander John F., USNR
Served as non-flying executive officer of Bombing Squadron Ten in the aircraft carrier Enterprise (CV-6) during World War II, 66

Dosé, Captain Robert G., USN
Top-notch naval aviator who headed a replacement air group in the late 1950s, 206; served as judge for carrier landing competitions involving HATWing 1, 216-217

Douglas Aircraft Corporation
Did tests in the 1950s of the wing strength in the A3D attack bomber, 216; sponsored flying competitions in the late 1950s, 216-218; proposal in the late 1950s to build more A3Ds, 223

Duncan, Midshipman George, USN (USNA, 1939)
Sneaked off the grounds while a midshipman at the Naval Academy in the late 1930s, 20

Early, Captain Calvin B., MC, USN
Treated Ramage in the mid-1970s because of spinal problems, 370-371

Eddy, Lieutenant Daniel T., USN (USNA, 1927)
Served as flag lieutenant to Admiral James Richardson, CinCUS, in 1940, 39-40

Education
Ramage's school and college experiences in Iowa in the 1920s and 1930s, 4-8, 10-11; at the Naval Academy in the late 1930s, 13-17; curriculum at the Naval War College in the years immediately after World War II, 128-131

Elder, Captain Robert M., USN
Top-flight naval aviator who commanded VF-191 in the early 1950s, 159-160, 180; while on AirPac staff in the mid-1950s, drafted a glowing fitness report on Ramage, 191; served in the late 1950s as judge for carrier landing competitions involving HATWing 1, 216-217; was commanding officer of the carrier Coral Sea (CVA-43) in 1963 when she ran aground, 379-380

Electronic Countermeasures
Used in a 1956 nuclear-weapons war game at the National War College, 200

Elliott, Lieutenant Commander August William, Jr., USN (USNA, 1941)
Commanded an attack squadron in Air Group 19 in the early 1950s, 158, 160, 173-174

Eniwetok, Marshall Islands
Site of Operation Sandstone nuclear weapons testing in 1948, 133-134

Enlisted Personnel
Administration of in the AirPac type command in the late 1940s, 134-137; the role of enlisted bombardier-navigators in A3D crews in the late 1950s was comparable to that of later NFOs, 220-222

Enterprise, USS (CV-6)
Personal styles of commanding officers Charles Pownall and George Murray shortly before World War II, 26-28; junior officer training program, 29-30; reported to Pearl Harbor in late 1939 as part of the Hawaiian Detachment of the fleet, 30-33; limited role for the ship's strike aircraft prior to World War II, 33-35; the ship was built in the 1930s

as part of Depression relief measures, 35-36; Admiral James O. Richardson, Commander in Chief U.S. Fleet, had his flag and staff on board the ship briefly in 1940, 38-40; in 1940-41 former aviation cadets were in the air group, 40-41; limited operations west of Hawaii prior to war, 43-44; change in appearance after the war began, 54; Battle of Midway, 54-55; operated in the South Pacific in early 1943, 58-68; role of landing signal officers, 66, 68-69; in Hawaii between operations in 1943, 69-71; Air Group Ten was reconstituted in the summer and fall of 1943, 73-80; operations in support of the Marshall Islands invasion in early 1944, 81-82; for a while was the only effective U.S. carrier in the Pacific in 1942-43, 86; contributed planes to the attacks on Truk in February and April 1944, 86-89, 94-97; crew animosity toward the carrier Yorktown (CV-10), 90-91; various operations in early 1944, 93-94; operations in support of the Marianas Islands invasion in June 1944, 97-121

Epes, Captain Horace H., USN
Worked in the mid-1960s as a captain detailer in the Bureau of Naval Personnel, 286-287

Erdmann, Captain William L., USN (USNA, 1924)
Demonstrated his difficult personality in 1944-45 while commanding the escort carrier Matanikau (CVE-101), 128

Espiritu Santo, New Hebrides
Served as a base for U.S. warships in late 1942, 57-63; hostility ashore in early 1944 between crews from the carriers Enterprise (CV-6) and Yorktown (CV-10), 90-91

Everest, Brigadier General Frank K., USAF
While serving with the Tactical Air Command in the mid-1960s believed supersonic speed was essential for low-altitude bombing, 276-278

Ewen, Rear Admiral Edward C., USN (USNA, 1921)
Oversaw air group training while serving as Commander Fleet Air Alameda in the early 1950s, 162-164

F2H Banshee
Used as a fighter and attack plane in Air Group 19 in the early 1950s, 160-161, 164, 166-167, 172, 177; involved in a bad-weather Seventh Fleet exercise in March 1954, 174-176; flown in Fleet Composite Squadron Three in the mid-1950s, 180-181

F4U Corsair
A detachment of night-qualified F4Us joined the aircraft carrier Enterprise (CV-6) in late 1943, 79-80

F-4 Phantom II
Landing difficulties on board the aircraft carrier Independence (CVA-62) in 1963, 246-249; change in missile loading to Sidewinder in 1963, 250; used in April 1966 strike on Cam Pha, North Vietnam, 290-292; Air Force version used in the early 1970s in strikes

against North Vietnam, 324-328; replaced in the 1970s by the A-4 Skyhawk as the aircraft flown by the Blue Angels, 347

F6F Hellcat
Flew in support of the invasion of the Marianas in June 1944, 102

F7U Cutlass
Difficult plane introduced into the fleet in the early 1950s, 183-188

F9F-6 Cougar
Difficulty in landing on a straight-deck aircraft carrier in the early 1950s, 163-164, 177, 180, 184; problems because of limited fuel capacity, 225

F-111
Tests in the mid-1960s by Joint Task Force Two to determine requirements for a low-altitude bomber for the Navy and Air Force, 276-286

FJ Fury
Flying qualities of the FJ-3 model in the mid-1950s, 184-185

Families of Servicemen
In the late 1930s newly commissioned officers were prohibited from marrying during the first two years after graduation from the Naval Academy, 22-23; in the mid-1970s a chief petty officer's wife was penalized when her husband was convicted by a court-martial and lost his pension, 358

Fechteler, Admiral William M., USN (USNA, 1916)
As Chief of Naval Operations in the early 1950s, received a briefing on the damage potential of small nuclear weapons, 152-155

Fires
On board the aircraft carrier Independence (CVA-62) in the early 1960s, 247-248

Fitness Reports
Insights Ramage gained by seeing reports written on senior officers in the late 1940s, 136-137; Ramage received a mediocre report from Captain Carroll Jones in the mid-1950s, 191; revision of the format in the early 1970s to reflect goal achievement, 345-346

Flatley, Lieutenant Commander James H., Jr., USN (USNA, 1929)
Top-notch aviator who commanded VF-10 in the aircraft carrier Enterprise (CV-6) in World War II, 59, 66

Fleet Air Gunnery Unit
Provided training to naval aviators at El Centro, California in 1952, 158-159

Fleet Composite Squadron Five
After being commissioned in September 1948, had a high priority for quality personnel, 137

Fleet Composite Squadron Three
Included a transitional training unit for jet aircraft in the mid-1950s, 180-183; testing and evaluation of the difficult F7U Cutlass in 1954, 183-188; involvement in 1955 with nuclear weapons tests, 189

Fleming, Colonel Patrick D., USAF (USNA, 1941)
Killed in 1956 in the first crash of an Air Force B-52 bomber, 148

Flight Training
Various phases at Pensacola in 1940-41, 44-47, 66

Forbes, Rear Admiral Bernard B., Jr., USN (USNA, 1945)
As a BuPers detail officer in 1973, told Ramage of his limited options for further service, 353-354

Foss, Captain Newton P., USN (USNA, 1944)
Served as executive officer of the aircraft carrier Independence (CVA-62) in the early 1960s, 248, 260, 265-266

Football
The sport conflicted with Ramage's studies at the Naval Academy in the mid-1930s, 13-16

Fourteenth Naval District
In mid-1943 Ramage had difficulty at district headquarters getting transportation for his wife to the mainland, 69-71

Fowler, Commander Richard E., USN
Service in the mid-1960s as executive officer of the aircraft carrier Independence (CVA-62), 271

France
Cannes visited by the aircraft carrier Independence (CVA-62) in 1963, 253-255, 259-267

Franklin D. Roosevelt, USS (CVA-42)
Conducted carrier qualifications in the late 1950s for heavy attack pilots flying the A3D, 215-216; encountered heavy weather in January 1967 while en route to a port visit to Hong Kong, 299-301

Gallery, Rear Admiral Daniel V., Jr., USN (Ret.) (USNA, 1921)
Reaction to racial unrest on board Navy ships in the early 1970s, 342-344

Gardner, Captain Matthias B., USN (USNA, 1919)
Commanded the aircraft carrier Enterprise (CV-6) in 1943-44, 80, 96

Gayler, Captain Noel A. M., USN (USNA, 1935)
While in OpNav in the mid-1950s was involved in setting aviation requirements, 227

Gentner, Vice Admiral William E., Jr., USN (USNA, 1930)
As Commander Sixth Fleet in 1963, inquired about a message on the subject of movies shown in aircraft carriers, 245; boarded the aircraft carrier Independence (CVA-62) at Gibraltar during a joint operation with the Spanish, 266-267

Gibraltar
The strait was the site of a joint operation between the U.S. Navy and the Spanish in the mid-1960s, 266-267; concern about weather one day in early 1964, when the aircraft carrier Independence (CVA-62) was running liberty boats at Gibraltar, 269-272

Giddens, Lieutenant (j.g.) Homer A., USN
Served on the staff of Commander Air Force Pacific Fleet in the late 1940s, 134-137

Giffen, Captain Robert C., USN (USNA, 1907)
Served as athletic director at the Naval Academy in the mid-1930s, 14

Gray, Lieutenant James S., USN (USNA, 1936)
Assessment of his performance as CO of VF-6 during the June 1942 Battle of Midway, 130

Green Bowl Society
A secret group of Naval Academy midshipmen and graduates that existed through the World War II period, 23, 63-64

Greer, Rear Admiral Howard E., USN (USNA, 1944)
Observed changes in the Naval Reserve in the early 1970s while serving as Chief of Naval Air Reserve Training, 330-331, 334-335

Griffin, Rear Admiral Charles Donald, USN (USNA, 1927)
Served as a model carrier skipper while commanding the Oriskany (CVA-34) in the early 1950s, 165, 167-170, 172-174, 176, 225-226; served in the mid-1950s as an assistant to the Chairman of the Joint Chiefs of Staff, 201

Guam
Was a target for U.S. bombs during the invasion of the Marianas in June 1944, 101

Guinn, Vice Admiral Dick H., USN (USNA, 1941)
As Chief of Naval Personnel in 1972, was not authorized to offer Ramage much choice in terms of his next billet, 330-332

Gunnery-Naval
Training schools on board the Brooklyn (CL-40) and Utah AG-16) shortly before World War II, 37-38; shore bombardment in support of the U.S. invasion of the Marshall Islands in February 1944, 85

Hamilton, Lieutenant (j.g.) Thomas J., USN (USNA, 1927)
Served as football coach at the Naval Academy in the mid-1930s, 14; member of the secret Green Bowl society, 63; as air officer and executive officer in the aircraft carrier Enterprise (CV-6) during World War II, 80, 90-91

Hanecak, Captain Richard G. USN
Did a fine job in the early 1970s as chief of staff to Commander Naval Air Reserve Force, 341

Hanley, Commander Michael J., USN (USNA, 1940)
As NavAirLant training officer in the late 1950s, was skeptical about the value of the loft maneuver for A3Ds, 213-214

Hanoi/Haiphong, North Vietnam
Hit in June of 1966 by Navy and Air Force bombing strikes, 293

Hardison, Captain Osborne B., USN (USNA, 1916)
Unimpressive individual who served in 1942-43 as commanding officer of the aircraft carrier Enterprise (CV-6), 59-63

Harmer, Lieutenant Commander Richard E., USN (USNA, 1935)
Commanded a detachment of night-qualified F4U Corsairs on board the aircraft carrier Enterprise (CV-6) in World War II, 79-80

Hawaii
Aviation training at Maui in 1943-44, 77-78

See also: entries under Honolulu and Pearl Harbor

Hawkins, Captain Carson, USN (USNA, 1931)
Commanded Fleet Airborne Electronics Unit Pacific in the early 1950s, 156-158

Hayward, Commander John T., USN (USNA, 1930)
Commanded VC-5 during the introduction of nuclear weapons to the fleet in the late 1940s and early 1950s, 137

Heavy Attack Wing One
Charged in the late 1950s with improving the process of getting A3Ds ready for the fleet, 207-209; shortage of carrier experience among heavy attack pilots, 210-212; tactics for use in the low-altitude loft delivery of nuclear weapons, 212-214; carrier qualifications in the late 1950s for pilots new to the aircraft, 214-215; various competitions to raise pilot

morale, 216-218; role of A3D crewmen, 219-222; poorly trained pilots in the early 1960s, 249-250

Hebert, Representative F. Edward
Louisiana congressman who in the early 1970s arranged to have naval activities relocated to his district at New Orleans, 334-337, 344-345, 349-350, 382

Heinemann, Edward H.
Designer of the Douglas SBD Dauntless of World War II said he could not get a more powerful engine for the plane until the Curtiss Wright SB2C was in the fleet, 124; designer of the A3D Skywarrior and A4D Skyhawk, which got into the fleet in the 1950s, 195-196, 219-220, 224-225

Himmel, Ensign William, USNR
Officer who got into some mischief while serving in the aircraft carrier Enterprise (CV-6) in 1940, 39-40

Hobbs, Rear Admiral Ira E., USN (USNA, 1925)
Served as chief of staff to ComAirPac in the mid-1950s, 187

Hoch, Lieutenant James E., USNR
Served as a division officer in the aircraft carrier Independence (CVA-62) in the early 1960s, 262-263

Hoffman, Commander Melvin C., USN
Ran the Fleet Air Gunnery Unit at El Centro, California, in the early 1950s, 158

Hollandia, New Guinea
Carrier strikes in connection with amphibious operations in the spring of 1944, 93-94

Holloway, Admiral James L. III, USN (USNA, 1943)
While serving as Chief of Naval Operations in the mid-1970s corresponded with Ramage, 367-368

Hong Kong, British Crown Colony
In January 1967 the aircraft carrier Franklin D. Roosevelt (CVA-42) encountered heavy weather while en route to a port visit to Hong Kong, 299-301

Honolulu, Hawaii
Ramage and his roommate were stopped in Honolulu for driving without a license shortly before World War II, 30-32

Hoover, Captain John H., USN (USNA, 1907)
Proved difficult to deal with while serving as chief of staff to Commander Aircraft Battle Force shortly before World War II, 27-28

Houser, Vice Admiral William D., USN (USNA, 1942)
As OP-05 in the early 1970s, felt he was not part of CNO Elmo Zumwalt's inner circle, 345; display of the CNO Safety Trophy won in the early 1970s by the Naval Air Reserve Force, 348

Hubbard, Commander Samuel W., USN
Served as Commander Carrier Air Wing 19 during strikes against North Vietnam in 1971, 327

Hyland, Admiral John J., USN (USNA, 1934)
In 1967 became Commander in Chief Pacific Fleet, 307-308; sent Ramage to Washington in March 1968 for a briefing on Vietnam, 309; in 1969 extended Ramage on his staff for an additional year, 310-311; role in response to the seizure in March 1970 of the U.S.-flag merchant ship Columbia Eagle, 311-312; was publicly scolded by CinCPac, Admiral John McCain over the Columbia Eagle episode, 313-314; initiated a feud when he sent a tough message to Vice Admiral Elmo Zumwalt, naval commander in Vietnam, about riverine operations, 316; concurred in Ramage's replacement on the Pacific Fleet staff in 1970 by Rear Admiral Roy Isaman, 317; relieved in December 1970 as CinCPacFlt, 321

Independence (CVL-22)-Class Aircraft Carriers
Role in supporting operations in the Central Pacific campaign in World War II, 92-93

Independence, USS (CVA-62)
Ramage had to shoo off a clothing salesman who sought to do business on board the ship in 1963, 239-240, 253-255; Ramage's hurried command turnover with Captain Leroy Swanson, 240-241; training needed to get a ragged air wing up to speed, 241-243, 246-253; difficulties between Ramage as flag captain and Rear Admiral Allen Shinn, the embarked carrier division commander, 241-253, 264-266, 259-274; landing accidents on board, 246-249; temporary stand-down in nuclear weapons capability, 250-251; visited Cannes, France, during a Mediterranean deployment in the early 1960s, 253-255, 259-267; joint operation with Spain in the Strait of Gibraltar, 266-267; visit to Beirut, Lebanon, 267-268; concern about weather one day in early 1964, when the ship was running liberty boats at Gibraltar, 269-272; return to Norfolk in March 1964, 272-274; participation in a fleet exercise in 1964 off North Carolina, 274; in 1964 won the Arleigh Burke Award for improvement, 278

In-Flight Refueling
See: Refueling in Flight

Investigations
In 1950 Ramage investigated the crash of an AJ Savage in New Mexico, 139-140

Iowa State Teachers College, Cedar Falls, Iowa
Ramage attended the college briefly in the early 1930s, 10-11

J2F Duck
Amphibian plane used for utility roles on board the aircraft carrier Enterprise (CV-6) during World War II, 59-60

Jaap, Rear Admiral Joseph A., USN (USNA, 1932)
Followed regulations while serving in the mid-1960s as Commander Fleet Air Whidbey, 303-304

Jackson, Captain Frederick E., MC, USN
Treated Ramage in the mid-1970s because of spinal problems, 370-371

Japanese Navy
Sent aircraft out to harass U.S. warships at Espiritu Santo in the New Hebrides in early 1943, 62; defense against the U.S. invasion of the Marianas in June 1944, 97, 101-110, 116-117

Johnson, President Lyndon B.
Role in directing aspects of the war against North Vietnam in the mid-1960s, 293-294, 297, 317, 320, 321

Johnson, Admiral Roy L., USN (USNA, 1929)
Headed the OP-05W organization in OpNav in the mid-1950s, 190; while serving as CinCPacFlt in the mid-1960s, was concerned about bombing operations in North Vietnam, 298; pleased with Ramage's work as Task Force 77 chief of staff, 301; in 1967 asked for Ramage for his staff, 307; arranged in 1967 for Ramage to join the Pacific Fleet staff, 307-308

Johnson, Captain Silas R., USN
Served as operations officer on the CarDiv 6 staff in the early 1960s, 243-244

Johnston, Admiral Means, Jr., USN (USNA, 1939)
Made four-star rank, though he didn't get good grades in aptitude for the service as a midshipman in the 1930s, 18, 375-376; in the early 1970s, as the Navy Inspector General, was involved in a Naval Reserve reorganization, 334-337

Joint Chiefs of Staff
Evaluation in 1956 of the effects of an all-out nuclear exchange between the United States and Soviet Union, 196-200

Joint Strategic Target Planning Staff, Offutt Air Force Base, Nebraska
Established around 1960 to give a joint aspect to nuclear weapons targeting, 232-235

Joint Task Force Two
In the mid-1960s ran tests to determine the speed necessary for low-altitude bombing by Navy and Air Force aircraft, 276-286

Jones, Captain Carroll B., USN (USNA, 1926)
 While serving as acting ComFAir Alameda in 1954, took a dislike to Ramage, 188; wrote a mediocre fitness report on Ramage, 191

Jumper, Colonel George Y., USAF (USMA, 1939)
 Involved with the Armed Forces Special Weapons Project in the early 1950s, 148-149

Kane, Lieutenant Commander William R., USN (USNA, 1933)
 Commanded VF-10 in the aircraft carrier Enterprise (CV-6) during World War II, 73, 84; became commander of Air Group Ten in the spring of 1944, 93-95, 98, 105, 116, 119; in late 1944 became athletic director at the Naval Academy, 125

Kauffman, Rear Admiral Draper L., USN (USNA, 1933)
 As Commander U.S. Naval Forces Philippines in March 1970, was designated to be in control of an anticipated operation to retake the captured U.S.-flag merchant ship Columbia Eagle, 313

Kirn, Captain Louis J., USN (USNA, 1932)
 While on the AirPac staff in the early 1950s, arranged for Ramage to get a carrier air group in the Pacific, 156

Kissinger, Henry A.
 In the mid-1970s, as Secretary of State, stopped in Puerto Rico during a vacation, 367

Kitty Hawk, USS (CVA-63)
 In April of 1966 her aircraft took part in bombing strikes against North Vietnam, 290-292; racial unrest on board in the early 1970s, 342-344; site of Ramage's retirement from active duty in December 1975, 372

Koch, Commander Ferdinand B., USN (USNA, 1946)
 Commanded Attack Squadron 86 on board the aircraft carrier Independence (CVA-62) when the ship made a Med cruise in the early 1960s, 256

Kwajalein, Marshall Islands
 Invasion of in February 1944 supported by planes from the aircraft carrier Enterprise (CV-6), 81-85

Lampman, Commander Lester B., USN
 Unpleasant moment in March 1964 when, as operations officer of the aircraft carrier Independence (CVA-62), he was helping bring the ship into Norfolk in a fog, 273

Larson, Commander William J., USN (USNA, 1914)
 Took a forgiving approach when he saw midshipmen sneaking onto the Naval Academy grounds in the mid-1930s, 20-21

Lavelle, General John D., USAF
    In the early 1970s commanded the Seventh Air Force during unauthorized air strikes against North Vietnam, 325-327, 380

Lebanon
    The son-in-law of Soviet Premier Nikita Khrushchev complained about a visit the aircraft carrier Independence (CVA-62) made in the mid-1960s to Beirut, 267-268

Lee, Lieutenant Commander James R., USN (USNA, 1928)
    Commanded Scouting Squadron Ten in the aircraft carrier Enterprise (CV-6) during World War II, 64, 66

LeMay, General Curtis E., USAF
    Strong personality who commanded the Strategic Air Command in the early 1950s, 147; stopped a war game in 1956 because he didn't like the way things were going, 198; as Air Force Chief of Staff in the mid-1960s was concerned about joint Air Force-Navy bombing tests, 278-279

Leonard, Lieutenant Commander William N., USN (USNA, 1938)
    While on the staff of CTF 38 in late 1944, pursued the idea of replacing SB2Cs with fighters, 123-124

Lewis, Lieutenant (junior grade) Donald, USNR
    Wrote an account of the Task Force 58 strike against Japanese warships on 20 June 1944, 105-119

Lexington, USS (CV-16)
    Role in supporting the invasion of the Marianas in June 1944, 122-123

Lindsey, Ensign Robin M., USNR
    Former aviation cadet who served in the aircraft carrier Enterprise (CV-6) in the early 1940s, 41, 61; role as landing signal officer in the Enterprise, 66, 68

Mack, Vice Admiral William P., USN (USNA, 1937)
    In the early 1970s commanded the Seventh Fleet during bombing operations against North Vietnam, 325-327

Mahler, Captain George H. III, USN (USNA, 1942)
    Retired suddenly in 1966 rather than taking a billet a chief of staff to Commander Task Force 77, 286

Majuro Atoll, Marshall Islands
    Served as an anchorage base for the U.S. fleet in early 1944, 86

Marianas Islands
Invasion of in June 1944 supported by planes from the aircraft carrier Enterprise (CV-6), 97-121; Admiral Raymond Spruance's decisions concerning support for the amphibious forces, 122, 129

Marine Corps, U.S.
Role in the invasion of the Marshall Islands in February 1944, 84-85; VMA-324 operated A-4 Skyhawks off the aircraft carrier Independence (CVA-62) in the early 1960s, 252; poor operation of A-6 Intruders during mid-1960s bombing tests conducted by Joint Task Force Two, 284

Marrs, Theodore C.
White House official who complained to Ramage in the mid-1970s when the Navy stopped supplying water from Puerto Rico to the Virgin Islands, 363-364, 370

Marshall Islands
Invasion of in February 1944 supported by planes from the aircraft carrier Enterprise (CV-6), 81-85; Operation Sandstone nuclear weapons testing at Eniwetok in 1948, 133-134

Martell, Vice Admiral Charles B., USN (USNA, 1930)
As Commander Second Fleet in early 1964, had discussions with Ramage about the aircraft carrier Independence (CVA-62), 273-274

Martin, Vice Admiral Harold M., USN (USNA, 1919)
Interested in carrier group training while serving as ComAirPac in the early 1950s, 164; arranged in 1954 for Ramage to command Fleet Composite Squadron Three, 179-181; interest in the problems of the F7U Cutlass in the mid-1950s, 187-188; thought well of a personnel suggestion by Ramage, 189-190; gave Ramage a glowing concurrent fitness report after Ramage received a mediocre one from his regular reporting senior, 191; light-hearted comment on the negative aspects of Pentagon duty, 202

Martin, Lieutenant Commander William I., USN (USNA, 1934)
Commanded squadrons in the aircraft carrier Enterprise (CV-6) in World War II, 65, 73, 105

Matanikau, USS (CVE-101)
Served as a training platform in 1944-45 for pilot carrier qualifications, 128

McCain, Admiral John S., Jr., USN (USNA, 1931)
While serving in March 1970 as Commander in Chief Pacific, did not order overt action as part of the U.S. response to the seizure of the merchant ship Columbia Eagle, 313-314

McCauley, Rear Admiral Brian, USN (USNA, 1943)
While serving in March 1970 as Pacific Fleet operations officer, had a role in the response to the seizure of the U.S.-flag merchant ship Columbia Eagle, 312-313; concern

about riverine operations in Vietnam, 316

McClusky, Captain C. Wade, Jr., USN (USNA, 1926)
Took a low-key approach in Hawaii following his participation in the June 1942 Battle of Midway, 53-54; shortly after World War II, served as executive officer of the General Line School at Newport, 129; his view of the Battle of Midway, 130

McDonald, Admiral David L., USN (USNA, 1928)
As CNO in 1964, he specified Ramage for a job on the staff of Joint Task Force Two, 276

McKee, Lieutenant General William F., USAF
Attempted in about 1947 to recruit Ramage for the Air Force, 148

McKellar, Captain Edwin D., USN
Served in the early 1970s as operations officer on the staff of Commander Task Force 77 during bombing operations against North Vietnam, 325-326

McNamara, Robert S.
As Secretary of Defense in the early 1960s, attacked the Navy's nuclear weapons capabilities, 230-231; negative view of the Skybolt missile program, 234; in the mid-1960s directed tests to determine the speed necessary for penetrating in low-altitude bombing, 276, 278-279

Medical Problems
Ramage had to get a pilonidal cyst corrected before he could report to flight training in 1941, 42; Ramage managed to squelch a proposed venereal disease examination for Air Group 19 on board the aircraft carrier Oriskany (CVA-34) in the early 1950s, 172-173; concern about VD in Okinawa in the early 1960s, 229; Ramage had surgery in 1975 to correct spinal problems, 370-372

Mediterranean Sea
The aircraft carrier Independence (CVA-62) deployed to the Mediterranean in 1963-64 for operations with the Sixth Fleet, 240-272

Mehle, Rear Admiral Roger W., Jr., USN (USNA, 1937)
His relief in 1967 as Commander Task Force 77 led to a daisy chain of personnel moves, 306-307

Mellon, USCGC (WHEC-717)
Coast Guard cutter that was involved in the U.S. response to the seizure in March 1970 of the merchant ship Columbia Eagle, 312-313

Merchant Ships
Crews of merchant ships were paid substantially more than servicemen in World War II, 56; in March 1970 the U.S.-flag merchant ship Columbia Eagle was hijacked and taken to

Cambodia, 311-315

Michaelis, Vice Admiral Frederick H., USN (USNA, 1940)
While in OpNav in the early 1960s was involved in selling the Polaris program, 238; as ComNavAirLant in the early 1970s he expressed opposition to a proposed Naval Reserve reorganization, 335-336; was suggested in the early 1970s as Chief of Naval Reserve, but he did not want the job, 350; attended the ceremony in August 1975 when Ramage was relieved as Commandant of the Tenth Naval District, 371-372; served on a joint staff in Omaha during part of the Zumwalt years in the early 1970s, 378

Midway, Battle of
The Army Air Forces made exaggerated claims for credit in the victorious battle in June 1942, 52-53; effect on some individual participants, 54-55; role of Lieutenant Commander Wade McClusky, 129-130

Military Sea Transportation Service
In March 1970 the U.S.-flag merchant ship Columbia Eagle, under contract to MSTS, was hijacked and taken to Cambodia, 311-315

Miller, Captain Gerald E., USN (USNA, 1942)
Served as a member of the Joint Strategic Target Planning Staff in the early 1960s, 233-234

Mines
By 1970 carrier planes were dropping mines on North Vietnam, 317

Missiles
In the early 1960s the United States had a short-lived program for the Skybolt missile, which was to be launched from the B-52 bomber, 234-235; substitution of Sidewinders for Sparrows on F-4s of the aircraft carrier Independence (CVA-62) in the early 1960s, 250-251; U.S. policy in the mid-1960s about not attacking North Vietnamese SAM sites until they were activated, 282-283; threat to U.S. planes in 1971 during attacks on North Vietnam, 325, 327-328

Mitscher, Vice Admiral Marc A., USN (USNA, 1910)
As Commander Task Force 58 during the attacks on Truk in February 1944, 89; "Mitscher Shampoo" attack on Palau in the spring of 1944, 91-92; in the attack on New Guinea in April 1944, 93-94; during attacks on Truk in April 1944, 96-97, 325; during the Marianas campaign in June 1944, 97, 101, 118, 122-123

Moffett Field, Sunnyvale, California
Served as a base for Carrier Air Group 19 in the early 1950s, 158; as base for Composite Squadron Three in the mid-1950s, 180-185

Moore, Captain Frederick T., Jr., USN
Commanded the aircraft carrier Saratoga (CVA-60) in the early 1960s, 244-245; in 1963

became chief of staff to Commander Carrier Division Six, 264-265, 272

Moorer, Admiral Thomas H., USN (USNA, 1933)
In the mid-1950s objected to the cancellation of a proposed nuclear-powered seaplane, 192-193; involved in the late 1950s in pushing an in-flight refueling system for naval aircraft, 223-224; as CNO in March 1968 asked for an officer from the Pacific Fleet staff to come to Washington to present a briefing on the Vietnam War, 309-310; interest in the seizure in March 1970 of the merchant ship Columbia Eagle, 314; communication with CinCPacFlt John Hyland about Vice Admiral Elmo Zumwalt's operations in Vietnam, 316; as Chairman of the JCS in the early 1970s was eager to talk to Ramage about Ramage's experiences in Vietnam, 322, 330; speculation as to Moorer's reaction to the explanation for changes made in the early 1970s when Admiral Elmo Zumwalt was Chief of Naval Operations, 328; in 1972 arranged for Ramage to meet and talk with Walter Cronkite, 340-341; reaction to racial unrest on board Navy ships, 344; in the 1970s headed the Association of Naval Aviation, 373; as CNO in the late 1960s gave advice to new flag officers, 378

Movies
In 1963 Rear Admiral Allen Shinn, ComCarDiv 6, issued a message directing aircraft carriers in his task force not to show charthouse movies under way, 244-246

Murray, Captain George D., USN (USNA, 1911)
As commanding officer of the aircraft carrier Enterprise (CV-6) in 1941, brooked no interference from the embarked chief of staff, Captain John Hoover, 27-28

Music
Men from the aircraft carrier Independence (CVA-62) were entertained by a flamenco troupe when they visited Palermo, Sicily, in the early 1960s, 256-259; Rear Admiral Allen Shinn, ComCarDiv 6, issued a message in 1963 limiting public appearances by musical groups under his command, 264-265

National War College, Washington, D.C.
Site of a 1956 war game that evaluated the effects of an all-out nuclear exchange between the United States and Soviet Union, 196-200; composition of the student body in 1957-58, 202-204; curriculum, 203-204; argument between naval aviators over the role of carriers, 205

Naval Academy, Annapolis, Maryland
Ramage's efforts in the early 1930s to get an appointment, 7, 9-11, 25; plebe summer in 1935, 12-13; academics, 13-17; football, 13-16; evaluation of midshipmen in aptitude for the service, 17-18, 21-22; punishment of disciplinary infractions, 18-21; prohibition against marriage for two years after graduation, 22-23; the Green Bowl Society was a secret group of Naval Academy midshipmen and graduates that existed through the World War II period, 23, 63-64; in career planning lectures in the late 1930s, only a few officers on the faculty were counseling midshipmen to go into aircraft carriers and naval aviation, 24; in Ramage's opinion, too few Naval Academy graduates were in combat

aviation in World War II and the Korean War, 178-179; concerns in the 1980s about the organization's curriculum, 375-376

Naval Air Reserve Force, U.S.
Changes were made in the early 1970s as part of an overall reorganization of the Naval Reserve, 330-337; successful effort by Representative F. Edward Hebert in the early 1970s to get the command's headquarters moved to New Orleans, 334-337, 344-345, 349-350; composition of in the early 1970s, 335; in the early 1970s added the C-9 to its transport inventory, 337-338; in the early 1970s won the CNO Safety Trophy, 348; won bombing competition at Lemoore, California, 348

Naval Flight Officers
Role of enlisted bombardier-navigators in A3D crews in the late 1950s was comparable to that of later NFOs, 220-222

Naval Reserve, U.S.
During its 1953-54 deployment to the Western Pacific, Carrier Air Group 19 included about 50% recalled reservists as pilots, 177-179; reorganization of in the early 1970s, 331-332, 334-337; headquarters move to New Orleans n the early 1970s, 349-351

Naval War College, Newport, Rhode Island
In the years following World War II, was slow to incorporate lessons learned about aviation during the war, 128; study of nuclear weapons in the postwar era, 130-131

Navigation
Difficulties in March 1964 in bringing the aircraft carrier Independence (CVA-62) into the port of Norfolk in a heavy fog, 273

Nearman, Commander Leonard M., USN
Commanded Carrier Air Wing Seven on board the Independence (CVA-62) in the early 1960s, 241-242, 251

Nelson, Lieutenant Robert S., USNR
TBF pilot who located the Japanese fleet during operations west of the Marianas on 20 June 1944, 103, 105

New Guinea
Carrier strikes on Hollandia in connection with amphibious operations in the spring of 1944, 93-94

New Hebrides
Espiritu Santo served as a base for U.S. warships in late 1942, 57-63

New Jersey, USS (BB-62)
Brief service in the late 1960s in providing shore bombardment during the Vietnam War, 298-299

Newman, Commander Roscoe L., USN (USNA, 1930)
Commanded Air Group Ten in the aircraft carrier Enterprise (CV-6) during World War II, 73; transfer in 1944 to the staff of Rear Admiral J. W. Reeves, 93

New Orleans, Louisiana
Representative F. Edward Hebert arranged in the early 1970s to have naval activities relocated to his district at New Orleans, 334-337, 344-345, 349-350

News Media
In the mid-1960s received briefings from U.S. naval officers concerning air strikes against targets in North Vietnam, 295-297; coverage in April 1972 of the Carrier Division Seven change of command, 332-333; at a testimonial dinner in the summer of 1972 Ramage expressed his views on the Vietnam War to newsman Walter Cronkite, 340-341

Night Flying
Return of Task Force 58 planes to their carriers during the June 1944 Battle of the Philippine Sea, 111-120; by VC-3 night fighters in the mid-1950s, 183-184; training for Carrier Air Wing Seven on board the aircraft carrier Independence (CVA-62) in the early 1960s, 250-253

Nixon, President Richard M.
Did not interfere in the November 1970 attempt to rescue American prisoners of war from Son Tay prison in North Vietnam, 320

North American Aviation, Inc.
As the manufacturer of the AJ Savage, worked to correct problems uncovered in a 1950 accident, 139-141

Nuclear Propulsion
In the mid-1950s the Navy investigated the concept of a nuclear-powered seaplane, 192-194

Nuclear Weapons
Studied at the Naval War College in the years following World War II, 130-131; Operation Sandstone tests at Eniwetok in 1948, 133-134; squadron VC-5 went into commission in 1948 to give the fleet a nuclear weapons capability, 137; potential in the early 1950s for developing smaller weapons than previously, 138-139, 148-155; types of weapons in the early 1950s, 141-143, 149; President Harry S. Truman would not let the armed forces have control of the weapons, 145-146; Carrier Air Group 19 was nuclear capable in the early 1950s, 160-162, 168-171; when Dwight Eisenhower became President in 1953, the military began to have control of nuclear components, 161; reservations on use of nuclear weapons on the part of an Air Group 19 pilot in the early 1950s, 170-171; Operation Teapot tests in 1955, 189; evaluation in 1956 of the effects of an all-out nuclear exchange between the United States and Soviet Union, 196-200; argument at the National War College in the late 1950s over the availability of aircraft

carriers armed with nuclear weapons, 205; low-altitude loft delivery of nuclear weapons by A3Ds in the late 1950s, 212-214; role of OP-604 in nuclear weapons planning in the early 1960s, 230-239; temporary stand-down in the nuclear-weapons capability of the aircraft carrier Independence (CVA-62) in 1963 to get the air wing better trained, 250-251

OS2U Kingfisher
Used in flight training at Pensacola in the early 1940s, 45; in-shore patrol detachment at Pearl Harbor in the spring of 1942, 48-51

Oberg, Commander Owen H., USN
Commanded Fighter Squadron 41 on board the aircraft carrier Independence (CVA-62) in the early 1960s, 246-247; threw a big squadron party when the ship visited Palermo, Sicily, 256, 258-259

Okinawa
The large seaplane tender Salisbury Sound (AV-13) operated around Okinawa in the early 1960s, 228-229; concern about venereal disease, 229

OpNav
Role of OP-05W in the mid-1950s as the Sea-Based Striking Forces Planning Unit, 190-194; involvement in a 1956 war game testing the usefulness and effects of nuclear weapons, 196-200; Ramage's assessment of the negative aspects of Pentagon duty, 202; role of OP-604 in nuclear weapons planning inn the early 1960s, 230-239

Oriskany, USS (CVA-34)
Workup with Air Group 19 for a deployment, 165-167; deployment to the Western Pacific in 1953-54, 168-176; short cycle times because of limited fuel capacity in the aircraft, 225-226; in December 1970 served as the site of the Pacific Fleet change of command, 321; was involved in the early 1970s in strikes against North Vietnam, 324, 326-327

Outlaw, Rear Admiral Edward C., USN (USNA, 1935)
Was one of the early pilots in the nuclear attack program in the late 1940s, 169; got into a disagreement with Ramage while both were students at the National War College in the late 1950s, 203, 205; while serving as Commander Task Force 77 in the mid-1970s was unhappy about U.S. policy that prevented attacking North Vietnamese SAM sites before they were activated, 283

PBY Catalina
Flying boat operations out of New Caledonia in 1943, 57

Pacific Fleet, U.S.
Staff changes in 1967 as a result of a daisy chain of promotions, 306-308

Palermo, Sicily
   Visited by the aircraft carrier Independence (CVA-62) in the early 1960s, 255-259

Parker, Vice Admiral Edward N., USN (USNA, 1925)
   Involved in a 1956 war game testing the effects of nuclear weapons, 196-199; in 1960 became the first Navy deputy director of the Joint Strategic Target Planning Staff, 233

Pay and Allowances
   Crews of merchant ships were paid substantially more than servicemen in World War II, 56

Pearl Harbor, Hawaii
   The aircraft carrier Enterprise (CV-6) was stationed there, beginning in late 1939, as part of the fleet's Hawaiian detachment, 30-31; in-shore patrol detachment of OS2Us in the spring of 1942, 48-51; results of the Japanese attack in December 1941, 46, 48

Pearson, Rear Admiral John B. Jr., USN (USNA, 1923)
   As an AirPac staff member in the mid-1950s was unhappy about unfavorable reports on the F7U Cutlass, 187

Pederson, Commander Oscar, USN (USNA, 1926)
   Service in 1943 as navigator of the aircraft carrier Enterprise (CV-6), 59

Pennsylvania, USS (BB-38)
   Served in 1940 as the flagship for Admiral J. O. Richardson, who was Commander in Chief U.S. Fleet, 38-40

Pensacola, Florida, Naval Air Station
   Site of Navy flight training in the early 1940s, 44-47, 66

Personnel
   Ramage didn't believe carriers got the best personnel in the years right after World War II, 131-132; management of enlisted personnel in the late 1940s, 134-137; initiatives in the mid-1950s for better career planning for naval aviation personnel, 189-192, 194-195; shortage in the late 1950s of carrier experience among heavy attack pilots, 210-212; the role of enlisted bombardier-navigators in A3D crews in the late 1950s was comparable to that of later NFOs, 220-222; transition of AD pilots to the A-6 in the late 1960s, 303-304

Pirie, Vice Admiral Robert B., USN (USNA, 1926)
   Promoted naval aviation in the late 1930s while on the faculty of the Naval Academy, 24; as OP-05 in the late 1950s, was impressed by the A3Ds of HATWing 1, 217-218; acceptance of the A3J in the late 1950s, 226; lost out on a fourth star in the early 1960s because of a perception that he was not cooperating with Secretary of Defense Robert McNamara and his Whiz Kids, 231

Planning
   Role of OP-05W in the mid-1950s as the Sea-Based Striking Forces Planning Unit, 190-194; role of OP-604 in nuclear weapons planning in the early 1960s, 230-239

Polaris Program
   Two of the main salesmen for the program in OpNav in the early 1960s were naval aviators, 238

Poor, Commander Richard L., USN (USNA, 1933)
   Commanded a section of Bombing Squadron Ten, operating from the aircraft carrier Enterprise (CV-6) during the middle part of World War II, 73, 93

Pownall, Rear Admiral Charles A., USN (USNA, 1910)
   Demonstrated gentlemanly qualities while commanding the aircraft carrier Enterprise (CV-6) from 1938 to 1941, 26-29, 38-40

Pride, Vice Admiral Alfred M., USN
   Vetoed Ramage as head of the West Coast replacement air group in 1958, 206-207

Prisoners of War
   Unsuccessful attempt in November 1970 to rescue U.S. prisoners of war from Son Tay prison in North Vietnam, 318-321

Promotion of Officers
   Ramage encountered some blackshoe opposition in the 1960s in getting selected for flag rank, 301-303

Puerto Rico
   In the early 1970s the headquarters of Commandant Tenth Naval District moved from San Juan to Roosevelt Roads, 355-356; the Navy's response to pressure in the mid-1970s to give up its training facilities on Vieques and Culebra, 361-366; in the 1960s and 1970s the Navy sold Puerto Rican water to the Virgin Islands, 362-364, 370; supplied water to Vieques, 369

Racial Integration
   In 1973 Chief of Naval Personnel David Bagley called Ramage on the carpet about his views on CNO Elmo Zumwalt's racial policies, 350-352

Racial Prejudice
   On the part of a Naval Academy midshipman in 1935, 12

Racial Unrest
   Difficulties in the early 1970s on board Navy ships, particularly aircraft carriers, 342

Radar
    Use of in March 1964 in bringing the aircraft carrier Independence (CVA-62) into the port of Norfolk in a heavy fog, 273; role in the late 1960s in giving the A-6 Intruder an all-weather bombing capability, 305-306

Radio
    Radio discipline among aviators supporting the invasion of the Marshall Islands in February 1944, 83-84

Railroads
    Targeted in the mid-1960s by Task Force 77 attack planes that hit North Vietnam, 294-296

Ramage, Rear Admiral James D., USN (Ret.) (USNA, 1939)
    Parents of, 1-3, 5-12, 15-16, 25; other ancestors, 1-2; siblings, 2, 6, 8, 10, 11; boyhood in Iowa in the 1920s and 1930s, 2-8; education of, 4-7, 10-11, 15-16, 236-237; preparation for attending the Naval Academy, 6-7, 9-11; as a Naval Academy midshipman from 1935 to 1939, 12-25; duty as a junior officer in the aircraft carrier Enterprise (CV-6) following graduation from the Naval Academy, 26-44; first wife Emeleen, 43, 47, 55, 69, 134, 237; flight training in 1941-42, 44-47; in-shore patrol duty at Pearl Harbor in the spring of 1942, 48-51; brief duty in 1942 in the heavy cruiser Salt Lake City (CA-25), 51-52; part of ship's company in the aircraft carrier Enterprise (CV-6) in early 1943, 58-62; nickname "Jig Dog," 55; in SBD squadrons in the Enterprise in 1943-44, 64-125; served 1944-46 as CO of Bombing Squadron 98, 125-128; as a student in 1946-47 at the Naval War College, 128-133; served 1947 to 1948 as navigator of the escort carrier Bairoko (CVE-115), 133-134; served 1948-50 on the staff of ComAirPac, 134-137; duty from 1950 to 1952 with the Armed Forces Special Weapons Project, Albuquerque, New Mexico, 138-154; children of, 139, 237; from 1952 to 1954 commanded Carrier Air Group 19, 158-180, 225-226; in 1954-55 commanded Fleet Composite Squadron Three, 180-190; served 1955-57 in the Pentagon in OP-05W, the Sea-Based Striking Forces Planning Unit in OpNav, 190-202; as student in 1957-58 at the National War College, 202-205; command of Heavy Attack Wing One, 1958-60, 208-227; in 1960-61 commanded the seaplane tender Salisbury Sound (AV-13), 227-230; served 1961-63 as head of Special Weapons Plans on the OpNav staff, 230-239; commanded the aircraft carrier Independence (CVA-62) in 1963-64, 239-275; service in 1964-65 on the staff of Joint Task Force Two, which tested low-altitude bombing alternatives, 276-286; married second wife Ginger in 1964, 278, 287, 354; stepchildren, 287; served in 1966-67 as chief of staff to Commander Task Force 77, 287-301; brief temporary assignment in January 1967 as commanding officer of the carrier Franklin D. Roosevelt (CVA-42), 299-301; served briefly in 1967 as Commander Fleet Air Whidbey, 303-307; served from 1967 to 1970 as deputy chief of staff for plans and operations on the staff of CinCPacFlt, 307-317; duty from 1970 to 1972 as Commander Carrier Division Seven, 317-333; served in 1972-73 as Commander Naval Air Reserve Force, 330-355; final tour of duty, from 1973 to 1975, was as Commandant Tenth Naval District, Commander Caribbean Sea Frontier, and Commander Antilles Defense Command, 355-372 surgery in 1975 to correct spinal problems, 370-372; activities following his 1975 retirement from active duty, 373-383

Ramsey, Vice Admiral Paul H., USN (USNA, 1927)
    As commander of Heavy Attack Wing One in the early 1950s, tried unsuccessfully to get Ramage to command one of his AJ squadrons, 169; served in the mid-1960s as ComNavAirLant, 271, 275-276

Reconnaissance-Aerial
    Armed reconnaissance was practiced against North Vietnam in the mid-1960s by aircraft of the Navy's Task Force 77, 288, 290-291, 294-295, 297-298; against North Vietnam in the early 1970s, 323-324

Reedy, Rear Admiral James R., USN (USNA, 1933)
    Served in the mid-1960s as Commander Task Force 77 during bombing of North Vietnam, 287-288, 290-292, 295

Rees, Vice Admiral William L., USN (USNA, 1921)
    As ComNavAirLant in the late 1950s, was concerned by the performance of A3D squadrons, 209, 211-213, 215, 218-219, 221, 226

Reeves, Rear Admiral John W., Jr., USN (USNA, 1911)
    Commanded a carrier task group in the Central Pacific campaign in World War II, 93, 96-97, 99, 120-121, 325

Refueling at Sea
    Done in early 1964 by the aircraft carrier Independence (CVA-62) while returning to Norfolk, 272-274

Refueling in Flight
    Done by various naval aircraft in the late 1950s, 223-226

Reina Mercedes, USS (IX-25)
    Former Spanish warship that served as a floating brig at the Naval Academy in the late 1930s, 19

Reinhart, Commander Leonard J., USN
    While commanding Heavy Attack Squadron One in the aircraft carrier Independence (CVA-62) in the early 1960s, was not allowed to fly at night, 253

Religion
    Ramage's family had strong church connections in Iowa in the 1920s and 1930s, 7-8; prejudice against Catholics, 9; chapel service on board the large seaplane tender Salisbury Sound (AV-13) in the early 1960s, 229

Repp, Lieutenant Frank J., USNR
    Had a spectacular ramp strike on board the aircraft carrier Oriskany (CVA-34) in the mid-1950s, 172

Rescue at Sea
Pickup of aviators from accidents on board the aircraft carrier Independence (CVA-62) in the early 1960s, 246-249

Richardson, Vice Admiral David C., USN (USNA, 1936)
Served in the mid-1960s as Commander Task Force 77 during bombing of North Vietnam, 288, 292, 295, 298, 301, 306; in the early 1970s was deputy CinCPacFlt, 328; in December 1975 attended Ramage's retirement ceremony, 372

Richardson, Admiral James O., USN (USNA, 1902)
U.S. Fleet Commander in Chief who moved aboard the aircraft carrier Enterprise (CV-6) in 1940, 38-39

Roane, Lieutenant Commander Virginius R., USN (USNA, 1924)
Fine gentleman who served as gunnery officer of the aircraft carrier Enterprise (CV-6) shortly before World War II, 30, 32

Rogers, Ensign Grant H., USN (USNA, 1939)
Served in the aircraft carrier Enterprise (CV-6) after his 1939 graduation from the Naval Academy, 26, 31, 38

Roosevelt Roads Naval Station, Puerto Rico
In the early 1970s the headquarters of Commandant Tenth Naval District moved from San Juan to Roosevelt Roads, 355-356; tax-free whiskey was illegally used in the mid-1970s at a bar near the base, 357; Ramage had a closed-door meeting with chief petty officers about perceived lapses in discipline as a result of initiatives by CNO Elmo Zumwalt, 358-360

Roper, Ensign Joseph C., USN (USNA, 1939)
Was the victim of a practical joke in 1940 when the U.S. Fleet staff was briefly embarked in the aircraft carrier Enterprise (CV-6), 39-40

Rudd, Lieutenant Commander Richard Orten, USN
Served as navigator in the large seaplane tender Salisbury Sound (AV-13) in the early 1960s, 229

Runyon, Commander Donald E., USN
Accomplished pilot who flew in Heavy Attack Wing One in the late 1950s, 214-215

Russell, Rear Admiral James S., USN (USNA, 1926)
Congressional testimony while serving as Chief of the Bureau of Aeronautics in the mid-1950s, 201

Russell, Rear Admiral Thomas B., Jr., USN
In 1973 relieved Ramage as Commander Naval Air Reserve Force, 353-354

SB2C Helldiver
  Dive bomber that flew in combat during the latter part of the Pacific campaign in World War II, 87, 110, 119, 122-124

SBD Dauntless
  Dive bomber that entered the fleet in 1941, 34; flown by Scouting Squadron Ten in the aircraft carrier Enterprise (CV-6) in 1943, 64-69; upgrade to SBD-5 model for Bombing Squadron Ten to retrain in 1943-44 for a return to combat, 72-80; SBDs used in bombing operations in support of the invasion of the Marshall Islands in February 1944, 81-85; U.S. attacks on Truk in February and April 1944, 86-89, 94-97; New Guinea operation in April 1944, 93-94; SBDs used in bombing operations in support of the invasion of the Marianas Islands in June 1944, 97-115; allegation of political influence in powering the SBD-5 model, 124

SOC Seagull
  Floatplane used by the heavy cruiser Salt Lake City (CA-25) early in World War II, 51

Saipan, Marianas Islands
  See: Marianas Islands

Salisbury Sound, USS (AV-13)
  Large seaplane tender that operated in the Western Pacific in the early 1960s, 227-230

Sallada, Vice Admiral Harold B., USN (USNA, 1917)
  As ComAirPac in the late 1940s, objected to moving the type command to the West Coast, 135

Salt Lake City, USS (CA-25)
  Heavy cruiser to which Ramage was assigned in 1942 for floatplane duty, 47-52

Sandstone-Operation
  Nuclear weapons testing conducted at Eniwetok in the Marshall Islands in 1948, 133-134

Sanford, Florida, Naval Air Station
  Base of operations for Heavy Attack Wing One in the late 1950s, 208-223

Saratoga, USS (CVA-60)
  While operating in the Mediterranean in the summer of 1963, received a message directing that no movies be shown in the charthouse while under way, 244-246

Schaefer, Lieutenant (junior grade) William W., USNR
  Flew an SBD during the Battle of the Philippine Sea in June 1944, 110

Schantz, Lieutenant Commander John Malcolm, USN (USNA, 1963)
Served in the mid-1970s as aide to the Commandant of the Tenth Naval District in Puerto Rico, 365

Schirra, Lieutenant Walter M., Jr., USN (USNA, 1946)
Involved in jet aircraft training in the mid-1950s, 183-185

Scouting Squadron Ten
Flew SBD Dauntless scout bombers from the aircraft carrier Enterprise (CV-6) in 1943, 64-69

Selection Boards
Ramage encountered some blackshoe opposition in the 1960s in getting selected for flag rank, 301-303

Sharp, Admiral Ulysses S. Grant, USN (USNA, 1927)
Demanding leader while serving as DCNO (Plans and Policy) in the early 1960s, 230, 232, 235-238; as CinCPac in the mid-1960s, assigned bombing target packages in Vietnam, 289; approval of April 1966 bombing strike on Cam Pha, North Vietnam, 292; relationship with the Air Force in connection with Vietnam bombing, 298; was often out of the loop as CinCPac because communications went directly from Washington to Vietnam, 308-309; did not place much value on riverine operations in Vietnam, 316

Shepard, Lieutenant Alan B., USN (USNA, 1945)
Flew with Fighter Squadron 193 in the aircraft carrier Oriskany (CVA-34) in the mid-1950s, 160, 168, 174-176

Shinn, Vice Admiral Allen M., USN (USNA, 1932)
Used the aircraft carrier Independence (CVA-62) as flagship while commanding Carrier Division Six in the early 1960s, 241-252; difficulties with flag captain Ramage, 242-249, 264-266, 269-274; put out a message in 1963 complaining about charthouse movies in carriers, 244-246; seemed a bit discomfited when his wife arranged for a flamenco troupe to play music on board the flagship, 258; issued a message in 1963 limiting public appearances by musical groups under his command, 264-265; concern about weather one day in early 1964, when the Independence was running liberty boats at Gibraltar, 269-272; as ComNavAirPac in 1967, gave Ramage a boost toward flag rank, 301-302; arranged for Ramage to go to Whidbey Island because of a concern about A-6 squadrons, 303-304, 308

Shinneman, Lieutenant (junior grade) John R., USNR
Flew an F6F during the Battle of the Philippine Sea in June 1944, 108

Sicily
Palermo visited by the aircraft carrier Independence (CVA-62) in the early 1960s, 255-259

Sickel, Lieutenant Commander Horatio G. V, USN (USNA, 1944)
Operated a transitional training unit for jet pilots in the mid-1950s, 182-185, 187

Sixth Fleet, U.S.
The aircraft carrier Independence (CVA-62) deployed to the Mediterranean in 1963-64 for operations with the fleet, 240-272

Skybolt Missile
In the early 1960s the United States had a short-lived program for the Skybolt, which was to be launched from the B-52 bomber, 234-235

Sloatman, Commander John K., Jr., USN
Worked for the Armed Forces Special Weapons Project in the early 1950s to study the probable effects of nuclear weapons, 149-154

Small, Captain Ernest G., USN (USNA, 1912)
Commanded the heavy cruiser Salt Lake City (CA-25) early in World War II, 51-52

Snipes, Captain Beecher, USN
As commanding officer of Whidbey Island Naval Air Station in the late 1960s, had to be encouraged to institute morale-enhancing rules, 304-305

Son Tay Prison
Unsuccessful attempt in November 1970 to rescue U.S. prisoners of war from Son Tay prison in North Vietnam, 318-321

Soviet Union
The son-in-law of Premier Nikita Khrushchev complained about a visit the aircraft carrier Independence (CVA-62) made in the mid-1960s to Beirut, Lebanon, 267-268

Spain
The Strait of Gibraltar was the site of a joint operation between the U.S. Navy and the Spanish in the mid-1960s, 266-267

Sprague, Vice Admiral Thomas L., USN (USNA, 1918)
As ComAirPac, supported Ramage in personnel decisions in 1949-50, 135-136; gave Ramage blessing to go to the Armed Forces Special Weapons Project in 1950, 139

Spruance, Admiral Raymond A., USN (USNA, 1907)
After the war discussed his reasons for the decisions he made during the June 1944 Battle of the Philippine Sea, 122, 129; as president of the Naval War College after World War II, 128-129; his first flag billet, in 1940-41, was as Commandant Tenth Naval District, 355-356

Stebbins, Lieutenant Commander Edgar E., USN
Was talkative on the voice radio while commanding the air group from the carrier Yorktown (CV-10) in early 1944, 83-84

Stever, Lieutenant Elbert M., USN (USNA, 1935)
Service on the ComAirPac staff at Pearl Harbor in early 1942, 49-50

Stockdale, Vice Admiral James B., USN (Ret.) (USNA, 1947)
Vietnam War prisoner who later became involved in examining the Naval Academy's curriculum, 376-377

Stone, Lieutenant Doyle L., USN
Mustang officer who worked in the early 1950s in getting nuclear weapons aboard aircraft carriers, 150-151, 161

Stong, Midshipman Jake, USN
Entered the Naval Academy in 1935 as a plebe, later dropped out for academic deficiency, 7, 14

Stranathan, Brigadier General Leland S., USAF
As a field director for the Armed Forces Special Weapons Project in the early 1950s, was concerned about Navy interest in small nuclear weapons, 153-154

Strategic Air Command
Role in nuclear weapons planning and development in the early 1950s, 142, 145-147; flew a B-36 bomber with a nuclear reactor in the 1950s, 192; involved in a 1956 evaluation of the effects of an all-out nuclear exchange between the United States and Soviet Union, 196-200; major player in the Joint Strategic Target Planning Staff in the early 1960s, 233-234

Strategy
Limited U.S. approach in the mid-1960s as it fought a war against North Vietnam, 294, 332-333

Strean, Rear Admiral Bernard M., USN (USNA, 1933)
As a student at the National War College in the late 1950s, 203; when he had a carrier division command in the mid-1960s, Ramage declined the opportunity to be his chief of staff, 275

Strong, Commander Stockton Birney, USN (USNA, 1937)
SBD pilot in the aircraft carrier Enterprise (CV-6) in the early part of World War II, 64-65, 71; was one of the early pilots in the nuclear attack program in the late 1940s, 169

Stump, Commander Felix B., USN (USNA, 1917)
Was not a very good pilot while serving shortly before World War II as executive officer of the aircraft carrier Enterprise (CV-6), 29-30, 39

Swanson, Captain Leroy V., USN
Left hurriedly upon completing his command tour of the aircraft carrier Independence (CVA-62) in 1963, 240-241

Sweeney, General Walter C., Jr., USAF
As Commander Tactical Air Command in the mid-1960s, was unhappy with bombing test results produced by Joint Task Force Two, 282

TBD Devastator
Slow torpedo plane that entered the fleet in the late 1930s, 34

TFX
See: F-111

Tactics
SBDs changed their formations in early 1942 to give rear gunners better fields of fire, 103; methods for nuclear weapons delivery by Navy aircraft in the mid-1950s, 162 low-altitude loft delivery of nuclear weapons by A3Ds in the late 1950s, 212-214

Tailhook Association
Activities in the 1970s and 1980s on behalf of naval aviation, 373-374

Talley, Captain George C., Jr., USN (USNA, 1944)
After suffering a heart attack, had to be replaced in January 1967 as commanding officer of the aircraft carrier Franklin D. Roosevelt (CVA-42), 299

Tamny, Lieutenant Lewis D., USN (USNA, 1937)
Commanded an in-shore aviation patrol squadron at Pearl Harbor in early 1942, 50

Task Force 77
Role of in the mid-1960s during carrier bombing operations against Vietnam, 287-298; supported in November 1970 of the attempt to rescue U.S. prisoners of war from Son Tay prison in North Vietnam, 318-321; turnover of command in the early 1970s, 322-323; bombing operations in the early 1970s, 323-328

Tenth Naval District
In the early 1970s the headquarters of Commandant Tenth Naval District moved from San Juan, Puerto Rico, to Roosevelt Roads, 355-356; staff members in the mid-1970s were weak and sometimes dishonest, 356-358; Ramage had a closed-door meeting with chief petty officers about perceived lapses in discipline as a result of initiatives by CNO Elmo Zumwalt, 358-360

Thompson, Rear Admiral William, USN
As the Navy's Chief of Information in the early 1970s, objected to Ramage's pronouncements on the Vietnam War, 339

Towers, Vice Admiral John H., USN (USNA, 1906)
As ComAirPac in 1943, interceded on behalf of Ramage in his effort to get transportation for his wife, 70-71

Training
Navy flight training at Pensacola, Florida, in the early 1940s, 44-47, 66; after service in the aircraft carrier Enterprise (CV-6) in the South Pacific, Carrier Air Group Ten returned to the West Coast and then to Hawaii for retraining in 1943-44, 73-80; transitional training unit for jet pilots in the mid-1950s, 182; training needed to get a ragged Carrier Air Wing Seven up to speed on board the USS Independence (CVA-62) in the early 1960s, 241-253; concern about the experience and training of carrier skippers, 268-269; the Navy's response to pressure in the mid-1970s to give up its training facilities on the islands of Vieques and Culebra, 361-366

Trapnell, Rear Admiral Frederick M., USN (USNA, 1923)
Served in the early 1950s as the senior naval officer at the Armed Forces Special Weapons Project in Albuquerque, New Mexico, 151, 153-155

Trim, Midshipman Kermit M., USN
Displayed racial prejudice in 1935 when he entered the Naval Academy, 12

Truk, Caroline Islands
Japanese bastion hit by air-sea attacks from U.S. naval forces in February and April 1944, 86-89, 94-97

Truman, President Harry S.
In the early 1950s did not allow the Strategic Air Command to control nuclear weapons components, 145-146, 161

Tully, Rear Admiral Joseph M., Jr., USN (USNA, 1942)
Commanded Heavy Attack Wing One in the early 1960s, 249-250; while at Lemoore, California, in the early 1970s, hosted a bombing competition for Navy squadrons, 348

Turner, Admiral Stansfield, USN (USNA, 1947)
In the early 1970s was among CNO Elmo Zumwalt's close associates in the Navy hierarchy, 345-347; reputation as an intellectual, 375

Tyler, Captain Orville, USA (Ret.) (USMA, 1903)
Honolulu banker who became Ramage's father-in-law in 1941, 42-43, 55

Uniforms-Naval
At Whidbey Island in 1967, Ramage encouraged aviators to wear flight jackets, 304

Upham, Commander Frank K., USN (USNA, 1934)
Helped Ramage get a job on the AirPac staff in 1948, 134-135

VB-10
See: Bombing Squadron Ten

VC-3
See: Fleet Composite Squadron Three

VC-5
See: Fleet Composite Squadron Five

VS-10
See: Scouting Squadron Ten

VX-3
See: Air Development Squadron Three

Venereal Disease
Ramage managed to squelch a proposed venereal disease examination for Air Group 19 on board the aircraft carrier Oriskany (CVA-34) in the early 1950s, 172-173; concern about the disease in Okinawa in the early 1960s, 229

Vieques Island
The Navy's response to pressure in the mid-1970s to give up its training facilities on the island, 361-366; received water supplied from Puerto Rico, 369

Vieweg, Captain Walter V. R., USN (USNA, 1924)
Reviewed operations by Air Group 19 while serving as ComFAir Hawaii in 1953, 165-166

Vietnam-North
Role of Task Force 77 in the mid-1960s in carrier bombing operations against targets in Vietnam, 287-298; by 1970 carrier planes were dropping mines on North Vietnam, 317; unsuccessful attempt in November 1970 to rescue U.S. prisoners of war from Son Tay prison in North Vietnam, 318-321; U.S. bombing operations in the early 1970s, 323-328; missile threat to U.S. aircraft, 325, 327-328

Vietnam War
Unlike the Korean War, nearly all carrier pilots got a shot at combat duty in Vietnam, 178-179; U.S. policy in the mid-1960s about not attacking North Vietnamese SAM sites until they were activated, 282-283; role of Task Force 77 in the mid-1960s in carrier bombing operations, 287-298; Admiral U.S. Grant Sharp was often out of the loop as CinCPac because communications went directly from Washington to Vietnam, 308-309; in March 1968 Ramage went to Washington to provide a briefing from the CinCPacFlt perspective on the war in Vietnam, 309-310; Vice Admiral Elmo Zumwalt's emphasis on riverine operations while serving from 1968 to 1970 as Commander U.S. Naval Forces Vietnam, 315-316; by 1970 carrier planes were dropping mines on North Vietnam, 317;

unsuccessful attempt in November 1970 to rescue U.S. prisoners of war from Son Tay prison in North Vietnam, 318-321; U.S. bombing operations in the early 1970s, 323-328; Ramage's observations on the U.S. approach to the war, 332-333, 339; at a testimonial dinner in 1972, Ramage talked to newsman Walter Cronkite about the war, 340-341

Virgin Islands
In the 1960s and 1970s the U.S. Navy supplied water to the islands, 362-364, 370

Vito, Lieutenant Commander Albert H., Jr., USN (USNA, 1944)
In 1956 gave Ramage advice on public speaking, 199

Vought
See: Chance Vought Division of United Aircraft Corporation

Walker, Vice Admiral Thomas J. III, USN (USNA, 1939)
While stationed with the Armed Forces Special Weapons Project in 1950, worked at getting nuclear weapons in carrier planes, 138, 144, 155; in the early 1950s served as the first commanding officer of squadron VX-5, 144-145, 155; as ComNavAirPac in the early 1970s he expressed opposition to a proposed Naval Reserve reorganization, 335-336

Ward, Rear Admiral Norvell G., USN (USNA, 1935)
Service in the early 1970s as Commandant Tenth Naval District, 355, 362

War Games
Role of a 1956 war game testing the usefulness and effects of nuclear weapons, 196-200

Warner, John W.
As Secretary of the Navy in the early 1970s, was involved in reorganization of the Naval Reserve, 335-337, 350

Weapons Systems Evaluation Group
Involved in 1967 in an evaluation of bombing accuracy by the A-6 Intruder, 305-306

Weather
A fleet exercise in the Sea of Japan in March 1954 was conducted in heavy weather, 174-176; changeable winds in the mid-1960s when the aircraft carrier Independence (CVA-62) was involved in a joint operation with the Spanish near the Strait of Gibraltar, 266-267; concern about wind and rain one day in early 1964, when the Independence was running liberty boats at Gibraltar, 269-272; difficulties in March 1964 in bringing the aircraft carrier Independence (CVA-62) into the port of Norfolk in a heavy fog, 273; in January 1967 the aircraft carrier Franklin D. Roosevelt (CVA-42) encountered heavy weather while en route to a port visit to Hong Kong, 299-301

Weinel, Admiral John P., USN (USNA, 1939)
Made four-star rank, though he didn't get good grades in aptitude for the service as a midshipman in the 1930s, 18, 375-376

Weisner, Admiral Maurice F., USN (USNA, 1941)
As Commander Seventh Fleet in the early 1970s, made an unsuccessful attempt to have Ramage selected as Commander Task Force 77, 323; as OP-05 in the early 1970s responded to a proposal from Ramage to put C-9s into the Naval Air Reserve Force, 338; in the summer of 1972 asked Ramage to attend a testimonial dinner for Walter Cronkite, 340-341; warning to Ramage to restrain his comments about Chief of Naval Operations Elmo Zumwalt, 344-345; as VCNO made Ramage temporary Chief of the Naval Reserve, 349; consulted in 1973 about Ramage's departure from the reserve job, 353

Wessell, Lieutenant Commander Leonard P., USN (USNA, 1917)
Was aggressive in enforcing regulations while serving as a battalion officer at the Naval Academy in the mid-1930s, 18-19

Westmoreland, General William C., USA (USMA, 1936)
As Commander U.S. Military Assistance Command in the mid-1960s, involvement with air strike targeting, 289; gave the Navy a chance to tell its story to the news media, 295-296; Admiral U.S. Grant Sharp was often out of the loop as CinCPac because communications went directly from Washington to Westmoreland, 308-309

Weymouth, Lieutenant Commander Ralph, USN (USNA, 1938)
Commanded VB-16, an SBD squadron during the June 1944 Battle of the Philippine Sea, 123

Whidbey Island, Washington, Naval Air Station
Served in the late 1960s as a base for A-6 and A-3 attack planes, 303-307; Ramage put his personnel stamp on the base, 304-305

Windsor, Commander Robert W., Jr., USN (USNA, 1941)
Commanded Fighter Squadron 24 in the mid-1950s, 160, 180, 182

Wisconsin, USS (BB-64)
Subjected to a mock air attack during a fleet exercise in the Pacific in March 1954, 174

Withington, Rear Admiral Frederic S., USN USNA, 1923)
While in the Atomic Energy Division of the Navy Department in the early 1950s, was caught unaware by a briefing on the capability of a small nuclear weapon, 153-154

Wooldridge, Vice Admiral Edmund T., USN (USNA, 1920)
Role as president of the National War College in the late 1950s, 204

Wouk, Herman
Novelist's activities as a member of California's Bohemian Club, 374-375

Yates, Captain Earl P., USN (USNA, 1944)
Served in the mid-1960s as a Seventh Fleet liaison officer in Saigon, South Vietnam, 295

Yorktown, USS (CV-5)
Was built in the 1930s as part of the Depression relief program, 35-36

Yorktown, USS (CV-10/CVA-10)
Participation in the Central Pacific campaign in 1944, 83-84, 89-90, 114; animosity toward the crew of the Enterprise (CV-6), 90-91; Ramage spent a short time on board after landing on the ship during the Battle of the Philippine Sea, 117, 119-120; carrier qualifications for different groups in the mid-1950s, 163, 184

Young, Captain David B., USN (USNA, 1927)
Served in the early 1950s as the senior naval officer at the Armed Forces Special Weapons Project in Albuquerque, New Mexico, 144; had a later tour in the 1950s as executive assistant to the Secretary of the Navy, 151-152

Youngs, Dr. Theodore
University of Indiana professor who was loaned to the Sandia Corporation in the early 1950s to study nuclear weapons effects, 149-152

Zero (Japanese Fighter Plane)
See: A6M Zero

Zumwalt, Admiral Elmo R., Jr., USN (USNA, 1943)
As Commander U.S. Naval Forces Vietnam in March 1970, wanted to be in control of an anticipated operation to retake the captured U.S.-flag merchant ship Columbia Eagle, 313; relationship with the Pacific Fleet command from 1968 to 1970 while serving in country in Vietnam, 315-316; as CNO in the early 1970s expressed no desire to see Ramage when Ramage had just come from Vietnam duty, 321-322, 330; Ramage was not happy with the changes Zumwalt made as CNO in the early 1970s, 328-329, 358-361; in 1972 was not willing to let Ramage have any choice jobs nor be promoted to vice admiral, 330-331; as CNO favored a reorganization of the Naval Reserve, 334-337; perception that his policies led to racial unrest, 342-344; reaction to negative comments about him by Ramage, 344-345, 350-352; not popular with retired senior leaders, 346-347

www.ingramcontent.com/pod-product-compliance
Lightning Source LLC
Chambersburg PA
CBHW080623170426
43209CB00007B/1503